THE QUISLINGS

The Norwegian 'treason trials' were the most extensive post–Second World War 'reckoning' with wartime collaboration in all of Europe. Following the war, tens of thousands of Norwegians were sentenced for their wartime actions, including the notorious leader of Norway's collaborationist party *Nasjonal Samling*, Vidkun Quisling. And yet many wartime actions also went unpunished, including, in the vast majority of cases, violence perpetrated against Norway's Jewish minority. *The Quislings* examines how the Norwegian authorities planned, implemented and interpreted this reckoning between 1941 and 1964. In doing so, it looks at the broader political purposes the treason trials served, how these changed over time and the mechanisms that brought these changes about. This wide-ranging study argues that the trials were not driven by the agenda of any one institution or group. Instead, their final shape was the result of a complex process of weighing up demands for legal form and consistency against a fast-changing political and social environment.

ANIKA SEEMANN is a senior research fellow at the Max Planck Institute for Social Law and Social Policy, focusing on the history of the Nordic countries and their relationship to wider Europe. She has previously published on the history of citizenship, migration and the welfare state, as well as the aftermath of the Second World War in the Nordic countries.

NEW STUDIES IN EUROPEAN HISTORY

The aim of this series in early modern and modern European history is to publish outstanding works of research, addressed to important themes across a wide geographical range, from southern and central Europe, to Scandinavia and Russia, from the time of the Renaissance to the present. As it develops the series will comprise focused works of wide contextual range and intellectual ambition.

A full list of titles published in the series can be found at:
www.cambridge.org/newstudiesineuropeanhistory

THE QUISLINGS

The Trials of Norwegian Wartime Collaborators, 1941–1964

ANIKA SEEMANN

Max Planck Institute for Social Law and Social Policy

CAMBRIDGE
UNIVERSITY PRESS

CAMBRIDGE
UNIVERSITY PRESS

Shaftesbury Road, Cambridge CB2 8EA, United Kingdom

One Liberty Plaza, 20th Floor, New York, NY 10006, USA

477 Williamstown Road, Port Melbourne, VIC 3207, Australia

314–321, 3rd Floor, Plot 3, Splendor Forum, Jasola District Centre, New Delhi – 110025, India

103 Penang Road, #05-06/07, Visioncrest Commercial, Singapore 238467

Cambridge University Press is part of Cambridge University Press & Assessment, a department of the University of Cambridge.

We share the University's mission to contribute to society through the pursuit of education, learning and research at the highest international levels of excellence.

www.cambridge.org
Information on this title: www.cambridge.org/9781009212304

DOI: 10.1017/9781009212298

First published 2025

A catalogue record for this publication is available from the British Library

Library of Congress Cataloging-in-Publication Data
NAMES: Seemann, Anika, author.
TITLE: The Quislings : the trials of Norwegian wartime collaborators, 1941-1964 / Anika Seemann, Max Planck Institute for Social Law and Social Policy.
DESCRIPTION: Cambridge, United Kingdom ; New York, NY : Cambridge Press University, 2024. | Series: New studies in european history | Includes bibliographical references and index.
IDENTIFIERS: LCCN 2023039198 (print) | LCCN 2023039199 (ebook) | ISBN 9781009212304 (hardback) | ISBN 9781009212311 (paperback) | ISBN 9781009212298 (ebook)
SUBJECTS: LCSH: Trials (Treason)–Norway–Oslo–History. | War crime trials–Norway–Oslo–History. | World War, 1939-1945–Collaborationists–Norway. | Norway–History–German occupation, 1940-1945. | Trials (Treason)–Europe–History. | Quisling, Vidkun, 1887-1945–Trials, litigation, etc.
CLASSIFICATION: LCC KKN40.T73 S44 2024 (print) | LCC KKN40.T73 (ebook) | DDC 345.481/0238–dc23/eng/20231002
LC record available at https://lccn.loc.gov/2023039198
LC ebook record available at https://lccn.loc.gov/2023039199

ISBN 978-1-009-21230-4 Hardback

Contents

List of Figures *page* vi
Acknowledgements vii
Note on Translations x
List of Abbreviations xi

Introduction 1

1 Occupation: Norway's Wartime Experience and the Preparation of the Trials, 1940–1945 26

2 Transition: Rebuilding State Institutions, May–June 1945 79

3 Foundation: Laws and Legal Precedent, July–December 1945 110

4 Adjudication: Bringing Collaborators to Justice, 1946–1947 147

5 Limitation: Pragmatism and Political Promises, 1948–1949 190

6 Interpretation: Competing Narrations of the Trials, 1948–1964 226

7 Correlation: The Norwegian Treason Trials in European Perspective 257

Conclusion 298

Appendix 1 Numbers of Individuals Investigated in Norway during the Treason Trials and War Crimes Trials 305
Appendix 2 The Key Legal Provisions of the Treason Trials 306
Bibliography 308
Index 324

Figures

1.1 Josef Terboven and Vidkun Quisling at Akershus Fortress in Oslo on 1 February 1942 *page* 36
2.1 Celebrations on Karl Johan Gate in Oslo on 8 May 1945 82
3.1 The verdict is handed down in the trial of Vidkun Quisling at the Oslo Court of Appeal (*Eidsivating Lagmannsrett*), 10 September 1945 128
3.2 Public protest in Youngstorget, Oslo, in connection with the treason trials, 20 August 1945 137
4.1 'Kongeriket Norges Rettskvern' (The Kingdom of Norway's legal mill), sketch by Odd Einarson, 1946 161
4.2 Members of the Rinnan group on trial 182
6.1 Oliver Langeland, pictured with his defence attorney Rolf Foss at court in Oslo 246

Acknowledgements

There are many individuals I need to thank for their advice and encouragement over the years.

Writing this book would not have been possible without the support and trust of my PhD supervisor, Christopher Clark. I will forever be grateful for his decision to take me on as a PhD student and for guiding me through the process of writing my thesis, upon which this book is built. I also want to thank my PhD examiners, David Reynolds and Patrick Salmon, who offered invaluable advice on how to turn my thesis into a book, as well as my adviser at Cambridge, Henning Grunwald, who supported me, in particular during the first year of the PhD. In addition, this work has benefited tremendously from conversations about Nordic history with Ditlev Tamm, Hans Fredrik Dahl, Hans Petter Graver, Guri Hjeltnes and Klaus Petersen. At the Max Planck Institute for Social Law and Social Policy (MPISoc), I owe a huge debt to Ulrich Becker, who has supported my work in so many ways since I joined the institute as a research fellow in 2018. Within the Max Planck Law network, I am especially indebted to Stefan Vogenauer and the late Michael Stolleis, who offered helpful guidance at various stages of this book project. Moreover, I am indebted to Lars-Erik Vaale and Baard Herman Borge for many in-depth exchanges on the post-war trials in Norway and for reading the manuscript of this book in full and sharing their thoughts on it.

At Cambridge, the Colloquium provided a wonderful intellectual and social environment, and I am grateful to Eirik Røsvik, Thomas Clausen, Oliver Haardt, Darren O'Byrne and Hanna Weibye for many stimulating conversations during seminars, coffee breaks and dinners over the years. I am highly indebted to Alice Schneider and Adeel Hussain for encouraging me to embark upon this project in the first place. I am grateful for their continuous support and for providing me with a home in Cambridge at the beginning of my PhD. I also want to thank Johanna Lukate, Allegra

Fryxell, Sasha Montelli, Domna Michailidou, Shalina Daved, Emily Sloan Rhodes and Spencer Rhodes for their friendship and for making my time in Cambridge such an enriching experience.

My friends Julia Redies, Ingra Sallaba, Gerd Weyer, Rieke Arendt, Agnes Michels, Ophélie Perrault, Mathias Häußler, Theresa Grundler, Daniel Spinks, Sarah Lampe and Rajka Kölble offered both emotional support and happy distractions over the years, and I am extremely grateful to them for all the good times spent together.

The Freie Universität Berlin provided me with a highly pleasant work environment during the final stages of my PhD, and I would like to thank Peter-André Alt, Tomaž Čebašek, Antonia Fegeler, Susanne Kruppa, Ina Lödden and Goran Krstin for welcoming me so warmly to my interim role as personal assistant at the university's Presidential Office. My wonderful colleagues at the MPISoc accompanied this project during its later stages. The dynamic and welcoming atmosphere has made my time at the institute both academically stimulating and socially enriching.

It has been an immense privilege to work in some of the best libraries I could imagine for this project. The Cambridge Univerity Library, the Bayerische Staatsbibliothek, Nasjonalbiblioteket, the HumSam-biblioteket and the Juridisk bibliotek of the University of Oslo, the library at HL-senteret, the MPISoc Library and the Seeley Historical Library provided me with invaluable resources and stimulating work environments. I would especially like to thank Jakob Berg Olsen for guiding me through the collections of the HL-senteret's library, as well as Henning Frankenberger, Head of the MPISoc Library, for being so helpful with regard to acquiring literature on the Nordic countries. In addition, I am extremely grateful to the staff at the Norwegian National Archives and the Oslo State Archives for their help with tracking down so many archival documents over the years.

Carrying out this research would not have been possible without the financial support of the Cambridge European Trust; the Faculty of History of the University of Cambridge; the Prince Consort and Thirlwall Fund; Corpus Christi College, Cambridge; the FAZIT Foundation; the Max Planck Society; and the Fritt Ord Foundation. I thank them for their confidence in this project.

In Cambridge University Press I have found the perfect academic home for this book. I would like to thank the Press, and especially my editor Liz Friend-Smith, for believing in the potential of this book and for making the publication process such a pleasant experience. I also would like to thank the editors of the series New Studies in European History, as well as the three anonymous reviewers, who offered extremely helpful feedback on earlier drafts.

To my family, especially my husband Marcus, my parents and my sister – thank you for your endless love and support on this journey. It means the world to me.

Note on Translations

Unless otherwise indicated, all translations are those of the author.

Abbreviations

Innst.	*Innstilling* – a parliamentary or select committee's recommendation to the parliament (*Storting*)
L.tid.	*Lagtingstidende* – parliamentary proceedings of the *Lagting* (the *Storting*'s former lower chamber)
O.tid.	*Odelstingstidende* – parliamentary proceedings of the *Odelsting* (the *Storting*'s former upper chamber)
Ot.prp.	*Odelstingsproposisjon* – proposal on a new legislative act
P.M.	*Pro Memoria* – a ministerial or government memorandum
RA	*Riksarkivet* – the National Archives of Norway
Rt.	*Norsk Retstidende* – a periodical publishing the decisions of the Norwegian Supreme Court
SAO	*Statsarkivet Oslo* – Regional State Archives in Oslo
S.tid.	*Stortingstidende* – parliamentary proceedings of the *Storting*
St.meld.	*Stortingsmelding* – report to be presented by the government to the parliament (*Storting*)
St.prp.	*Stortingsproposisjon* – proposal to the *Storting* not concerning a new legislative act

Introduction

I.1 The Last Word

When the trial against Oliver Langeland opened before the Court of Appeal in Oslo on 15 November 1950, it was followed closely by the media, the government and the wider public. Countless spectators filled the public gallery, in which not a seat had been left vacant.[1] A total of 125 witnesses had been summoned for the trial, which was scheduled to last for three weeks. Langeland was one of the most ardent critics of the 'treason trials': the Norwegian authorities' reckoning with those who had collaborated with the enemy during the German occupation between 1940 and 1945.[2] Langeland had published two books, in 1948 and 1949, attacking government policy before, during and after the war. Most of all, he had criticised the ways in which the treason trials had been carried out since the liberation. His books were widely read, and his first book *Judge Not* (*Dømmer ikke*) sold around 25,000 copies.[3] It was for his books that Langeland was on trial, officially because some sections were deemed to contain libellous presentations of some of Norway's senior officials. But it was no secret that the trial concerned a much broader question: the legitimacy of the reckoning as a whole. Opinion on Langeland was hugely divided. To some, he had, despite his wartime background as the head of the military resistance (*Milorg*) in Oslo, turned towards an antipatriotic stance. He was endangering national unity when it

[1] 'Fri kritikk av rettsoppgjøret', *Morgenposten* (15 November 1950); '125 vitner, forhandlingene vil ta 2–3 uker', *Dagbladet* (15 November 1950); 'Lagmannsrettssaken mot Langeland og Bergsvik begynt', *Aftenposten* (15 November 1950).

[2] This book uses the terms 'reckoning' and 'treason trials' interchangeably to refer to the judicial and administrative proceedings conducted in Norway against wartime collaborators following the Second World War ('*landssvikoppgjøret*' or '*rettsoppgjøret*' in Norwegian). The term 'treason trials' is used in a descriptive sense to capture that Norway's post-war reckoning was mainly concerned with the offence of treason.

[3] SAO/A-10085c/J/Jc/Jca/Jcac/3215: document nr. 113, letter by Roar Fjeld to Oslo Criminal Police, 2 September 1950.

was much needed, only a few years after the end of the German occupation and at the dawn of the Cold War. To others, he was a speaker of hard truths: someone who finally challenged the core assumptions of the treason trials, questioning whether just judgement had been meted out and the right individuals had been held to account.

While Langeland's books were widely read and discussed in newspapers across the country, it is the way Norwegian authorities chose to respond to them that is most revealing of the delicate political climate in Norway in the late 1940s. In December 1948, the government had appointed a special advocate, Øystein Thommessen, to undertake a thorough investigation into Langeland's 'campaign against the treason trials'.[4] The investigation led to legal proceedings being brought against Langeland, as well as a comprehensive report being published and widely circulated in 1950 on each of Langeland's claims, which was subsequently debated by the Norwegian parliament (the *Storting*) in 1952. These measures were a desperate attempt by officials to bring to a conclusion the heated debate that had raged in Norway ever since the liberation on how to handle the painful legacy of the occupation. The debate concerned the ways in which Norwegian authorities had administered the trials of collaborators after the liberation in 1945, and the many inconsistencies and controversies that had accompanied this process. But, as both the authorities in charge and their critics knew, these debates also touched on the validity of the historic interpretations driving them, and by extension, on the political legitimacy and authority of those in power in post-war Norway.

I.2 A Difficult Reckoning

The early post-war period in Norway was an era of reckonings. These took place simultaneously and at multiple levels, within the criminal justice system, the broader administration, in industry and in civil society.[5] Not a single citizen had remained unaffected by five years of German occupation. Upon the liberation, Norwegians sought to come to terms with the tensions and difficulties the occupation had brought upon their country. This soon involved building a national narrative of overwhelming collective resistance, marred only by the actions of a small group of disloyal

[4] St.meld. nr. 64 (1950), p. 1; 'Rettslig etterforskning i anledning av Langelands bok', *Aftenposten* (11 December 1948); 'Mer gransking', *Aftenposten* (11 December 1948).

[5] Ole Kristian Grimnes, 'Fra krig til fred', in Hans Fredrik Dahl, Hans Kirchhoff, Joachim Lund and Lars-Erik Vaale (eds.), *Danske tilstande – norske tilstande: forskelle og ligheder under tysk besættelse 1940–45* (Copenhagen: Gyldendal, 2010), pp. 259–281, at p. 277.

collaborators. The reckonings were about allocating blame for collaboration with the enemy and defining who had forfeited their right to membership of the national community. Internal 'honour courts', established within businesses, institutions and societies, decided upon the collaborative involvement of their employees and members, and along with it their professional and personal futures. Examples of professional honour courts included those for journalists, artists and solicitors.[6] The reckonings that took place in private led to many individuals being excluded from their social or professional environment, or even their own families. It was a period of intense social tragedy, but also of opportunism. Many who had played ambivalent or trivial roles during the occupation opted into a narrative of collective resistance, and called for harsh punishment of the 'traitors'. In some cases, private reckonings led to acts of violence against collaborators or those who were said to have 'failed the national struggle'.[7] In many regards, these different processes overlapped and shaped one another. All in all, an estimated 12 per cent of the Norwegian population were affected by the reckonings that took place after 1945.[8]

The 'treason trials' (*landssvikoppgjøret* or *rettsoppgjøret*), implemented by the Norwegian authorities between 1945 and 1957, were the most central element within this broader set of reckonings. They had been planned by the Norwegian government-in-exile in cooperation with the resistance between 1941 and 1945. A swift legal process of collaborators, it was hoped, would prevent mob justice and stabilise society during the period of social and political transition that would follow the liberation. The resistance had warned of the enormous hatred towards collaborators, and had argued that a strict reckoning was at once a necessary response to the 'sense of justice' in the population and to prevent social violence and chaos.[9] But the trials were about more than preventing violence. The exiled authorities – and the underground resistance members who hoped

[6] Guri Hjeltnes, *Avisoppgjøret etter 1945* (Oslo: Aschehoug, 1990), pp. 68–96; Dag Solhjell and Hans Fredrik Dahl, *Men viktigst er æren: oppgjøret blant kunstnerne etter 1945* (Oslo: Pax Forlag, 2013); Harald Espeli, Hans Eyvind Næss and Harald Rinde (eds.), *Våpendrager og veiviser: advokatenes historie i Norge* (Oslo: Universitetsforlaget, 2008).

[7] Johannes Andenæs, *Det vanskelige oppgjøret* (Oslo: Tanum-Norli, 1979), pp. 61–65.

[8] Anders Gogstad, *'Men seier'n var vår': søkelys på omveltningenes år mellom krig og fred* (Bergen: University of Bergen, 2003), p. 156. In addition, research has shown how subsequent generations were affected by these processes: Baard Herman Borge, 'I rettsoppgjørets lange skygger: andre generasjons problemer i lys av moderne transisjonsteori' (PhD Dissertation, University of Bergen, 2012).

[9] The preparation of the trials is discussed more fully in Chapter 1.

for a central role in the post-war order – realised that they would be a central factor in reuniting the nation during the transition period, and that they would mark a powerful symbolic change from five years of German rule to the return of a sovereign Norwegian nationhood.[10] The reckoning with the Norwegian collaborators was to take place in legal form, carried out by the restored criminal justice system, and was to be 'worthy of a state based on the rule of law'.[11] The trials were therefore intended to reinstil faith in public institutions and to demonstrate their moral authority. During the occupation, the exile government had issued a series of decrees (*provisoriske anordninger*)[12] from London, expanding the scope of the Criminal Code of 1902, by which it communicated its intention to bring collaborators to trial from 1941 onwards.[13] The most important aspect of these preparations was the express criminalisation of formal membership of the Norwegian fascist party, *Nasjonal Samling* (NS), with whom the Germans cooperated. In 1944, the earliest decrees were developed into a more comprehensive set of provisions that would form a key basis for the post-war reckoning. However, due to the complex constitutional questions raised by the occupation, these decrees were juridically ambivalent, raising numerous concerns about their legal validity that would later threaten the overall legitimacy of the trials.[14]

The exile government had estimated that the trials would be over within one year of the liberation, ensuring a swift return to a peaceful and unified society, which could firmly leave the upheavals of its recent past behind. Due to a radical underestimation of the scope of the legal provisions implemented for the reckoning, however, the trials were not concluded

[10] On the role of the reckoning in Norwegian nation-building, see Baard Herman Borge, 'Forsoningen som uteble. Norges oppgjør med landssvikerne', in Bård-Anders Andreassen and Elin Skaar (eds.), *Forsoning eller rettferdighet?* (Oslo: Cappelen, 1998), pp. 204–234, at pp. 219–220.

[11] 'Strengt rettsoppgjør med landssvikerne – Men på en måte som er en rettsstat verdig. Quisling antagelig for forhørsrett alt i denne uken', *Nationen* (23 May 1945).

[12] The legal measures adopted by the exile government during the war (*provisoriske anordninger*) are referred to as 'provisional decrees' throughout this manuscript. They are also sometimes referred to as 'provisional ordinances' or 'provisional laws' in English. They were based – by extension – on emergency powers enshrined in Art. 17 of the Norwegian Constitution.

[13] Straffeloven av 1902; provisional decrees of 3 October 1941, 22 January 1942 and 15 December 1944, discussed in more detail later in this chapter.

[14] Their legality is disputed to this day: Hans Petter Graver, 'Rettsoppgjøret i Norge – tid for et nytt juridisk blikk?', *Lov og Rett: Norsk Juridisk Tidsskrift*, 54 (2015) 2, pp. 65–86; Baard Herman Borge and Lars-Erik Vaale, *Grunnlovens største prøve: rettsoppgjøret etter 1945* (Oslo: Scandinavian Academic Press), pp. 130–150 and pp. 151–172.

until 1957.[15] Far exceeding the estimations of the Norwegian government-in-exile, a total of 92,805 cases were ultimately investigated – almost twice the figure wartime authorities had anticipated and the equivalent of 3.2 per cent of the Norwegian population.[16] In the end, the Norwegian post-war trials became the most encompassing reckoning with former 'collaborators' in the whole of Europe.[17] Around 49,000 individuals were sentenced by a court, 46,000 on counts of collaboration, which was brought under the offence of treason.[18] The same number of individuals lost some or all of their civil rights. A total of 18,000 people received a prison sentence.[19] Thirty death sentences were handed down, and 25 of these executed.[20] In addition, the courts ordered a total of 289.9 million Norwegian kroners in compensation payments from members of the NS (approx. 572 million GBP by today's standards).[21] The trials raised numerous legal concerns, including retroactivity, lack of a constitutional basis, and the collapse of the separation of powers, as well as the establishment of criminal culpability without subjective intent (*mens rea*). In addition, the trials – as well as the reckoning more generally – raised difficult social and political questions about the attribution of guilt and the redefinition of the patriotic community in the early post-war era. In the end, the reckoning would be remembered not for the efficient way in which the law handled the occupation legacy and stabilised post-war Norwegian society, but for the

15 The actual end date of the trials can be somewhat difficult to determine. 1957 was the year the last individuals sentenced during the trials were released from prison, and it will mark the end date of the trials as such within the context of this study. Hans Fredrik Dahl states 1955 as the end year of the trials, the year the criminal court cases had been concluded – Hans Fredrik Dahl, *En kort historie om rettsoppgjøret etter krigen* (Oslo: Pax Forlag, 2018), p. 7, while other sources state 1964 as the conclusion, as this was the year the formal report of the Treason Commission was debated and all cases had been processed by the court system.

16 The authorities had underestimated membership of the NS, and had planned for around 45,000–50,000 cases; see Einar Gerhardsen, *Fellesskap i krig og fred: erindringer 1940–45* (Oslo: Tiden Norsk Forlag, 1970), p. 236; Norges Offisielle Statistikk XI 179, *Statistikk over landssvik 1940–1945* (Oslo: Statistisk Sentralbyrå, 1954), p. 12; Hans Fredrik Dahl, *Norsk idéhistorie, Bind V: De store ideologienes tid: 1914–1955* (Oslo: Aschehoug, 2001), p. 332.

17 Philip Morgan, *Hitler's Collaborators* (Oxford: Oxford University Press, 2018), p. 19.

18 *Statistikk over landssvik 1940–1945*, p. 22.

19 Hans Petter Graver, *Dommernes krig: den tyske okkupasjonen 1940–1945 og den norske rettsstaten* (Oslo: Pax Forlag, 2015), p. 157.

20 This figure excludes German war criminals.

21 Calculated on the basis of the mean year 1948 via the conversion tool of the Norwegian Bank: 'Priskalkulator', www.norges-bank.no/tema/Statistikk/Priskalkulator/, last accessed 29 September 2022, and converted from Norwegian Kroners to Pound Sterling on www.xe.com using the exchange rate of 29 September 2022.

problematic legal bases that it rested on and the deep social frictions it generated or failed to overcome.[22]

The reckoning had broad social ramifications. The main reason for this was the collective attribution of guilt through the criminalisation of membership of the NS. 'Active' and 'passive' party members alike were prosecuted for the offence of treason. As Johannes Andenæs, an influential law professor in post-war Norway who played a central role in shaping the reckoning, later stated, this became a dangerous 'psychological identification process'.[23] NS members were singled out and held responsible for the plight of the occupation. While other forms of collaboration also, in principle, came within the remit of the relevant criminal provisions, the members of the NS were tried early on and had a higher visibility in society compared, for example, to economic collaborators. The enormous public resonance of the trials amplified this effect. Throughout the reckoning, questions of guilt and its allocation captured the public mind and dominated newspaper headlines.[24] As the court machinery processed cases and put the 'treason stamp' on individuals, the country became increasingly divided. The allocation of culpability to this clearly defined group made it easy to eclipse the complexity and proximity of five years of occupation and the inevitable day-to-day contact with the occupier that it brought. As the trials unfolded, they increasingly became the very lens through which the occupation period was interpreted. They seemingly legitimised a nationally held desire (and conviction) that a majority of Norwegians had engaged in widespread resistance activity, and that only a clearly defined minority had collaborated with the Germans.[25] Lensed through the black–white binaries of 'guilt' or 'innocence', the greyscales of collaboration were rarely acknowledged.

A further characteristic of the trials is that their main focus was on very specific types of crimes. This is easily overlooked, given the significant scope of the Norwegian reckoning. Due to the central focus on crimes

[22] Susanne März, *Die langen Schatten der Besatzungszeit: 'Vergangenheitsbewältigung' in Norwegen als Identitätsdiskurs* (Berlin: Berliner Wissenschaftsverlag, 2008); Hans Fredrik Dahl and Øystein Sørensen (eds.), *Et rettferdig oppgjør? Rettsoppgjøret i Norge etter 1945* (Oslo: Pax Forlag, 2004).

[23] Andenæs, *Det vanskelige oppgjøret*, p. 61.

[24] Stein U. Larsen, 'Die Ausschaltung der Quislinge in Norwegen', in Klaus-Dietmar Henke and Hans Woller (eds.), *Politische Säuberung in Europa: die Abrechnung mit Faschismus und Kollaboration nach dem Zweiten Weltkrieg* (Munich: DTV, 1991), pp. 241–280, at p. 249.

[25] The true picture was significantly more bleak: only around 4 per cent of the population had, in fact, been engaged in active resistance activity: Arnd Bauerkämper, *Das umstrittene Gedächtnis: die Erinnerung an Nationalsozialismus, Faschismus und Krieg in Europa seit 1945* (Paderborn: Schöningh, 2012), p. 157.

against the state and the majority population, first and foremost treason (*landssvik*), the reckoning ultimately sidelined many of the crimes committed by Norwegian citizens during the occupation, both on Norwegian soil and abroad. During the war, Norwegian NS officials, police officers and members of various military and paramilitary organisations had participated in acts of violence against Norway's Jews, including the liquidation of their assets and their ultimate deportation to the extermination camps. Several thousand Norwegians had volunteered for the Waffen-SS, serving in divisions which partook in the murder of both civilians and prisoners of war.[26] Norwegian citizens had also served as guards in POW camps across Norway, where thousands of prisoners perished. However, the trials, as well as the comprehensive social, political and legal debates that accompanied them, revolved largely around the treasonous nature of joining and participation in the NS, taking up arms against the Norwegian state, obstructing the resistance and, to a lesser degree, economic collaboration and violent acts against individuals. And yet, even despite these limitations, the trials were of such scope that they ultimately overwhelmed the institutions involved in administering and implementing them.

From the perspective of the authorities, the trials drifted out of control within mere months of the liberation. Already by early 1946, the authorities were forced to come to terms with the fact that it would take the legal apparatus years to bring the reckoning to a conclusion. This brought with it a variety of problems. It burdened the individuals awaiting trial and put a strain on the nation's resources. Many individuals spent years awaiting their trial, jeopardising their return to their former workplaces and communities. With the backlog in cases, public faith in the ability of state institutions to handle the occupation legacy dwindled. Feeling that the reckoning with the 'traitors' was too slow, too lenient, or both, many communities developed their own strategies to handle the occupation legacy, often leaving those deemed to have collaborated socially vulnerable. Upon leaving the courtrooms and prisons of the country, many collaborators faced social condemnation and exclusion from their respective communities. Gradually, the reckoning, knowing only the binary categories of guilt and innocence, produced a group of social outcasts. The combination of institutional delays and social condemnation meant that the trials did not serve their original purposes: to have collaborators brought to justice,

[26] Linking individuals to specific crimes remains difficult. However, there are strong arguments that Norwegians partook in war crimes across Eastern Europe: Terje Emberland and Matthew Kott, *Himmlers Norge: nordmenn i det storgermanske prosjekt* (Oslo: Aschehoug, 2012), pp. 246–247.

but to see them return to society as rehabilitated citizens once they had served their sentence.

Rather than unite the fraught nation, the trials therefore soon appeared to be deepening social divisions. This development concerned both officials and critics of the trials. The government increasingly cautioned for moderation as angry masses threatened to undermine the success of the trials. The authorities in charge sought to accelerate proceedings in order to prevent long-term detrimental effects on society. But at the same time, they were reluctant to grant amnesties or to implement broad changes within the trials' legal framework. The credibility of the post-war legal system rested on the successful implementation of the treason trials as per the legal provisions that had been adopted during the occupation. The promise that the reckoning would be carried out within the contours of the rule of law soon proved the most fundamental challenge to their implementation: adherence to fundamental principles such as equality before the law meant that provisions could not be changed depending on the ebbs and flows of the caseload the courts faced or according to opinions expressed outside the courtroom. Those tried later should not benefit from institutional delays. As the trials progressed, authorities had to continuously balance the punitive purposes of the trials with the adverse effects they had on the nation.

By 1948, the bulk of cases against collaborators had been processed. However, the debate on the legacy and success of the treason trials was far from over. Opinions on the trials had become increasingly fragmented. While a small but ever more vocal group of hardliners continued to criticise the 'leniency' towards collaborators, a growing number of sceptics, from a variety of backgrounds, began to criticise the scope and administration of the trials, as well as their legal bases. With a growing distance in time to the occupation, debate also became more nuanced, with the anger that had defined the first few years following the occupation receding into the background. The focus was now on the present rather than the past. At this stage, many argued that the trials should have been restricted only to the key collaborators of the occupation. These critics were not exclusively the subjects of the trials themselves, but an ever-widening range of representatives from the academe, the Church, industry, and the political establishment itself. Collectively, they compelled the authorities to justify the trials both with a view to their legal validity as well as their political and social legitimacy. Numerous public scandals in the late 1940s surrounding the maltreatment of treason prisoners in the immediate post-war period put further pressure on authorities. But in the infancy of the Cold War, the trials also attained a new meaning: they were to symbolise the way the state would handle threats from within and how loyalty to the nation would be defined. Many felt that a new war was looming, and the representatives of the Norwegian state were intent on presenting the trials as an emblem of state authority.

Through a series of public statements, reports and investigations, the authorities looked to dampen down the debate that was raging by the late 1940s on whether or not the reckoning had been a success. The question increasingly revolved around the integrity of the state apparatus. But the efforts of the authorities to convey the complexity of the undertaking fell on deaf ears. Rather, the trials became a focal point of larger political disagreements within Norwegian politics at the time. In an attempt to make an authoritative statement on the reckoning as a whole, senior officials set in motion a comprehensive legal machinery to present an authoritative verdict on the treason trials. This, then, was the larger context in which Oliver Langeland was tried. His trial was an attempt to bring to a successful conclusion a legal undertaking that had been initiated during the occupation, more than a decade earlier. This, the authorities hoped, would finally draw a line under the occupation. But even then, the debate was far from over.

I.3 Contested Legacies

The manner in which the Norwegian post-war authorities brought collaborators to justice attracted significant interest worldwide. Such had been the resonance of Vidkun Quisling's actions following the German invasion of Norway that already during the war, the term 'quisling' had become a synonym for 'collaborator' across the globe.[27] The Western Allies followed Quisling's trial closely as they prepared the Nuremberg trials. A representative of the United States' Chief of Counsel for the prosecution of Nazi war criminals, Robert Jackson, accompanied the Norwegian delegation in its preparations of Quisling's trial.[28] Beyond its work in Norway, this delegation travelled to Germany, France and Great Britain to gather evidence for the case against Quisling and, in doing so, worked

[27] 'Quislings Everywhere', *The Times* (19 April 1940); Prime Minister Winston Churchill's Speech to the Allied Delegates, St James's Place, London, 12 June 1941 (Churchill had described it as 'a new word which will carry the scorn of mankind down the centuries').

[28] George Axelsson, 'Quisling on Trial for His Life Today', *New York Times* (20 October 1945).

closely with other allied representatives.[29] The evidence collected during the joint investigations – in a 'demonstration of international collaboration'[30] – would both help bring Quisling to trial and aid in the prosecution of war criminals at Nuremberg. In addition, allied representatives were present throughout Quisling's trial, which was followed closely by the international press.[31]

And yet, despite their wide resonance across the Western world at the time, the Norwegian trials remain curiously neglected in the anglophone historiography, where no full study on the trials exists. References to the trials are made in some of the central works on early post-war Europe. These include the books *Postwar* by Tony Judt, *Out of Ashes* by Konrad Jarausch and *Dark Continent* by Mark Mazower.[32] However, reference to the Norwegian handling of the collaboration legacy is mostly only made in passing – as a side note to the reckonings that have been studied more fully, such as the French, the Belgian and the Czechoslovak cases.[33] A recent publication – *Hitler's Collaborators* by Philip Morgan – looks at the Norwegian trials in more detail in one of its chapters, but as a whole does not go beyond a broader institutional and statistical comparison with parallel processes across Europe.[34] In German scholarship, the trials are referred to primarily as an afterthought in studies of the German occupation of Norway. A number of essays in collected volumes look at the administration of the reckoning both with German war criminals and the Norwegian collaborators. Summaries of the trials can also be found in comparative studies of the post-war reckonings across Europe.[35] These, however, often take the form of statistical and institutional overviews,

[29] See for example Arne W. Brøgger to James B. Donovan, accompanied by diary notes, 4 September 1945, in 'The War Crimes Trials at Nuremberg', Archives of Harry S. Truman; RA/S-1555/D/L0048: Letter from Jens Chr. Hauge to Colonel Amen, 14 December 1945.

[30] Ibid.

[31] See for example 'Quisling Executed by a Firing Squad', *New York Times* (24 October 1945); Axelsson, 'Quisling on Trial for His Life Today'.

[32] Tony Judt, *Postwar: A History of Europe since 1945* (London: Penguin, 2010); Konrad Jarausch, *Out of Ashes: A New History of Europe in the Twentieth Century* (Princeton: Princeton University Press, 2015); Mark Mazower, *Dark Continent: Europe's Twentieth Century* (New York: Vintage Books, 2000).

[33] Henry Rousso, *The Vichy Syndrome: History and Memory in France since 1944* (Cambridge, MA: Harvard University Press, 1994); Martin Conway, *The Sorrows of Belgium: Liberation and Political Reconstruction, 1944–1947* (Oxford: Oxford University Press, 2012); Benjamin Frommer, *National Cleansing: Retribution against Nazi Collaborators in Postwar Czechoslovakia* (New York: Cambridge University Press, 2005).

[34] Morgan, *Hitler's Collaborators*, pp. 13–31.

[35] Henke and Woller (eds.), *Politische Säuberung in Europa*.

without going into much detail on the implementation of the trials, or the obstacles and tensions faced in the process.

In Norwegian historiography, the treason trials were long considered a 'taboo' topic. Widespread newspaper coverage and the many debates on the subject in the Norwegian parliament up until 1952 had ensured that the trials as a political issue remained present in the public realm throughout their duration. In 1962, the Treason Commission published its concluding report on the treason trials, which was debated in the *Storting* in 1964. Politically, however, they remained contentious for much longer. In the 1970s, debate flared up again, when individuals who had been sentenced during the treason trials were elected to the Norwegian parliament for the first time.[36] At the same time, authorities were hoping for closure on what had been a crippling debate. It is perhaps unsurprising, therefore, that the trials were not subjected to comprehensive scholarly investigation. In the decades following the trials, it was mainly those – directly or indirectly – affected by them that wrote about them. Most books about the trials in the 1950s, 1960s and 1970s were personal accounts from subjects of the trials.[37] Ole Kristian Grimnes has pointed towards the mechanisms that produced this subgenre of often apologetic writing, stating that it was the very 'collective condemnation of NS' that led to such a strong counter-reaction in the form of apologist literature.[38] However, not all contributions were by members of the NS: criticism also came from the left of the political spectrum.[39] Whatever the political agenda, writing on the trials became a form of protest against the political establishment.

One book from the 1970s stands out in that it provides both a legal analysis of and insider view on the trials: *Det vanskelige oppgjøret* (*The Difficult Reckoning*) by Johannes Andenæs, a law professor at the University of Oslo who was involved in the planning and conduct of the trials at various levels.[40] The book is part legal investigation, part historical account and part memoir. It is less a scholarly account than a reflection on how Andenæs himself interpreted and experienced the trials. Andenæs

36 Hanna Kvanmo, *Dommen* (Oslo: Gyldendal, 1990).

37 Ole Kristian Grimnes, 'Historieskrivingen om okkupasjonen. Det nasjonale konsenssyndromets gjennomslagskraft', *Nytt Norsk Tidsskrift* (1990), pp. 108–121; März, *Die langen Schatten der Besatzungszeit*, p. 198.

38 Ibid., Grimnes, p. 110.

39 Helge Krog, *6te kolonne?: om den norske storindustriens bidrag til Nazi-Tysklands krigføring* (Oslo: Pax Forlag, 1969); Terje Valen, *De tjente på krigen: hjemmefronten og kapitalen* (Oslo: Oktober, 1974).

40 Andenæs, *Det vanskelige oppgjøret*.

does not merely present the official version of events, however: he also adopts critical positions, and acknowledges some of the trials' shortcomings.[41] But as a whole, Andenæs largely defends the trials from the perspective of someone who was involved in them, and therefore his work cannot be understood as a scholarly contribution as such.

The long absence of nuanced scholarship on the trials has to be seen in the context of the broader field of historical research on the occupation period itself. Norwegian historiography on the occupation and on the treason trials are closely intertwined. Having come out of a period of five years of enemy occupation, there was a strong desire in the relatively young nation-state of Norway to restore its proud national self-image. We find in early Norwegian scholarship on the occupation a strong tendency to moralise, and to write a war history of national cohesion, portraying a society collectively engaged in resistance activity.[42] This has resulted in a 'value dichotomy' in most writing on the occupation period.[43] As Synne Corell's research into Norwegian historiography of the occupation period has shown, the key works of the post-war period were marked by a strong consensus on the occupation period and a near-universal focus on the experience of the national community. The distinction between 'friend' and 'foe', the 'traitors' and the 'resisters' defined much thinking about the occupation.[44]

This binary approach to the history of the occupation made it difficult to find fault with the treason trials. The official narratives offered an interpretation of wartime events that, on the whole, corresponded to the punishment that had been meted out during the trials. Communists and persecuted minorities were long excluded from these official histories.[45] Moreover, the ambivalences of the occupation period were conveniently eclipsed. Corell points towards incoherent depictions of the resistance, and a conflation of active and passive resistance in order to allow for a broad identification and association with it.[46] It is unsurprising, therefore, that in the official narratives, the trials, with their broad condemnation of NS

41 Ibid., p. 259.

42 Synne Corell, *Krigens ettertid: okkupasjonshistorien i norske historiebøker* (Oslo: Scandinavian Academic Press, 2010).

43 Robert Bohn, *Reichskommissariat Norwegen: 'Nationalsozialistische Neuordnung' und Kriegswirtschaft* (Munich: Oldenbourg, 2009), p. 18.

44 Corell, *Krigens ettertid*, p. 52; Synne Corell, 'The Solidarity of a National Narrative: The German Occupation in Norwegian History Culture', in Henrik Stenius, Mirja Österberg and Johan Östling (eds.), *Nordic Narratives of the Second World War: National Historiographies Revisited* (Lund: Nordic Academic Press, 2011), pp. 101–126.

45 Corell, 'The Solidarity of a National Narrative'.

46 Corell, *Krigens ettertid*, pp. 72, 125.

membership and the sidelining of other forms of collaboration, seemed like a natural outflow of that version of occupation history. While increasing calls were made in the 1990s for the trials to be subjected to in-depth scholarly investigation, hardly any works saw the light of day. In 1993, Dag Ellingsen published a book on the reckoning with economic collaborators.[47] His work pointed out the inconsistencies and inequalities of the handling of the economic side of the occupation. But before the turn of the millennium few other researchers followed suit.

The turn of the millennium, finally, brought with it an increasing scholarly focus on the treason trials. Historians such as Hans Fredrik Dahl, Øystein Sørensen, Ole Kristian Grimnes and Odd-Bjørn Fure paved the way towards a more nuanced history of the occupation, and also called into question the dominant attitudes towards the treason trials. In 1999, a group of historians at the University of Oslo launched the research project 'Å overkomme fortiden' ('Overcoming the Past') on 'transitional justice' after 1945. It published its findings in four volumes, one of which was about the Norwegian treason trials. This volume, entitled 'Et rettferdig oppgjør?' ('A Just Reckoning?') and edited by Hans Frederik Dahl and Øystein Sørensen, contains eight essays on various aspects of the trials, such as the role of parliament, the punishment of members of the NS and the economic reckoning.[48] But while the collection is comprehensive in its aims and covers a broad range of topics, the scope of reflection in the book is at times narrowed by its concern with the question of whether the trials were 'just'.

Since the completion of 'Å overkomme fortiden', a number of studies on the trials have emerged. Some of these works have argued that the trials amounted to an unfair and illegitimate process towards those who stood trial. Ingerid Hagen's 2009 book provides a critical account of specific aspects of the trials, in particular the one-sided debate culture of the time, the maltreatment of prisoners and the systematic silencing of the trials' critics. She revisits some of the critiques raised by contemporaries, including Oliver Langeland, and the opposition they faced on the part of the state. It is in many ways a ground-breaking work, in that it is the first to specifically address the political debate on the trials, the fate of the trials' critics and questions of freedom of speech. However, Hagen's work can at times feel somewhat 'sensationalist'. Her main aim appears to be to uncover a historic 'wrong' by pointing to the maltreatment of prisoners

[47] Dag Ellingsen, *Krigsprofitørene og rettsoppgjøret* (Oslo: Gyldendal, 1993).
[48] Dahl and Sørensen (eds.), *Et rettferdig oppgjør?*.

in the first period of the trials, and the authorities' silencing of those critics who brought these conditions into the spotlight. Due to this specific concern, Hagen's analysis does not take into account the full spectrum of causes for specific decisions taken by the authorities in the course of the trials.

In December 2018, Baard Herman Borge and Lars-Erik Vaale published a comprehensive study of the trials and their relationship to the Norwegian Constitution, the *Grunnloven*.[49] In twelve thoroughly researched chapters, they investigate some of the core legal questions raised by the trials in relation to their legal bases and the role assumed by different political institutions in shaping them. The individual chapters of their volume mainly deal with the legitimacy of the role played by different institutions during the trials, and with core constitutional principles, such as the separation of powers, non-retroactivity and the right to free speech. The book provides the most thorough existing scholarly examination of the trials and their relationship to the Norwegian legal system and demonstrates just how far constitutional principles were stretched in the process of carrying them out. However, in this work, too, a key concern is to challenge the trials from a particular vantage point – in this case from the perspective of the law, and in particular the principles enshrined in the Norwegian Constitution.

Recent years have also witnessed an increasing number of works dealing with the shortcomings of the trials from other perspectives. In particular, the lack of focus on the victims of the Holocaust, as well as on prisoners of war and civilian forced labourers who perished, has been highlighted as a major omission of the trials.[50] This shift in focus has also been the result of a more differentiated understanding of the occupation history as such. In recent years, new details about Norwegians' participation in the deportation of the Jews and the seizure of their assets have come to light.[51] As more research into the complexities of the Norwegian wartime economy has been undertaken, it has also emerged that the considerable economic contributions made by slave labourers in Norway were

[49] Baard Herman Borge and Lars-Erik Vaale, *Grunnlovens største prøve: rettsoppgjøret etter 1945* (Oslo: Scandinavian Academic Press, 2018).

[50] Per Ole Johansen (ed.), *På siden av rettsoppgjøret* (Oslo: Unipub, 2006); Synne Corell, *Likvidasjonen: historien om holocaust i Norge og jakten på jødenes eiendom* (Oslo: Gyldendal, 2021).

[51] Bjarte Bruland, *Holocaust i Norge. Registrering. Deportasjon. Tilintetgjørelse* (Oslo: Dreyers Forlag, 2017); Corell, *Likvidasjonen*.

downplayed in the post-war era.[52] The suffering of Soviet and Yugoslav prisoners of war in camps guarded by both Germans and Norwegians, these studies have highlighted, had only a marginal presence in the trials.[53] In addition, many of the post-war narratives continue to be questioned, including that of the knowledge held by the wartime resistance concerning the Holocaust, which was debated intensely in a series of books published between 2018 and 2021.[54] Based on new insights into occupation history, therefore, scholars have been able to highlight how the reckoning fell short of delivering justice for groups of individuals who did not form part of the majority national narrative following the war.

The increased scholarly focus in recent years has placed the trials more firmly at the centre of Norwegian historical discourse. However, many of the above studies, in particular those that challenge the trials from the perspective of those who were sentenced, revolve largely around questions of legality or moral legitimacy. This has meant that many of the legal questions posed by the trials have typically been addressed *as* legal questions, rather than as elements of political history. In addition, the overriding focus on the law has often limited investigations to the national context. Rather than embedding the Norwegian experience within the political and social processes of 'post-war justice' across national boundaries, the trials appear to be examined mainly with reference to the Norwegian legal system. This needlessly limits our understanding of the political dynamics of the trials and their place within European post-war history. The studies of the groups that were overlooked, on the other hand, as important as they are, tend not to provide accounts of the trials as a whole. This book, by contrast, aims to provide a study of the trials in their entirety, explaining how they unfolded and what positions their key actors took over time.

I.4 A New Perspective

This book offers a first scholarly investigation into the central agents behind the treason trials and their changing roles and motivations, as well

[52] Hans Otto Frøland, Gunnar Hatlehol and Mats Ingulstad, 'Regimenting Labour in Norway during Nazi Germany's Occupation', *Unabhängige Historikerkommission zur Geschichte des Reichsarbeitsministeriums, 1933–1945*, Working Paper No. 12, 2017, p. 16.

[53] Bjørn Westlie, *Fangene som forsvant: NSB og slavearbeiderne på Nordlandsbanen* (Oslo: Spartacus, 2015).

[54] Marte Michelet, *Hva visste hjemmefronten? Holocaust i Norge: varslene, unnvikelsene, hemmeligholdet* (Oslo: Gyldendal, 2018); Bjarte Bruland, Elise B. Berggren and Mats Tangestuen, *Rapport frå ein gjennomgang av Hva visste hjemmefronten?* (Oslo: Dreyers Forlag, 2020).

as the arguments they invoked, in shaping the trials' contours throughout the entirety of their duration. It examines how the Norwegian authorities planned, implemented and interpreted the reckoning with wartime collaborators between 1941 and 1964. In doing so, it looks at the broader political purposes the trials served, how these changed over time and the mechanisms that brought these changes about. This book therefore has two central aims: first, it aims to push scholarship on the trials beyond questions of justice and legality and to open it up towards the complexities of competing power structures, institutional motivations and argumentative patterns within a broad political and social context. The often legalistic focus of much previous scholarship offers too narrow a framework for understanding these deeply political processes. Second, it aims to provide an account of the policy decisions surrounding the trials in their entirety, from the first planning efforts in exile and in the underground during the early 1940s, to when the legacies of the trials became the subject of intense political debate during the 1960s. Looking at the central administrators of the trials *over time* allows us to place individual events, decisions and arguments in relation to one another and to understand what purposes the trials served at different stages of their implementation, and how various policies and purposes intersected. Scholarly works on distinct groups or events of the trials – important as they are – cannot set the core decisions of the trials in their larger context.

The book argues that the trials were not driven by the agenda of any one institution or group, but that their final shape was the result of a complex process of weighing up demands for legal form and consistency against a fast-changing political and social environment. To understand the shape the trials ultimately took, it is important, I argue, to understand how institutions found themselves bound by their understanding of the law in administrating the trials, as well as how their decisions were embedded within the broader social and political dynamics of the time. The post-war authorities took pride in the fact that the treason trials were to take place in conformity with legal norms. But the emphasis on legal form also became the central challenge of these trials. The belief that ordinary principles of law could provide a response to the events of the occupation made the reckoning vulnerable to schematism and risked accelerating a process of polarisation in wider society. The law was also unclear on many of the unique situations brought about by the occupation. Throughout the treason trials, the decisions taken were results of a complex interaction between legal principles and the social and political forces found within Norwegian institutions and wider society at their various stages. This interaction exposed a gap between legal doctrine and social and political expectations, and resulted in the trials being guided by a certain element of pragmatism. Ultimately, therefore, the book argues that the Norwegian treason trials point towards the inherent limitations of the law in overcoming the friction and tension of an enemy occupation.

In its analysis, the book covers both 'internal' and 'external' influences on the trials, which over time came to shape one another. 'Internal' influences are understood as the personal, political and legal convictions articulated within the institutions that prepared, administered and governed the trials. The book analyses in particular how changing political, legal and pragmatic considerations both during and after the liberation led to disagreement regarding the scope, purposes and legitimacy of the trials. For the perspective from within, the main focus will be on the central institutions that determined the shape of the trials: the government (both the government-in-exile as well as the first three post-war governments), and in particular the Ministry of Justice and the Office of the Director of Public Prosecutions, Norway's most senior prosecutorial authority. Wherever relevant to the overall scope and overall course of the trials, the study also looks at court decisions, in particular the binding judgments of the Norwegian Supreme Court, the *Høyesterett*. 'External' influences, on the other hand, are understood as the broader public attitudes and debates surrounding the trials in civil society. In this context, the book analyses three spheres of debate and opposition to which the aforementioned central authorities had to respond in the administration of the trials: the Norwegian parliament, legal experts and public debate, in particular press coverage. The analysis is therefore concerned with both the legal and policy arguments advanced by the institutions in charge, as well as the role played by broader sociopolitical forces. What these two perspectives seek to uncover, therefore, is how and why specific decisions of law and policy were made, and what arguments they rested on.

In this way, the book connects the trials and their inner political, legal and institutional logic with the political debates and social realities in which they were embedded. It demonstrates how the legal, political and moral justifications employed by the central authorities in charge of administrating the trials interacted with those presented in the media and the political sphere. In doing so, it looks at the expectations and desires of a nation that had just come out of five years of occupation, and explores how and why the trials soon became so fiercely contested. At the same time, it examines the ways in which the authorities actively sought to shape public debates on the trials and tried to convey certain political messages through them. This in turn helps further an understanding of why the trials became so important to authorities that they waged attacks on those who dared to criticise them. In addition, this book examines how the belief systems of the time focused attention from the outset on specific sets of crimes against the majority population, leaving the fates of many victims unaddressed in the trials at large. The present study covers a longer period than most studies of the trials. This allows us to chart the transition from the early post-war period, when questions of political and legal legitimacy were central, to later years, when the trials turned increasingly on questions of historical legacy.

It bears repeating that this book is not concerned with questions of justice as such. The book neither seeks to justify the trials, nor to condone the actions or oversights of their key protagonists. The book is therefore not concerned with assessing the legal questions at the heart of the trials within the doctrinal logic of the law, nor in assessing their moral legitimacy. While legal and moral issues are at the centre of the book, the question is not what was or was not legal or 'just', but rather how different agents interpreted, or chose to interpret, the law, what motivations informed these interpretations, how these interpretations were mediated and contested between different agents, and what consequences they had for the administration of the trials. Its overall aim is therefore to further our understanding of the political, social, economic and individual forces that were engaged in the treason trials and how they engaged with the law. It is tempting of course to utilise concepts such as 'legality', '(transitional) justice' or 'morality' as an analytical tool for topics that centre so much around legal processes as the present one. However, a purely legal or normative analysis would not be able to answer the questions of *why* and *how* the treason trials took the shape they did.[55]

Rather than understanding the book's theme in relation to the concept of 'transitional justice', as would seem intuitive, this book chooses a different emphasis by focusing on the dynamics of what we may term 'transitional politics': a politics that is marked by recent disruption such as regime change, and which is characterised by competing and fast-changing attitudes towards the handling of the past regime's legacy. During times of 'transitional politics', public authorities can be questioned, and the

[55] Transitional justice can be used both in a descriptive or a normative sense. However, although frequently applied to the legal processes that followed the end of the Second World War, I find it best to avoid the term in this book, so as to focus the reader's attention to the political processes at play and avoid any suggestions of normativity.

institutions they represent need to (re)assert and stabilise the authority and legitimacy of their own power. 'Transitional politics' therefore entails a strong focus on the public resonance of any state measures, and a highly *demonstrative* and symbolic form of politics, as narratives of the recent past are collectively negotiated. The law typically plays a central role during such processes, but established legal principles frequently reach their limits. What this book aims to do, then, is to contrast the dynamics of politics with the inner logic of the law during Norway's early postwar years. This study therefore takes an encompassing approach to the public perception of the treason trials and the ways in which the law interacted with political decision-making and media and public discourses. This allows for a fuller investigation of the tensions surrounding the trials and the many questions raised by a situation in which a legal question is also a political one, and the outcome of a trial is also a verdict on history.

The verdict on history that the post-war trials produced – perhaps predictably – did not stand the test of time. As indicated above, the crimes against Jews and POWs did not form a focus of these trials, although the transgressions of the occupation period should have given rise to this. This was the case almost everywhere across formerly occupied countries in Europe. But the crimes against Jews and POWs were not ignored altogether. This book will explore some of the legal cases that were brought after the war concerning Jews and POWs, as well as the narratives surrounding them. As with the reckoning at large, however, it will not cast judgement on how these trials should have been conducted differently, neither from a legal nor from a moral perspective. In drawing on the recent literature on the fate of Norway's Jews in particular, it will rather seek to explain these absences by examining the contemporary political and social dynamics that drove the discourses surrounding the trials. This, in turn, will help cast a light on the social and political purposes of the trials, and by extension also on the society in which they unfolded.

To provide a nuanced account of the forces underlying the trials, the book places a particular emphasis on analysing their temporal dynamics. In doing so, it takes inspiration from the increasing focus on conceptions of time in the study of history.[56] Firstly, the study questions the presumption that any of the agents of the trials were rigid in their motivations, arguing instead that they were required to continuously modify their positions due to institutional limitations, a changing sociopolitical context,

[56] Marcus Colla, 'The Spectre of the Present: Time, Presentism and the Writing of Contemporary History', *Contemporary European History*, 30 (2021) 1, pp. 124–135.

changes in degrees of popular support and the inherent logic of the law itself. In order to grasp this, we need to go beyond a stagnant characterisation of the agents towards an analysis of how their positions changed over time. The book therefore distinguishes different chronological stages of the trials. Within each of these stages, the book traces the dynamics of the various overlapping legal and political discourses that shaped the trials. It then examines how discourses and individual as well as institutional positions shifted over time. This allows the book to chart the complex interaction across different discursive spheres across time and, ultimately, to provide a fuller picture of the decisions and rationales that shaped the contours of Norway's reckoning with its recent past.

Secondly, in understanding the complex interaction of law and politics in the immediate aftermath of Norway's occupation, the book aims to understand how the different actors located themselves *within time*, and how they saw their actions in relation to different conceptions of past, present and future. In doing so, the book examines in particular how these actors were bound by different, at times competing, temporal spheres: that of politics and that of law. As identified by Reinhart Koselleck, the law operates on a different temporal plane to history.[57] Law, 'in order to be law, is dependent upon its repeated applicability'.[58] History, on the other hand, is best understood by its 'diachronic singularity': while patterns and likenesses can be identified across historical periods, each event is ultimately unique.[59] Drawing on the ideas developed by Koselleck on temporality, the book therefore uncovers the competing temporal logics at play within the treason trials. It highlights how the distinct temporal logic of the law, which by its very nature aims to make generalisable, and to some extent, atemporal claims, aiming for consistency over time, ran into conflict with the shifting political agendas of Norway's post-war leaders and the fast-changing social environment in which they found themselves. In this way, the book aims to offer a case study on the multilayered temporalities of political trials. Because the trials marked a period of rapid change, and because they involved two systems with very different temporalities – the law and politics – the treason trials are a particularly useful event within which to examine competing and complementary temporal dynamics.

This study also contributes to a wider literature on post-war justice in Europe. It locates the Norwegian experience within a broader European

[57] Reinhart Koselleck, *Sediments of Time: On Possible Histories* (Stanford: Stanford University Press, 2018), pp. 117–136.

[58] Ibid., p. 130. [59] Ibid.

context by comparing and contrasting the Norwegian trials with political trials against wartime collaborators in other countries, thereby highlighting the distinctive characteristics of Norway's transition from war to post-war. After the Second World War, reckonings with those deemed to have collaborated took place across all countries that had been occupied by Germany. Many of these have been studied in detail.[60] One might wonder, therefore, what can be gained from an in-depth investigation into the underlying rationales of the Norwegian trials in particular. The book advances two reasons for why they are of particular interest. Firstly, the Norwegian reckoning was largely contained within the framework of the legal system. This sets it apart from many post-war purges across Europe after 1945, some of which were framed by widespread extra-legal violence.[61] Secondly, it was of a much broader scope than any of the other reckonings. As outlined earlier, 3.2 per cent of the Norwegian population were investigated, far more than in any other country.[62] One of the reasons for this was that no other occupied country criminalised membership of its fascist party per se. Even though a comparatively small percentage of those investigated received a prison sentence (18 per cent), Norway still had the highest imprisonment figures in Europe.[63] Out of every 100,000 individuals, 633 were sentenced to prison in Norway. By comparison, 94 out of every 100,000 were sentenced in France, 374 in Denmark, 419 in the Netherlands and 596 in Belgium.[64] While the trials themselves followed a pattern found in most European countries that had come out of occupation, the comparative breadth of the Norwegian case brought with it a set of distinct challenges that gave a very specific shape to the implementation of the trials and the broader debates surrounding them. It is this distinctive character of the Norwegian trials that stands at the centre of this book.

60 Istvan Deák, Jan T. Gross and Tony Judt (eds.), *The Politics of Retribution in Europe: World War II and Its Aftermath* (Princeton: Princeton University Press, 2000); Pieter Lagrou, *The Legacy of Nazi Occupation: Patriotic Memory and National Recovery in Western Europe, 1945–1965* (Cambridge: Cambridge University Press, 2004); Peter Novick, *The Resistance Versus Vichy: The Purge of Collaborators in Liberated France* (London: Chatto & Windus, 1968); Rousso, *The Vichy Syndrome*; Conway, *The Sorrows of Belgium*; Peter Romijn, *Snel, streng en rechtvaardig: politiek beleid inzake de bestraffing en reclassering van 'foute' Nederlanders, 1945–1955* (Amsterdam: De Haan, 1989); Frommer, *National Cleansing*; Ditlev Tamm, *Retsopgøret efter besættelsen* (Copenhagen: Jurist- og økonomforbundet, 1984); Andrew Kornbluth, *The August Trials: The Holocaust and Postwar Justice in Poland* (Cambridge, MA: Harvard University Press, 2021).

61 In France, estimated figures of extra-legal killings vary widely, ranging from just above 1,000 following the liberation to more than 10,000 when including the most intense period of fighting preceding the liberation; Henry Rousso, 'L'Epuration – Die politische Säuberung in Frankreich', in Henke and Woller (eds.), *Politische Säuberung in Europa*, pp. 192–234, at p. 202.

62 Judt, *Postwar*, p. 45. 63 Ibid., pp. 45–46. 64 Novick, *The Resistance Versus Vichy*, p. 187.

For the reasons I have outlined, this book in its chronological scope spans the entirety of the trials, from the initial planning stages in 1941 to the debate of the Treason Commission's report in 1964. Given the long period and the complex processes under investigation, the main focus of the study had to be restricted to the central authorities which administered the trials, the central court cases and the most influential parliamentary and public debates and events that determined their shape. Wherever possible, however, the study has also drawn upon singular cases as well as personal accounts of the trials to highlight the myriad ways in which the trials affected individuals in Norway after 1945. The book looks at parliamentary debates, newspaper coverage and events from across the country that had an influence on the contours and agendas of the trials. Particular emphasis is, however, placed on events in and around Oslo, which due to the density of NS activities in the city during the war, as well as it being the seat of the nation's most senior constitutional bodies, became the epicentre of the trials. With regard to the subjects of these trials, this book looks almost exclusively at the reckoning with Norwegian citizens. This is because the prosecution of collaboration on the one hand, and foreigners' war crimes on the other, raised very different legal, political and moral questions, and rested on different legal bases. In addition, the investigation of collaboration constituted both the overwhelming majority of cases and the central concern of authorities within the grander reckoning that took place (only 346 foreign citizens were investigated, compared to 92,805 Norwegian citizens).[65]

In terms of primary sources, I have relied primarily on the archives of the Norwegian Ministry of Justice (*Justisdepartementet*) and the Office of the Director of Public Prosecutions (*Riksadvokaten*), both held at the Norwegian National Archives (*Riksarkivet*) in Oslo. Within the archive of the Ministry of Justice, the study has drawn in particular on the files of the Law Division (*Lovavdelingen*), the Treason Division (*Landssvikavdelingen*) and the Prisons Division (*Fengselsstyret*) spanning the years 1940–1965. In the archive of the Director of Public Prosecutions, the study has relied on both the 'General Archive' as well as the 'Treason Archive'. In addition, the protocols of cabinet meetings between 1945 and 1953, the period during which the key decisions concerning the trials were taken by the Cabinet, as

[65] *Statistikk over landssvik 1940–1945*, p. 13; Tore Pryser, *Tyske hemmelige tjenester i Norden: spionsaker og aktører 1930–1950* (Oslo: Universitetsforlaget, 2012), p. 427; Lars-Erik Vaale and Baard Herman Borge, 'Caught between International Law and National Constitution: The Legal Reckoning with Foreign War Criminals in Norway after 1945', in *Max Planck Institute for Legal History and Legal Theory Research Paper Series*, No. 1, 2022, pp. 20–24.

well as the correspondences between the Cabinet and the Ministry of Justice, have been used to examine the distinct role of the government in the trials. Wherever relevant, the study has also drawn on files from the Ministry of Social Affairs and the Ministry of Church Affairs. In addition, I have consulted the personal archives of a number of central figures during the trials, including Professor Johannes Andenæs and Eivind Berggrav, the Bishop of Oslo. Finally, the case files of the trial against Oliver Langeland were examined in full at the State Archive in Oslo (*Statsarkivet*).

A further central set of sources that I have consulted are the court judgments produced by the treason trials, as well as select trial records held in the *Landssvikarkivet* at the National Archives in Oslo. The set of trial records, around 90,000 individual files in total, is too comprehensive for examination within the context of this study, as is the full set of judgments at all levels of the court system.[66] A review of the full set of judgments and individual files has also not been necessary to explore the reasons why the trials unfolded in the way that they did. However, looking at individual judgments allows us to examine in more detail some of the legal and moral arguments driving the trials, as well as the criticisms waged against some of their main premises. Dissenting judgments in particular can allow for insights into the core frictions of the trials. With the study's central focus in mind, the review of cases has therefore been focused on those judgments and files which concern some of the fundamental legal, political and social questions of the trials. The analysis is based on a full review of criminal and civil law judgments on the treason trials passed down by the Supreme Court and published in *Retstidende* from 1945 until 1950.[67] The focus on the judgments of the Supreme Court is meaningful in this context, as it was the most authoritative voice in the treason trials, and its reasoning determined the course of the trials overall. Following the review of Supreme Court judgments, those cases deemed of particular relevance to the course of the trials overall, addressing some of the core questions of legal principle and social and political concern, or highlighting some of the moral dilemmas of the trials, have been included in this book. Whenever the judgment suggested that additional information of interest could be found in the trial records, these have been consulted at the National Archives, as the trial records can add relevant context to the

66 There were 23,133 court cases before 30 June 1950: *Statistikk over landssvik 1940–1945*, pp. 61–64.

67 The reason that civil cases are included is that the compensation cases during the treason trials were typically adjudicated as civil law cases. The end date has been chosen as, by this time, the bulk of decisions had been made, and the cases of principle decided.

key arguments and facts of the case. And, finally, as the trial records also provide the very important opportunity to let the trial participants tell their stories, these have also been added to illustrate some of the typical cases and dilemmas of the treason trials.

As regards printed or digitised primary sources beyond court judgments, the study has also drawn extensively on the parliamentary proceedings of the Norwegian parliament (*Stortingsforhandlingerne*). With regard to the wartime exchange between the exile government and the resistance forces in Norway, the compendium *Regjeringen og hjemmefronten under krigen* proved a valuable complementary resource to the files consulted at the National Archives.[68] For newspaper coverage of the trials, the project has benefited enormously from the ambitious digitalisation projects currently under way at the Norwegian National Library (*Nasjonalbiblioteket*), which provide electronic access to most major Norwegian newspapers. In addition, the study has drawn upon extensive collections of newspaper clippings found across Ministerial archives, which indicate the topics deemed important by authorities. To convey the perspective of trial participants as well as critics of the trials, the book has examined in detail a series of books, pamphlets and memoirs published during and after the trials were carried out. Two influential printed primary sources which have also been consulted are the government's own White Papers into the 'criticism of the trials', printed in 1950, and the report of the Treason Committee, published in 1962, on the trials as a whole.[69] But these publications, however valuable, must be treated with caution, for they were in part drafted by key actors of the trials, and published in a particular political context. The study has therefore relied on these publications only selectively, and referenced them only with regard to claims that are generally verifiable through other sources. To highlight the international dimension of the trials, select foreign newspapers as well as international archives have also been consulted, including the collections of the Harry S. Truman Library.

Because the passing of time became a central factor in the administration of the trials, this book is structured chronologically. However, time did not unfold at a consistent speed during the trials. The periods investigated in each chapter therefore vary in length. Chapter 1 considers the

[68] Reidar Omang (ed.), *Regjeringen og hjemmefronten under krigen, Aktstykker utgitt av Stortinget* (Oslo: Aschehoug, 1948).

[69] Justis- og Politidepartementet, *Om landssvikoppgjøret* (Gjøvik: Mariendal, 1962); St.meld. nr. 62 (1950).

complex power constellations triggered by the German invasion of Norway in 1940, and the preparations made by the exile government and the resistance forces in Norway for the reckoning with 'traitors' that was to follow the liberation. It spans the period September 1939 until May 1945. Chapter 2 covers the political and social forces unleashed by liberation, and the administrative and legal preparations made ahead of the treason trials. It covers the period May until June 1945. Chapter 3 looks at the earliest trials against collaborators, the broader public responses to them, and the first difficulties faced by public authorities when they realised the true scale of the reckoning that lay ahead. It begins in July 1945 and ends with the declaration of the first freely elected post-war government in December 1945. Chapter 4 explores the period between January 1946 and October 1947, in which the majority of court cases – roughly 80 per cent – were processed. In particular, it reviews the challenges authorities faced in maintaining the legal framework set up during the occupation in light of institutional shortcomings and swiftly changing public attitudes. Chapter 5 looks at how authorities sought to phase out the trials and accelerate the release of prisoners from 1948 onwards. It relates these measures to the new meaning the trials were attaining for authorities at the beginning of the Cold War, but also to decreasing public interest. Chapter 6 examines the challenges and criticisms brought against the trials, the ways in which authorities responded to them, and the final stages in their practical administration. Finally, Chapter 7 embeds the Norwegian post-war reckoning in a European context to demonstrate how there were both shared experiences as well as fundamental differences between the ways in which Norway and other European countries brought wartime collaborators to justice.

CHAPTER 1

Occupation

Norway's Wartime Experience and the Preparation of the Trials, 1940–1945

The treason trials after 1945 were shaped by Norway's particular experience of German occupation. Unlike in other German-occupied countries, Norway's national fascist party *Nasjonal Samling* (NS) was elevated to governing status, its leader, Vidkun Quisling, being made 'Minister President' in early 1942. The central importance of the NS to German Nazification efforts in Norway meant that those planning for a post-war reckoning soon focused their attention on how to criminalise the actions of party members. The trials accordingly came to centre on the concept of 'treason': on crimes against the state and the majority population. This meant that many other crimes committed in Norway during the occupation, including those against the Jewish population and prisoners of war, would play only a marginal role after 1945, as would the crimes of Norwegian volunteers on the Eastern Front. The status of the exiled Norwegian government in London, and its complex relationship with the resistance forces in Norway, is a further central element in understanding how the legal bases of the trials were developed. For the resistance, meanwhile, the plans to punish collaborators were an important element of its own political ambitions for post-war Norway. A joint aim of both the exiles and the resistance was to ensure a smooth transition from war to peace. This chapter outlines the Norwegian occupation and, in drawing on documents produced by the exile government, details how the preparations for the post-war reckoning were made. In doing so, it highlights the reasoning behind the introduction of the extraordinary legal provisions that would both determine the course of the trials and cause significant controversy after the war.

1.1 Invasion, Flight and Exile

Upon the outbreak of the Second World War, Norway's Labour government, led by Johan Nygaardsvold, initially sought to maintain a policy of neutrality. It had pursued a neutral line internationally since the mid-1930s, in particular in an attempt to steer Norway away from the adverse effects of the global economic crisis.[1] Politically, too, neutrality was deemed necessary to avoid putting at risk a nation-state which had only gained formal independence from Sweden in 1905.[2] Norway had undergone significant changes since the last world war. The inter-war period had been marked by domestic political struggles, economic turmoil and the rise of the radical left and the labour movement. The 'spirit of 1905' had withered away by the 1920s and made way for social and political frictions.[3] Strikes and instability had swept the country since the 1920s, which many citizens perceived as a threat to sovereignty and national harmony. This, in turn, had provided fertile ground for various new streams of political thinking. The turmoil of the inter-war period had resulted in the formation of numerous new political parties and social movements, including the fascist party NS led by Vidkun Quisling, a military officer and minister of defence under the government of the Centre Party (*Bondepartiet*) between 1931 and 1932. The NS saw itself in competition with the Labour Party (*Arbeiderpartiet*) in claiming to be the 'people's party'. In its ideology and aesthetics, the NS resembled the German *Nationalsozialistische Deutsche Arbeiterpartei* (NSDAP), but it was much less successful than its German counterpart. Before the occupation, it was relatively insignificant, receiving only 1.8 per cent of votes in the 1936 elections to the Norwegian parliament.[4]

A period of economic growth in the 1930s had given the Labour Party enormous upswing, and from 1935, it provided its first long-term government under Johan Nygaardsvold, who was to remain in office throughout the German occupation.[5] The party had by that point become more moderate, leaving behind its previous global revolutionary outlook.

[1] Nygaardsvold had been in power since 1935 and increasingly advocated neutrality. On 1 September 1939, Norway declared itself neutral: Harald Berntsen, *I malstrømmen: Johan Nygaardsvold 1979–1952* (Oslo: Aschehoug, 1991), pp. 409–419. This strategy had proven successful before: during the First World War, Norway had pursued a neutrality policy in order to maintain much-needed trade relations with both Britain and Germany: Olav Riste, *The Neutral Ally: Norway's Relations with Belligerent Powers in the First World War* (Oslo: Universitetsforlaget, 1965).

[2] Norway had only become independent from Denmark in 1814, and from Sweden in 1905, and the comparatively recent independence still shaped the nation's broader identity and politics.

[3] Hans Fredrik Dahl, *Norsk idéhistorie, Bind V: De store ideologienes tid: 1914–1955* (Oslo: Aschehoug, 2001), p. 8.

[4] Norges Offisielle Statistikk IX 107, *Stortingsvalget 1936* (Oslo: Stortingets Kontor and Aschehoug, 1937), p. 138.

[5] The Labour government had previously formed a minority government for a sixteen-day spell in early 1928 before being voted out by parliament on a vote of no confidence.

Instead, it had distanced itself from the Norwegian Communist Party (*Norges Kommunistiske Parti*) and embraced the state as the centre of its politics. Broadening its focus was also a conscious move to prevent workers and farmers from drifting towards National Socialism.[6] In the pre-war era, the Labour government initiated large-scale social reforms and focused on economic recovery from the Great Depression. But even within his own party, Nygaardsvold's policy of neutrality became increasingly contested. With war looming in Europe, some party colleagues referred to the decision not to mobilise as 'criminal naivety'.[7] And at the same time that the government was seeking to maintain its neutrality in an ever more volatile Europe, Vidkun Quisling paid a visit to Berlin to discuss the political role of the NS in the event of a German invasion.[8]

The Labour government's policy of neutrality meant that when Germany launched its Operation Weserübung (Weser Exercise) on 9 April 1940 and invaded Norway with no prior declaration, Norway was ill-prepared. For Germany, the occupation of Norway was a measure to secure long-term supplies of iron ore and aluminium from Scandinavia and, at a more fundamental level, to integrate it into the New Order.[9] Hitler deemed the Norwegian resources and its geopolitical location of key importance in the German war effort. But the invasion of Norway and Denmark differed from the previous invasion of Poland, in that the Scandinavian countries were intended to be politically and economically integrated into the 'Greater German Empire' through a comparatively moderate occupation policy.[10] Hitler saw Norwegians as a superior Germanic race, which had to be won over ideologically.[11] A further reason for the launch of Operation Weserübung was that Hitler had become concerned over the increasing presence of British warships in Norwegian territorial waters, which in early 1940 had violated Norway's neutrality.

[6] Hans Fredrik Dahl, *Fra klassekamp til nasjonal samling: Arbeiderpartiet og det nasjonale spørsmål i 30-årene* (Oslo: Pax Forlag, 1969), pp. 55–64.

[7] Haakon Lie, during a meeting of the Labour Party in 1937, referenced in Berntsen, *I malstrømmen*, p. 439.

[8] Hans-Dietrich Loock, *Quisling, Rosenberg und Terboven: Zur Vorgeschichte und Geschichte der nationalsozialistischen Revolution in Norwegen* (Stuttgart: Deutsche Verlags-Anstalt, 1970), pp. 207–234.

[9] Ibid., p. 258; Alan Milward, *The Fascist Economy in Norway* (Oxford: Clarendon Press, 1972), pp. 67–94.

[10] Ibid., Milward, pp. 67–94; Hans-Dietrich Loock, 'Nordeuropa Zwischen Außenpolitik und "großgermanischer" Innenpolitik', in Manfred Funk (ed.), *Hitler, Deutschland und die Mächte: Materialien zur Außenpolitik des Dritten Reiches* (Düsseldorf: Droste, 1976), pp. 684–706.

[11] On Hitler's visions for Norway, see Despina Stratigakos, *Hitler's Northern Utopia: Building the New Order in Occupied Norway* (Princeton: Princeton University Press, 2020).

The invasion of Norway did not go as planned, however. The warship *Blücher*, carrying soldiers and goods essential to the invasion, sank in the Oslofjord on 9 April 1940 after being hit by Norwegian torpedoes. The delays caused by this left the Norwegian government, the royal family, the parliament and the most important senior ministerial advisers sufficient time to flee Oslo and find temporary refuge in the small town of Elverum, close to the Swedish border. The sinking of the *Blücher* also slowed down the invasion of the country more generally, with German troops moving northwards only gradually, and battles continuing for another two months. It would take until 10 June 1940 before the Norwegian forces capitulated.[12]

Despite the delays, Oslo was quickly placed under German control on 9 April 1940, and Curt Bräuer, the German envoy to Norway, put an ultimatum before the Nygaardsvold government to accept a regime of collaboration, as had been done in Denmark earlier that day.[13] However, the Norwegian government declined, a situation entirely unexpected by the Germans.[14] Meanwhile, with no forewarning whatsoever, Vidkun Quisling seized the hour and that same day declared himself prime minister, announcing via public broadcast: 'We are the only ones, who ... can save this country from the desperate situation into which party politicians have brought us. The Nygaardsvold cabinet has resigned. The national government has assumed all governing power, with Vidkun Quisling as its Head of Government and Minister of Foreign Affairs.'[15]

Despite his December 1939 visit to Berlin to negotiate his status in a German-occupied Norway, Quisling had acted without the agreement of the Germans.[16] Hitler had intended only to keep Quisling in reserve, the primary strategy being to form a collaborative government with Norway within the framework of a 'peaceful occupation' (*friedliche Besetzung*).[17] Hitler had realised that a collaboration government headed by the controversial figure of Quisling was unlikely to be carried by a consensus. When it became clear that the Norwegian government would oppose German occupation rule, however, Bräuer was instructed by Hitler to back

[12] The end of the struggles was interpreted differently by Norway and Germany, with the Norwegian resistance stating that there had not been a full capitulation, while Germany insisted that there had been: Arnd Bauerkämper, *Das umstrittene Gedächtnis: die Erinnerung an Nationalsozialismus, Faschismus und Krieg in Europa seit 1945* (Paderborn: Schöningh, 2012), p. 73.

[13] On the Danish invasion, see Claus B. Christensen, *Danmark besat: krig og hverdag 1940–45* (Copenhagen: Høst, 2005), pp. 103–113.

[14] Loock, *Quisling, Rosenberg und Terboven*, pp. 280–285. [15] Ibid., p. 289.

[16] Ibid., pp. 285–291. [17] Ibid., p. 271.

Quisling and put before the government a second ultimatum to accept him as the new head of state.[18] And yet, Quisling was forced to step down on 15 April 1940 when King Haakon VII and the government refused to appoint him prime minister, a step which all parties, including the Germans, recognised at the time as a formal constitutional requirement.[19] The German plans for Norway had failed spectacularly.

After declining the second ultimatum, King Haakon VII and the government saw no option but to flee and, after weeks in hiding, left the country from Tromsø harbour for Great Britain aboard the British warship HMS *Devonshire* on 7 June 1940.[20] Only narrowly avoiding German torpedoes on their voyage, the Nygaardsvold government and king found exile in London. Shortly after the German invasion, the Norwegian parliament, the *Storting*, had held a final meeting in the town of Elverum. Here it had issued full powers to the Norwegian government in the so-called Elverum Authorisation (*Elverumsfullmakten*) of 9 April 1940.[21] The two-page document held that

> Parliament grants authority to the Government, until the time arrives when the Government and the Presideum of Parliament can call Parliament for an ordinary meeting again, to oversee the interests of the realm and to take those decisions and warrants on behalf of Parliament and the Government that seem necessary with a view to the realm's interests and future security.[22]

The exile government relied on the Elverum Authorisation to issue decrees during the occupation, some of which would later form the basis of the treason trials.[23] However, throughout the occupation, the legal relationship between the governing efforts of the exile government and the law-making powers of the occupier would prove difficult. Pursuant to Article

[18] Ibid., pp. 289–291. [19] Ibid., pp. 300–324.

[20] There was a general consensus that upon declining the second German ultimatum, Norway had de facto become an ally of Britain.

[21] The precise nature of the vote is disputed; see Baard Herman Borge and Lars-Erik Vaale, *Grunnlovens største prøve: rettsoppgjøret etter 1945* (Oslo: Scandinavian Academic Press, 2018), pp. 160–167.

[22] Magne Skodvin, 'Elverumsfullmakten', *Store Norske Leksikon* (15 February 2018), https://snl.no/Elverumsfullmakten, last accessed 14 February 2021; Magne Skodvin, 'Trondheimsavtalen 1940', in Trond Bergh and Helge Ø. Pharo (eds), *Historiker og veileder: festskrift til Jakob Sverdrup* (Oslo: Tiden Norsk Forlag, 1989), pp. 81–111.

[23] The exile government was of the opinion that, based on the Elverum Authorisation, it held the powers of the legislature and executive. However, both during and after the war, the Elverum Authorisation was the subject of much controversy, and the Supreme Court after the liberation argued that legally the government-in-exile had derived its powers during the occupation period from a 'state of emergency' rather than the Authorisation.

43 of the Hague Conventions of 1907, an occupier held legitimate law-making powers in the occupied territory, although the range of permissible measures was limited by the treaty. Over the years, Germany in many ways violently transgressed the requirements placed on occupation regimes under the Hague Conventions.[24] Nevertheless, this state of affairs left the law-making powers in an ambivalent position, both in occupied Norway and within the exile government. The situation was further complicated by the fact that, while the exile government gradually built its ministries in London, many civil servants remained in office in the ministries that had been taken over by the occupier. After the war, indeed, some laws made by the German occupier were retained, but only in so far as they did not either contradict the provisional laws issued by the exile government or violate the constitution.[25]

1.2 War and Peace

The power vacuum left by the government and the Quisling putsch led to negotiations for the formation of an Administration Council (*Administrasjonsrådet*) on 15 April 1940. The initiative was made by members of the Supreme Court of Norway (*Høyesterett*), who wanted to offer an alternative to Quisling's rule within the contours of a peaceful occupation. This body was primarily composed of members of the Supreme Court of Norway under Chief Justice of the Supreme Court, Paal Berg, who considered it an apolitical body necessary to govern the occupied territories as a 'temporary set-up' before a more permanent agreement could be reached with the Germans.[26] The German intention, on the other hand, was to expand the Council into the government of German-occupied Norway, which was meant to serve German interests. Curt Bräuer's diplomatic career was ended after he deliberately misrepresented the role of the Council to Hitler as a political body serving German interests.[27] When Hitler found out about its true status and the difficult negotiations with the Norwegian Supreme Court justices, he immediately

[24] Convention (IV) respecting the Laws and Customs of War on Land and its annex: Regulations concerning the Laws and Customs of War on Land, The Hague, 18 October 1907, https://ihl-databases.icrc.org/ihl/INTRO/195, last accessed 14 February 2021.

[25] 'Lov om okkupasjonslovgivningen', *Norsk Lovtidend 1* (27 September 1946), pp. 600–606.

[26] Other members were representatives of industry: Olav Riste and Berit Nøkleby, *Norway 1940–1945: The Resistance Movement* (Oslo: Tanum, 1970), p. 10.

[27] Robert Bohn, *Reichskommissariat Norwegen* (Munich: Oldenbourg, 2000), p. 7; Susanne März, *Die langen Schatten der Besatzungszeit: 'Vergangenheitsbewältigung' in Norwegen als Identitätsdiskurs* (Berlin: Berliner Wissenschaftsverlag, 2008), p. 48.

withdrew Bräuer from his position on 16 April 1940. In his stead, Josef Terboven, formerly the NSDAP *Gauleiter* of Essen and an ardent admirer of Hitler, was made *Reichskommissar* of Norway on 24 April 1940.[28]

Because Hitler's aim was to establish – at least on surface – *legal* rule in Norway through a shift in power within the contours of the Norwegian constitution, political cooperation was necessary. Terboven was entrusted with carrying out the conversion of the Administration Council into a governing body that could secure German interests, but that would equally be carried by Norwegian support. In contrast to the brief Quisling rule, the Administration Council was generally accepted by the Norwegian people. It was considered a necessary governing entity to prevent the collapse of the administration and the economy. Industry representatives issued orders for workers and businesses to 'keep the wheels in motion' and to continue working, despite the potential advantages of Norwegian industry for the German war effort.[29] However, the disagreement between the German powers and the members of the Supreme Court as to the status of the Administration Council soon deepened. While the Germans upheld their demand for it to become the government of occupied Norway, its Norwegian members insisted on its apolitical nature and continued to regard the government-in-exile as the country's legitimate government. On 10 June 1940, however, the Norwegian forces surrendered and signed a capitulation treaty, and the members of the Administration Council lost their political leverage.[30] On Hitler's orders, Terboven began new negotiations with the more willing Presideum of the Norwegian parliament, who had remained in Norway, about installing a collaboration government.[31]

[28] For a full biography of Terboven, see Berit Nøkleby, *Josef Terboven: Hitlers mann i Norge* (Oslo: Gyldendal, 1992).

[29] Dag Ellingsen, *Krigsprofitørene og rettsoppgjøret* (Oslo: Gyldendal, 1993), p. 19.

[30] The legal and political status of Norway was unclear after the signing of the capitulation treaty; see Jörg Zägel, *Vergangenheitsdiskurse in der Ostseeregion: Auseinandersetzungen in den nordischen Staaten über Krieg, Völkermord, Diktatur, Besatzung und Vertreibung* (Münster: LIT Verlag, 2007), p. 70; Bohn, *Reichskommissariat Norwegen*, p. 9. The German perspective was that Norway had formally capitulated. The Norwegian government, on the other hand, argued that the war continued, but was now being fought outside the territory of Norway (and later by the military resistance). The Norwegian forces, their argument went, had not held a mandate to fully capitulate, but the capitulation was limited to the areas that Germany had at that time not occupied, so as to prevent further destruction. The question of the formal status of the government-in-exile came to have a huge relevance in the context of the treason trials, where the invocation of § 86, which prohibited aiding the enemy during a war, was dependent on the status of Norway during the occupation.

[31] Loock, *Quisling, Rosenberg und Terboven*, pp. 518–541; Hans Fredrik Dahl, Guri Hjeltnes, Berit Nøkleby, Nils Johan Ringdal and Øystein Sørensen (eds.), *Norsk krigsleksikon* (Oslo: Cappelen, 1995), p. 354.

The aim of these negotiations, later known as the Realm Council negotiations (*Riksrådsforhandlingene*), was to establish a body that would be formed of well-known members of Norwegian society and accepted as legitimate by the Norwegian people. It was also an attempt to prevent personal rule by Quisling, whom Terboven resented and considered unfit to be a statesman. In the course of these negotiations, many prominent members of Norwegian society, including members of parliament (MPs), were positive towards the establishment of such a body, as they saw it as the only way to safeguard Norwegian interests within the framework of a German occupation, in particular in light of the surrender of France on 17 June 1940. In September 1940, a majority of MPs voted in favour of revoking the Elverum Authorisation, and voted to establish a body replacing both the former government and the Administration Council. In a joint letter, a majority of MPs (75 out of 130) urged King Haakon VII to resign so as to make way for these institutional changes until the war was over. Norwegian parties additionally competed for an agreement with the Germans, in that there were fears in all camps that one party might prevail over another in reaching an agreement with the occupier. But the king refused to step down and received the full support of his government.[32]

Disagreement between the Presidium of the *Storting* and the Germans about the status of the Realm Council, with Germany intending for a 'legal revolution' and 'self-Nazification' of the country, led to the ultimate failure of the negotiations.[33] In particular, Norwegian officials refused to accede to Hitler's demand that Quisling and the NS – much to the frustration also of Terboven – should have a central role in the occupation order.[34] But Terboven, too, had contributed to the failing of the negotiations by attempting to secure his own powers and German interests in the Council to a degree that Norwegians felt unable to accept. Yet, politically, the negotiations carried a strong symbolic meaning, in that they showed the willingness of some senior politicians, in particular the *Storting*'s Presideum, to go against the king and government. The negotiations conducted by these prominent figures had weakened the overall will for resistance in the population and led to considerable controversy after the

[32] Reidar Omang (ed.), *Regjeringen og hjemmefronten under krigen: aktstykker utgitt av Stortinget* (Oslo: Aschehoug, 1948), p. 41.

[33] Loock, *Quisling, Rosenberg und Terboven*, pp. 527–541; Iselin Theien, 'Det politiske system og den tyske besættelse i året 1940', in Hans Fredrik Dahl, Hans Kirchhoff, Joachim Lund and Lars-Erik Vaale (eds.), *Danske tilstande – norske tilstande: forskelle og ligheder under tysk besættelse 1940–45* (Copenhagen: Gyldendal, 2010), pp. 33–48.

[34] Dahl et al., *Norsk krigsleksikon*, p. 355; Bohn, *Reichskommissariat Norwegen*, p. 13.

war.[35] They also introduced an element of uncertainty regarding the status of the governing authorities and were to become a core problem for the later handling of the occupation legacy.[36]

When the negotiations eventually failed, Terboven – under Hitler's instruction – unilaterally set up the *Reichskommissariat Norwegen* as a civil administration, which became both the legislative and executive power in occupied Norway.[37] Hitler, who was keen to see a fascist party in power in Norway and to build up political cooperation with the NS, instructed Terboven to allow representatives of the NS onto the *Reichskommissariat* in addition to prominent figures of Norwegian public life. Due to Hitler's support of Quisling – largely the result of Quisling's persistence and visits to Berlin as well as his close relationship with the prominent Nazi ideologist Alfred Rosenberg – Terboven's hands were tied with regard to the NS and would remain so throughout the occupation. Reluctantly, Terboven declared that Norway's path to freedom and independence now led 'via *Nasjonal Samling*'.[38] The *Reichskommissariat* became the central body in the new occupation order. It consisted of *Reichskommissar* Terboven, along with thirteen 'Acting State Councillors' (*Kommissarische Staatsräte*), of whom nine were NS members. Though initially envisaged as an organ of oversight, with the central administration staying in place, its powers increased significantly over the course of the occupation.

The NS became the vehicle through which Germany sought to increase its influence while generating a semblance of legitimacy. On 25 September 1940, Terboven banned all political parties but the NS by decree. The influence of the NS was superficial, however, as all real authority resided with the *Reichskommissar*. The *Reichskommissar* held sweeping powers, which were increased on several occasions during the occupation. Described by historian Robert Bohn as a 'relentless autocrat, who interfered with the smallest things and was used to enforcing his will', Terboven was to lead occupied Norway 'with almost limitless powers' for

[35] *Innstilling fra Undersøkelseskommisjonen av 1945* (Oslo: Familieforlaget, 2010).

[36] The negotiations were construed as a necessity by those who had conducted them as well as their supporters. A further argument put forward in their defence was that they provided a counterweight to Quisling and his NS, and were the only chance at securing a collaboration regime without the involvement of the NS. Since the early post-war period, the negotiations have been subject to criticism and changing interpretations, in particular the role of Paal Berg, who was to become a leader of the resistance and a key figure in the Norwegian post-war order; Per Hem, *Megleren Paal Berg 1873–1968* (Oslo: Aschehoug, 2012), pp. 434–435.

[37] Bohn, *Reichskommissariat Norwegen*, p. 12.

[38] Ole Kristian Grimnes, 'Okkupation og politik', in Dahl, Kirchhoff, Lund and Vaale (eds.), *Danske tilstande – norske tilstande*, pp. 79–103, at p. 88; Loock, *Quisling, Rosenberg und Terboven*, p. 543.

the remainder of the occupation.[39] Despite the general policy of cooperation, Terboven frequently cracked down on those who opposed his rule. Early on in the occupation, suspected resistance members and members of the banned political parties were deported to Germany on the basis of Hitler's 'Night and Fog Directive' (*Nacht und Nebel-Verordnung*), often to concentration camps, with many detained in Sachsenhausen. Later, Terboven expanded his apparatus of oppression through a restructuring of the police forces and changes to the legal apparatus. All State Councillors were bound by the orders of the *Reichskommissar*, which ultimately gave Terboven extensive powers to keep decision-making powers away from representatives of the NS.[40] One of the key functions of the *Reichskommissariat* was, after all, to secure the Third Reich's economic interests in Norway.

Instructed by Hitler, Terboven sought to develop the relatively weak NS into a more widely accepted political party modelled on the NSDAP. The German hope was that more support of the NS would allow for the occupation regime to secure a status of legitimate and accepted rule. This was primarily aimed at securing cooperation at the economic level and to safeguard the steady supply of much needed resources from Norway. At the same time, Hitler's visions for Northern Europe and the 'Germanic race' were pursued through a restructuring of the economy, educational initiatives and the Lebensborn birth programme, which aimed to promote births by 'Aryan' parents.[41] The establishment of the NS as a 'state bearing party' proved a difficult process, however. It was not until February 1942 that Terboven instated Quisling as 'Minister President' during an elaborate ceremony at Akershus Fortress in Oslo, followed by a state banquet hoped pompous enough to satisfy Quisling's vanity (Figure 1.1). Until that point, an *Einsatzstab* within Terboven's *Reichskommissariat*, along with the Commissariat's Propaganda Department (*Hauptabteilung Volksaufklärung und Propaganda*), had worked continuously to promote the NS within occupied Norway, to Nazify professions and organisations and to increase its public support.[42] In February 1942, as pressure from various resistance

[39] Bohn, *Reichskommissariat Norwegen*, p. 31. [40] Ibid., p. 46.

[41] Georg Lilienthal, *Der 'Lebensborn e.V.': ein Instrument nationalsozialistischer Rassenpolitik* (Stuttgart: Gustav Fischer, 1985); Volker Koop, *'Dem Führer ein Kind schenken': die SS-Organisation Lebensborn e.V.* (Cologne: Böhlau, 2007); Kjersti Ericsson and Eva Simonsen (eds.), *Children of World War II: The Hidden Enemy Legacy* (Oxford: Berg, 2005); Stratigakos, *Hitler's Northern Utopia*.

[42] Bohn, *Reichskommissariat Norwegen*, p. 114; Terje Emberland and Matthew Kott, *Himmlers Norge: nordmenn i det storgermanske prosjekt* (Oslo: Aschehoug, 2012), pp. 163–166.

Figure 1.1 Josef Terboven (third from left) and Vidkun Quisling (second from right) at Akershus Fortress in Oslo on 1 February 1942.
Source: Riksarkivet Oslo, RA/PA-0750/H/0002/1019.

movements began to increase, Hitler deemed it a wise move to formally elevate Quisling to the highest office. The Germans portrayed the move as a revolution from within, and argued that it was warranted by the widespread support of the NS among the Norwegian population. However, it was also a move designed to ease the strenuous relationship with Quisling, who had relentlessly pushed for Norwegian sovereignty, raising the issue with Hitler whenever he could. Hitler's stance was that sovereignty would not be granted until the war was over, if ever.[43]

In February 1942, the State Councillors stepped down to make way for a rule centred around the NS, which they now declared to be 'the only political organisation which is able to safeguard Norwegian interests'.[44] From then on, the NS presented itself as a regime in its own right, centred on a *Führer principle* despite a lack of constitutional basis for it.[45] The

[43] Stratigakos, *Hitler's Northern Utopia*, p. 6.

[44] 'Ministrenes Beslutning' of 30 January 1942, *Norsk Lovtidend 1* (1942), pp. 81–82.

[45] As Graver points out, '*Nasjonal Samling* never attempted to ground its seizure of power legally in the constitution as the German Nazis had done in Germany in 1933. On the contrary, the situation in Norway was presented as a lawless space … that had to be filled.' Hans Petter Graver,

judges of the Supreme Court had collectively resigned on 21 December 1940, and a set of judges willing to cooperate with the Germans, typically from lower instance courts, had taken their place. On 30 January 1942, these judges had issued a statement declaring the formation of a 'Norwegian national government' as constitutional, something for which they would later be judged.[46] Quisling conceptualised his appointment as a rebirth in a time of lawlessness, stating that 'higher than all law and actual positions of power is the realisation that in this hour of fate in our people's life . . . a national renewal movement has been born . . ., which directly and manifestly represents all that matters in the nation's will and which is the only path to the nation's rescue.'[47]

But this rebirth never materialised. During the entire occupation, the powers held by the *Reichskommissar* remained decisive. Constitutionally, the Quisling regime was always a part of the occupying framework of the Germans. As Quisling did not overturn the exile Norwegian government, it was later argued that there was also no case of a revolutionary uprising against the constitution of Norway – a question that would become relevant during the treason trials.[48] However, the state act had been a serious attempt at establishing NS rule in Norway 'from within', based on Norwegian popular support, and without any such constraints as the Germans in principle were subjected to as occupying power under international law.[49]

For the duration of the occupation period there remained a situation of joint governance between the German occupier and the NS, but with the Germans stipulating the framework for the exercise of power in the occupied territories. This was to the ever-growing frustration of Quisling, whose demands for an independent Norway fell on deaf ears. But the NS was not a submissive entity. While, institutionally, the *Reichskommissariat* held the key powers over occupied Norway, Quisling often made use of his bargaining power and on numerous occasions went directly to Hitler to ensure his continued support.[50] The occupier's ambitious ideas for a German rule legitimised by the NS were not readily

Dommernes krig: den tyske okkupasjonen 1940–1945 og den norske rettsstaten (Oslo: Pax Forlag, 2015), p. 44.

46 Hans Petter Graver, *Okkupasjonstidens Høyesterett* (Oslo: Pax Forlag, 2019), pp. 121-129; Graver, *Dommernes krig*, pp. 40-47; Rt. 1946, pp. 1205-1235, at p. 1209.

47 'Kunngjøring' of 1 February 1942, *Norsk Lovtidend* 1 (1942), pp. 83–88, at p. 86.

48 Bohn, *Reichskommissariat Norwegen*, p. 49.

49 RA/S-1042/D/Dh/L0004: Report by Gunnar Astrup Hoel to the Ministry of Justice in Oslo of 21 February 1942.

50 Hans Fredrik Dahl, *Quisling: A Study in Treachery* (Cambridge: Cambridge University Press, 2007 [1999]), pp. 250–253.

embraced within the party. This considerably impeded the effort to govern jointly. From 1943 the party's increasing frustration over the unlikelihood of gaining sovereignty led NS members to turn openly against Terboven. This indicates that the relationship between the NS and the occupying power was significantly more complex 'than the widespread clichés of a full and willing collaboration on the part of *Nasjonal Samling*' suggest.[51] The opposition faced by Terboven led him to increasingly shape Norwegian public life according to his own visions, far exceeding the party programme of the NS. These tensions were often ignored after the war, and 'from the outset, the resistance movement and Allied press characterised the Quisling government as a set of German puppets that supported the cause of Hitler's Reich'.[52]

1.3 Nazification and Collaboration

The *Reichskommissariat*, together with the NS and its organisations, sought to Nazify the country and to integrate it into the New Order.[53] They pursued these aims through reorganising the Norwegian state apparatus, establishing and expanding the institutions and organisations of the NS, forming SS organisations throughout Norway, and Nazifying professional and social life. Throughout the occupation, the Nazification efforts therefore took many different forms. But they were also profoundly shaped by the tensions between the German occupying regime, Quisling's NS and opposition forces in the Norwegian population. Disagreement about the forced Nazification of certain professions, first and foremost teachers and pastors, for example, led to widespread protests which inhibited the capacity of the occupying forces to undertake more comprehensive Nazification efforts. On the other hand, the occupation also brought both tempting opportunities and dilemmas for Norwegians. With several hundred thousand Wehrmacht soldiers present, and large-scale industrial projects under way, the economy was a central focus for the Germans, and both companies and individual workers became involved in various ways: while some actively seized the opportunities for economic gain, others had few options but to work for the occupying power to be able to feed their families. Against this background, the forms of collaboration witnessed during the occupation varied significantly. Mapping their wide

[51] Bohn, *Reichskommissariat Norwegen*, p. 56. [52] Ibid.

[53] 'Nazification' throughout this book is meant as the promotion of the ideology and aims of the NS rather than the NSDAP. However, there was considerable overlap between the two.

range is essential if we wish to understand the complexity of the occupation experience and the reckoning which followed.

In terms of governance and administration, several major structural changes were implemented. Terboven established four main departments within the *Reichskommissariat* to oversee the work of the NS-led ministries. The Germans and the NS also restructured the existing state apparatus, moulding it into a *führer* state composed, beyond the central government, of regions (*fylker*), each led by a regional leader called a county governor (*fylkesfører*) who was directly responsible to Quisling.[54] Quisling planned for a corporative body called the *Rikstíng* to replace the parliament, which would consist of representatives from industry and wider society, but it never materialised. The police held a central position in German Nazification efforts, and the Norwegian police force was realigned to make it mirror the centralised German police structure and brought under the aegis of the SS.[55] Terboven and Himmler had agreed that Wilhelm Rediess should act as *Höhere SS- und Polizeiführer Nord* of the country.[56] Rediess would have two commanders (*Befehlshaber*), each responsible for one of the two branches of the German police in Norway: the *Sicherheitspolizei* (*Sipo*) (which included the Gestapo) and the *Ordnungspolizei*.[57] These organisations were in principle independent from the *Reichskommissar*. However, Terboven was able to concentrate power in himself and make considerable use of this security apparatus in his oppression. In addition, the German military intelligence organisation *Abwehr* also had an extensive network across Norway.[58] The NS founded its own police force, the State Police (*Statspolitiet* – short: *Stapo*), which supplemented the German police forces and acted independently of the ordinary Norwegian police force.[59] Terboven therefore had an extensive police apparatus at his personal disposal with which to crack down on his enemies. The groups that were in Terboven's searchlight early on included members of the now-banned political parties, anyone suspected of smuggling information to the

[54] *Reichskommissariat* officials who had been sent from Germany acted as advisers to the NS *fylkesførere*: Ole Kristian Grimnes, *Norge under andre verdenskrig, 1939–1945* (Oslo: Aschehoug, 2018), p. 113.

[55] Nils Johan Ringdal, *Mellom barken og veden: politiet under okkupasjonen* (Oslo: Aschehoug, 1987), pp. 65–71; Øystein Hetland, 'In the Shadow of the SS: Three Norwegian Police Districts, 1940–1945' (PhD Dissertation, University of Oslo, 2021).

[56] Emberland and Kott, *Himmlers Norge*, p. 123.

[57] Ibid., pp. 126–128, 130–132.

[58] Tore Pryser, *Tyske hemmelige tjenester i Norden: spionsaker og aktører 1930–1950* (Oslo: Universitetsforlaget, 2012).

[59] After the war, some 4,037 were prosecuted for being informers, 284 for espionage, and 220 were sentenced for having been Norwegian Gestapo members; ibid., pp. 425, 436.

exile government or across the Swedish border to the Norwegian Legation which had been established there, and – of course – communists.[60]

As in most of the German-occupied countries, the legal system became a key element in the oppressive apparatus of the occupying regime. By instrumentalising the law, a veneer of legitimacy could be maintained, while sweeping political measures were implemented in its guise. However, unlike the situation in most other occupied countries, political matters were separated from ordinary matters within the Norwegian court system.[61] This led to the ordinary Norwegian court system being left relatively unaffected, sparing many a judge at the ordinary courts a conflict of conscience, while a number of special political courts instituted by Terboven became instruments of political oppression.[62] Matters concerning German interests or acts of resistance were initially brought before German courts, *Folkedomstolen* (a political court installed by the Germans to resemble the People's Court in Berlin) and later the Special Courts (*særdomstolene*), while civilian matters were brought before the ordinary Norwegian courts.[63] The separation of political courts from ordinary courts in no way prevented institutional and political conflict, however. Early on in the occupation, the occupying regime had run into conflict with the Supreme Court of Norway over the implementation of measures decreed by the *Reichskommissariat*. In December 1940, the Supreme Court judges collectively resigned. In their stead, Terboven appointed NS judges in January 1941.[64] While the court continued to constitute the highest court of appeal within the Norwegian court system, its judges argued that they did not have the authority to set aside acts by the *Reichskommissar*.[65]

The SS controlled a range of organisations in occupied Norway and it was central to suppressing the population and allowing Terboven and his NS accomplices to implement their policies.[66] The *Sipo*, Gestapo and the intelligence wing of the SS, the SD (*Sicherheitsdienst*), were the main organisations in monitoring and fighting resistance activity among the

[60] Stig Ekman and Ole Kristian Grimnes, *Broderfolk i ufredstid: norsk-svenske forbindelser under annen verdenskrig* (Oslo: Universitetsforlage, 1991); Birger Bakken, Reidar Toralf Larsen, Arne Jørgensen and Åge Fjeld, *Død over de tyske okkupanter: de norske kommunistenes motstandskamp 1940–1945* (Moss: Informasjonsforlaget, 1998).

[61] Graver, *Dommernes krig*, p. 227.

[62] This also ensured that the majority of the Norwegian judiciary were able to serve in the treason trials after the liberation.

[63] Graver, *Dommernes krig*, pp. 66–67.

[64] The wartime Supreme Court will be referred to as 'Acting Supreme Court' (*Kommissarisk Høyesterett*).

[65] Graver, *Dommernes krig*, p. 41.

[66] Emberland and Kott, *Himmlers Norge*.

population. Over the course of the war, they built an expansive network across Norway, and their headquarters in Oslo's Victoria Terrasse became a byword for torture and terror. Thousands of Norwegians would work in various roles for the Allgemeine SS, the *Sipo*, the Gestapo and the SD, acting as guards, interrogators, informants and in some cases torturers. In addition, the Germans used the NS organisational apparatus, including the *Stapo*, towards their own ends. Through these elaborate networks, the Germans were able to rely extensively on Norwegians' local knowledge when implementing their ambition to align the population with Nazi ideology. At the same time, the Norwegians were seen as high up in the racial order, and Himmler had a strong interest in incorporating them into the SS elite, in particular the *Waffen-SS*. As a result of intense recruitment drives, around 4,500–5,000 young Norwegians signed up to various SS divisions and fought against the Soviet Union on the Eastern Front (these were later known as 'frontfighters').[67] Around 800–1,000 of them died in the war. The precise degree of involvement of Norwegian SS volunteers in the crimes committed on the Eastern front would become difficult to determine in the post-war era. However, it is established that some of them served in units that participated in the brutal murder of Jews, Soviet prisoners of war and suspected partisans, and it is beyond reasonable doubt that Norwegians partook in war crimes across Eastern Europe.[68] But crimes against foreign nationals were not only committed on foreign soil: across Norway, the SS ran political prisons and concentration camps for resistance members from Germany and for Soviet, Yugoslav and Polish captured civilians and prisoners of war.[69] The concentration camps had a death rate of around 65 per cent. Over the course of the war, there were around 100,000 forced labourers in Norway, around 18,000 of whom perished under the brutal conditions they faced in the camps and during construction work.[70] Around 360 Norwegians, many of them SS volunteers, served as prison camp guards during the occupation.[71] After the war, Norwegian SS volunteers would stand trial almost exclusively for taking up

[67] Sigurd Sørlie, *Solkors eller hakekors: nordmenn i Waffen-SS 1941–1945* (Oslo: Dreyers Forlag, 2015), pp. 89–128.

[68] Emberland and Kott, *Himmlers Norge*, pp. 219–247.

[69] Over the course of the war, there were around 100,000 Soviet, 4,500 Yugoslav and 1,600 Polish prisoners of war in Norway: Marianne N. Soleim, *Sovjetiske krigsfanger i Norge, 1941–45: antall, organisering og repatriering* (Oslo: Spartacus, 2018), pp. 41–50; Trond Risto Nilssen and Jon Reitan, *The Legacies of the Nazi Camps in Norway: Falstad 1941–49* (Münster: Lit, 2020), p. 24.

[70] Emberland and Kott, *Himmlers Norge*, pp. 366–377; Torgeir E. Sæveraas, *Wehrmacht i Norge: på vakt i krigens skjebnesone* (Oslo: Pax Forlag, 2022), pp. 209–210.

[71] Nilssen and Reitan, *Legacies of the Nazi Camps in Norway*, p. 27.

arms against their own country rather than the humanitarian crimes they had committed.

Alongside the SS apparatus, the NS came to gain ever more importance in shaping the situation in occupied Norway, in particular from 1942 onwards. However, it was a rocky road for Quisling and his party at first. One of the reasons that the NS played such a small role in the early occupation years was its relative insignificance at the time of the German invasion. The NS had been founded in 1933, and was inspired by Italian fascism.[72] In 1930, Quisling had expressed two key aims of his 'movement' Nordic Folk Rising of Norway (*Nordisk Folkereisning i Norge*), the predecessor of the NS: to pursue a politics involving social and economic reform based on the 'race-related characteristics' of the Norwegian people, and to defeat Marxism.[73] Its focus on a Nordic cultural nationalism could not act as a main selling point in elections, however, as a strong national-cultural orientation had already defined the broader political agenda since Norway's separation from Sweden in 1905.[74] In the run-up to the 1936 elections, the party modelled its structure and aesthetics around the NSDAP. It was able to secure only negligible successes in the parliamentary elections in 1933 and 1936, and was marked by considerable internal conflict.[75] The association with the German NSDAP also posed a problem to the party, as the Norwegian electorate increasingly distanced itself from German policies after Hitler's victory in 1933. The internal struggles split the NS into two factions: one advocating Christian values and the other opting for a narrower German-style National Socialism. This sealed the fate of the NS in the pre-war era. By the outbreak of the Second World War, it was a minor and largely irrelevant party. Had it not been for the German occupation, it is likely that Quisling and his party would have disappeared into historical obscurity.

The German occupier, however, recognised the party's potential value for its own purposes. From September 1940 onwards, the *Reichskommissariat* conducted the Nazification of the country in a systematic fashion, through political and administrative institutions and legal decrees and by supporting the NS and moulding it into a Norwegian equivalent of the NSDAP. At the *Reichskommissariat*, a dedicated *Einsatzstab* worked to promote the

[72] For a detailed account of the NS in the pre-war era, see Loock, *Quisling, Rosenberg und Terboven*, pp. 96–157; Hans Fredrik Dahl, Bernt Hagtvet and Guri Hjeltnes, *Den norske nasjonalsosialismen: Nasjonal samling 1933–1945 i tekst og bilder* (Oslo: Pax Forlag, 2009); Hans Olav Brevig, Hans Olav and Ivo de Figueiredo, *Den norske fascismen: Nasjonal Samling 1933–1940* (Oslo: Pax Forlag, 2002).

[73] Dahl, *Norsk idéhistorie V*, p. 175; Loock, *Quisling, Rosenberg und Terboven*, pp. 60–71.

[74] Ibid., Dahl, p. 192.

[75] Loock, *Quisling, Rosenberg und Terboven*, p. 113.

popularity of the NS among the Norwegian population. For the Germans, this strategy was aimed at securing, stabilising and legitimising their own influence. Quisling, on the other hand, hoped that his party programme and ideology would finally be carried by wider parts of the population. In the NS programme of 1934, Quisling had propagated the abolition of party politics and traditional state structures. In the early months of the occupation, he set out to quickly build the party according to his long-held visions. In doing so, however, he was dependent on the consent of the German occupying power, which was ultimately in control. With the support of the Germans, Quisling was able to build a more comprehensive party structure, and to bring about a partial restructuring of the state according to his ideological outlook. In addition to its police force *Stapo*, the NS also founded a number of military and paramilitary organisations to support its party operations, including the Hird (*Hirden*), which was modelled on the German SA, as well as a corresponding organisation for women (*Kvinnehirden*). *Germanske SS Norge* was founded as both a branch of the *Allgemeine SS* and part of the NS, and counted around 1,300 active members. It operated alongside other units of the SS in which Norwegians also served.

At an ideological level, Quisling's hope following the German invasion was that he would finally bring about the 'revolution' he had advocated for so long. At the outset of the occupation, the party showed many ideological resemblances to the NSDAP. The NS had in the late 1930s moulded itself along the ideological lines of the German NSDAP, and it had become increasingly radical in its outlook. Its declared enemies were Marxism, Judaism, liberal democracy and materialism. It aimed to abolish representative democracy in favour of a *führer* principle. Much like its German counterpart, the party was strongly centred around a racist ideology, with the 'Germanic race' seen as superior and in need of protection from 'inferior races'. From 1935, antisemitism became increasingly central to the party ideology (although it was absent from the 1934 party programme, which remained in place throughout the occupation). The NS also embraced the idea that 'living space' was needed for the 'Germanic race' to be safeguarded. However, there were key differences between the NS and the NSDAP, too, which began to reveal themselves during the occupation. In Quisling's nationalist vision, he always saw a proud, independent Norway and he frequently cited Norse mythology to underscore the Nordic foundations of his ideology. For this reason, the interests between the Germans and the NS did not always converge. Instead, over the course of the occupation, and in particular from 1942, there were increasing tensions between the national outlook of the NS and its desire for Norwegian independence, and the more pan-Germanic ambitions of the SS. However, despite these differences in ideological orientation, the Germans deemed the NS the core vehicle through which to secure their rule and their own political aims in Norway.

The co-option of its policies by the German occupier made the NS a serious threat for the exile government and an enemy to all those who remained loyal to it. If the NS could secure widespread support in Norway, this could lead to the ultimate break with the exile government. And the combined efforts of Quisling and Terboven did show some success. From 2,700 members before the occupation, membership rose to around 26,000 in early 1941.[76] By mid-1942, this figure had almost doubled.[77] Motivations for membership varied hugely, however.[78] Some believed that an active NS could help secure Norwegian interests vis-à-vis the Germans. Others feared for personal and professional disadvantages if they did not sign up. Many new members were opportunists who saw NS membership as inevitable if they wished to maintain career prospects or secure their own livelihoods in the new occupation order.[79] In the early months of the occupation, when a German victory could not be ruled out, it seemed that many wished to opt for the safety of party membership, with the advantages it could entail. NS membership figures were also closely connected to activity in military formations. The Soviet war in Finland, the German invasion of the Soviet Union and the desire to fight against Bolshevism were therefore further factors for a rise in membership figures.

But restructuring the governing apparatus and recruiting directly into the NS and various military and paramilitary organisations alone could not generate the desired levels of support for the party. A further strategy for the consolidation of German and NS rule was therefore deemed to be the gradual Nazification of professions. Here, the occupier relied on a combination of forcing individuals to sign up and replacing opposing individuals with NS members. A decree of 4 October 1940 allowed for non-NS members to be removed from their positions in the public service. In addition, the NS established its own workers' association (*Nasjonal Samlings Faggruppeorganisasjon*, NSFO) to replace the existing trade unions. Across professions, Nazification figures varied significantly, often

[76] Justis- og Politidepartementet, *Om landssvikoppgjøret* (Gjøvik: Mariendal, 1962), p. 16.

[77] Ibid.

[78] See in particular Hans Fredrik Dahl and Øystein Sørensen, 'Et parti av lovbrytere', in Hans Fredrik Dahl and Øystein Sørensen (eds.), *Et rettferdig oppgjør? Rettsoppgjøret i Norge etter 1945* (Oslo: Pax Forlag, 2004), pp. 100–107.

[79] Bauerkämper, *Das umstrittene Gedächtnis*, p. 74.

but not exclusively in accordance with how important a profession was for the political ambitions of Terboven and Quisling.[80] The situation from September 1940 onwards placed public servants in particular in a difficult position. If they resigned, they would make way for individuals more loyal to the NS. But if they stayed, they were constrained by the occupier's power structures. Many signed up to the NS and stayed in an ambiguous position during the occupation, implementing NS orders, but trying to reduce their scope in what many later claimed was an act of resistance from within the institutions. By the end of the occupation, almost all mayoral positions across Norway were occupied by NS members. Policemen showed particularly high membership rates in the NS, around 50 per cent.[81] A considerable number of lawyers also signed up to the party.

Due to the many ways in which the Norwegian church resistance was celebrated, both in international news outlets and Allied propaganda during the war and thereafter, it is easy to forget that the Church was initially conflicted about how to meet the new joint regime of Germans and the NS.[82] As with most governing officials, its initial policy was in fact one of accommodation.[83] Eivind Berggrav, the Bishop of Oslo and later a prominent figure in the church resistance, had in the first weeks after the German invasion negotiated with German representatives – and, controversially, announced on one occasion that Norwegian civilians should stop fighting Germans.[84] This provided the occupier with propaganda material claiming that the Bishop of Oslo had acquiesced to the occupation.[85] It was only with the widespread Nazification attempts by Terboven and the NS from September 1940 onwards, and in particular the measures

[80] On the Nazification of the police, see Justis- og Politidepartementet, *Om landssvikoppgjøret*, pp. 456–460. On the Nazification of the judiciary, see Graver, *Dommernes krig*, pp. 61–65.

[81] Ringdal, *Mellom barken og veden*, pp. 37–42.

[82] See for example the front page of *Time* magazine, 25 December 1944.

[83] A nuanced study on the complex relationship between the Norwegian Church and the German occupier is offered in Arne Hassing, *Church Resistance to Nazism in Norway, 1940–1945* (Washington: University of Washington Press, 2014).

[84] In an 'energetic and naïve' effort, Berggrav had previously visited Hermann Göring and Lord Halifax in person in order to mediate between German and British interests in the hope of bringing about an end to the war: Per Voksø, 'Brobyggeren', in Per Voksø (ed.), *Eivind Berggrav: brobygger og kirkeleder, 1884–1984* (Oslo: Gyldendal, 1984), p. 18; Berggrav's highly active, 'unwise and impetuous' involvement during the early period of the invasion later made him subject to considerable criticism, even though his call to lay down weapons had not been meant as a call for an official ceasefire, but for the protection of the civilians involved – mainly youths, including Berggrav's own son: Edwin Robertson, *Bishop of the Resistance: The Life of Eivind Berggrav* (Haddington: Handsel Press, 2001), p. 106; Gunnar Heiene, *Eivind Berggrav: en biografi* (Oslo: Universitetsforlaget, 1992), pp. 297–311.

[85] Voksø, 'Brobyggeren', p. 20.

taken after the State Act of 1942, that church opposition grew. The Church was an ideal starting point for the ideological changes both Quisling and Terboven wanted to see in Norway. When ceremonial church services were ordered to mark Quisling's new title as 'Minister President', church representatives refused to comply, leading to seven bishops collectively resigning over the matter. Quisling reacted by sacking some key bishops, including Berggrav.[86] However, hundreds of pastors resigned in the following months in an act of protest, leaving the NS regime with a shell of a church and only around 10 per cent of bishops remaining at the service of the NS.[87] Ultimately, the Church broke with the state and continued an independent, largely undercover, existence.[88]

Large-scale attempts were also made to Nazify and reform the education system and to establish an encompassing system of indoctrination through the school curriculum and youth organisations. Quisling and his party hoped that by convincing the country's youth it would be able to gain broader support among the Norwegian population.[89] With the NS playing an increasingly central role in the Germans' occupation regime, changes to school curricula were implemented from the winter of 1940–1941.[90] Through various decrees, English texts were banned from curricula, and lessons in National Socialism were put on the teaching plan. In addition, specific rituals were introduced to school life, such as the equivalent of the Hitler greeting. Quisling's portrait was to be hung in all schools, and attending certain events was made compulsory for pupils, such as the Hitler Youth Exhibition, held in Oslo in 1941.[91] However, the NS regime faced unexpected and profound opposition from teachers' unions and parents, leading to widespread strikes from early 1941. From then on, means of political influence became more subtle, with pressure being exerted on teachers at regular meetings, through threatening removal from school or other professional limitations.[92] Gradually, opposing teachers were removed, and school leaderships were replaced with NS members, allowing for easier access and control.

[86] For a full biography of Bishop Berggrav, see Robertson, *Bishop of the Resistance*; Heiene, *Eivind Berggrav*; on the role of the Church during the occupation, and church opposition, see Robertson, *Bishop of the Resistance*, pp. 113–122; Heiene, *Eivind Berggrav*, pp. 297–374.

[87] Hassing, *Church Resistance to Nazism in Norway*, pp. 191–201; Ragnar Norrman, *Quislingkyrkan: Nasjonal samlings kyrkopolitik 1940–1945* (Skellefteå: Norma, 1998).

[88] Ibid., Hassing, pp. 180–190; Pål A. Berg, *Kirke i krig* (Oslo: Genesis forlag, 1999).

[89] *Norway's Schools in the Battle for Freedom* (Montreal: Royal Norwegian Government's Information Office, 1942), p. 10; Nicola Karcher, *Kampen om skolen: nazifisering og lærerens motstand i det okkuperte Norge* (Oslo: Dreyers Forlag, 2018).

[90] Ibid., *Norway's Schools*.

[91] Karcher, *Kampen om skolen*, p. 147.

[92] *Norway's Schools*, p. 11.

Opposition continued, however, and teachers increasingly joined resistance organisations in protest. Upon his institution as 'Minister President' in 1942, Quisling began to take an increasingly harsh stance on teachers. He believed that he now possessed the powers to instigate the National Socialist revolution he had dreamt of and was keen to show himself as its head. In February 1942 Quisling established a 'Teachers' Front' (*Lærersambandet*), a Nazi organisation with compulsory membership for teachers.[93] On the same day, he made membership in the youth organisation *Nasjonal Samling* Youth Movement (*NS Ungdomsfylking*, NSUF), which was modelled on the German *Hitler Jugend*, compulsory for schoolchildren. Through this organisation, Quisling hoped to gain control over 400,000 children and youths.[94] School discipline was sharpened and symbols and indoctrination of the NS were made compulsory elements of everyday school life, with anyone who disobeyed facing a six-month suspension.[95] However, opposition to Quisling's measures was even larger than the first time that direct and comprehensive changes had been attempted, and more than 90 per cent of teachers rejected Quisling's decrees, in particular through refusing to join the Teachers' Front. Threats of loss of professional status or mass arrests did not halt the wave of protests. Of Norway's 14,000 teachers, 12,000 rejected the measures by sending identical letters of resignation on the same day.[96] The Church supported the protests, and both Quisling and Terboven became nervous about this broad front of resistance, cracking down harshly on their opponents. A total of 1,000 teachers were arrested and 500 were taken on a ship to a concentration camp in the Arctic as 'exemplary punishment'. To keep schools in operation, several of the controversial measures were repealed, including the compulsory membership of the Teachers' Front and the NSUF.[97] The widespread protests in the Church and schools were a blow to Quisling's regime and signalled a fundamental change within the occupation regime in that it became clear both to him and the Germans

[93] Karcher, *Kampen om skolen*, pp. 79–105.

[94] Rupert Butler, *Legions of Death: The Nazi Enslavement of Europe* (Barnsley: Pen & Sword, 1983), p. 91.

[95] *Norway's Schools.*

[96] Butler, *Legions of Death*, p. 91. According to Karcher, it is difficult to establish reliable figures on the number of letters, but what is clear is that there was widespread opposition among teachers, which put Quisling under considerable pressure: Karcher, *Kampen om skolen*, pp. 155–156.

[97] Karcher, *Kampen om skolen*, pp. 159–160; John Mikal Kvistad, '"Det unge Norges fylking klar til slag", Nasjonalsosialistisk ungdom i Norge – Historien om Nasjonal Samlings Ungdomsfylking, 1933–1945' (PhD Dissertation, University of Oslo, 2011), pp. 483–489.

that the NS would never succeed in summoning widespread support, let alone successfully Nazifying the country.[98]

While the protests of teachers and pastors became celebrated all over the world,[99] and later became a synonym in Norway for the nation's collective resistance efforts, the Norwegian people's attitudes towards opposition overall were, in fact, significantly more varied. Over the course of the occupation, individuals faced complex economic, political and moral choices, and many seized the opportunities the war provided. The Norwegian economy was at the centre of Germany's occupation policies in Norway. Germany's plans for Norway differed radically from those of Western European countries such as France. Rather than exploit the country's resources for the war effort, Norway's economy was to form part of a New Order within the German Reich. The German economic policies in Norway were therefore strategic and long-term and many businesses collaborated willingly.[100] Providing access for German companies to Norwegian resources was a central element in this, as was direct collaboration with Norwegian industry. German companies such as IG Farben and Krupp had representatives on the *Reichskommissariat* to ensure access to key Norwegian resources. German companies set up branches in Norway, relying on forced labourers, such as the company Nordsee in its fish manufacturing plant in Bodø in northern Norway. The German plans for the Norwegian aluminium industry were of enormous scope, and some Norwegian companies such as Norsk Hydro stood to benefit enormously from them.[101] At the more local level, Germany had to rely on the supplies of Norwegian businesses to feed and house its people. For many of these smaller businesses, it was difficult to protest against the demands made by a strong and draconian occupier to cooperate, or to resist the many business opportunities the building of German infrastructures provided. In the post-war order, these various forms of economic collaboration would cause heated debate, and it proved almost impossible to delineate between collaboration and coercion.

Workers, too, faced difficult decisions. Cooperation was essential from the perspective of the German occupier. Terboven's central aim was to ensure that the Norwegian economy would continue to function well, and that key resources could be extracted smoothly. This involved securing the support of the Norwegian workforce, and policies were initially cooperative. The occupier provided financial incentives for Norwegian labourers

98 Dahl, *Norsk idéhistorie V*, p. 312.
99 Karcher, *Kampen om skolen*, pp. 162–163.
100 Milward, *The Fascist Economy*, p. 67.
101 Ibid., p. 171.

to work for them. However, cooperation did not always go as hoped, and from July 1941 the *Arbeidsdirektoratet* was able to forcibly move Norwegian workers to sites where the occupier needed them. When a rationing of milk supplies was announced on 8 September 1941, this led to widespread protests and strikes among Norwegian workers, culminating in a state of exception announced by Terboven on 10 September. Terboven introduced martial law and had the leading figures of the strike, Viggo Hansteen and Rolf Wickstrøm, executed.[102] But despite the occurrence of strikes, the workforce overall largely cooperated, even after the uncertainty of the summer of 1940 had ended. Many workers found employment on German construction sites or working for Germans. Everyday contact was mostly accommodating, and the majority of Norwegians appeared willing to meet German demands.[103] An estimated 150,000 so-called Germany workers were in some form professionally involved with the occupier, many out of financial incentives, but others out of economic necessity.[104] After the liberation, this group would face mixed public attitudes and considerable criticism, and the case of the Germany workers highlighted how fine the line often was between collaboration and acceptable cooperation.

The press and all other media outlets were also heavily regulated and gradually Nazified throughout the occupation. Many newspapers were stopped entirely, in particular the party organs. Critical editors were replaced by party members or individuals who sided with the party.[105] The NS's organ *Fritt Folk* ('Free People') held a central position during the occupation, in that Norwegian companies were forced to place advertisements in it.[106] Radios were confiscated across the whole of Norway following a decree issued by the *Reichskommissar* in 1940, and listening to the radio was criminalised for all but NS members.[107] A high number of illegal newspapers were circulated during the occupation, but often in very limited quantities, and few lasted very long. Production and distribution were difficult, and newspapers would instead be passed on secretly, rather than

[102] Bohn, *Reichskommissariat Norwegen*, p. 84.

[103] Bauerkämper, *Das umstrittene Gedächtnis*, p. 77.

[104] Official estimates are that there were around 100,000–150,000 Germany workers; see Justis- og Politidepartementet, *Om landssvikoppgjøret*, p. 369.

[105] Some newspapers remained in operation during the occupation, such as *Aftenposten*, *Morgenposten* and *Nationen*. The question to what degree these newspapers as a whole collaborated is complex, with many editors having been replaced by NS editors, and considerable pressure exerted by the occupation regime.

[106] Idar Flo, *Norsk presses historie 1660–2010, Bind IV: Norske aviser fra A til Å* (Oslo: Universitetsforlaget, 2001), p. 134.

[107] Norway was the only country during the Second World War in which such a measure was taken, and a total of 500,000 radios were confiscated.

publishers running the risks of high publication numbers. The distribution of illegal newspapers amounted to some of the most significant resistance work during the occupation, with around 12,000–15,000 people involved in it.[108] The organised resistance gradually formed its own newspapers and other publication channels, which were not only hugely important during the occupation but grew into powerful newspapers in the post-war period. The most important newspapers circulated were those that contained the typed statements given by the exile government on the BBC Norwegian Section.[109] The production and distribution of illegal newspapers was heavily penalised. Initially being punishable with five years' imprisonment, Terboven made the involvement in illegal newspaper printing punishable by death in a decree of 12 October 1942.

There was widespread Nazification also of the everyday, albeit with varying degrees of success. Cultural institutions, in particular, were affected, with theatres and cinemas being subjected to considerable restrictions in their programmes. The NS founded a long list of organisations corresponding to the purposes of its broader ideologies and societal restructuring. Many resembled organisations within the NSDAP. Some of these, such as *Nasjonal Samlings Kvinneorganisasjon*, were for women only and presided over by women – a significant factor in explaining the comparatively high number of women later sentenced for active involvement in NS organisations.[110] For authors, the occupation period became a time of draconian censorship. The larger publishing houses were taken over by the NS and many authors fled to Sweden in order to continue their writing and publishing. As with the Nazification attempts in schools and churches, the attempts to monopolise cultural institutions and utilise them ideologically were largely unfruitful. Similar to the economic interaction with the occupier, however, everyday contact with the population in general was primarily characterised by close contact, curiosity and a high degree of acceptance of the situation. Day-to-day transactions had to continue, and coexistence between the Norwegians and German soldiers was the norm. With more than 300,000 German soldiers stationed in

[108] Henrik G. Bastiansen and Hans Fredrik Dahl, *Norsk Mediehistorie* (Oslo: Universitetsforlaget, 2019 [2003]), p. 195.

[109] Ibid.

[110] The largest of these was the *Nasjonal Samling* Women's Organisation (*Nasjonal Samlings Kvinneorganisasjon*, NSK), which oversaw all other women's organisations; see in particular Kjersti Brathagen, 'Oppgjøret med NS-kvinnene', in Hans Fredrik Dahl and Øystein Sørensen (eds.), *Et rettferdig oppgjør? Rettsoppgjøret i Norge etter 1945* (Oslo: Pax Forlag, 2004), pp. 136–159; roughly one-third of court sentences (16,083) were handed down against women: *Statistikk over landssvik 1940–1945*, p. 22.

Norway during the occupation, romantic relationships between German soldiers and Norwegian women were not uncommon. The everyday experience of the collaboration was thus one in which a 'broad spectrum of behaviours' could be witnessed, 'in particular many (purportedly) necessary arrangements with the occupiers'.[111]

This is not to say that the relationship between occupier and occupied was stable and consistent throughout the war. The experience across the country varied significantly, and it changed over time.[112] It goes without saying that for Norway's Jewish population, the German occupation was a time of targeted terror.[113] For those engaged in resistance activity, it was a time of great personal risk and sacrifice. But overall, public opinion and personal allegiances changed and diversified, and they were far from as homogenous as people in the post-war period often liked to see them. In the early occupation years, when it was unclear who would win the war, many felt that supporting the NS might be a better way of securing Norwegian interests.[114] This uncertainty is reflected in changing public sentiment both towards the German occupier and the domestic NS during the occupation period. Initially, Norwegians took issue with Quisling and his NS, finding him incompetent.[115] Many Norwegians warmed to the idea that a collaboration agreement with the Germans could successfully avoid Quisling rule. As the events of summer 1940 unfolded, resentment of the Germans spread and Norwegians underwent a 'maturation period', after which Germans were met with much greater suspicion.[116] Germany's occupying status was still largely accepted at this time on more pragmatic grounds, however. A reluctant allegiance was still with the occupier, as 'in the first years of the war, a German victory had to be considered likely, or at least possible'.[117]

This changed when Germany's war prospects shrank from 1941–1942, and a victory began to seem impossible.[118] The party's many reform attempts contributed to both anti-NS and anti-German sentiments in the wider population.[119] Resentment reached a peak at the time of the 'revolutionary' reforms in early 1942, when Quisling sought to bring about a more widespread Nazification of society. This affected membership

111 Bauerkämper, *Das umstrittene Gedächtnis*, p. 76.

112 Guri Hjeltnes, *Norge i krig, Bind VI* (Oslo: Aschehoug, 1986); Ebba Drolshagen, *Der freundliche Feind: Wehrmachtssoldaten im besetzten Europa* (Munich: Droemer, 2009).

113 See Section 1.4 on persecution.

114 Dahl, *Norsk idéhistorie V*, p. 272.

115 Dahl, *Quisling*, pp. 177–178.

116 Theien, 'Det politiske system og den tyske besættelse i året 1940', p. 46.

117 Dahl, *Norsk idéhistorie V*, p. 272.

118 Ibid.

119 Grimnes, 'Okkupation og politik', p. 94.

figures, too. In 1942, the party had around 50,000 members, in the following year only around 43,000.[120] It was during this period that the equation of the NS with Germans that was to dominate much of post-war discourse became prevalent. The persistent but ultimately unsuccessful attempts of the NS to push for Norwegian independence did not succeed in restoring an image of the NS acting on behalf of the 'national' cause. The weakening powers of the Germans in conjunction with Quisling's unsuccessful attempts of negotiating with Hitler rather accelerated the decline in status of the NS.[121] Within the NS, meanwhile, the Germans' harsh stance on Norwegian independence led to considerable anti-German sentiments.[122] This complexity of agents and the changing power constellations was sidelined in post-war discourse. But while most Norwegians did not join the NS and opposed German rule to varying degrees, the vast majority of the population could – and did – make arrangements to adapt to occupation rule.[123]

1.4 Persecution

For the Jewish community of Norway, the occupation of Norway and the joint rule of the NS and the *Reichskommissariat* had catastrophic consequences. The occupation regime turned Norway into a hostile environment marked by discrimination, killings and deportations. Around 2,200 Jews lived in Norway at the time of the invasion, making it one of Europe's smallest Jewish communities.[124] Most of them lived in Oslo and Trondheim, where they were well represented in the garments industry.[125] Norwegian Jews held a very different socio-economic position from that in most other countries, for the simple reason that they had only been in the country since 1851, when a 'Jew paragraph' of the Norwegian Constitution had been upturned to allow for Jewish immigration. Few had received higher education, and most were self-employed, positioned in the lower middle class rather than belonging to the political, economic or cultural elite of the country. At the time of the invasion, around a quarter

[120] Stein Ugelvik Larsen, 'The Social Foundations of Norwegian Fascism 1933–1945: An Analysis of Membership Data', in Stein Ugelvik Larsen, Bernt Hagtvet and Jan Petter Myklebust (eds.), *Who Were the Fascists? Social Roots of European Fascism* (Bergen/Oslo/Tromsø: Universitetsforlaget, 1980), pp. 595–620, at p. 601.

[121] Dahl, *Norsk idéhistorie V*, pp. 272–274.

[122] Bohn, *Reichskommissariat Norwegen*, p. 55.

[123] Bauerkämper, *Das umstrittene Gedächtnis*, p. 76.

[124] Bjarte Bruland, *Holocaust i Norge. Registrering. Deportasjon. Tilintetgjørelse* (Oslo: Dreyers Forlag, 2017), p. 28.

[125] Grimnes, *Norge under andre verdenskrig*, p. 357.

of the Jewish population were refugees from other countries, including Germany, Austria and Czechoslovakia, who had arrived in Norway in the 1930s, and who would later be at particular risk of deportation.[126] By the end of the war, hardly any Jews remained in Norway. A total of 773 had been deported from Norway to the death camps, where 738 of them perished. Almost all other Jews had fled the country.

Antisemitism was not new in occupied Norway. While not politically organised to the same extent as it was in other European countries, antisemitism was still widely present in society.[127] Rather than forming an encompassing ideology, it tended to take the form of 'latent antisemitism',[128] finding its way into everyday language, cultural depictions and political debate.[129] Jews were instrumentalised by both the political left and the political right, being framed either as the drivers of capitalism or as bolshevist revolutionaries. As Kjetil Braut Simonsen has pointed out, there were no pogroms in Norway prior to 1940, nor was any comprehensive discriminatory legislation adopted before the invasion.[130] But there was fertile ground for conspiracy theories during the turbulent interwar years, and antisemitic publications were widespread. Using her public platform, the Christian public figure Marta Steinsvik for example acted as a 'multiplicator' for antisemitic conspiracy theories in the 1920s.[131] But there were critical voices, too, and during the late 1930s, a gradual distancing from the antisemitism of the German National Socialists could be observed in public circles, especially after the *Reichskristallnacht* of 1938.[132] The NS, as we have seen, adopted an increasingly explicit antisemitic stance in the late

[126] Bruland, *Holocaust i Norge*, pp. 17, 369.

[127] Kjetil Braut Simonsen, 'Antisemittismen i Norge, ca. 1918–1940: former, funksjoner og virkninger', in Øystein Sørensen and Kjetil Braut Simonsen (eds.), *Historie og moral, nazismen, jødene og hjemmefronten* (Oslo: Dreyers Forlag, 2020), pp. 21–50, at p. 22; Einhart Lorenz, '"Vi har ikke invitert jødene hit til landet" – norske syn på jødene i et langtidsperspektiv', in Vibeke Moe and Øivind Kopperud (eds.), *Forestillinger om jøder – aspekter ved konstruksjonen av en minoritet 1814–1940* (Oslo: Unipub, 2011), pp. 35–52; Terje Emberland, 'Antisemittisme i Norge 1900–1940', in Trond Berg Eriksen, Håkon Harket and Einhart Lorenz (eds.), *Jødehat: antisemittismens historie fra antikken til i dag* (Oslo: N.W. Damm & Søn, 2005), pp. 401–420, at p. 401.

[128] Lorenz, '"Vi har ikke invitert jødene hit til landet"', p. 50.

[129] In 1929, Jewish *shechita* procedures were prohibited by the Norwegian parliament following a highly antisemitic, decades-long public and political debate.

[130] Simonsen, 'Antisemittismen i Norge, ca. 1918–1940', p. 25. [131] Ibid., p. 29.

[132] Ibid., pp. 38–39; Emberland, 'Antisemittismen i Norge 1900–1940', p. 418. The solidarity did not extend far enough to allow Jews to seek refuge in Norway more widely, and the country pursued a highly restrictive refuge policy with regard to Jewish refugees ahead of the war: Ibid., Emberland, p. 419.

1930s. However, given the party's marginal position, this was of no direct consequence to the Jewish population before the occupation.

The threat radically changed after the German invasion.[133] Following the establishment of Quisling's occupation rule – monitored and shaped by Terboven's *Reichskommissariat* – life was made increasingly difficult for Jews in Norway. Immediately following the formation of the occupation apparatus under the NS and *Reichskommisar* Terboven, a series of restrictions were implemented. Radios of Jewish citizens were seized already in May 1940[134] and many Jews had their professional licences removed in the early occupation period.[135] Some Jews were fired, including those working in the civil service, and the *Sipo* began to map the Jewish populations as well as Jewish businesses in Norway. However, during the early occupation years, Jews in Norway experienced comparatively fewer restrictions than those in Germany or other Western European countries occupied by the Germans.[136] Most significantly, they were not registered to the same systematic degree as in other countries immediately after the occupation began. To some extent, this was deliberate, so as not to risk public protest. But this does not mean that this period was without violence. The German occupier and its collaborationist partners conducted swathes of random arrests, imprisonments and killings.[137]

Alongside these early measures, the NS was preparing a more comprehensive set of antisemitic laws. As we have seen, the party had more explicitly embraced antisemitism in the form of the racial ideology of the German National Socialists in the late 1930s. In 1938, Quisling explicitly referred to the 'removal' of all Jews from Europe in a series of public speeches.[138] In his world view, Jews were at the centre of a conspiratorial threat to the Aryan race. Over the first two years of the occupation, Quisling's rhetoric became increasingly aggressive towards Jews.[139] Quisling regularly mixed antisemitic rhetoric with Norse mythology, stating that the Jews were 'Loke's terrible offspring, the Midgard Serpent and Fenris Wolf',[140] and an enemy of the Norwegian people. In line with the ever-harsher rhetoric, Quisling's administration worked on a series of

[133] For a detailed account of the Holocaust in Norway, see Bruland, *Holocaust i Norge*.
[134] Ibid., pp. 82–87. Those of the wider population were seized in autumn of 1941.
[135] Ibid., pp. 163–165. [136] Ibid., p. 77. [137] Ibid., pp. 98–118.
[138] Dahl, *Quisling*, p. 137.
[139] Øystein Sørensen, 'NS-regimet og jødene', in Øystein Sørensen and Kjetil Braut Simonsen (eds.), *Historie og moral: Nazismen, jødene og hjemmefronten* (Oslo: Dreyers Forlag, 2020), pp. 51–90, at p. 52.
[140] *Quisling har sagt, Mot Nytt Land*, Vol. IV (Oslo: 1944), p. 175; referenced in Sørensen, 'NS-regimet og jødene', p. 55.

laws aimed at 'racially' identifying and sanctioning Jews. This legislation was in large part modelled on German race laws.

But despite the legislative activity of the NS and the party's attempt to embed the measures in a longer Nordic racial narrative, the measures against the Jews ultimately came about through a cooperation between the NS and the German occupier. Behind the scenes, it was the Germans who were in control of anti-Jewish policies, as with other elements of the occupation regime. The *Reichskommissariat* and Berlin oversaw the situation in occupied Norway and gave orders. And yet it was largely NS members and local police who implemented the policies against Norway's Jews. This cooperation was convenient to the Germans, as they aimed to convey an image of legitimacy and to make any measures against the country's Jews appear as driven by the NS and, by extension, Norwegians themselves. Given the comparatively small size of the Jewish community in Norway, the German occupiers did not want to make the measures appear as top-down German-instructed ones, for fear that this might generate a backlash to the occupation regime in society – and perhaps even sympathy with the Jews.[141]

For Norway's Jews, the climate became significantly more violent following Germany's invasion of the Soviet Union in June 1941.[142] In addition, as resistance activity grew within Norway, this was used as an excuse to increasingly crack down on the Jewish population. However, when widespread and tough measures were implemented in 1942, they still came as a shock to many. In January 1942, Jews were forced to have a 'J' stamped in red in their documents (on the initiative of the *Sicherheitspolizei*).[143] Registration of Jews had already been planned from autumn 1941 and began fully in February 1942.[144] Ultimately, 1,582 Jews were registered in the spring of 1942.[145] Especially after 1 February 1942, when the Quisling regime had been granted governing status, a series of harsh measures came in quick succession. Quisling had the 'Jew Paragraph' reintroduced into the Norwegian Constitution in March 1942.[146] Later on, additional legislation was adopted which made it mandatory for Jews, 'half-Jews' and 'quarter-Jews' to register. In including 'quarter-Jews', the definition of Jews in the Norwegian legislation was in fact even wider than

141 Bruland, *Holocaust i Norge*, pp. 37–44, 89.

142 Ibid., pp. 78–79; Oskar Mendelsohn, *Jødene i Norge: historien om en minoritet* (Oslo: Universitetsforlaget, 1992), p. 75.

143 Bruland, *Holocaust i Norge*, pp. 183–192.

144 Ibid., pp. 179–205.

145 Ibid., pp. 366–367.

146 Ibid., pp. 166–167.

that of the Nuremberg Laws.[147] The treatment of Jews was part of a broader plan to signal to Hitler that the NS was fully cooperating, and by extension it therefore aimed at facilitating the peace agreement and Norwegian independence so desired by Quisling.[148] But it was also a direct consequence of the party's antisemitism.

In October 1942, Terboven declared a state of emergency in the county of Trøndelag, following increased resistance activity in the region. As part of this, all Jews in the region were rounded up and arrested. Women and children were taken to a few locations in the city of Trondheim, while men over the age of fifteen were deported to Falstad prison camp.[149] This was the beginning of the most severe phase of persecution. The shooting and killing of a border police officer on 22 October 1942 while a group of Jews were trying to flee on a train towards the Swedish border marked the start of a further escalation. The event was used as an excuse to blame the Jewish population of Norway as a whole for sabotage. Widespread arrests were carried out across the country on 26 October by the Norwegian state police, supported by regular police, the *Hird* and *Germanske SS Norge*, following the adoption of a new legal basis on detention two days prior.[150] These arrests were mainly carried out by the Norwegian police. Women were initially allowed to remain in their place of residence, but they were required to report to the local police station each day, allowing authorities to keep track of their whereabouts and strongly discouraging them from fleeing, not least because they feared for their arrested men.[151]

On 26 October 1942, the Quisling government adopted an act on the expropriation of Jewish property.[152] This, too, was likely accelerated in the wake of the shooting incident on the train. The act stipulated that the property of Jews, and their spouses and children, would be liquidated.[153] The operation was conducted by the Liquidation Board (*Likvidasjonsstyret*), which reported directly to the Ministry of Finance and which was run by a judge on the Acting Supreme Court.[154] The aim was to fill NS coffers with

147 Sørensen, 'NS-regimet og jødene', p. 65. 148 Ibid., p. 61.

149 Nilssen and Reitan, *Legacies of the Nazi Camps in Norway*, p. 46.

150 'Lov av 24. oktober om tillegg til midlertidig forordning av 6. oktober 1941 om anvendelse av sikringsforføyninger overfor personer som mistenkes for visse overtredelser'.

151 Bruland, *Holocaust i Norge*, pp. 277–280.

152 Ibid., pp. 477–549; Synne Corell, *Likvidasjonen: historien om holocaust i Norge og jakten på jødenes ejendom* (Oslo: Gyldendal, 2021).

153 'Lov om inndragning av formue som tilhører jøder' of 26 October 1942; Bruland, *Holocaust i Norge*, pp. 482–483.

154 Christopher S. Harper, 'Rettsoppgjørets behandling av deportasjonen av jødene fra Norge under okkupasjonen 1940–1945' (HL-senterets temahefte nr. 16, 2012), p. 16; Corell, *Likvidasjonen*, pp. 244–254.

money seized through the expropriations. However, following an agreement between the NS and the Germans, the gold, silver and jewellery of Jews was to be given to the Germans. The NS had prepared further legislation to strip all Jews – following the wide definition proposed by Quisling – of their Norwegian citizenship, to forbid marriages and intercourse between Jews and non-Jews, and to require Jews to wear a Star of David in public. Within the Quisling administration, there had been some internal doubts about whether such sweeping measures were necessary, given the 'comparatively few Jews living in this country'.[155] But ultimately, some of this legislation never came into effect, as the deportations that followed soon after stripped any such legislation of its purpose.

The dreadful culmination of anti-Jewish policy during the occupation occurred on 26 November 1942, when 529 Norwegian Jews were deported on the cargo ship *Donau* from Oslo harbour to occupied Poland. On 24 November 1942, Wilhelm Wagner, who was responsible in the German *Sipo* for 'Jewish Matters', had issued an order to arrest *all* Jews over fifteen years of age with a 'J' in their documents and have them moved to Oslo.[156] Within forty-eight hours, these men, women and children had been transported to the Oslo harbour. Knut Rød, a chief superintendent (*politiinspektør*) and head of the Oslo-Aker department of *Stapo*, was in charge of the arrests of Oslo's Jews, helped by Oslo police officers, members of the *Hird*, *Germanske SS-Norge* and the *Stapo*, as well as local taxi chauffeurs and employees of Norwegian public transport organisations.[157] The deportations came on German initiative, and took the NS leadership by surprise, which was still in the midst of deliberating on the precise contours of its race legislation.[158] The Germans had decided at the last minute to use the *Donau* to deport the Jews, as the ship had become available at short notice after carrying cargo to Norway. But it was mostly Norwegians who carried out the arrests and brought men, women and children to Oslo quay, where the Gestapo took over.[159] When the *Donau* departed Oslo at 14.55 on 26 November, 529 Jews were on board, almost all of whom would face death in Auschwitz. A further ship, the *Gotenland*, departed Oslo on 23 February 1943, carrying 158 Jews. In total, 776 Jews were deported from Norway, of whom only 38 survived.[160]

155 RA/S-3212/D/Dh/L0269: 'Notat fra Justisdepartementets lovavdeling', p. 19, referenced in Sørensen, 'NS-regimet og jødene', p. 70.

156 Bruland, *Holocaust i Norge*, p. 289. 157 Ibid., pp. 314.

158 Sørensen, 'NS-regimet og jødene', p. 78.

159 Simonsen, 'Antisemittismen i Norge, ca. 1918–1940', p. 40.

160 Bruland, *Holocaust i Norge*, p. 365.

Parts of the Jewish population managed to avoid the horrors of Germany's extermination camps, the vast majority of them by fleeing the country, and a few by hiding. The percentage of those who managed to flee was higher among Norwegian Jews with established networks in the community than the newly arrived refugees. An estimated 1,216 individuals were able to flee from Norway during the occupation,[161] while 124 were able to avoid deportation because they were married to non-Jews.[162] A total of 930 individuals fled to Sweden between October 1942 and January 1943 alone.[163] Many of them were lucky to be tipped off by local police, taxi chauffeurs, resistance groups or individuals informed or suspecting of the fate that might await them. Most often, those fleeing received help from various groups and organisations, including from the organised civil resistance, the military resistance and the communist organisation *Komorg*. Carl Fredriksen Transport, a group associated with the military resistance *Milorg*, managed to help 350 Jews across the border.[164]

As Bjarte Bruland has argued, 'Norway was a microcosm of what took place at the European level.'[165] But there were also key differences when it came to the persecution of Jews in Norway. The Jewish population was comparatively small and more spread out geographically. For this reason, the Germans did not want to cause unrest in society by imposing too draconian measures from the outset. Systematic measures against the Jews came comparatively late, but when they came, they did so very suddenly and were concentrated around a span of a few short months. A further aspect of the Holocaust in Norway that stands out is that, in comparison to other occupied countries in Western Europe, a relatively high percentage of registered Jews, around 53 per cent, were deported.[166] But despite this high percentage, the crimes against Norway's Jews would receive very little attention during the trials of the immediate post-war era – as was the case elsewhere in Europe.

1.5 Outfront and Home Front

From London, the exile government tried to observe developments in Norway as closely as it could. After holding its first cabinet meetings in the Norwegian Embassy, it had gradually set up at Kingston House in Knightsbridge and built departmental infrastructures. In the early period,

161 Ibid., p. 470; Frode Færøy, 'Hjelperne fra Norges Kommunistiske Parti', in Sørensen and Simonsen (eds.), *Historie og moral*, pp. 211–228, at p. 222.

162 Grimnes, *Norge under andre verdenskrig*, p. 363. 163 Ibid., p. 362. 164 Ibid., p. 362.

165 Bruland, *Holocaust i Norge*, p. 18. 166 Ibid., p. 367.

the exile government was in a weak position, despite seeking to assert some degree of authority through a series of public statements and declaring void any agreement that might be reached with the occupying power on home soil.[167] The news that leading Norwegians back home were negotiating with the Germans deeply affected the exiles, in particular as it came with an instruction from Chief Justice Paal Berg that the government remain silent so as not to jeopardise ongoing negotiations.[168] With the aim of returning to liberated Norway as its legitimate government, the most acute threat facing the exile government throughout was that it would lose the loyalty of its people before that time. But thanks to the failure of the Realm Council negotiations, the exile government remained the legitimate Norwegian government. The first two years in exile in particular were a 'probationary period', in which the government had to secure the trust of its own population. It also had to do everything it could to present its situation as being the result of an unbroken continuity of state power.[169] Institutionally, it operated at first on a 'minimum programme', only sufficient to maintain a link to mainland Norway and adapt cabinet policies to wartime circumstances. With reliable information channels not yet in place, the exile government had difficulty assessing the situation back home during the early months of the occupation. Gradually, however, it established communicative avenues into occupied Norway, and after the establishment of the *Reichskommissariat* in September 1940 it could be more certain of its status. One of its key assets was the Norwegian merchant fleet, of which 80 per cent had set sail for Allied harbours and which contributed significantly to the Allied war effort. Its value ensured that the exile government could maintain financial independence.[170]

Within Norway, an organised resistance gradually extended into a large and influential network. A first act of resistance was the collective resignation of the judges of the Supreme Court in December 1940.[171] This circle of judges, who had earlier been members of the Administration Council and taken part in the failed Realm Council negotiations, became central figures in the

[167] Olav Riste, *London-Regjeringa, Norge i krigsalliansen, Bind I: 1940–1942: Prøvetid* (Oslo: Samlaget, 1973), pp. 18–19; Ole Kristian Grimnes, 'The Two Norways, 1940–41', in Michael H. Clemmesen and Marcus S. Faulkner (eds.), *Northern European Overture to War, 1939–1941* (Leiden: Brill, 2013), pp. 383–402.

[168] Riste, *London-Regjeringa, Norge i krigsalliansen, Bind I: 1940–1942: Prøvetid*, p. 18.

[169] Ibid.

[170] Chris Mann, 'The Norwegian Armed Forces in Britain', in Martin Conway and José Gotovitch (eds.), *Europe in Exile: European Exile Communities in Britain 1940–45* (Oxford: Berghahn, 2001), pp. 153–166, at p. 157; Harald Espeli, 'The Economic Effects of the German Occupation of Norway, 1940–1945', in Jonas Scherner and Eugene N. White (eds.), *Paying for Hitler's War: The Consequences of Nazi Hegemony for Europe* (Cambridge: Cambridge University Press, 2016), pp. 235–265.

[171] Graver, *Dommernes krig*, pp. 35–39.

organised resistance.[172] Founded in 1941, the 'Circle' (*Kretsen*) around Chief Justice Paal Berg became the core of the civilian resistance movement in Norway. Berg had held key positions in pre-war Norway, and acted as Minister for Social Affairs and Minister of Justice, before becoming Chief Justice of the Supreme Court. He was an unlikely figure to lead the resistance due to both his prominence and his age (he was 67 when Norway was invaded). However, Berg described these features as his 'best disguise', as few suspected he would be so actively involved in resistance work.[173] Numerous organisations of civilian resistance sprang up in the first two years after the invasion, but coordination was difficult, with hardly any wider resistance infrastructure in place.[174] The Circle managed to hold regular meetings, however, and recruited leading individuals from the judiciary, the public administration, the economy and the political parties.[175] The exile government made contact with the resistance early on in the occupation period, despite the difficulties it faced in getting an overview of the various resistance groups that had formed in Norway.[176] From summer 1942, a reliable and frequent exchange between the government and resistance had been established.

Founded in early 1941, a group of military opponents known as *Milorg* made up a second pillar of resistance. It was formed by officers, who operated with the possibility of a liberation in mind and intended to have armed forces in place should the situation arise. Its main role came to be to prepare for the various scenarios that a liberation could entail, and to be ready to act as 'guerrilla forces, sabotage groups and guard divisions, depending on how the liberation took shape'.[177] It was recognised as a resistance group by the exile government from late 1941 onwards. Several of its leaders rose to prominence in the post-war era, in particular its head from 1942, Jens Christian Hauge, who became Minister of Defence and later Minister of Justice. From January 1942 onwards, a third group stepped onto the scene. Initially an organising committee aimed at

[172] Ole Kristian Grimnes, *Hjemmefrontens ledelse* (Oslo: Universitetsforlaget, 1977), pp. 121–212.
[173] Hem, p. 600. [174] Omang (ed.), *Regjeringen og hjemmefronten under krigen*, p. 6.
[175] Ole Kristian Grimnes, 'Fra krig til fred', in Dahl, Kirchhoff, Lund and Vaale (eds.), *Danske tilstande – norske tilstande*, pp. 259–281, at p. 264.
[176] Contact was made through individuals who travelled between Oslo and London, as well as through the 'Press Bureau' (*Pressekontoret*) in Stockholm, formed by journalists who had fled from Norway. Using code names such as 'Sophie, Jenny, Franz, Georg' the correspondence took place through letters, telegrams and, in urgent situations, radio messaging. On several occasions, meetings took place between members of the government and the resistance; Omang (ed.), *Regjeringen og hjemmefronten under krigen*, pp. 5, 12–13.
[177] Grimnes, 'Fra krig til fred', p. 262.

coordinating resistance in various different professions against Nazification, the Coordination Committee (*Koordinasjonskomitéen*) gradually developed into a more independent body, issuing its own statements and going beyond its initial role of a coordinator.[178] It soon joined forces with the Circle and *Milorg*. From 1943, the three groups had established a frequent exchange and began to coordinate resistance activities and develop joint plans for the post-war order.

From 1943 onwards, the resistance in Norway was collectively referred to as the Home Front (*Hjemmefronten*), and its inner circle as the 'Leadership of the Home Front' (*Hjemmefrontens Ledelse*). Its members were primarily the leading figures within the Circle.[179] While the Coordination Committee did not step into direct contact with the exile government, it corresponded through the Circle. A key interest of the government in the correspondence was to receive information about the situation on the ground in Norway. By corresponding with key figures of the resistance and issuing decrees it could also reassert its powers as the government of Norway. The legitimacy of the exile government rested in large parts on the condition that the underground forces in Norway respected it as its government. But the resistance figures, too, had a core strategic interest in the exchange. As early as 1941, resistance members had communicated to the government-in-exile that they wished to be represented in the post-war government.[180] This was met with considerable suspicion by the government-in-exile, which feared for its status in liberated Norway.[181] A further topic of much debate in the correspondences between the Circle and the exile government was what forms of resistance could be endorsed. The government was as sceptical as the Home Front towards acts of sabotage and distanced itself from 'acts of terror or planless partisan war'.[182] Its aim was initially to be cautious and act 'without weapons', and to make the resistance an ideological battle against the NS.[183] This was seen differently by the British, as well as many members of *Milorg*, who argued that military resistance was the only meaningful way of countering German rule.[184]

In the final months of the war, the exile government felt unable to define how resistance could best be carried out, and entrusted the Circle

[178] Omang (ed.), *Regjeringen og hjemmefronten under krigen*, p. 9.
[179] März, *Die langen Schatten der Besatzungszeit*, p. 64.
[180] Omang (ed.), *Regjeringen og hjemmefronten under krigen*, p. 7.
[181] Grimnes, 'Fra krig til fred', p. 264.
[182] Omang (ed.), *Regjeringen og hjemmefronten under krigen*, pp. 31–32. [183] Ibid., p. 31.
[184] Olav Riste, *London-Regjeringa, Norge i krigsalliansen, Bind II: 1942–1945: Vegen heim* (Oslo: Det Norske Samlaget, 1979), pp. 22–34.

with deciding what line of resistance should be taken.[185] This reflects the general power dynamics between the 'Outfront' – the London exiles – and the 'Home Front'. The Home Front opted for an intensification of resistance activity, and the government supported these actions.[186] A relationship of trust had formed between the government-in-exile and the Circle more generally from 1943 onwards, and in June 1943, the exile government recognised Paal Berg as the de facto leader of the Home Front. Responsibility for preparations for the event of a German capitulation was placed with the Home Front rather than *Milorg*. In a letter to the Home Front, the government expressly stated that 'we do not believe that *Milorg* should have a role outside the purely military … organisations'.[187] In autumn 1944, the Home Front was formally gathered into one organisation, comprising representatives of the Circle, the Coordination Committee, the military organisations and police. On 5 May 1945 the exile government granted this joint body the powers to take the 'necessary measures' in the event of a German capitulation. Due to the key powers the Home Front held at this critical stage, many members of the resistance secured key offices in the political and juridical apparatus in the early post-war years.

1.6 Planning for a Reckoning

Despite their close coordination during the final months of the occupation, the relationship between the resistance and the government-in-exile had not always been free from tension. The government was criticised early on by individuals from the resistance that it was out of touch with the situation in Norway.[188] They argued that there was a significant gap between the perception of the exile government and the Norwegians who had remained on Norwegian territory. As the war continued, the points of conflict increasingly came to concern arrangements for the post-war order.[189] Calls in 1941 for the exile government to resign and make space for the Home Front members in the post-war order had made for a sour start to the relationship.[190] But the two sides reached a compromise in 1943, according to which the Home Front would provide an interim government until the government delegation from London returned to Norway, but that the government would then take over. A core element of

[185] Omang (ed.), *Regjeringen og hjemmefronten under krigen*, p. 32. [186] Ibid., pp. 503–504.
[187] Ibid., p. 240. [188] Ibid., p. 15. [189] Grimnes, 'Fra krig til fred', pp. 266–269.
[190] Einar Gerhardsen, *Fellesskap i krig og fred: erindringer 1940–1945* (Oslo: Tiden Norsk Forlag, 1970), p. 60; Omang (ed.), *Regjeringen og hjemmefronten under krigen*, p. 7.

the cooperation between the exile government and the Home Front was the planning of the post-war reckoning with 'collaborators', the legal bases of which were shaped by the power dynamics between the two groups. The earliest initiatives came from the exile government, while later on the Home Front became more influential in the planning.[191] Through a series of decrees, the exile government criminalised various forms of collaboration and set out the structural and administrative bases for the treason trials. While there were some discrepancies between the Home Front and the exile government concerning the legal basis for the reckoning, the decrees that came to form the basis of the treason trials were ultimately an effort of coordination between the two.

Wilhelm Keilhau, the Chief Military Prosecutor and board member of the Norwegian Central Bank in London, had first floated a proposal for 'The Legal Reckoning with the Norwegian Traitors and Semi-Traitors' with the government in January 1941.[192] He argued that additional provisions were necessary because the pre-war Criminal Code provided an insufficient basis for the situation at hand. That a reckoning with disloyal individuals was necessary appears to have been generally accepted within the exile government.[193] But its jurists were divided as to whether or not additional provisions were necessary or desirable, signalling the entirely unprecedented nature of the question.[194] One jurist within the exile government, Arnold Ræstad, argued that the situation upon the liberation was so unpredictable that the exile government should not narrow its scope for manoeuvre at this early stage by issuing legal provisions, especially as it knew little of the situation on the ground. Rather, it should adopt provisions only once the country had been liberated. Ræstad dismissed the idea that such provisions could be deemed retroactive, due to the inherently *political* nature of the reckoning. He reasoned that constitutional provisions would not apply, as the authors of the constitution had simply not envisaged a case of such widespread treason.[195] These early

[191] On the dynamics between exile government and Home Front: Baard Herman Borge and Lars-Erik Vaale, 'Stretching the Rule of Law: How the Norwegian Resistance Movement Influenced the Provisional Treason Decrees of the Exile Government, 1944–1945', *Scandinavian Journal of History* 46 (2021) 1, pp. 105–124.

[192] Ot.prp. nr. 92 (1945–1946), p. 70.

[193] Helge Olav Bugge, Kirsti Coward and Stein Rognlien (eds.), *Festskrift Lovavdelingen 100 år 1885–1985* (Oslo: Universitetsforlaget, 1986), p. 27.

[194] RA/S-3212/D/De/L0299: 'Utskrift av referat av møte på Legasjonen den 6. februar 1941', 6 February 1941.

[195] RA/S-3212/D/De/L0299: 'Bör regjeringen i London utferdige en provisorisk anordning om straff for landssvikhandlinger i Norge utover den vår gjeldende straffelov rammer?' P.M. by Arnold Ræstad, 5 February 1941.

considerations foreshadowed how difficult the conceptualisation and implementation of adequate legal provisions for the reckoning would become.

But it was not feasible for the exile government to wait until the liberation. It received frequent messages from Norway that unequivocal statements on the matter were expected. Legal questions aside, the planning of the post-war reckoning also carried significant *symbolic* meaning. The many uncertain legal questions surrounding the reckoning, combined with the pressure to make announcements that the collaborators would be put to justice, prompted the Ministry of Justice to appoint a select criminal law committee on 12 March 1941. Headed by none other than Wilhelm Keilhau, the committee was entrusted with investigating which legal provisions were needed for a comprehensive reckoning with the 'traitors'.[196] The Ministry urged the committee to look at how other exile governments had handled similar situations, in particular the exile government of Belgium, both during the ongoing war and the First World War.[197]

Before the Keilhau Committee had concluded its investigation, the London government adopted its two first provisional decrees on 3 October 1941, by which it introduced the death penalty into ordinary criminal law and extended the applicability of the death penalty in military law. The first decree allowed for death penalties under the Military Criminal Code to be executed also after a war had ended. The second decree allowed for the death penalty to be applied to certain offences under Chapters 8 and 9 of the 1902 Civilian Criminal Code, which concerned crimes against the state, in particular treason.[198] The offence of treason would become the most widely used offence under which collaborators were charged. The second decree also introduced the new penalty of forced labour for crimes under Chapters 8 and 9 of the Criminal Code, mainly to prevent an overcrowding of prisons. Finally, it allowed for the penalty of loss of civil rights *for life* (previously it had been limited to ten years), for '[t]he state can no longer trust such people, which is why – even after 10 years – they should not be allowed to hold [these] rights'.[199] The decrees of 3 October 1941 were a response to increasing hostilities in Norway. At this stage, the exile government had established some communication channels to occupied Norway and knew of the violence being used against the

[196] Ot.prp. nr. 92 (1945–1946), p. 65. [197] Ibid., p. 70.

[198] 'Provisorisk anordning om tillegg til den alminnelige borgerlige straffelov av 22. mai 1902' of 3 October 1941 and 'Provisorisk anordning om tillegg til den militære straffelov av 22. mai 1902' of 3 October 1941, printed in Ot.prp. nr. 141 (1945–1946), p. 2.

[199] Ibid., p. 3.

population, including resistance members, by the German occupiers and their Norwegian aides. Executions were common in occupied Norway, and 417 Norwegians were killed in this way on Norwegian territory during the war.[200] The measures adopted, so the exile government hoped, would have some deterrent function, addressed at both the German occupiers and Norwegian collaborators, while also asserting the exile government's continued claim to authority. But the introduction of the offence of loss of civil rights also indicates that, early on, the purpose of the reckoning was to place individuals outside the post-war national community.

Regarding the reintroduction of the death penalty into civilian law, the government expressly stated that the death penalty would only apply to acts committed *after* the decree had been issued.[201] This signals an early recognition that the reckoning with collaborators would still have to take place within the contours of established principles of law, such as the prohibition of retroactive laws, which was also laid down in § 97 of the Constitution. As a broader justification for the introduction of the death penalty – which had been formally abolished in 1902 and not been carried out in Norway since 1876 – the government argued that most citizens demanded it, and that this was both a 'healthy and correct legal opinion'.[202] But it is unlikely that the government had any insight into the broader public's demands. Its only source were the reports drafted by the resistance representatives, which it relied on heavily throughout the occupation. Instead, the reintroduction of the death penalty was rather an expression of what the government expected would be the public's demand upon the liberation, foreshadowing the way in which actual or perceived public demands would shape the course of the trials. Most of all, however, the exile government hoped that the adoption of the death penalty – so alien to Norwegian law – would have a strong deterrent function against wartime crimes.[203]

However, this modification in itself was not deemed sufficient as a basis for a wider reckoning. It was clear to the government that most citizens had not committed crimes serious enough to justify use of the death penalty, but that still would warrant punishment upon the liberation. On 5 December 1941, the Keilhau Committee presented its findings. It had reached the conclusion that the existing criminal provisions were insufficient and made a number of proposals for additions to the existing

200 Berit Nøkleby, *Skutt blir den …: tysk bruk av dødsstraff i Norge, 1940–1945* (Oslo: Gyldendal, 1996), p. 9.

201 Ot.prp. nr. 141 (1945–1946), p. 4. 202 Ibid., p. 3.

203 RA/S-4242/D/L0100: 'Det rettslige grunnlag for oppgjöret med quislingene', undated memo.

Criminal Code. In terms of new provisions, the Committee found that in particular members of the NS and 'any other organisations that support the treacherous government' should be criminalised.[204] It argued that additional provisions were necessary in particular because the pre-war provisions were too inflexible to cover activities such as NS membership. The existing provision for treason – the provision that was most suitable as a basis for the reckoning – stipulated a prison term of three years, which was deemed too high for the broad masses of collaborators.[205] The degree of collaboration necessary to fulfil the offence of treason under § 86 was also unclear, raising the controversial question of whether passive membership of the NS alone would constitute an offence. The Committee pointed also to the 'general-preventive' effect an explicit prohibition of NS membership might have, and that it might prevent 'German-friendly, dissatisfied luck-chasers or weak souls from joining *Nasjonal Samling*'.[206]

In order to limit clashes with § 97 of the Norwegian Constitution, which laid down the prohibition of retroactive laws, the Committee deemed it important that any further decrees be adopted 'as soon as possible', and not to wait until the end of the occupation.[207] But the Committee also emphasised that only actions committed *after* the decree was issued should be deemed to be criminal.[208] The Committee cited Belgian provisions used during the reckoning with collaborators after the end of the First World War, the validity of which had never been challenged. The Committee concluded that 'these [Belgian] experiences therefore unequivocally point in the direction of supporting the issuance of new Norwegian criminal provisions at this point in time'.[209] We thus see that the Committee had a strong regard for constitutional principles. But at the same time, it was led by a considerable degree of pragmatism: in its report, the Committee considered the criminalisation of other actions, such as against individuals who continued in leading positions within the collaborationist regime but without joining the NS. But ultimately, it deemed it too complex and therefore limited itself to recommending the criminalisation of pure membership of the NS.

The Ministry of Justice used the Keilhau Committee's suggestions as a basis for two further decrees, issued on 22 January 1942, one of which was sometimes referred to as the 'Quisling Decree'.[210] The decrees contained

[204] Ot.prp. nr. 92 (1945–1946), p. 74. [205] Ibid., p. 72. [206] Ibid., pp. 72–73.
[207] Ibid., p. 73. [208] Ibid., pp. 73–74. [209] Ibid., p. 73.
[210] 'Provisorisk anordning om tillegg til den alminnelige borgerlige straffelovs kapitler 19, 21 og 22' of 22 January 1942, printed in Ot.prp. nr. 141 (1945–1946), p. 5; 'Provisorisk anordning om tillegg til straffelovgivningen om forræderi' of 22 January 1942, printed in Ot.prp. nr. 92 (1945–1946),

three key elements, which were to define the contours of the treason trials. Firstly, they expressly established the criminality of NS membership, stressing that it was the party's actions after the German invasion that turned it into a 'party of traitors'.[211] All membership after the date on which the decree was issued was to be criminal, regardless of individual intent or motivation. This meant that active and passive membership alike was punishable under the new provisions.[212] In its statement on the bill, the Ministry of Justice stated that it had no doubt that 99 per cent of the members of the NS knew that they were engaged in criminal activity. Secondly, the decrees extended the applicability of the death penalty to crimes against 'public morality', 'personal freedom' or 'life, limb and health'.[213] Finally, they allowed for crimes committed during the occupation to be sanctioned by fine and loss of civil rights in addition to or *in lieu of* prison sentences, a new principle in criminal sanctions. 'Loss of civil rights' was to be considered a primary penalty and NS members were to be punished through the withdrawal of their full set of civil rights for varying durations. The Ministry argued that a loss of civil rights would affect individuals as much as prison sentences, so that by way of this penalty, public expenses for prisons could be reduced. The loss of civil rights included

> loss of any public offices which the guilty person may hold, loss of the right to vote in all public matters, loss of the right to serve in the armed forces of the State, loss of the right to carry on any trade, profession or business for which public authorisation or approval is required, and loss of the right to hold any position, whether paid or unpaid, as head or leading official in companies, financial societies, organisations, or other associations.[214]

The decrees were announced through the *Norwegian Law Gazette* (*Norsk Lovtidend*), printed in London, on 22 January 1942. They signalled that the reckoning would primarily revolve around members of the NS and

p. 9. For an example of use of the term 'Quisling Decree', see RA/S-3212/D/De/L0299: Letter by P. Stabell of the Norwegian Delegation to V. Benes of the Czechoslovak Ministry of Justice, 21 May 1943.

211 Ot.prp. nr. 92 (1945–1946), p. 66.

212 There was some disagreement among the exiles as to whether all activities were already covered by treason provisions in the Criminal Code from before the war. The Ministry of Justice argued that the 1942 decree was intended to send a strong signal to occupied Norway, to make it clear that all NS members would face punishment and to allow for the penalty of loss of public trust to be applied, but that NS membership was in the vast majority of cases already covered by pre-war provisions on treason. The Keilhau Committee, on the other hand, did not consider simple membership of the NS to be covered by the pre-war provisions. The difference between these interpretations would become relevant again after the war, when the wartime decrees were tested in court.

213 Ot.prp. nr. 141 (1945–1946), p. 5.

214 Ot.prp. nr. 92 (1945–1946), p. 9.

those guilty of capital offences and assaults.[215] This set the contours for the reckoning that lay ahead. The decrees sought to delineate the scope of punishable activities in Norway, and set out new forms of punishment. The decrees broke with established legal traditions in an attempt to introduce provisions unequivocal enough to deter collaborationist activity. But the deliberations ahead of their adoption also signalled the strong desire among some experts within the exile government to adhere to constitutional principles and ground the provisions in (international) precedent. The day after the Quisling Decree was announced, Justice Minister Terje Wold gave a speech on the Norwegian public broadcaster, laying out the provisions and declaring that '[a]ll members of *Nasjonal Samling* are traitors'.[216] He expressly declared that this included passive NS members. The reckoning was to be a reckoning with *political* traitors, and the NS in particular. From then on, the word 'traitor' became synonymous with NS members. Henceforth, the government frequently repeated its intentions for a full reckoning with party members.[217] Yet, as we have seen, it is difficult to assess what effect these announcements had on home soil. The willingness and ability of individuals to modify their wartime behaviour or revoke their party membership depended on many factors, such as their economic position, their location in the country, the attitudes within their own respective communities and their ability to receive these broadcasts in the first place.[218]

In order to be able to prepare for a post-war purge of collaborationist civil servants, the exile government issued the Civil Servant Decree on 26 February 1943.[219] According to the decree, any civil servant who had been a member of the NS after 22 January 1942, the date on which the Quisling Decree expressly criminalised NS membership, would be suspended. In addition, all those who had been appointed to their positions

[215] RA/S-3212/D/De/L0299: Memo on the decree of 22 January 1942, attached to letter from the Norwegian exile government to the Swedish delegation, 27 January 1942.

[216] Speech by Terje Wold of 23 January 1942, printed in Justis- og Politidepartementet, *Om landssvikoppgjøret*, pp. 41–42.

[217] On 25 December 1942, State Minister Johan Nygaardsvold declared via radio that 'the Norwegian traitors – the Quislings – those who are members of *Nasjonal Samling* ... will all be held accountable before a Norwegian court of law for their crimes against Norway, the Norwegian laws and against the Norwegian people'; excerpt from State Minister Nygaardsvold's speech in his London broadcast of 25 December 1942, in Omang (ed.), *Regjeringen og hjemmefronten under krigen*, p. 140.

[218] Listening to broadcasts from London was illegal in Norway, although many defied the prohibition and the broadcasts became an important information channel; Hans Fredrik Dahl, *'Dette er London', NRK i krig 1940–1945* (Oslo: Cappelen, 1978).

[219] Ot.prp. nr. 91 (1945–1946), pp. 16–17.

by someone without legal authority would be removed. In turn, any civil servant suspended by the NS regime or the German occupier would be reinstated. In addition, the exile government on 26 February 1943 also issued the Criminal Procedure Decree (*Rettergangsanordningen*), which allowed for special criminal proceedings in the context of the treason trials in order to stem the caseload.[220] The main elements of this were extended detention periods and a limitation of the possibilities for appeal. Both these decrees were replaced by new, more encompassing decrees towards the end of the war.[221]

Alongside preparations for the punishment and purge of Norwegian collaborators, the Norwegian exile government was also involved in the joint planning of the nine exile governments based in London to prosecute German war criminals, which led to the Declaration of St James Palace of 13 January 1942. The Declaration laid down the principle that war crimes in occupied countries should be prosecuted and that, as a rule, they would do so in the countries in which the crimes had been committed. In October 1943, the United Nations War Crimes Commission (UNWCCW) was established, which was to collect evidence of war crimes. The Norwegian exile government subsequently adopted a framework which would allow for the prosecution and punishment of German war criminals in Norway.[222] It was already possible to sentence them to death for torture under the ordinary Criminal Code in conjunction with the decrees of 3 October 1941, if the victim had suffered long-term damage. However, the exile government intended to go further, and to be able to sentence to death those who had caused severe suffering or who were repeated offenders. The decree was not adopted before 4 May 1945, however, leading to concerns about retroactivity in the post-war period.[223]

As the communication channels between the exile government and the Home Front became more established from 1943 onwards, the Home Front pushed for a more active role in the planning of the reckoning.[224] A first meeting on the subject of the treason trials between the Home Front's law group and representatives of the exile government on the matter took place in Sweden in autumn 1943. The Home Front leadership

[220] Justis- og Politidepartementet, *Om landssvikoppgjøret*, pp. 50–51.

[221] 'Tjenestemannsanordningen' of 24 November 1944 and 'Rettergangsanordningen' of 16 February 1945.

[222] For a study on the prosecution of war criminals in Norway, see Berit Nøkleby, *Krigsforbrytelser: brudd på krigens lov i Norge 1940–45* (Oslo: Pax Forlag, 2004).

[223] Borge and Vaale, *Grunnlovens største prøve*, pp. 54–56.

[224] Andenæs, *Det vanskelige oppgjøret*, pp. 53–55.

consisted of a number of jurists who were to have an enormous impact on the treason trials. This group included Sven Arntzen, who later acted as Director of Public Prosecutions (*Riksadvokat*) from the liberation until October 1946; Erik Solem, who became an influential judge during the treason trials, presiding over such high-profile cases as that of Vidkun Quisling; and Jens Christian Hauge, the leader of *Milorg* and later the head of the Compensation Directorate (*Erstatningsdirektoratet*), which administered compensation payments from former members of the NS in the post-war period.[225] It was this group that also secured the interests of the Home Front in the preparatory stages of the trials. From 1943, the planning of the treason trials became oriented towards both the demands of the Home Front and the specifics of the political transition that lay ahead. In cooperation with the Home Front, the exile government adopted a number of decrees involving the procedural and administrative implementation of the transition and the reckoning.[226]

The Home Front's law committee was not satisfied with the decrees of 1941 and 1942 and pushed for a new decree, which would include the most central elements of the previous provisions while adding a legal basis for a comprehensive *economic* reckoning with the 'traitors'. The Home Front presented a proposal to the exile government in May 1944 which it argued truly reflected the 'wish of the people'.[227] While provisions for the confiscation of winnings of NS members had already been put in place by the exile government, the Home Front proposal called for *compensation* from NS members for the economic damage they had brought upon the nation.[228] The principle proposed for this compensation mechanism was that members of the NS were liable *collectively* for the damages the party had caused. This liability was to be established regardless of individual culpability, according to the principle 'one for all and all for one' (although the courts could adjust payments to reflect individual liability).[229] The compensation claims were, according to the Home Front proposal, to apply to anyone who had been a member of the NS *after 8 April 1940* (and therefore before the 'Quisling Decree' of 22 January 1942 had been issued). The assets that could be seized were, however, not merely those of NS members themselves. In addition, the draft foresaw that any assets of

[225] Ibid., p. 54. [226] Justis- og Politidepartementet, *Om landssvikoppgjøret*, p. 42.

[227] Andenæs, *Det vanskelige oppgjøret*, p. 63.

[228] A corresponding provision of 3 September 1943 had already been adopted on the basis of a cooperative effort of the Home Front and the Ministry of Justice. The decree stipulated that there could be no caps to the monetary redistribution.

[229] Ot.prp. nr. 66 (1945–1946), p. 137.

the spouses or heirs of NS members could also be seized.[230] In order to administer this large-scale undertaking, the Home Front proposed the establishment of a separate organ, the Compensation Directorate (*Erstatningsdirektoratet*). The proposal also expanded the scope of loss of rights to include the loss of the right to own property.[231] More than anything, therefore, the provision was meant to freeze out NS members financially so as to greatly reduce their opportunities in the post-war era.

The decree for which the Home Front pushed was intended as a full list of offences that could be used by the courts whenever they could not apply the harsher rules found in Chapters 8 and 9 of the Criminal Code.[232] Its proposal was intended to replace the Quisling Decree of 1942. It sought to introduce more rigid rules for the punishment of NS members. Most controversially, it applied to NS membership after 8 April 1940, while the 1942 decree had only introduced penalties for NS membership from the date of its issuing.[233] In addition to the solidary compensation principle, it stipulated the *mandatory* loss of civil rights for any individual who received a prison term of more than six months. The Home Front proposal also laid out the foundation for a comprehensive reckoning with *economic* collaborators. Any economic collaboration that was 'improper' was to be criminal. This added a new dimension to the reckoning ahead, along with a much higher degree of administrative and legal complexity, as the exile government noted.[234] The Home Front recognised the limits of the legal system and excluded the so-called Germany workers from criminal culpability. The Home Front proposal stated that it was regrettable that so many individuals had worked for the enemy, and that it was precisely the large number that would make it unwise to punish them all, for one cannot 'put a considerable portion of the Norwegian people in the dock'.[235] Only individuals in leading positions or those who had acted

[230] The Home Front admitted that NS members would be unable to compensate for the totality of the economic damage done to the country, Ibid.

[231] Anika Seemann, 'Citizen Outcasts – The Penalty of "Loss of Civil Rights" during the Norwegian Treason Trials, 1945–1953', *Scandinavian Journal of History*, 45 (2020) 3, pp. 360–383.

[232] The Home Front wanted to clarify the distinction between more violent criminals and NS members, with the latter being punished only according to the wartime decrees.

[233] Both decrees, however, rested on the assumption that NS membership was already punishable under the pre-war provisions on treason.

[234] RA/S-3212/D/De/L0299: 'Forslag til anordning om straff og andre åtgjerder mot N.S. medlemmer og andre landssvikere', confidential note by Andreas Aulie, 12 May 1944.

[235] 'Utkast med motiver til provisorisk anordning om straff og andre åtgjerder mot N.S.-medlemmer og andre landssvikere, utarbeidet av en komite nedsatt av Hjemmefrontledelse', printed in Ot.prp. nr. 66 (1945–1946), pp. 132–159, at p. 144.

'improperly' for their own benefit were to be punished. The dividing line would be difficult to draw.

The Home Front urged the exile government to adopt the bill swiftly as a provisional decree.[236] But some jurists within exile circles had their reservations about this sweeping expansion of the scope of the trials 'at the eleventh hour' and were concerned about the constitutional concerns it raised.[237] The exile government therefore appointed a further expert committee to evaluate the provisions, which presented its findings on 26 September 1944.[238] The expert jurists consulted were sceptical of a number of the provisions set out, in particular with regard to the potential retroactivity of the solidary compensation principle and the wide competencies envisaged for the Compensation Directorate. It found that its proposed authority was much too extensive and that there was a significant risk of overlapping competencies.[239] A broader anxiety surrounded the exile government's thinking regarding the legality of the wartime decrees. It expressed a deep desire to act within the contours of established legal principle. This was reflected also in the ways in which the exile government had monitored the planning for any legal action in France, Belgium, Czechoslovakia and the Netherlands.[240] It had also consulted a number of external legal experts on matters of constitutional law.[241]

Ultimately, however, the Home Front prevailed. The government-in-exile made only 'few and non-invasive' changes to the Home Front proposal.[242] In particular, the Home Front was successful in having the

[236] RA/S-3212/D/De/L0299: Letter from the Home Front to the Ministry of Justice of 1 September 1944, referenced in undated memo, Annæus Schjødt to Justice Minister Terje Wold.

[237] RA/S-3212/D/De/L0299: 'Adv. Schjødts bemerkninger til Justisdepartementets innstilling til prov. anordning om endring i forrederianordningen av 22. januar 1942', P.M., 3 September 1944.

[238] RA/S-3212/D/De/L0299: Report for the Ministry of Justice by the Committee appointed on 8 September 1944, 26 September 1944.

[239] Ibid.

[240] See for example RA/S-3212/D/De/L0299: Notat: Utkast til prov. anordning om endring i forrederianordningen av 22. Januar 1942: Belgiske lovbestemmelser, 23 September 1944; RA/S-3212/D/De/L0299: 'Opprydningen blandt forredere. Saken mot "den franske Gestapo"', letter from E. Hougen to the Ministry of the Exterior, 14 December 1944; RA/S-3212/D/De/L0299: 'Notat om Rettsoppgjøret med landssvikere i Frankrike', memo, 'H.S.', 4 December 1944; the Norwegian delegation also frequently corresponded with foreign delegations: RA/S-3212/D/De/L0299: Letter to M. Stavropoulos of the Greek Shipping Committee, 5 March 1942; letter to M. Bodson of the Luxembourg Ministry of Justice, 29 February 1942; letter to Dr de Moor of the Netherlands Ministry of Justice, 5 March 1942; letter to Monsieur Szathmary of the Czechoslovak Legation to Norway, 2 February 1942.

[241] RA/S-3212/D/De/L0299: Correspondence with Professor Brierly, University of Oxford.

[242] Ot.prp. nr. 92 (1945–1946), p. 83.

Compensation Directorate established, which the experts of the London government found both 'unconstitutional and impractical'.[243] The Ministry of Justice in an internal assessment noted that the specific implementation of the compensation payments could 'after the return home' be devised in such a manner as to be compatible with the constitution.[244] The Ministry added that 'ordinary legal principles' could not form the basis upon which to adjudicate the complexities of the occupation.[245] Instead, one had to take into consideration that 'public opinion at home will not only approve, but demand, that one bases the reckoning on an exceedingly liberal interpretation of § 97 of the Constitution in deciding what limitations there are for adopting new compensation provisions retroactively'.[246] The Ministry concluded that as long as they were strictly 'necessary', such measures could, therefore, be implemented.[247]

With this, the exile government adopted the Home Front proposal as a provisional decree on 15 December 1944 (the 'Treason Decree').[248] The official reason given by both the exile government and the Home Front representatives was that the population demanded a strict reckoning. It was to send a signal that justice would be done, that promises would be kept and, most importantly, that the population was not to take justice into its own hands. But the invocation of the 'sense of justice' or 'public opinion' also added a new category of justification for whenever pre-war legal interpretation alone might have led to a different result. This introduced a decidedly political element into judicial procedure. Within the Ministry of Justice, there remained considerable concern regarding this disregard for legal rationale at the heart of the 'reckoning', in particular as the Home Front tended to sideline many legal questions in its proposals. In a departmental memo, a civil servant in the Ministry of Justice cautioned that during 'a time in which "everything flows", it is of the utmost importance to take into account the more long-term interests of

243 Omang (ed.), *Regjeringen og hjemmefronten under krigen*, p. 499.

244 RA/S-3212/D/De/L0299: 'Adv. Schjødts bemerkninger til Justisdepartementets inntilling til prov. anordning om endring i forrederianordningen av 22. januar 1942', P.M. 3 September 1944.

245 Ibid.

246 RA/S-3212/D/De/L0299: P.M. 'Utkast til prov. anordning om straff m.v. mot N.S. medlemmer og andre landssvikere', 10 October 1944; this echoed the attitude of the Home Front, as expressed in 'Anvendelse av Grunnlovens §§ 97, 105 g 96 under oppgjøret etter okkupasjonen', printed as Appendix 3 in Ot.prp. nr. 92 (1945–1946), pp. 78–82.

247 RA/S-3212/D/De/L0299: 'Utkast til prov. anordning om straff m.v. mot N.S. medlemmer og andre landssvikere', P.M., 10 October 1944.

248 'Provisorisk anordning av 15. desember 1944 om tillegg til straffelovgivningen om forræderi (Landssvikanordningen)', in Ot.prp. nr. 66 (1945–1946), pp. 99–107.

safeguarding the principles [of law] which we have relied upon for more than a century'.[249]

Further decrees were deemed necessary to regulate the specifics of transition and the administration of the trials, both in legal and practical terms. The exile government had, of course, already adopted a first decree on legal procedures in February 1943 to accommodate for the increased workload. The early decree had foreseen the risk that the legal apparatus would drown in cases, and that the delay in bringing cases to trial could increase the likelihood of public unrest.[250] But the exile government soon realised that this first decree in itself was insufficient to guarantee the necessary expediency. The broader scope of the Treason Decree of 15 December 1944 had also increased the number of cases the courts would have to face upon the liberation. Both the exile government and the Home Front therefore worked on new proposals. Both sides agreed that special 'treason' courts were undesirable.[251] First and foremost, this was based on a wish to ground the trials firmly in ordinary legal procedure. At the same time, several figures remarked that 'special courts' were associated with the Nazi legal system.[252] But the Home Front pushed for major changes that departed significantly from previous interpretations of due legal process. It wanted to allow for all prison sentences of up to six months' imprisonment to be handed down by administrative decree, rather than by a court verdict, so as to accelerate the speed of the reckoning. More significantly, perhaps, these decrees could be handed down *in absentia* against the individual.[253] This measure was met with significant scepticism by the exile government's expert law committee and the Ministry of Justice and was consequently not adopted.[254] The exile government issued its Legal Procedures Decree (*Rettergangsanordningen*) on 16 February 1945. This decree reveals the ways in which Home Front representatives in particular were willing to depart from established legal principles.

A further element of the joint preparations for the post-war order was the adoption of new decrees for the purge of NS members and other 'unpatriotic' staff in the civil service. On the initiative of the Home Front, the exile government issued a new decree concerning civil servants on 24 November 1944, which sharpened the previous decree in that it

[249] RA/S-3212/D/De/L0299: 'Utkast til prov. anordning om straff m.v. mot N.S. medlemmer og andre landssvikere', P.M., 10 October 1944.

[250] Ot.prp. nr. 66 (1945–1946), p. 174. [251] Ibid., p. 180. [252] Ibid. [253] Ibid., p. 204.

[254] Ibid., pp. 182–183.

allowed for the removal of civil servants based on NS membership, even if they had left the party before 22 January 1942, as well as on grounds of other 'unpatriotic' conduct. Any advantages individuals had received, including promotions to senior positions, were to be undone upon the liberation. In addition, the decree explicitly stated that suspended civil servants were to receive no pay.[255] Those who had remained in office without having sought or received advantages, on the other hand, were to receive 'full public trust'. It is not difficult to see the problems this would raise in practice. NS members were to be able to return to their position if they could demonstrate that they had joined only as a ruse, and that in reality, they had furthered Norwegian interests. On the other hand, all those who – for political reasons – had been removed from their positions during the occupation were to be able to return to them. This would later lead to difficult case-by-case decisions for the authorities.

With the adoption of the wartime decrees, the exile government and Home Front had laid the legal foundations for the reckoning. The deliberations during the war also indicated which actions were to be the most central in the prosecution of war-time crimes: acts against the state and the national community. While there was an awareness of the heinous crimes of the Nazi regime in the persecution of the Jews, prosecuting these crimes was less central. A provisional decree was adopted stipulating the legal duty to return assets confiscated during the war,[256] but in terms of criminal law the Jews were not considered specifically. The same held true for the crimes committed against foreigners, both in Norway and abroad. Capital offences and grievous bodily harm could of course be prosecuted, but later they would typically stand in the shadows of the more central charge of treason. This aspect of the post-war reckoning was not peculiar to Norway. All across Europe, resistance movements and exile governments made plans to rebuild their national communities. This typically involved a pragmatic and simplified process of determining individuals' loyalty to the nation – not one of meting out punishment for the totality of crimes committed during the war.

Throughout this final planning stage, the question of how the – by now highly likely – liberation of the country would unfold remained entirely unclear. The exile government and resistance forces prepared for three alternative scenarios: an armistice or German capitulation, an invasion of Norwegian and Allied troops, or a German evacuation while the war continued. The liberation in France and events in Greece had shown the

[255] Ibid., p. 72. [256] 'Prov. Anordning av 18. desember 1942', § 3.

intense violence that could come out of four years of enemy occupation.[257] Even the scenario of a peaceful liberation, therefore, carried much potential for conflict. It was unclear how the various groups within Norwegian territory would act in the event of a capitulation, and there were widespread fears of vigilante justice. In frequent messages transmitted through printed flyers and radio broadcasts, both the Home Front and the exile government thus sought to prepare the population for a peaceful liberation. There was a particular anxiety surrounding the high number of Wehrmacht soldiers stationed in Norway – around 323,000 – and the possibility that they might not surrender without a fight.[258] In October 1944, the Home Front sent a letter to the London government stating that it was of critical importance to demonstrate a 'fact-based orientation' and to prepare people for 'an active and disciplined commitment during the final phase of the war' through radio broadcasts.[259]

In preparing the trials, the Home Front had begun to compile lists of members of the NS as well as other individuals to be tried. In addition, it drew up lists of individuals who could act as investigative police, prosecutors, defence lawyers and judges in the trials. Most importantly, the government and Home Front gave out messages to the population to prepare them both for the liberation and for the trials ahead. One of these messages stated:

> We ask all Norwegians to help so that this reckoning can take place swiftly and in a just manner. It is an obligation to take note of crimes committed by the Nazis – both the Norwegian and the German ones. That way, each of us can contribute to ensuring that justice is served against those who failed the Norwegian cause and who played with Norwegian lives. No one shall go unpunished, but no one shall be punished unheard. It is a legal reckoning we shall have. We will not use the methods of Nazis. Moreover, vigilante justice turns its victims into martyrs, and Nazis and war criminals do not deserve such a thing. The French began using such methods during their reckoning as shearing the heads of Germany girls, but they soon stopped, because it led to these girls receiving all kind people's sympathy. The only really efficient way of punishing Nazis and war criminals is to put them before a court of law and have them sentenced just like other criminals.
>
> . . .

[257] Mark Mazower, *Hitler's Empire: Nazi Rule in Occupied Europe* (London: Penguin, 2008), p. 519.

[258] On this, Omang (ed.), *Regjeringen og hjemmefronten under krigen*, pp. 482–491; Lars Roar Langslet, *John Lyng: samarbeidets arkitekt* (Oslo: Cappelen, 1989), p. 52; Sæveraas, *Wehrmacht i Norge*, p. 7.

[259] Omang (ed.), *Regjeringen og hjemmefronten under krigen*, p. 482.

> All those who want a thorough reckoning with the Nazis and their entire essence can only achieve this by gathering evidence that will aid the courts. Therefore, start today with securing pieces of evidence for crimes that you know have been committed and be most vigilant now in this critical phase of transition. We need to drag each case of assault of German and Norwegian Nazis into the light, from now on and until the war is over. Let neither them nor us doubt this for a single moment.
>
> . . .
>
> There shall not be vigilante justice in Norway, but the criminals will not be treated mildly, rest assured. They will be punished with the loss of their lives and freedom, their honour and their wallet. It shall be demonstrated once and for all what treason is.[260]

1.7 The Liberation

After Hitler's suicide on 30 April 1945, Terboven met with Admiral Karl Dönitz in Flensburg, just south of Germany's border with Denmark, to discuss the status of the German forces in Norway. Terboven insisted on fighting for Norway, but was discouraged by Dönitz, who ordered that Norway be demilitarised peacefully.[261] The *Reichskommissariat* was dissolved and its affairs transferred to the 'military authority' (*Befehlsgewalt*) of the Wehrmacht.[262] On 7 May, the incumbent *Wehrmachtsbefehlshaber Norwegen* Franz Böhme communicated the unconditional surrender of the German military in Norway. At 00.01 on the night of 9 May, the capitulation came into effect. In military terms, the capitulation in Norway was ultimately as peaceful as anyone could have hoped for.[263]

Within hours of the capitulation, Terboven took his own life in the bunker of his Skaugum estate outside Oslo. Of the *Reichskommissariat*'s other members, some 'tried to escape by blending into the demobilised Wehrmacht, others committed suicide, and yet others were identified and faced their fate'.[264] Believing he had done no wrong, Quisling declined an

260 Ibid., p. 486.

261 Bohn, *Reichskommissariat Norwegen*, p. 2; Martin Moll, 'Kapitulation oder heroischer Endkampf in der "Festung Norwegen"? Die Entscheidung für ein friedliches Ende der deutschen Okkupation Dänemarks und Norwegens im Frühjahr 1945', in Robert Bohn and Jürgen Elvert (eds.), *Kriegsende im Norden: vom heißen zum kalten Krieg* (Stuttgart: Steiner, 1995), pp. 43–84.

262 Ibid., Bohn, p. 2.

263 Jens Christian Hauge, *Frigjøringen* (Oslo: Gyldendal, 1994); Edvard Bull, *Norge i den rike verden* (Oslo: Cappelen, 1979), p. 85.

264 Hassing, *Church Resistance to Nazism in Norway*, p. 245.

offer by Böhme to escape to Spain, and instead awaited his imprisonment at his Gimle Estate, just outside Oslo, where he was arrested along with his ministers in the early hours of 9 May.[265] Britain held formal governing authority in Norway after the liberation to oversee the removal of the German military. By agreement with the Allies, the German troops were ordered to conduct their demilitarisation peacefully. The Norwegian underground police and military forces, which since 1943 had been trained in Sweden, Scotland and Norway, were put into place by the Home Front to oversee the phase of transition between regimes, assisted by Home Front forces.[266] The joint plans of the exile government and Home Front were implemented, and the Home Front held governing authority until the first delegation with the Crown Prince and three ministers from London returned to Oslo on 13 May 1945. But while formal governing authority had been established, no one believed that the power struggles or the reckoning that lay ahead would be free from hostility.

[265] Dahl, *Quisling*, pp. 372–373.

[266] Chris Mann, 'The Norwegian Armed Forces in Britain'.

CHAPTER 2

Transition
Rebuilding State Institutions, May–June 1945

2.1 A Bishop's Reckoning

In May 1945, Eivind Berggrav, the Bishop of Oslo who during the occupation had become a leading figure in the resistance, published an influential pamphlet entitled 'The People's Judgment over NS [*Nasjonal Samling*]' (*Folkedommen over NS*).[1] Berggrav was a leading advocate of the treason trials, considering them a core element of the nation's recovery from the occupation period. In his pamphlet, he argued that, through their membership alone, passive and active NS members alike had contributed to all crimes committed in the name of the party.[2] In doing so, he defended the core principle of the trials as laid down by the exile government and the Home Front during the occupation: that all NS members were liable for punishment. This, he argued, was the necessary position with which Norwegian post-war society should meet the 'traitors' of the collaboration period. Only then could social reconciliation follow. In his view, a strong and encompassing legal reckoning with all members of the NS was the only way in which widespread social unrest could be avoided. But Berggrav also had a further motive in calling for such widespread punishment: he hoped that this could prevent extensive use of the death penalty.[3]

Berggrav's pamphlet expressed what many members of the political establishment understood: that for the trials to have any meaning at all, they would have to be carried out in close correspondence with public demands. According to Berggrav, public opinion (*folkeopinionen*) therefore

[1] Berggrav had completed the draft for the pamphlet in autumn 1944.

[2] Eivind Berggrav, *Folkedommen over NS* (Oslo: Land og Kirke, 1945), p. 10.

[3] Berggrav was later said to have presented both the 'ice front' claims, by demanding an encompassing reckoning, and the 'silk front', by arguing against the death penalty. Rather than an increase in popularity, however, this led to him being accused from both sides of being either too harsh or too lenient.

had to inform the law. He argued that while there were judges to hand down *legal* verdicts, the people as a whole were responsible for handing down the *moral* verdict. Berggrav reasoned that while the general legal convictions of a people will always have to be reflected in its legal system, these convictions would under usual circumstances be institutionalised gradually, in the course of decades and centuries, and continuously modified and readjusted by lawmakers and judges. In the context of the treason trials, however, a legal scenario that no one could have foreseen, there was a different level of immediacy, as no legal practice had evolved that could match social expectations for a legal response. The more immediate attitudes people held upon the liberation and what could be deemed a more general 'legal consciousness' – society's perceptions of justice on the matter over time – therefore flowed together in the present context. For this reason, the treason trials were as much a direct social process as a judicial one, demanding a constant 'interplay' between legal judgment and the broader social processes of the reckoning.[4]

In his pamphlet, Berggrav warned of the potential consequences if the reckoning were reduced to a process of *formal* law, or if the legal and the wider social reckoning were to take place in separate institutional and discursive spheres. He pointed to the limitations of the law alone in overcoming the frictions generated by collaborationism, but argued that the law should nevertheless be the ideal to be approximated, accompanied by a wider social debate that at all times would scrutinise the implementation of the law. In the absence of a broader social discourse, the legal reckoning could, at a future point, appear as rigid, unjustified or a failure altogether. Berggrav was concerned in particular that courts or authorities might stretch the letter of the law too far in an assumption that this was what society demanded. To prevent this, therefore, he argued that the social purpose and the moral validity of the reckoning would always have to be at the centre of debate. At the same time, Berggrav warned against the dangers that wider public opinion could spiral out of control and abandon the legal dimension of the reckoning altogether, leading to an increased risk of vigilante justice. By advocating that the wider public reckoning and the legal reckoning shape and correct one another, he hoped that a separation of the two processes of coming to terms with the past could be avoided. This, he argued, was the key to success. But it would turn out that Berggrav's ambitious vision was impossible to live up to.

[4] Berggrav, *Folkedommen over NS*.

This chapter analyses the political and social dynamics that unfolded in Norway following the country's liberation on 8 May 1945 and how these shaped the contours of the treason trials in the long term. At the political level, it demonstrates, the early consensus between the returning exile government and the resistance forces in Norway on the topic of the trials was a key reason as to why they were largely implemented according to plan. At the social level, the swift commencement of the trials satisfied a strong public demand and was deemed a requirement for securing a peaceful transition period. The purpose of the trials in the period immediately following the liberation was, most of all, to avoid disorder and to contain the desire for vengeance against collaborators by channelling it into the legal system. To harmonise this purpose with social expectations of the trials, Norwegian officials appealed both to ideas of 'national pride' and to Norway's rule of law traditions. But, as this chapter explains, the trials also served another fundamental purpose in Norway's post-war reconstitution: they asserted the authority of the institutions that implemented them and held a powerful symbolic meaning. Public support for the first post-war government therefore rested on its ability to fulfil its promises to undertake a comprehensive reckoning, and to conduct it quickly. Finally, the last section of the chapter details the public pressure felt by representatives of the Norwegian parliament (*Storting*) in July 1945 as they debated and passed some of the basic instruments of the trials, most notably an act approving of the use of the death penalty. Together, these political necessities and social expectations had a decisive influence on the course of the trials as well as the discourses surrounding them. 'Good' Norwegians were soon separated from 'bad' Norwegians, and against this backdrop, a national narrative of overwhelming collective resistance against the Nazi oppressor was forged.

2.2 May 1945

Berggrav published his pamphlet *Folkedommen over NS* in a climate of profound anxiety and expectation. Immediately after the liberation, jubilant crowds took to the streets, rejoicing in the new-won freedom of their country (see Figure 2.1). The festivities would continue for weeks, with seas of Norwegian flags waving on the Karl Johan Boulevard in central Oslo, culminating in the return of the government on 31 May 1945 and that of King Haakon VII shortly after on 7 June 1945. While the country was initially under British control, Norwegian authority was soon re-established. It is a remarkable aspect of the post-war transition in

Figure 2.1 Celebrations on Karl Johan Gate in Oslo on 8 May 1945.
Source: Ingvald Møllerstad, *Aftenposten*, NTB.

Norway that the demilitarisation was so peaceful: there are only sporadic reports of violent encounters between Wehrmacht soldiers and Norwegians.[5] But it was the tensions among Norwegians themselves that were the primary concern of the exile government and the interim governing authorities. In the immediate aftermath of the liberation, there was a widespread fear among the country's intellectual and political leadership that the liberation would see phases of intense violence. Beyond the symbolism that a reckoning would entail for the political institutions and the nation as a whole, the promise of an encompassing reckoning was also deemed necessary to avoid violence. The promise would be repeated over and over during the following weeks.

Imprisonment of alleged collaborators began almost immediately after the liberation, partially based on lists compiled and evidence collected during the occupation, both in exile and on home soil.[6] Norwegian police

[5] Torgeir E. Sæveraas, *Wehrmacht i Norge: på vakt i krigens skjæbnesone* (Oslo: Pax Forlag, 2022), pp. 413–422.

[6] The most notorious of prison camps during the occupation, 'Grini', was renamed 'Ilebu' and used for treason suspects and prisoners. Women suspected of treason were placed in separate camps, usually 'Bredtveit Fengsel' and 'Arbeidshus for Kvinner' in Oslo: Kjersti Brathagen, 'Oppgjøret med

officers who had undergone training in Sweden and Scotland were assisted by members of the resistance organisations (*Hjemmestyrkene*) and within weeks arrested thousands of suspected traitors. The NS membership registry – a valuable index containing more than 61,400 membership cards – was confiscated from the central NS offices in Oslo and put under the responsibility of the office of the National Police Chief (*Rikspolitisjefen*).[7] The exile government had introduced a series of provisions that would allow for a simplified arrest and detention procedure and for individuals suspected of having committed a list of crimes, including treason, to be held in custody for up to 120 days.[8] However, under the hectic conditions of the first weeks following the liberation, many more arrests were made than had been intended. Local resistance forces had often secured lists of NS members or suspected collaborators, and arrested these without first liaising with the formal police authorities. On many occasions, local forces and citizens simply delivered groups of suspected traitors to police stations. At times, individuals who had been released by the police were subsequently rearrested by resistance groups.[9] Anyone who was suspected of treason could therefore fall victim to random arrests. The number of individuals arrested during the first weeks of the liberation was ultimately much higher than initially estimated.[10] In the course of the first few weeks of the liberation, 28,750 arrests were made, with many who were considered 'traitors' subjected to 'rough and humiliating treatment'.[11]

The chaos during the early weeks was – in part – a consequence of the difficulty of establishing police authority in liberated Norway. While many thousands of police officers had been trained in Sweden and the United Kingdom for the task of the transition, the resistance and local communities had their own groups prepared for the changeover of power. *Milorg* and Home Front groups had previously been asked to assist the police during the transition, but in many cases did not adhere to police protocol.

NS-kvinnene', in Hans Fredrik Dahl and Øystein Sørensen (eds.), *Et rettferdig oppgjør? Rettsoppgjøret i Norge etter 1945* (Oslo: Pax Forlag, 2004), pp. 136–159.

7 RA/S-1558/D/L0020: Letter from DPP Andreas Aulie to the Ministry of Justice entitled 'Avviklingen av rettsoppgjøret', 25 November 1947.

8 Ot.prp. nr. 66 (1945–1946), pp. 36, 42.

9 Johannes Andenæs, *Det vanskelige oppgjøret* (Oslo: Tanum-Norli, 1979), pp. 58–59; St.meld. nr. 64 (1950), pp. 12–17.

10 Andenæs, *Det vanskelige oppgjøret*, p. 59.

11 Ole Kristian Grimnes, 'Fra krig til fred', in Hans Fredrik Dahl, Hans Kirchhoff, Joachim Lund and Lars-Erik Vaale (eds.), *Danske tilstande – norske tilstande: forskelle og ligheder under tysk besættelse 1940–45* (Copenhagen: Gyldendal, 2010), pp. 259–281, at p. 275.

As we have seen, private groups also took to the streets to arrest suspected collaborators. The National Police Chief later reported that he had been concerned that any decision of officials not to tolerate such private or semi-private actions might lead to the establishment of competing private police organisations, and threaten official police authority.[12] Moreover, these groups and individuals were much needed in order to secure the provisional prisons and camps built for collaborators. The National Police Chief later recalled that '[i]f the prisoners had not been arrested, this could have led to protest. Much needed [private] prison guards in particular frequently threatened to stop working if the actions of private groups were not respected by the authorities.'[13] He later characterised the transition period as 'a semi-illegal time'.[14] Much later, in 1950, the chaotic conditions of the early post-war period, especially in detention camps, including the brutal treatment of prisoners suspected of wartime collaboration, would become subject to a comprehensive government investigation.[15]

In rebuilding the police force, almost all NS members were immediately removed from office according to plans made by the exile government and Home Front during the occupation.[16] However, the purge within the police force also had a demonstrative dimension in the period immediately following the liberation. No distinction was initially drawn between different durations of NS membership, the motivations behind it, or even whether the membership in question had only been a ruse for the sake of undercover resistance work.[17] Within a few months, therefore, 1,200 police officers who had been investigated for treason were readmitted to the police force. Police authorities also formed a separate 'Treason Police', entrusted with the investigation of treason cases, and a separate intelligence division, the so-called Liaison Division (*Sambandsavdelingen*). The latter was comprised of many untrained staff, and entrusted with investigating the activities of NS members whom the authorities feared were forming underground networks.[18]

But institutional reconstruction was not the only concern. The government-in-exile and the Home Front had recognised early on the centrality

[12] St.meld. nr. 64 (1950), pp. 15.

[13] 'Rikspolitisjefens årsberetning', Justis- og Politidepartementet, *Om landssvikoppgjøret* (Gjøvik: Mariendal, 1962), p. 462.

[14] Andenæs, *Det vanskelige oppgjøret*, p. 64; 'Rikspolitisjefens årsberetning', Justis- og Politidepartementet, *Om landssvikoppgjøret*, p. 462.

[15] See Chapter 6.

[16] Justis- og Politidepartementet, *Om landssvikoppgjøret*, pp. 432–433.

[17] Per Hem, *Megleren Paal Berg 1873–1968* (Oslo: Aschehoug, 2012), p. 616.

[18] RA/S-1555/D/L0053: 'Sambandsavdelingen – Redegjørelse fra fhv. politifullmektiger . . . og . . .', March 1950.

of information policy in securing social stability and building trust in its own authority during the 'hectic atmosphere' it expected upon liberation.[19] The Home Front had meticulously planned the first radio broadcasts to be made in liberated Norway. In a letter sent by the Home Front to Prime Minister Nygaardsvold on 7 March 1945, the Home Front had addressed the importance of radio broadcasts and urged that immediate use be made of Norwegian broadcasting channels after the capitulation in addition to the available broadcasting slots via the BBC. It argued that failure to make a presence on the airwaves could suggest a power vacuum and raise suspicions among the population about the stability of the governing powers: 'If the authorities are to be able to solve their tasks . . . they have to be in as close contact as possible with the population at any time, both with regard to information and directives.'[20] From the moment of the liberation, broadcasts were therefore made instructing people to remain calm and to respect law and order.[21] This highlights both the concerns that the exile government and Home Front held early on regarding public sentiments during the period of transition, as well as the symbolic importance of marking the transition rhetorically.

Similarly, the role of the print media had been planned in detail during the occupation. The Home Front had suggested that a number of 'joint newspapers' should be issued for an interim period, while the traditional newspaper market reorganised itself. Through these joint publications, the exile government and Home Front would be able to speak with one voice. The exile government agreed, as this would ensure 'an intimate, swift and direct contact with the population' and prevent rumours, uncertainty and potential violence.[22] The Oslo newspaper *Oslo-Pressen* was the newspaper with the highest print run, but similar newspapers were printed locally across the country. *Oslo-Pressen* was published twice daily between 8 May and 12 May. It was issued by the Home Front and was run by a committee consisting of one representative of each of the major pre-war newspapers.[23] In its first issue on 8 May, the Home Front cautioned: 'Let us amidst this joy preserve our serenity, honour and discipline. Do not provoke the defeated enemy, and do not take the law into your own hands.'[24] In its

[19] Reidar Omang (ed.), *Regjeringen og hjemmefronten under krigen: aktstykker utgitt av Stortinget* (Oslo: Aschehoug, 1948), p. 547.
[20] Ibid.
[21] *Oslo-Pressen*, 10 May 1945 (evening edition); on 9 May Paal Berg gave a speech via public radio in his capacity as Chief Justice of the Supreme Court.
[22] Omang (ed.), *Regjeringen og hjemmefronten under krigen*, p. 547.
[23] *Oslo-Pressen* (8 May 1945) (morning edition). [24] Ibid.

evening edition on the same day, the Home Front issued a 'greeting' to the government-in-exile and the king, thanking them for their efforts during the war. This would undoubtedly have been understood also as a statement of who was in power in the days following the liberation.[25]

Throughout the following weeks, from exile and on home soil, government and Home Front representatives cautioned against public disorder and vigilante justice. On 9 May, Paal Berg gave a speech via public radio in his capacity as Chief Justice of the Supreme Court, warning that law and order must be respected.[26] King Haakon VII and Prime Minister Nygaardsvold made similar statements, which were printed in *Oslo-Pressen* and other joint newspapers. Officials were swift to emphasise that they would be thorough in handling the difficult occupation legacy, repeating like a mantra their promises for a 'swift and energetic' reckoning with those who had 'failed in the national struggle'.[27] On 16 May, Justice Minister Terje Wold gave a public speech on the Norwegian public broadcaster, stating that 'the reckoning that lies ahead will have to be carried through with all available resources and in line with the adopted provisions and shall be completed by the end of the year'.[28] He emphasised that the reckoning would be implemented by the courts of the land, but added that 'in reality' this meant 'by the Norwegian people itself'.[29] Sven Arntzen of the Home Front's law committee had secured the position of Director of Public Prosecutions, and in this capacity called a press conference on 22 May in which he gave an account of the reckoning that lay ahead.[30] In seeking to assure the public, he stated that collaborators would be 'met with a tough hand', but emphasised that the specific punishment of the individual would have to be for the courts to decide.[31]

The mixed rhetoric of the early public announcements, draconian but emphasising the centrality of the rule of law, was indicative of the challenges in finding a middle ground between channelling public emotion and observing due legal process. Officials were aware that the gulf between

[25] *Oslo-Pressen* (8 May 1945) (evening edition). [26] *Oslo-Pressen* (10 May 1945) (evening edition).

[27] See for example Terje Wold's speech on the Norwegian public broadcaster, NRK, 6 June 1945 and the speech by Paal Berg at the ceremonial opening of the Supreme Court, 14 May 1945, printed in Rt. (1945), pp. 2–6.

[28] Speech by Terje Wold, printed in *Friheten* (17 May 1945). [29] Ibid.

[30] 'Rettsoppgjøret med landssvikerne skal gjennomføres strengt men på en måte som kan være et fritt Norge verdig', *Aftenposten* (22 May 1945); 'Krigsforbryterne vil bli dømt etter norsk lov og rett', *Dagbladet* (22 May 1945); 'Rettssakene mot krigsforbryterne på trappene', *Friheten* (23 May 1945), 'Strengt rettsoppgjør med landssvikerne – Men på en måte som er en rettsstat verdig Quisling antagelig for forhørsrett alt i denne uken', *Nationen* (23 May 1945).

[31] 'Rettsoppgjøret med landssvikerne skal gjennomføres strengt men på en måte som kan være et fritt Norge verdig', *Aftenposten* (22 May 1945).

public demands and the rule of law would be a difficult one to bridge, as reflected in Arntzen's statement that 'it must be established once and for all that the Norwegians who betray their country during war are punished strictly', before adding that 'at the same time [however] we will try to keep a cool head'.[32] Leading politicians and officials would over the following weeks seek to calm the public, with Arntzen at one point describing the right to punish as 'clear as the sun', but adding that even though those involved with the treason trials would be 'soldiers in the nation's service', the reckoning would have to take place 'in accordance with Norwegian law and justice'.[33] These frequent statements were intended to reassure the public that the trials would soon commence. Politicians were aware that a failure to do so could lead to widespread violence and the harassment of suspected collaborators.

In their statements, officials also appealed to Norway's long tradition as a state observing the rule of law and linked a return to legal traditions to the nation's identity and pride.[34] On one occasion, Arntzen stressed that 'we will strive to conduct this reckoning in a way that is worthy of Norway, one of Europe's oldest legal communities, so that this reckoning can stand before the judgment of history'.[35] With such appeals to the pride and honour of the nation and its legal traditions, officials sought to prevent mob justice and create a sense of unity around the process of the trials. Such references were also a much-needed tool in buying time, because of the administrative preparations necessary before the trials could begin.

It is likely that the extensive promises for this all-encompassing reckoning contributed to Norway's relatively peaceful transition after the war. Unlike the situation elsewhere in Europe, there were no reported killings of suspected collaborators during the weeks following the liberation, and acts of violence and harassment were much rarer than in France, the Czech Lands, the Netherlands or even Denmark. But there were tragic exceptions to this comparatively peaceful image: several individual acts of violence were nevertheless reported against suspected collaborators, both inside and outside prison walls.[36] And at the same time, the resolute

[32] Ibid. [33] Ibid.; *Arbeiderbladet* (6 June 1945).
[34] Arnd Bauerkämper, *Das umstrittene Gedächtnis: die Erinnerung an Nationalsozialismus, Faschismus und Krieg in Europa seit 1945* (Paderborn: Schöningh, 2012), p. 157.
[35] 'Rettsoppgjøret med landssvikerne skal gjennomføres strengt men på en måte som kan være et fritt Norge verdig', *Aftenposten* (22 May 1945).
[36] 'Mishandling av landssvikfanger', memo to Justice Minister O. C. Gundersen, 26 February 1948, in RA/S-1555/D/L0039; Trond Risto Nilssen, *Da freden brøt løs* (Oslo: Universitetsforlaget, 2015), pp. 97–118.

emphasis on legal form channelled some of the emotion of the liberation period into the trials, and over the coming months and years the legal system would often prove too fragile to cope with popular demands for punishment.[37]

2.3 Political Transition

While the exile government and interim authorities repeated their calls for peace and order, the political establishment deliberated over who would hold long-term governing power in liberated Norway. The swift implementation of wartime promises – most of all the rebuilding of the country and the reckoning with collaborators – depended on a consensus as to who was to form the first post-war government. A general understanding had evolved during the occupation, due in part to the wartime tensions between the exile government and the Home Front, that the pre-war leaders should make room for the next generation and that the Home Front would be granted a central position in the post-war government.[38] But it was unclear who Nygaardsvold's successor would be. At the party levels, the occupation had shaken up pre-war allegiances, and new personal bonds had formed mostly according to the geographical location of their respective members, many of whom had spent time in concentration camps in Germany or taken refuge in Sweden. At the same time, Home Front members pushed for influence.

But despite the potential for tensions between the returning established parties, the Home Front and the exile government, the return to the traditional constitutional order happened swiftly and without major frictions. This process was aided by the fact that the exile government was willing to hand over the reins to a new set of leaders. The resistance forces and the pre-war political parties also reached a consensus. Despite initial hesitation from the Conservative Party (*Høyre*), an agreement was reached that Paal Berg, the leader of the Home Front and Chief Justice, should form a government. Berg's name had been in circulation as a possible successor during the occupation, as he enjoyed widespread popularity while lacking a party affiliation.[39] Berg agreed to form a government on

[37] Evidenced by the many calls received by the Ministry of Justice that collaborators be brought to trial. In one letter, dated 16 May 1945, an unnamed member of the public insists that his neighbour, who he asserts was a 'traitor', be arrested; in RA/S-3212/D/De/L0299.

[38] Carl Joachim Hambro, *Dagboksblade og aktstykker til regjeringsdannelsen i 1945* (Oslo: Gyldendal, 1964), p. 25.

[39] Hem, *Megleren Paal Berg*, pp. 619–620.

the condition that he would not be bound by the particular allocation of party seats in the pre-war *Storting*. Seeing himself as somewhat 'above' the parties, Berg argued that he strove to form a government that rested on a 'national consensus' rather than pre-war party lines.[40] However, Berg did not succeed in bringing about the agreement he so desired. Given the occupation experience, Berg had expected to receive universal backing for his government, but when his choice of government ministers was challenged by the pre-war political parties, he soon became disappointed and abandoned plans to form a government altogether. On 18 June, he informed the king that it had not been possible to unite the various groups to build the desired collective government.[41]

Subsequently, the king turned to Einar Gerhardsen, the young and ambitious leader of the Labour Party. Gerhardsen had spent four years in German imprisonment during the occupation and was immensely popular both within and outside his own party. He successfully formed a government and the king announced him prime minister on 25 June 1945.[42] The consensus had been that the government that would replace that of Nygaardsvold would consist of representatives from all parties represented in the pre-war *Storting*. The point was to emphasise that Norway's political leadership stood united in liberated Norway and embraced the challenging tasks ahead as a collective. Gerhardsen's government therefore consisted of representatives of the former government, the Home Front as well as new members of the Liberal Party (*Venstre*), the Conservative Party (*Høyre*), the agrarian Centre Party (*Bondepartiet*) and the Communist Party (*Norges Kommunistiske Parti* – NKP).[43] Ultimately, however, the government was dominated by the Labour Party and members of the Home Front.

The consensus reached between the new leaders of the Labour Party and the Home Front representatives was a significant contributing factor to the stability of the early post-war order. Due to the constellation of the unity government, political opposition from other party representatives was – at least temporarily – muted. Underlying tensions were nevertheless visible early on. *Høyre* was dissatisfied with the powerful position the Labour Party, its main political opponent, had secured. There also remained a strong mutual distrust between the Communist Party on the one hand and

[40] Ibid., p. 617. [41] S.tid. (1945), p. 65. [42] Ibid., p. 29.

[43] It is a symbol of the profound changes following the liberation that Gerharden's cabinet consisted of only two individuals who had been members of the pre-war government: Trygve Lie (Foreign Minister) and Oscar Torp (Defence Minister).

the Labour Party and Home Front on the other, primarily due to the fact that the Home Front leadership had not been open to a formalised cooperation with the communists during the occupation.[44] But overall, the joining of forces between pre-war political parties and resistance members was remarkable for its absence of frictions or government crises.[45] Unlike the situation in Belgium, for example, Norwegian politics entered a long phase of stability soon after the liberation.[46] This allowed the Gerhardsen government to focus immediately on the most imminent tasks at hand, one of which was the commencement of the trials.

The government's policies were shaped by the 'Joint Party Programme' (*Fellesprogrammet*), on which all parties had agreed ahead of the liberation. This programme was aimed at securing a consensus on key questions for the post-war order and laid the foundations for the first set of government policies.[47] In Gerhardsen's government declaration, presented to parliament on 28 June 1945, the trials were laid down as a central policy. The declaration contained a renewed promise for a '[q]uick and strictly fair reckoning with those who failed in the national struggle'.[48] In June 1945, the estimate was that the trials would involve around 40–50,000 cases.[49] The newly formed government was intent on carrying out the trials in accordance with the framework laid out in the provisional decrees adopted during the occupation. The Labour Party reasserted its ambition at its National Meeting (*Landsmøtet*), where it unanimously voted in favour of a 'quick and energetic conclusion' to the reckoning with 'the traitors, the war criminals and all who have assisted the enemy, and with others who exploited the war situation for their own benefit'.[50] The reckoning provided a useful means of demonstrating state authority and distancing the new administration from the occupation period.[51] By tying the trials so closely to their political programmes, both the government and the Labour Party hitched their authority to the successful implementation of the trials.

44 Hem, *Megleren Paal Berg*, p. 629.

45 For a comparison with the situation in other European countries, see Chapter 7.

46 Martin Conway, *The Sorrows of Belgium: Liberation and Political Reconstruction, 1944–1947* (Oxford: Oxford University Press, 2012).

47 See '*Fellesprogrammet*', https://snl.no/Fellesprogrammet, last accessed 21 February 2021.

48 Government declaration of 28 June 1945, S.tid. (1945), p. 37.

49 Justis- og Politidepartementet, *Om landssvikoppgjøret*, p. 441.

50 Det norske arbeiderparti, *Landsmøtet, 31. august – 2. September 1945*, Referat ved Bjarne Jullum (Oslo: Arbeidernes Aktietrykkeri, 1947), p. 135; Nikolai Brandal, 'Eit politisk strafferettsleg oppgjer: det norske arbeidarpartiet og etterkrigsoppgjeret 1945–50' (Master's Dissertation, University of Oslo, 2002).

51 Nikolai Brandal, '"En rettsstat verdig": oppgjøret i Stortinget 1945–50', in Dahl and Sørensen (eds.), *Et rettferdig oppgjør?*, pp. 52–86, at p. 64.

While this seemed unproblematic at the time, it would later put the government and the Labour Party under considerable pressure.

Norway's parliament became a central arena of debate during the treason trials. The primary reason was that the provisional decrees adopted by the exile government had to pass through a formal legislative process after the liberation in order to become valid law. The provisional decrees issued by the exile government were ultimately deemed to rest on extraordinary constitutional powers granted as a result of the unique circumstances of the occupation. By extension, these had been derived from § 17 of the Constitution, which granted the king and his government extraordinary powers to issue decrees.[52] Any such decree would automatically lose its validity at the end of the *following* parliament's term (a term being any one-year period ending each calendar year). The provisional decrees of the exile government thus only had a validity until the end of 1946. Hence, the *Storting* would have to legislate on all provisions introduced during the occupation period if it wanted to extend their validity beyond the expiration of the ninetieth *Storting* and ground them in formal law.

But it was not simply out of constitutional formality that parliament debated the trials on numerous occasions in the years following the liberation. There was a political imperative at play as well. The *Storting* endowed the trials with democratic legitimacy. Moreover, the legal foundation of the trials had to be continuously modified in order to reflect the changing political, economic and social rationales that legitimised them. The most comprehensive piece of legislation, the Treason Act (*Landsvikloven*) did not reach parliament until 1947. However, various smaller bills on specific aspects of the trials were put before the *Storting* before that time, and parliamentarians as well as government representatives often used the occasion of these bills as a platform to convey their more general opinions and criticism of the trials. The death penalty was debated twice, once in June 1945 by the 1936 *Storting*, and then again in December 1946 by the first post-war assembly. In February 1946, the *Storting* debated a bill proposing accelerated criminal justice procedures involving sentencing without trials, sparking huge controversy. The attendant debates provide insights into the horizons, expectations and fears relating to the trials. But they also provide a sense of the limits of

[52] The Constitution of the Kingdom of Norway (LOV-1814-05-17), art. 17. This was only established by the Supreme Court in Rt. 1945, pp. 13–26. The Supreme Court also ruled that the Elverum Authorisation was superfluous, as the powers derived directly from the Constitution.

parliamentary politics in addressing a legal process of an unprecedented nature and scope. As we shall see, the nature of the debates fluctuated between technical questions of law and sweeping promises and visions for the post-war nation.

However, the involvement of the *Storting* was not a given in the post-liberation context.[53] In the immediate post-war period, the 1936 parliament rested on an unstable footing. Initially, it was not clear whether the eighty-ninth *Storting* should reconvene at all.[54] The continuation of the 1936 parliament into the post-war era was problematic from the perspective of constitutional legitimacy as it had overrun its mandate by more than four years (under normal circumstances, the *Storting* would have been dissolved on 10 January 1941). But more importantly, the 1936 parliament, and in particular its Presidium, were politically damaged. Their role in the negotiations for the Realm Council in 1940 and their cooperative relationship with the German occupying powers more generally in the early months of the occupation were criticised widely.[55] What was deemed most problematic was the Presidium's request of 27 June 1940 that the king step down, which two-thirds of MPs had endorsed by September 1940.[56] The question of whether the old parliament would be summoned had therefore been left open during the occupation.[57] After the liberation, members of the Home Front repeated their preference of awaiting the first parliamentary elections in liberated Norway. But many members of the traditional political parties argued that the *Storting* as a constitutional body could not be sidelined. The argument for constitutional continuity prevailed, and the government decided that the eighty-ninth *Storting* should continue its term.[58] On 14 June 1945, the *Storting* officially assembled for the first time in liberated Norway. It was its first session since the final meeting in Elverum on 9 April 1940.[59]

Given the validity of the provisional decrees until the end of 1946, formal involvement of the eighty-ninth *Storting* in the larger policies surrounding the treason trials was not strictly necessary, as all matters could have been solved by the ninetieth *Storting*, once elected. However, the President of the *Storting*, Carl Joachim Hambro (*Høyre*) made a

[53] Brandal, '"En rettsstat verdig"', pp. 52–53.
[54] Omang (ed.), *Regjeringen og hjemmefronten under krigen*, p. 16.
[55] Brandal, '"En rettsstat verdig"', p. 52.
[56] Hanne Marthe Narud, Knut Heidar and Tore Grønlie (eds.), *Stortingets historie 1964–2014* (Bergen: Fagbokforlaget, 2014), p. 29.
[57] The Home Front and exile government left the question open: Omang (ed.), *Regjeringen og hjemmefronten under krigen*, pp. 124, 502.
[58] Brandal, '"En rettsstat verdig"', p. 53. [59] S.tid. (1945), p. 1.

persuasive argument that the death penalty be formally debated in parliament, given the gravity of the matter.[60] He first addressed the issue in a meeting between party leaders, the government and Home Front members on 4 June 1945. He was concerned that for courts to hand down a death penalty sentence without a formal legal basis approved by parliament would allow for a dangerous constitutional precedent to be set for the post-war order.[61] Hambro's concerns were primarily constitutional in nature, as he himself supported the death penalty.[62] Within the Nygaardsvold government, the question of whether the death penalty bill should pass through parliament was contested. There were fears that comprehensive parliamentary deliberations on the question of the death penalty would cause uncertainty in the wider population in relation to the honesty of the proclaimed ambition to bring collaborators to justice. The government expressed concern that the prospect of lengthy parliamentary procedures would impede court procedures.[63] Hambro concurred, and as a compromise he suggested that the bill's passing through parliament would be kept behind closed doors so as not to generate uncertainty about the legal basis of the trials ahead of the debate.[64] The government agreed to this.

Politicians' fears that the announcement of a parliamentary debate to be held on the death penalty could generate uncertainty in the wider population highlights the centrality of wider public attitudes during the preparatory stages for the trials. While immediate and widespread violence had not occurred after the liberation, politicians were anxious to act in accordance with the 'general mood' and sought to ground the trials in wider public acceptance – not least because they felt that their political authority and appeal depended on it. At this stage, several weeks after the liberation, the threat of violence was no longer as severe as politicians often made it out to be. Yet, there was a perceived risk of unrest that guided many politicians for the remainder of 1945, resulting in a strong focus on tying decision-making to public demands. The widespread use of references to the 'people's will', the 'people's opinion' and the 'legal consciousness of the nation' in public statements – and later in legislative processes and in court verdicts – reflect the challenging relationship between the social and the legal justifications for the trials. Particularly where the legal bases of the

[60] Hambro, *Dagboksblade og aktstykker til regjeringsdannelsen i 1945*, p. 17. [61] Ibid., p. 23.

[62] The general uncertainty of the time prompted many bourgeois politicians to emphasise the need to ground the trials firmly within the institutional framework set out in the constitution: Narud, Heidar and Grønlie (eds.), *Stortingets historie 1964–2014*, p. 35.

[63] Hambro, *Dagboksblade og aktstykker til regjeringsdannelsen i 1945*, pp. 17–19. [64] Ibid.

trials were problematic, officials would refer to the overriding 'opinion of the people', which became a broad justification for the measures adopted in relation to the trials. However, in summer 1945, no one was in any doubt that a reckoning would need to take place if social reconciliation was to be possible. From the moment of the liberation, the topic of the treason trials engaged the nation and led to heated debate. The question of national allegiance during the occupation became a public and collective one and played out in local communities, workplaces, schools and universities and in nationwide media debates.[65]

Newspapers played a critical role in shaping and reflecting public attitudes towards the trials. Restrictions on the freedom of press during the occupation had spurred a demand for information and uncensored debate, and newspapers' print issues were at a record high within only months of the liberation.[66] Newspapers were quick to call for a swift and energetic reckoning in the weeks following the liberation. In an almost competitive demonstration of national allegiance, headlines declared the triumphant victory over the Quislings and called for harsh punishment. From immediately after the liberation and for many years to come, an intense debate surrounding the treason trials would be carried out in the nation's newspapers, driven by the general public, members of the political elite, public intellectuals, industry representatives, church leaders and academics. Policy makers at all times paid close attention to these debates.[67]

Of the roughly 260 newspapers in publication on 9 April 1940, only around 114 had continued their operation up until the liberation, with the remaining newspapers being halted at some point during the occupation.[68] The most widely read newspaper before, during and after the war was the conservative *Aftenposten*.[69] In the post-war period it could be described as right-leaning. While it sought to distance itself from collaboration, it still took a relatively moderate view on the treason trials. Other newspapers that had collaborated were the independent *Morgenposten* and *Nationen*, the party organ of the Centre Party. Some newspapers had been forced to narrow down their operations during the occupation, either voluntarily or by command of the Germans, with many ultimately being shut down from

65 Guri Hjeltnes, *Avisoppgjøret etter 1945* (Oslo: Aschehoug, 1990), p. 37.

66 Ibid., p. 39; Trond Reinaas, 'Isfront – Silkefront? Oslopressen og holdninger til landssvikoppgjøret 1945–1948' (Master's Dissertation, University of Trondheim, 1980), p. 4.

67 Political institutions soon commissioned agencies to collect newspaper clippings on the trials to keep track of the many attitudes on the trials displayed across newspapers.

68 Hjeltnes, *Avisoppgjøret etter 1945*, Appendix 1, p. 331.

69 Reinaas, *Isfront – Silkefront?*, p. 5.

1941 onwards as restrictions tightened and protests from within newspapers grew. The most prominent of these newspapers was the Labour Party organ *Arbeiderbladet* which had been discontinued as early as August 1940. *Morgenbladet*, a conservative newspaper, had been discontinued in 1943. Another newspaper whose production had been halted was *Dagbladet*, traditionally a left-leaning newspaper, which was shut down in 1943. After the war, *Dagbladet* was to become the most vocal advocate of strict punishment of collaborators.[70] Finally, a number of newspapers were founded anew as protest papers both during and after the occupation, such as *Friheten* and *Verdens Gang*.[71] *Friheten* was the Communist Party organ, while *Verdens Gang* was formed by members of the Home Front immediately after the liberation.[72]

Once the first newspapers had resumed operation on 14 May 1945, the treason trials became a central topic in their coverage. As early as 15 May 1945, a journalist from the Labour Party organ *Arbeiderbladet* informed the Ministry of Justice that the newspaper would produce a full overview of the legal provisions of the trials the next day, given the intense public interest.[73] *Arbeiderbladet*, in its first edition, declared that

> now it is time to clean up after the strangers and their henchmen. No one must lay their fingers in between [be too mild]. An atmosphere must be created so that people can breathe freely. The quislings and their helpers are a chapter to themselves. They are traitors who deserve the most stringent treatment possible.[74]

Dagbladet demanded that the 'evil forces in the population must be punished and rendered harmless, not on the basis of sentimental pity, but on the basis of justice'.[75] *Friheten*, too, insisted that the trials be seen through with 'strictness and justice'.[76] All newspapers agreed that there had to be a swift implementation of the trials. But similarly to official statements, they also referred often to 'justice' and the 'rule of law', both of which were tied closely to the proud national self-image the newspapers sought to present.

During the first few months following the liberation, the authorities benefited from a convenient consensus among newspapers. At the time,

[70] Hem, *Megleren Paal Berg*, p. 611.

[71] Newspapers from this category positioned themselves not only as communicators of new voices, but as symbols of Norway's 'resurrection' (*gjenreisning*) itself.

[72] Martin Eide, *Blod, sverte og gledestårer: VG, Verdens Gang 1945–95* (Oslo: Schibsted, 1995).

[73] RA/3212/D/De/L0299: Untitled note addressed to the Minister of Justice, 15 May 1945.

[74] 'Det nye Norge', *Arbeiderbladet* (14 May 1945).

[75] 'Frihet', *Dagbladet* (14 May 1945).

[76] 'Effektivt rettsoppgjør', *Friheten* (23 May 1945).

hardly anyone called into question the reckoning as such. But despite the consensus that the trials were needed, newspaper editorials disagreed on the broader objectives and the appropriate severity of punishment. *Nationen* and *Aftenposten* soon warned of too broad a reckoning – and cautioned against what they saw as an employment of 'Nazi-methods' in the context of the trials.[77] This provoked immediate and harsh responses from the majority of newspapers. *Nationen* and *Aftenposten* were quickly accused of propagating a 'false humanism seeking to prevent a fair settlement with the people of the country'.[78] *Dagbladet* warned that 'a spirit which condemns the harshest punishment for those who have responsibility and have carried out the acts, poses a danger'.[79] The stricter newspapers self-identified as 'ice front' (*isfront*), a term used by resistance organisations during the occupation. Early on, *Dagbladet* transferred the term to the context of the treason trials, stating that 'during the war we had something called ice front, and this front must be established in a strong and unbreakable form against those Norwegians who have failed us in this way [by way of treason]'.[80] The newspapers calling for moderation, in particular *Aftenposten* and *Nationen*, were soon mocked as 'silk front' (*silkefront*) by the stricter newspapers, *Dagbladet*, *Arbeiderbladet* and *Friheten* in particular.[81] This early categorisation marked the start of a process of polarisation that would continue for many years.

Newspapers also contributed significantly to the emphasis on the 'people's opinion' in the trials.[82] As we have seen, this was a central argument in legitimising the trials' legal and political framework. *Friheten*, for example, argued that 'the people's opinion ought to be decisive in the law's composition' and appealed to the population to monitor the legal process closely in order to ensure that justice was seen to.[83] Most newspapers argued that the occupation period had brought about such an unusual set of circumstances that it could not be evaluated on the basis of ordinary criminal law. Across the 'ice front' newspapers,

77 'De rettferdige', *Nationen* (24 May 1945); 'Der må sættes en grense', *Aftenposten* (3 July 1945).

78 'Alle positive krefter i folket må mobiliseres', *Friheten* (5 July 1945).

79 'Silkefronten', *Dagbladet* (23 May 1945).

80 'Isfront', *Dagbladet* (19 May 1945).

81 Roughly, the dividing line ran between conservative and Christian papers such as *Aftenposten*, *Nationen* and *Morgenposten*, which were labelled 'silk front', and the liberal *Dagbladet*, the Labour-Party organ *Arbeiderbladet* and left-wing papers such as *Friheten*, which all belonged to the 'ice front'; see Reinaas, *Isfront – Silkefront?*; Baard Herman Borge and Lars-Erik Vaale, *Grunnlovens største prøve: rettsoppgjøret etter 1945* (Oslo: Scandinavian Academic Press, 2018), pp. 148–149.

82 'Ømhet', *Dagbladet* (28 August 1945); 'Lovens bokstav og lovens ånd', *Friheten* (13 August 1945); 'Effektivt rettsoppgjør', *Friheten* (22 May 1945).

83 'Effektivt rettsoppgjør', *Friheten* (13 August 1945); Editorial, *Friheten* (23 May 1945).

frequent references were made to the 'uniform opinion of the people', the 'collective opinion of the people', the 'healthy opinion of the people' or the 'healthy sense of justice'.[84] With regard to the death penalty proposition and its debate in parliament, for example, *Arbeiderbladet* declared that 'no one can be in any doubt what the people's opinion is on this question'.[85] To some degree, newspaper discourse would have reflected the broader moods of the time, or at least of their own readership. However, their role in forming opinion must not be underestimated. And it is unlikely that politicians were confident enough to entirely ignore the arguments made by newspapers and the potentially threatening scenarios they outlined in the case that justice was not seen to.

2.4 Wartime Fraternization and Its Consequences

While the authorities were working to prepare the trials, they came under increasing pressure with regard to one particular group of individuals: the so-called Germany girls (*tyskerjenter*) – predominantly young women who had been romantically or sexually involved with Wehrmacht soldiers. The treatment of the *tyskerjenter* marks one of the most violent episodes of Norway's transition to peace. In the days immediately following the liberation, many women were subjected to harsh and humiliating treatment for having 'fallen for the green uniform'.[86] Throughout May and June, countless women were threatened, robbed and shorn, often in front of or even by the members of their own communities. Many of these women were attacked within the safety of their own homes and dragged out into the streets to face public condemnation. One newspaper reported of a woman who was found hanged.[87] As had been the case in most occupied countries, the relationships women had had with enemy soldiers were perceived as a deep humiliation to the nation, and to male authority and pride.[88] Throughout the treason trials, these women would widely be considered 'traitors' both by politicians and in wider discourses, despite not being under formal investigation for treason.

84 'Brakkebaroner', *Arbeiderbladet* (16 May 1945); 'Effektivt rettsoppgjør', *Friheten* (23 May 1945); 'Nasjonal opprydding i Stavanger', *Friheten* (24 July 1945).

85 'Dødsstraff', *Arbeiderbladet* (15 June 1945).

86 Grimnes, 'Fra krig til fred', p. 275.

87 'Tyskertøser klippes fort vekk', *Dagbladet* (16 May 1945).

88 Fabrice Virgili, *La France 'virile': des femmes tondues à la libération* (Paris: Payot, 2000); Dominique François, *Femmes tondues: la diabolisation de la femme en 1944: les bûchers de la Libération* (Coudray-Macouard: Cheminements, 2006); Anette Warring, *Tyskerpiger: under besættelse og retsopgør* (Copenhagen: Gyldendal, 2017); Ute Frevert, *Die Politik der Demütigung: Schauplätze von Macht und Ohnmacht* (Frankfurt am Main: Fischer, 2017), pp. 71–73.

The way that state institutions should handle the *tyskerjenter* constituted a core point of disagreement. In late May 1945, the Chief of Police in Oslo had to step before the press and declare that 'there is no law which directly covers those who interacted with the Germans exclusively for the sake of a "flirt"'.[89] The *tyskerjenter* soon represented one of the most serious social and political problems for officials, due to the hostile attitudes towards them and the many episodes of violence perpetrated against them throughout the early months of the liberation. Their unclear legal status, in combination with the antipathy directed towards them, made the *tyskerjenter* vulnerable to arbitrary infringements upon their rights. Because they could not be punished under law, they were at a much higher risk of extra-legal measures. In one reported case, resistance members found it unproblematic to fetch *tyskerjenter* from the streets in order to clean some nearby barracks. It was only when one of these women escaped and reported to the police that this practice was stopped.[90] Violent episodes against *tyskerjenter* such as these signalled to the police and government that the threat of extra-judicial justice was real. They were also concerned that a failure to satisfy public demand for the punishment of these women could lead to more widespread protests against the treason trials, and more general unrest.

The Ministry of Justice and the police force deemed it necessary to take action in regard to the *tyskerjenter*. In order to ease public dissatisfaction with the fact that they could not be subjected to criminal prosecution, but also – allegedly – to safeguard them, they were soon interred in 'education and betterment' camps.[91] § 6 of the Police Decree of 1943 allowed for arrests of citizens to be made for up to 30 days (120 days upon request by the Ministry of Justice) if authorities feared 'acts of aggression from the population on the basis of a presumption of un-national mentality'.[92] The provision was used extensively in the context of the *tyskerjenter*. In August, the National Police Chief, Andreas Aulie, sought to reassure the public, declaring that 'everything humanly possible will be done by the police and the other authorities to tidy up the mess which the problem of the

[89] 'Forbedringsleire for "tysker-tøsene"? Politimestreren i Oslo lufter spørsmålet', *Friheten* (31 May 1945).

[90] Leif Thomsen, 'Hvor stor myndighet har hjemmestyrkene? Svar til Johan Scharffenberg', *Arbeiderbladet* (27 June 1945).

[91] 'Tysker-jentene: Rikspolitisjef Aulie orienterer om dette meget vanskelige problem', *Arbeiderbladet* (20 July 1945).

[92] Ot.prp. nr. 66 (1945–1946), p. 36.

Germany girls has created'.[93] By this point, 1,097 *tyskerjenter* had been interned on the basis of this provision. The official position was that internment was for their own protection. Some public commentators were quick to point out, however, that this form of 'protective internment' should at least be *voluntary*.[94] The measures taken against the *tyskerjenter* would later be seen as highly controversial, in particular due to extensive use of the '120 days' rule, which effectively resulted in imprisonment without a legal basis or trial.[95]

Public intellectuals had joined the debate about the *tyskerjenter* early on, usually condemning all violence and cautioning against vigilante justice.[96] The writer Sigurd Evensmo for example appealed to the nation's legal self-image: 'In a society that is built on legal certainty and respect for human life, the aims cannot have one moral quality and the means another, lower, one.'[97] But these efforts were unable to prevent angry mobs from assaulting and shaming women who had in some form interacted with Germans. In the long term, attitudes towards these women remained hostile. The government distanced itself from Norwegian women who had sided with Germans, as well as their offspring. In August 1945, the cabinet discussed the case of Norwegian women who had left for Germany during the war and become German citizens by marrying Germans. The cabinet decided only to grant re-entry into the country for women who were widows *and* childless.[98] In public discourses, these women were widely seen as a problem, and depicted in the press as 'unintelligent' and 'immoral'.[99] It was only over time that attitudes became more nuanced. But in the early weeks of the liberation, neither the authorities nor the public were especially concerned with assessing the precise nature of the actions of the *tyskerjenter*, or reflecting on their long-term reintegration. The violent episodes against the *tyskerjenter* signalled the degree of violence parts of

93 Ibid.; 'Vi må ikke skape en stor pariakaste av prostituerte – Tyskertøsene et samfunnsproblem som må løses – Manende appell fra Rikspolitisjefen om å vise fornuft', *Friheten* (21 July 1945).

94 Johan Scharffenberg, 'Rettsstatens prinsipper', *Verdens Gang* (9 November 1945).

95 Knut Papendorf, *Siktet som tyskertøs: rettsoppgjøret i videre forstand* (Oslo: Novus Forlag, 2015), p. 173; Andenæs, *Det vanskelige oppgjøret*, p. 78.

96 'Hårklipping', *Arbeiderbladet* (15 May 1945); Sigurd Evensmo, 'Tyskerjenter', *Arbeiderbladet* (29 May 1945); Johan Scharffenberg, 'Vi er et kulturfolk i en rettsstat', *Arbeiderbladet* (14 May 1945).

97 Sigurd Evensmo, 'Tyskerjenter', *Arbeiderbladet* (29 May 1945); Johan Scharffenberg; 'Vi er et kulturfolk i en rettsstat', *Arbeiderbladet* (14 May 1945).

98 RA/S-1005/A/Aa/L0004: Referat fra regjeringskoneranse, sak nr. 9, 'Norskfødte kvinner i Hamburg', 2 August 1945.

99 '3000 tyskerjenter har gått gjennom leirene. Intelligensnivået lavt. Gruppen 21–25 år sterkest representert', *Aftenposten* (27 April 1946).

the population were willing to engage in, and the strength of the social tensions that the treason trials had to absorb.

2.5 The Will of the People

The most widely discussed aspect of the treason trials during the early summer months of 1945 was the death penalty. To many, this issue expressed the gravity of the reckoning that lay ahead. It was commented upon widely by newspapers, politicians, intellectuals and the broader public. The first executions, in particular of Vidkun Quisling and his close allies, were eagerly anticipated. Most major newspapers favoured the death penalty for 'traitors' – and none expressly opposed it during the early period of the trials.[100] Carl Joachim Hambro, who himself favoured the use of the death penalty, was therefore certain that the mood was so overwhelmingly in favour of the death penalty that it was highly unlikely that the already damaged *Storting* would dare oppose it.[101] By way of a relatively uncomplicated process, he reasoned, the death penalty could be given formal parliamentary legitimacy. In a meeting with Director of Public Prosecutions Sven Arntzen and Justice Erik Solem on 8 June, Hambro assured them both that he expected the bill to pass with only five or six opposing votes, whereas passing the bill a year later – when it would become necessary, given the provisional nature of the wartime decree that had reintroduced it to Norwegian law – could result in a radically different outcome, threatening to undermine the trials themselves. This reasoning highlights how important it was to politicians like Hambro that the reckoning be carried by broader public support. As an experienced politician (he had been a member of parliament since 1918), he recognised the problems that the trials as a whole might face if their legal basis were to be contested.[102] But it also signals an early awareness that public attitudes would change. Hambro's reasoning therefore expressed a dual expectation of the trials: that they capture the emotions

[100] 'Dødsstraff', *Arbeiderbladet* (15 June 1945); Martin Tranmæl, 'De som har gjort seg skyldige i grovt landssvik og angiveri som har ført til arrestasjon, mishandling og fengsling av norske patrioter, må bøte med sine liv', *Arbeiderbladet* (11 July 1945); Hans Fredrik Dahl, 'Dealing with the Past in Scandinavia: Legal Purges and Popular Memories', in Jon Elster (ed.), *Retribution and Reparation in the Transition to Democracy* (Cambridge: Cambridge University Press, 2006), pp. 147–163, at p. 153.

[101] Ibid., Dahl.

[102] Lars-Erik Vaale, *Dommen til døden: dødsstraffen i Norge 1945–50* (Oslo: Pax), p. 57.

of the moment, but also rest on a more long-term public mandate. This would prove a challenging process.

In order to understand why politicians were so confident of sweeping support for the death penalty in spring and summer 1945, it is worthwhile looking at some of the ways in which this support was expressed. No opinion surveys exist from this period. But in newspapers, journalists, public intellectuals, politicians and private individuals expressed their opinions on the matter. The argumentative patterns in favour of the death penalty overwhelmingly ran along similar lines to the justificatory mechanisms of the treason trials more generally. A general contempt for 'traitors', the gravity of the crimes committed during the occupation, the strong public demand for it, as well as the necessity to prevent any form of repetition in the future, were among the key arguments.[103] But in an interesting twist, the newspapers also sought to reconcile their calls for the death penalty with a return to Norway's legal traditions. *Dagbladet* wrote that while it did not favour the death penalty in 'times of peace', it could not be said that there *were* suddenly 'times of peace': just because the 'domestic enemies' were being put into prison, this did not mean that the war was in fact over. Rather, it concluded, the war would only be over once the *reckoning* with those enemies had been concluded.[104] *Dagbladet* referred extensively to peace times and utilised the idea of war to justify the use of the death penalty. *Arbeiderbladet* and *Aftenposten* argued along similar lines, stating that the death penalty was a 'law of necessity'. However, both newspapers also stressed that once the reckoning had been brought to an end, 'peace may arrive', and with it an end to the death penalty.[105] These statements convey an idea that the nation was in a largely transitional state, also with regard to its legal principles. The way in which newspapers utilised this argument highlights the duality of legitimating narratives at the time: on the one hand, there was a powerful unifying narrative surrounding the liberation and pride in the restoration of the rule of law and a return to 'normality'. On the other, however, those elements that fit less well with Norwegian legal traditions were justified as a delayed act of combat, attached to a period – the occupation – which in the national narrative was to be set in parentheses.

Few individuals publicly opposed the death penalty in the early months following the liberation. Those who did were met with fierce opposition. An exchange on the topic of the death penalty in *Arbeiderbladet* between

[103] 'Sløvhet og straff', *Dagbladet* (15 June 1945). [104] 'Silkefront', *Dagbladet* (23 June 1945).
[105] 'Henrettelse', *Aftenposten* (18 August 1945); 'Dødsstraffen', *Arbeiderbladet* (15 June 1945).

May and June 1945 reflected the breadth of the opinion spectrum at the time. Johan Scharffenberg, a humanist and prominent public intellectual, strongly opposed the death penalty, stating: 'I am not writing out of sentimental pity with the traitors or terrorists, but out of a firm belief that the abolition of the death penalty was a key act of cultural progress and that its reintroduction would mark a return to ancient barbaric legal practice.'[106] After Bishop Berggrav, Scharffenberg was the second prominent opponent of the death penalty to publicly voice his opposition in the first weeks following the liberation. But Scharffenberg's views sparked a number of critical responses, among others from Nils Christian Brøgger, a journalist and writer who had only recently returned from German imprisonment. Describing Scharffenberg's views as 'a voice from the grave, from a distant and unreal past', Brøgger accused Scharffenberg of not understanding the nature of the crimes committed by the 'traitors'. In Brøgger's opinion, '[y]ou eradicate rats. These human beings are worse than rats. They must be eradicated, quickly and simply. This has nothing to do with hatred or revenge, it is a simple process of restoration.'[107]

Brøgger then went on to argue that legal process ought to be sidelined. Once someone had been identified as a traitor, he wrote, they should immediately be executed, for 'hygiene is all that is needed to liberate the world from this pest at once, just as you would kill a rat'.[108] This call for extra-legal executions expressed a certain frustration and anger – a response to Brøgger's own experience during the war – and went far beyond what newspapers advocated at the time, not to mention government policy itself. The rhetoric of Brøgger's article signals the emotional resonance of the issue. Whether or not Brøgger's view was a majority one, it indicated the strength of the sentiments that the trials had to appease.

While there would no doubt have been much opposition to the death penalty in wider society, those with the strongest opinions shaped the discussions, and most people who partook in the debate that summer came out in support of the death penalty. But despite the intensity of this debate, it was not the case that the government was completely blind to the arguments against the death penalty. It would be wrong to argue, therefore, that the government was swept away on a wave of vengeance in summer 1945 in endorsing its use. While some government members harboured a strong contempt for collaborators and personally favoured the

[106] Johan Scharffenberg, 'Bør dødsstraff gjeninnføres? – Diskusjonsinnlegg', *Arbeiderbladet* (15 May 1945).

[107] N. Chr. Brøgger, 'Bør dødsstraff gjeninnføres?', *Arbeiderbladet* (28 May 1945).

[108] Ibid.

death penalty, opinions within the cabinet varied significantly. In fact, several members of the cabinet opposed it. The shape of the trials and the use of the death penalty are therefore much better understood through the logic of politics, and more indirectly through public expressions of anger and calls for harsh punishment. The government as a whole carefully assessed the situation and concluded that it was politically wise to act in accordance with popular sentiment, and to make use of the trials' symbolic potential – including that of the death penalty – in an attempt to overcome the past.

2.6 The *Storting* Debates the Death Penalty

The death penalty bill reached parliament on 29 June 1945 – four days after the new government had been appointed and Johan Cappelen had replaced Terje Wold as Minister of Justice. Cappelen was a member of the conservative *Høyre*, and had been heavily involved in resistance work in North Norway during the occupation. Ironically, the first bill he presented to parliament was one which he personally opposed. Cappelen was one of the cabinet's opponents of the death penalty, but throughout the debate sought to convince the *Storting*'s members to vote in its favour. In the government bill, Wold had emphasised that the provisional decrees concerning the death penalty were already valid law, and would in principle remain so until the newly elected *Storting* was dissolved. According to the bill, the sole motivation was that, for the future, 'the provisions on the death penalty – provided that parliament believes that they should be upheld – will be given the highest form of the State's will: the form of formal law'.[109] This led to considerable dissatisfaction among some MPs, who deemed it their prerogative to test the validity of the provision as a whole.

Ultimately, Hambro's predictions were sound and only 6 MPs in the *Storting* opposed the bill, against 140 in favour, with 4 absentees. However, this figure belies the high level of nuance in the debates surrounding the death penalty and the fundamentally different rationales by which parliamentarians came to their respective conclusions. The debate provided the first major opportunity to discuss the impending treason trials more generally and some MPs seized it. Despite the overwhelming majority for the bill, the debate therefore allows us to understand some of the thought patterns surrounding the early period of the treason trials, and

[109] Ot.prp. nr. 1 (1945), p. 2.

the kinds of pressures and criticisms the government faced. In many ways, the debate on the death penalty exposed some of the most fundamental contradictions of the trials, highlighted the strong influence of public pressure and foreshadowed the dilemmas authorities would face in their implementation in the following years.

The *Storting's* Justice Committee had debated the matter internally and fully supported the Ministry's proposal. It did not do so, however, without the qualification that

> [a]lthough under normal conditions the Committee . . . opposes the death penalty, it would . . . go against the general sense of justice in our population if the death penalty should not be available in the most severe cases of treason and against individuals who are guilty of the most outrageous and abominable crimes against patriotic Norwegians.[110]

This statement would set the tone for the main rationale for the trials; namely, that legal principle and constitutional convention had to recede into the background and the opinion of the people be given precedence when it was deemed politically unavoidable.[111] The challenge was to find a way of grounding the treason trials within a larger conception of the rule of law.

At least in the early period, positions relating to the treason trials did not tend to follow party lines. The joint government emphasised the common positions decided upon in the Joint Party Programme, and there was no question that the trials were to form a central part of post-war politics. There were, however, varying degrees of support and differing emphases on legal doctrine and the rule of law. The main points of conflict in the parliamentary debate ran along the dividing line of whether the treason trials should constitute a departure from, or rather a return to, pre-war legal principles. To some, the crimes committed against the state of Norway and its people by NS collaborators and the German occupying forces were so unprecedented that a response on the basis of pre-war attitudes towards the death penalty and the Norwegian legal system simply could not apply. This in many ways reflected wider international debates about the insufficiency of the law to confront the crimes of the Nazis. They added that the crimes committed had simply been inconceivable when the death penalty was abolished in 1902.[112] This line of argument made it easy to evade a debate altogether and signalled an overall tendency

[110] Innst. O. nr. 4 (1945), pp. 7–8.
[111] Brandal, *Eit politisk strafferettsleg oppgjør*, p. 21.
[112] O.tid. (1945), p. 26.

during the trials to avoid legal argument when it was deemed at odds with the broader demands of the reckoning.[113]

But some MPs wished to ground the use of the death penalty more firmly in pre-war theories of punishment. They were quick to point out that the very point of punishment according to pre-war punitive theories was to *avoid repetition*. If no such events as those experienced during the occupation were likely to reoccur, then this defeated the purposes of legal punishment. Use of the death penalty was only justified if there was a threat from the individuals who were to be sentenced and executed, or if the death penalty was likely to have a deterrent effect for the future. Without punitive purposes, the application of the death penalty was nothing more than revenge.[114] But in his address to parliament, Cappelen sidelined the topic of the broader punitive purposes of the death penalty, and indeed legal doctrine more generally. The government's position was that legalistic debate about the death penalty was unlikely to bring about new insights and that the delay caused by an in-depth engagement with legal arguments would jeopardise the swiftness of the trials' implementation.[115]

Fears that the death penalty contravened Norwegian religious principles and put into question the moral and religious integrity of post-war society also ran through the debate. Knut Strand of *Venstre* argued that Norway was a 'society of Christian culture', suggesting that this in itself ruled out the employment of the death penalty.[116] However, Christian arguments featured too in the statements made by those who supported the bill. Julius Graåsen (Centre Party) for example cited Bishop Berggrav's pamphlet *Folkedommen over NS*, which had stated that 'there are no absolute reasons from a Christian perspective either for or against the death penalty'.[117] Others still argued that it was not the role of parliament to grant forgiveness, but that it was for the king, and ultimately God, to decide.[118] This argument allowed MPs to rhetorically shift responsibility and vote in favour of the bill without having to publicly compromise the integrity of their Christian beliefs. The vague notions of Christianity in this debate also reflect the broader ambivalences of the Church on the question. Cappelen sought to reassure the sceptics by stressing that he believed the courts would apply the death penalty restrictively.[119]

[113] Ibid., pp. 26, 28. [114] Ibid., p. 19. [115] Ibid., p. 21. [116] Ibid., p. 15.
[117] Ibid., pp. 26–27; Berggrav, *Folkedommen over NS*, p. 32. [118] O.tid. (1945), p. 29.
[119] Ibid., p. 21.

Some MPs also addressed the potential retroactivity of the provisional decrees and the legitimacy of the treason trials more generally, exposing a fundamental post-war challenge: after years of lawlessness, the state authorities sought to establish the post-war era on the basis of the rule of law, and their legitimacy rested at least partially on their ability to live up to these promises. However, it proved challenging to present the trials as being in accordance with the grand proclamations of the rule of law expressed by the exile government during the occupation because its law-making powers and the validity of the decrees were yet to be tested in court. The government was anxious that in-depth criticism of the validity of the decrees would destabilise the trials as an institution and, more generally, the consensus upon which its post-war actions rested. The government therefore stressed that MPs be asked *not* to consider the validity of the decrees concerning the death penalty, but only the death penalty as such. Justice Minister Cappelen repeatedly invoked the separation of powers to refute concerns during the debate about the legality of the provisions. He emphasised that the invalidity of any provisional decrees, and indeed the extent of the use of the death penalty, would be for the *courts* to decide. In fact, he even argued that parliament would not need to concern itself with such matters, that the validity of the decrees would be a theoretical question, and that the courts would 'presumably solve it in such a way that can be justified vis-a-vis world opinion both now and for the future'.[120]

Unsurprisingly, this position was met with scepticism, both from those opposing the bill and those in favour of it. Christian Stray (*Venstre*), who voted for the death penalty, stated that the notion that the compatibility of the bill with the constitution was not open to debate represented a 'new constitutional doctrine'. He went on to argue that if retroactivity were expanded too much, 'Nazi justice' would soon be the consequence.[121] Several other MPs expressed dissatisfaction that they were not asked to debate the decrees as such. There were two dimensions to this opposition: firstly, there was a concern among some that the decrees violated traditional doctrines of legality. And, secondly, MPs feared that the role of parliament in the post-war order could be permanently undermined. The debate therefore extended beyond the legal bases of the treason trials themselves and came to concern the institutional integrity and powers of parliament as such.[122] In response to these concerns, Cappelen reapeatedly reiterated his point that the trials could not under any circumstances be delayed and that the curtailed debate did not mark a more fundamental

[120] Ibid., p. 22. [121] Ibid., pp. 29–30. [122] Ibid., p. 19.

institutional precedent.[123] He added that a full parliamentary debate on the treason trials was soon to be held. This highlights the unique circumstances of the time, in which the role of parliament was temporarily reduced to offering an opinion poll for the sake of speedy proceedings.

The concepts invoked most widely by MPs as arguments for the trials were the 'opinion of the people' (*folkeopinionen*), or the 'the legal sentiment of the people' (*folkets rettsbevissthet*). As we have seen, these concepts were a central element in debates about the trials, both within political decision-making and the wider social context. Minister Cappelen referred to the 'extremely important consideration' that the measures proposed by the government be 'consistent with a common and serious sense of justice in our country, and notably without the underlying reason for this sense of justice being hate, a feeling of vengeance or other objectionable motives. One must be extremely careful about violating a general sense of justice in a people.'[124]

Parliamentarians across all parties shared this opinion, which was frequently referred to as 'healthy' and 'adequate'.[125] A Labour Party representative stated that he believed 'that both this generation and the generations to come after us will find that it was a just and necessary reaction of society'.[126] While there was, at this early stage, a genuine concern for public unrest, the frequent references to the public also served as a tool for MPs to ground politics in an argumentatively constructed public opinion and to shift responsibility by stating that their hands were tied. For the government, the 'will of the people' was to become the central argument in legitimating its trial policies and the guiding principle to their implementation. This in turn highlighted that, despite the form of legal procedure, the trials were a legal anomaly that rested on an argument of social demand rather than legal doctrine. A number of politicians foreshadowed that this strategy might backfire. Knut Strand (*Venstre*), for example, directly referred to an expected change in sentiment and Ingvald Førre (*Independent*) argued that '[w]e must guard ourselves from random moods', noting that 'we are currently under a random mood created by brutality during the war'.[127]

What we see in this first debate is that many parliamentarians were conscious of the transitional times they operated in and accepted what they felt was their own limited power to oppose the bill. It is notable, however, how MPs used the platform of debate to voice their concerns. Some MPs

[123] Ibid., p. 22. [124] Ibid., p. 21. [125] Ibid., p. 24. [126] Ibid., p. 25.
[127] Ibid., pp. 15–16, 20.

openly stated how torn they were on the matter, indicating that true opposition to the death penalty was considerably higher than the voting outcome suggests.[128] However, only six MPs ultimately opposed the death penalty bill. The argument prevailed that it was necessary to vote in favour of the death penalty at this time due to fundamental social expectations. It is important to note, however, that MPs voted in the expectation that the trials would be carried through swiftly and that use of the death penalty would be an interim measure only. With this came the hope that the death penalty would be a short exception to Norway's durable legal traditions.

2.7 Conclusion

Bishop Berggrav's pamphlet of May 1945 would later be seen as a harrowing example of the forceful punitive demands of the period, even among senior figures of the Church.[129] But amid the strong language and the calls to punish all NS members, the subtlety of Berggrav's argument is often overlooked. In his pamphlet, Berggrav had sought to make a case for the close interdependence of public opinion and the general legitimacy of the trials. A correspondence of public and legal judgment was necessary for the trials to be a success both in law and in society.[130] The law could not be reduced to a fist fight ('enough of that!', Berggrav proclaimed), for the law contained an element of 'the eternal'.[131] Berggrav therefore urged public attitudes to be based on 'prudence' and, with a respect for the law, to lift the reckoning onto a 'timeless' plane.[132] This, he hoped would result in an awareness that the trials would have to be fair both from a present-day as well as from a future standpoint.[133] And, once the law had spoken, measures should be made available to rehabilitate individuals and allow them to return to society.[134] In fact, Berggrav realised that it might be difficult for the courts to act independently of public sentiment, and suggested that a review court should review all cases one year after the liberation, once the necessary calm for 'true legal reasoning' had arrived and the situation could be reconsidered. These judgments, reflecting the

[128] See for example statements by Julius Graåsen; O.tid. (1945), pp. 26–28.
[129] Andenæs, *Det vanskelige oppgjøret*, p. 60.
[130] The rule of law had been a central component of the Church resistance, and Berggrav's views of the law derived from natural law. He saw it as something 'holy'; see Torleiv Austad, 'Berggrav, Hitler og Luther', in Per Voksø (ed.), *Eivind Berggrav, Brobygger og kirkeleder, 1884–1984* (Oslo: Gyldendal 1984), pp. 88–103, at p. 92.
[131] Berggrav, *Folkedommen over NS*, p. 21. [132] Ibid. [133] Ibid.
[134] RA/PA-0320/2/H/L0017/0031: Undated draft by Bishop Berggrav entitled 'Fra det rettslige til det sosiale'.

more long-term attitudes of the population, should then be able to stand 'for posterity'.

But in the earliest political debates, the law's aspiration to timelessness had been sidelined. The law had instead become an immediate reflection of the dynamics of rapid social and political transition. As this chapter has demonstrated, the period immediately following the liberation was not a period of ordinary law-interpretation. Instead, public sentiments toward the trials had directly shaped their framework and the debates surrounding them. While officials frequently appealed to Norway's proud rule of law traditions, they understood that this set of trials was extraordinary in its legal basis, its scope and its wider purposes. In the preparatory stages of the trials, overwhelming public pressure, or at least a perception thereof, severely limited the government's and the *Storting*'s scope for manoeuvre. At the same time, the symbolism of the trials was a core element in the consolidation of the post-war order and considered critical in marking the overcoming of five years of German occupation. One question, then, was whether the trials would be able to commence swiftly enough to satisfy social expectations.

CHAPTER 3

Foundation

Laws and Legal Precedent, July–December 1945

In assessing the challenges faced by the legal apparatus at the outset of the trials, this chapter has three purposes. Firstly, it seeks to demonstrate how the political promises for a swift handling of the trials were jeopardised by the limited capacity of the institutions entrusted with administering them, generating a whole new set of political and institutional tensions. These tensions were in turn compounded by the difficulties faced by the judiciary in interpreting the provisions adopted during the war and applying them to the situation on the ground. Given the highly politicised nature of the trials, these problems came to bring judicial independence itself under scrutiny. In highlighting these tensions, the chapter argues that the judiciary's attempts to accommodate the political imperatives of the trials limited its scope to challenge or strike down the wartime provisions that underlay them. While overall, the Supreme Court sought to ground its reasoning in established legal doctrine, it nevertheless relied on generalised rationales such as 'absolute necessity' or 'the extraordinary situation' of the occupation, where the law in and of itself would not have provided a basis for the trials. This, I argue, points towards the many ways in which political arguments entered the realm of the law in the first legal cases of the reckoning. This could be seen, not least, in the trial of Vidkun Quisling, which was among the first cases to reach the courts. But the second purpose of this chapter is to show how the application of the law itself had a political consequence in that the earliest court verdicts also offered a first authoritative historical verdict on wartime events. The first Supreme Court verdicts presented a version of the occupation in which the focus on *Nasjonal Samling* (NS) members eclipsed most other forms of collaborative behaviour during the occupation, as well as the crimes committed against minorities. Finally, the chapter looks at three distinct groups to whose opposition to different aspects of the trials the Ministry of Justice and the Director of Public Prosecutions had to respond: industrial workers; jurists and opposition politicians. From August 1945 onwards, industrial workers increasingly protested what they perceived as a lenient and slow handling of the reckoning. At the same time, expert jurists came forward and cautioned against the framework of the reckoning from a legal perspective. Finally, opposition parties within the new *Storting*, elected in October 1945, confronted the government by criticising the slow progress made on the trials. Within months of the liberation, the trials that were meant to unite the liberated nation had become a politically contested topic.

3.1 The Trials Begin

Institutionally, it was a challenging time for the largest legal undertaking in Norway's history to commence. The processing of five years of occupation, the particular challenges of transition and a shortfall of resources already put a great strain on the capacities of the administration and the legal apparatus.[1] Wartime crime ensured that there were enough ordinary criminal cases to keep the prosecution services, the wider administration and the courts busy for several years. In addition, resources had to be invested into the re-establishment of the administration, restitution matters and the 'reopening of court cases and revision of legal and administrative decisions taken during the German occupation'.[2] Hundreds of thousands of Wehrmacht soldiers and POWs needed to return to their homelands, just as Norwegians abroad needed to be repatriated. Yet, there was no way of delaying or avoiding the trials. The Home Front members in particular exerted much pressure to ensure that the trials commenced as swiftly as possible, while the political establishment as a whole repeated its promise for a 'swift and energetic' reckoning to reassure a tense public.[3] The unity government knew that its political authority and popular support, as well as the prevention of public protest and unrest, depended on its ability and commitment to live up to wartime promises. But as a victorious response to occupation and Nazism, the trials also held an immense symbolic power, which meant that it would be meaningful to hold them as soon as possible after the liberation.

It became clear early on that the trials would demand considerable resources, requiring the institution of special departments across the administration to deal with the impending workload. Institutional

[1] Justis- og Politidepartementet, *Om landssvikoppgjøret* (Gjøvik: Mariendal, 1962), p. 441. [2] Ibid.

[3] See for example Nikolai Brandal, 'Eit politisk strafferettsleg oppgjør: det norske arbeidarpartiet og etterkrigsoppgjeret 1945–50' (Master's Dissertation, University of Oslo, 2002), p. 16; Jens Christian Hauge, *Frigjøringen* (Oslo: Gyldendal, 1994), p. 16.

limitations had early on been recognised as a potential bottleneck of the treason trials and dealing with them had consequently been a central component in their planning. Even the estimated number of 50,000 cases amounted to more than ten times the number of cases that the Norwegian legal system had handled each year in the pre-war era. Upon the liberation, it therefore became a key priority to restructure the legal and administrative apparatus for the challenges ahead. Within the legal system, the administration of the treason trials soon came to 'dominate the picture', gaining precedence over almost all other matters.[4] While the celebrations in the streets continued throughout May and June, the core institutions of the legal system were re-established, mass arrests were made, evidence was gathered, judges and prosecutors were reinstated, lawyers were requested to make themselves available and courtrooms were prepared for what was to become the largest set of trials in Norwegian history.

In the early period, the limited institutional infrastructure meant that many measures taken in the preparation and administration of the trials had to be improvised. At this time, personnel was primarily needed in the prison apparatus to handle the mass arrests and detentions following the liberation. Later on, the main burden would shift to the prosecution service and, finally, the courts.[5] At its highest, a total of around 4,500 individuals were involved in the administration of the trials.[6] As we have seen, during the early weeks of the liberation period, the police were assisted by low-trained resistance members and civilians, leading to transgressions of prisoners' rights. At the time, this was hardly a central concern to anyone, although it was to spark a heated debate a few years later.[7] There was also a shortage in trained prosecutors, defence lawyers and judges. However, the bodies engaged with the treason trials were soon expanded to accommodate the most pressing needs. Jurists and individuals who had been engaged in police activity in Sweden acted as provisional investigators and prosecutors, as did individuals who were trained over the summer in short courses conducted by the Ministry of Justice.[8]

The search for qualified judges had begun well before the end of the war.[9] However, it became clear within weeks of the liberation – once the

[4] Justis- og Politidepartementet, *Om landssvikoppgjøret*, p. 442. [5] Ibid., p. 443.
[6] Ibid., p. 442.
[7] On the public controversies surrounding the treatment of prisoners in the immediate post-war era, see Chapters 4 and 6.
[8] Justis- og Politidepartementet, *Om landssvikoppgjøret*, p. 460; Stenografisk referat fra Riksadvokatens og Erstatningsdirektoratets kursus (Oslo: 4. – 8. juni 1945).
[9] Justis- og Politidepartementet, *Om landssvikoppgjøret*, p. 444.

Ministry of Justice had gained full access to the membership catalogue of the NS – that the treason trials were going to involve many more cases than originally anticipated. In order to pre-empt staff shortages, the Ministry of Justice appointed additional judges as early as June 1945. The Ministry had been granted permission to appoint solicitors to serve as interim judges for a period of three months to deal with the overwhelming number of court cases. This appointment system was a new measure, and it emphasised the priority of a speedy reckoning. To ensure the greatest possible degree of continuity with the pre-war order, some exceptions were made to the retirement age of Supreme Court judges. Those who had reached the usual retirement age of 70 during the occupation were allowed to stay in office until the end of June 1946, so as to safeguard the continuity of the court in light of the 'extraordinary situation'.[10] But finding qualified jurists remained a problem throughout the duration of the trials.[11] The Ministry of Justice sent messages to courts asking them to notify the Ministry immediately should they either prefer a different division of court districts, or require more judges.[12] As we shall see, however, these measures were still not sufficient to deal with the high number of pending cases, and a number of additional modifications were introduced to the court structure and the adjudication process a short time later.[13] Securing a sufficiently high number of defence lawyers for NS members and others accused of collaboration proved highly challenging, and authorities deemed it necessary to stress repeatedly that there was a duty to act as defence lawyer once appointed.[14] Given the highly polarised atmosphere of the early post-war period, the Attorneys' Society (*Sakførerforeningen*) issued statements in newspapers in which it clarified that acting as a defence lawyer in a treason case was not 'unpatriotic' behaviour.[15]

Institutionally, the Ministry of Justice (*Justisdepartementet*) was the main institution overseeing the treason trials. It was responsible for the law-making processes surrounding the treason trials, the operation of the legal apparatus, the police force and the prisons, as well as the establishment and operation of the Compensation Directorate (*Erstatningsdirektoratet*). One

10 Erling Sandmo, *Siste ord: Høgsterett i norsk historie 1814–1965, Bind II: 1905–1965* (Oslo: Cappelen, 2005), pp. 55–60.
11 RA/S-1005/A/Aa/L0004: Referat fra regjeringskonferanse, sak nr. 2, 14 May 1946.
12 'Rundskriv av 25 juli 1945', printed in Justis- og Politidepartementet, *Om landssvikoppgjøret*, p. 445.
13 Ot.prp. nr. 12 (1945); Ot.prp. nr. 128 (1947).
14 Johannes Andenæs, *Det vanskelige oppgjøret* (Oslo: Tanum-Norli, 1979), p. 79.
15 Ibid.; 'Et forsvar for forsvarerne', *Arbeiderbladet* (21 August 1945).

of the key priorities of the Ministry of Justice, in line with broader government policy, was that 'the reckoning should be processed as quickly as possible'.[16] At the same time, the Ministry frequently emphasised that the reckoning would have to take place within the contours of the law.[17] Johan Cappelen served as Minister of Justice and Police during the term of the unity government and oversaw the critical early period of the trials until November 1945. Despite his resistance background, Cappelen advocated a moderate tone in the context of the reckoning, and, as we have seen, opposed the death penalty. He had, in fact, only joined the unity government on the condition that he would be exempt from having to consider requests for death penalty pardons.[18] In his stead, therefore, Prime Minister Einar Gerhardsen considered all requests for the duration of the unity government.[19] Cappelen's moderate line would often sit uneasily with the broader political sentiment of that summer and led to widespread protests in August and September. In the initial period, there was, however, little that Cappelen could do to alter the framework of the trials set out by the wartime decrees (although he did implement some influential modifications in August 1945, as I discuss later in the chapter).[20]

The Director of Public Prosecutions (*Riksadvokaten*; DPP) was the second central authority in shaping the course of the trials.[21] The DPP decided the types of cases first to be brought to court, as well as the criminal charge applied for. Throughout the treason trials, the DPP engaged much more actively than in ordinary times in the day-to-day oversight of prosecution and police work.[22] Given the geographical challenges of ensuring cohesion in prosecution practices, the DPP issued a regular communication, *Riksadvokatens Meddelelsesblad*, which was distributed between July 1945 and June 1953 to anyone actively involved in the treason trials.[23] This publication allowed for the swift communication necessary in such a vast country to ensure that the law could be applied consistently in a time-pressured period. The first post-war DPP was Sven Arntzen, who had been a leading figure in both the military and the civil

[16] 'Rundskriv av 25 Juli 1945'; Justis- og Politidepartementet, *Om landssvikoppgjøret*, p. 445.

[17] Andenæs, *Det vanskelige oppgjøret*, p. 79.

[18] Einar Gerhardsen, *Fellesskap i krig og fred: erindringer 1940–45* (Oslo: Tiden Norsk Forlag, 1970), p. 236.

[19] Ibid., pp. 236–237. In his memoir, Gerhardsen referred to the weight of the decisions that senior politicians had to make at the time and the central role of public opinion as a factor in decision-making.

[20] Harald Espeli, Hans Eyvind Næss and Harald Rinde (eds.), *Våpendrager og veiviser: advokatenes historie i Norge* (Oslo: Universitetsforlaget, 2008), p. 230.

[21] Justis- og Politidepartementet, *Om landssvikoppgjøret*, p. 450. [22] Ibid. [23] Ibid., p. 451.

resistance during the war. He had played a key role in the planning of the reckoning, and was one of the authors of the Home Front's draft for the 1944 Treason Decree. He assumed office on 15 May 1945, after having overseen the liberation period as acting National Police Chief. Arntzen took a position typical of former Home Front members and from the beginning called for a harsh reckoning. However, some of his contemporaries later emphasised that Arntzen also had a deep understanding of the human fates involved in the treason trials, and was ready to change his own position when needed.[24]

In terms of court structure, treason cases were to be tried before the ordinary courts of the country. It was deemed important at the time that the reckoning be carried out across the country, at a local level, so that it could absorb the resentment against collaborators and pre-empt local outbursts of violence.[25] Each court appointed one judge responsible specifically for treason cases. The rationale was that this concentrated expertise within each court would enable the legal system to process cases more swiftly. The composition of courts was also changed more generally, with the jury system being abolished towards a more integrated system in which professional judges and lay judges together decided on both the culpability and sentence to be passed down. The wartime decree of 16 February 1945 on court procedures had also introduced a streamlined and simplified procedure for cases concerning occupation offences, including easier rules for apprehension, as well as limited options for appeals.[26] The Supreme Court would, as a rule, consist of five judges. At the Oslo Court of Appeal (*Eidsivating lagmannsrett*), a department was founded on 12 June 1945 to deal exclusively with treason trials. It remained the only special division of a court to deal with treason cases. Erik Solem, a leading member of the resistance, became the presiding judge of the court's treason department, which was to try some of the most high-profile treason cases, including that against Vidkun Quisling.

With the rule of law reinstated and an initial administrative framework in place, the first cases of the treason trials were brought to court from early July 1945 onwards. But soon the lower courts were overwhelmed, given the many new legal provisions they had to apply and the lack of authoritative decisions to draw from. District attorneys, lawyers and judges frequently sent questions about how to interpret the new set of provisions to the Law Division in the Ministry of Justice. Legal precedent from the Supreme Court was urgently required so as to provide an authoritative interpretation of the myriad of overlapping provisions that formed the

[24] Andenæs, *Det vanskelige oppgjøret*, p. 70. [25] Ibid., p. 73. [26] Sandmo, *Siste ord*, p. 325.

basis of the treason trials. The question, then, was whether the broader framework of the treason trials, as laid down in the provisional decrees, would hold up in court, for in principle, the Norwegian Supreme Court could strike down any legal provision it deemed incompatible with the Constitution.[27] Three aspects of the framework of the treason trials were considered particularly controversial among critics of the trials' legal bases: the question of the law-making powers of the king and exile government in light of the potentially retroactive nature of the decrees, the introduction of two new forms of punishment – the death penalty and the loss of civil rights – into civilian criminal law, and the blanket criminalisation of NS membership. For this reason, the prosecution brought a series of cases to trial soon after the liberation concerning these core questions of the trials. Only after these cases had been decided could the reckoning start with 'full force'.[28]

3.2 Legal Precedent

On 12 July 1945, the first high-profile case of the treason trials reached the Oslo Court of Appeal.[29] The case concerned Reidar Haaland, a Norwegian constable in the State Police (*Stapo*), interpreter for the Gestapo and frontfighter accused of torturing Norwegian citizens. Haaland had become a member of the NS in 1940, and later volunteered as a frontfighter, fighting on the German-Soviet front in 1941. After his return to Norway, he became a member of the *Stapo*, there brutally torturing at least nine individuals.[30] Because the case had been brought on the basis of the provisional decrees of 3 October 1941 and 16 February 1945, the validity of which the defendant disputed, the court had to address the question what law-making powers, if any, the king and exile government had held during the occupation. The defence also raised objections on grounds of retroactivity and the omission of an announcement of the decrees in question and argued that NS membership was not unlawful under the Criminal Code. The Oslo Court of Appeal dismissed these objections and handed down a death sentence on 16 July 1945. The prosecution appealed the case to the Supreme Court, where Haaland's trial was held from 9 August 1945 onwards. It was the first treason case to reach the Supreme Court and the binding ruling of the

27 Ibid., pp. 114–168.

28 RA/S-1558/D/L0020: 'Rettsoppgjøret inntil nå', manuscript of the DPP's speech on the status of the treason trials.

29 Rt. 1945, pp. 13–26.

30 Hans Fredrik Dahl, Guri Hjeltnes, Berit Nøkleby, Nils Johan Ringdal and Øystein Sørensen, *Norsk krigsleksikon* (Oslo: Cappelen, 1995), p. 191.

Supreme Court on these central questions came to be a case of central importance for the treason trials. The reasoning of the Supreme Court became part of the official government narrative on the trials and on the course of the occupation more generally. It is therefore worth looking more closely at the questions addressed by the court.

The central question of the case was whether the events in 1940 had provided the king and exile government with the law-making powers according to which they had issued the provisional decrees. § 17 of the Constitution provided the government law-making powers in states of exception, but only on matters of 'trade, tax, the economy and public administration and regulation'. The court, however, unanimously dismissed the defence's argument that the king and exile government therefore had no law-making powers for the occupied territories and referred to a previous Supreme Court ruling of 6 August 1945, in which the court had stated – in a different context – that '[w]ithout such authority the King – the only [one] of our legitimate state bodies who, because he was not in an occupied area, still had full freedom of action – would have been prevented from being able to guard the country's interests, by measures that, in normal times, primarily lie with the Storting'.[31]

Rather than being derived directly from § 17 of the Constitution, the court argued that it was by way of 'absolute necessity' that the government after 9 April 1940 held the power to issue the provisional decrees in question, and that while the powers formally lay outside the scope of § 17, there was a parallel law-making authority based on 'the situation itself'.[32] Pointing to the 'extraordinary situation entirely unforeseen by the authors of the Constitution' expressed in the events of April 1940 and the Elverum Authorisation itself, the court agreed with the rationale behind the Authorisation and cited it as an indicator for this extraordinary situation.[33] However, legally it anchored the law-making powers in the Constitution itself and thereby dismissed the disputed Elverum Authorisation. With this, the law-making powers of the exile government had been confirmed. The court had established that the government had, based on a higher normative order, held the rights to hold onto its powers, despite an absence of constitutional precedent. It stated that in light of the occupation, the king and government had been entitled to act in the interest of their self-preservation. This became the widely accepted and celebrated dominant narrative in post-war Norway.

[31] Rt. 1945, pp. 13–26, at pp. 13–15, citing judgment of the Supreme Court of 6 August 1945.
[32] Ibid. [33] Ibid.

The question of public announcement and retroactivity of the provisional decrees had been a central concern of the exile government during the occupation. In the Haaland judgment, because the death penalty rested on the provisional decree of 3 October 1941, the defence argued that the death penalty could not be applied as the decree had not been validly announced in occupied Norway. The decree, therefore, was unknown at the time of the act and consequently void. The Court of Appeal dismissed these claims on the basis that the new provisions had been publicised by the best means possible in the occupation context. They had been 'announced via radio and illegal newspapers, and included in the Norwegian Law Gazette published in London'.[34] The court continued 'that a person who, like the accused, in a state of war enters into acts of the kind in question – treason in connection with torture of fellow countrymen – must be prepared for the available punishment to be sharpened so that the death penalty also becomes a possibility'.[35] The Supreme Court upheld this reasoning of the Court of Appeal. In stretching pre-war legal doctrine, the Supreme Court emphasised that the question of announcement was not a core criterion for legal validity and did not concern the separate question of *retroactivity*. The court stressed that the 1941 decree had not *established* criminal liability, but merely *increased* the punishment for acts already deemed to be criminal before the occupation, and only applied after its issuance.[36] It left the question open as to whether criminal liability as such could have been established without the announcement of the decree.

The question of announcement was also at issue in the *Stephanson* case, which concerned the culpability of a Norwegian NS general and was appealed to the Supreme Court on grounds of invalid legal basis. Proceedings had, in this case, been brought on the basis of the Treason Decree of 15 December 1944. Here, the question was more complex, as the 1944 decree had not been announced through any available means at all. The undisclosed rationale at the time was that this was necessary in order to prevent economic collaborators from making preparations for the trials by destroying evidence or embezzling assets.[37] A minority of judges argued that because the decree had been kept secret deliberately, the decree was invalid as the situation was equivalent to retroactivity.[38] However, the court's majority arrived at the opposite conclusion and reiterated the

[34] Ibid., at p. 25. [35] Ibid. [36] Ibid., at p. 17.

[37] RA/S-1042/D/Dh/L0010: 'Notat for Statsråd Gundersen' from J. Chr Mellbye to Justice Minister Gundersen, January 1946.

[38] Rt. 1945, pp. 26–42, at pp. 31–33.

rationale that those who 'betrayed' their country had to be prepared that their actions be subjected to new criminal provisions, especially in light of the earlier decrees already issued.[39] By its ruling, the court implicitly established a narrative that 'patriotic' Norwegians had known how to act during the occupation, and that formal announcement was not necessary.

Despite their willingness to set aside ordinary requirements of announcement and to adapt them to the occupation context, the separate question of the potential retroactivity of the decrees deeply troubled and occupied the courts. Aware of the possibility of accusations of victor's justice, they were cautious not to apply the occupation-time decrees to acts committed before their issuance. The question of retroactivity was of particular relevance when it came to the relationship between pre-war criminal law and the provisional decrees. This applied in particular to any acts committed between 8 April 1940 and the time the first relevant decrees were issued in 1941 and 1942. Many lower courts in the initial period did not state what the criminal nature would have been under the original rules on the one hand and the provisional decrees on the other, and applied the provisional decrees retroactively to acts committed during this period. The higher courts subsequently revoked those judgments, and consequentially only applied the provisional decrees to acts committed before their issuance *if* the punishment was no stricter than the provisions under pre-war criminal law.[40] Even the minority judges who argued that the decrees were invalid due to a lack of formal announcement agreed with their application if the penalty they stipulated was less than under the original rules.[41] For those cases where punishment was stricter than under the rules of the criminal law, the provisional decrees could only be applied to acts committed after the date of their respective issuing.[42]

The legal and social permissibility of the new forms of criminal punishment introduced by way of the provisional decrees during the occupation were also discussed in detail by the courts. The courts upheld them,

39 Ibid., at p. 28.

40 See for example Rt. 1945, pp. 154–159; Rt. 1945, pp. 263–264; Rt. 1945, pp. 264–265; Rt. 1945, pp. 285–287; Rt. 1945, pp. 308–311; Rt. 1946, p. 385. However, the use of the new penalties introduced during the occupation was fully retroactive, as § 51 of the Treason Decree allowed for them to be handed down for relevant offences committed from the beginning of the occupation.

41 Rt. 1945, pp. 26–43, at p. 32.

42 However, there were instances in which pre-war legal doctrine on retroactivity was stretched, such as in the death penalty verdict against Finn Knutinge Kaas, in whose case actions committed *before* the issuance of the 1941 death penalty decree were taken into consideration when determining the overall penalty: Baard Herman Borge and Lars-Erik Vaale, *Grunnlovens største prøve: rettsoppgjøret etter 1945* (Oslo: Scandinavian Academic Press, 2018), p. 231; Rt. 1947, pp. 25–36; Kaas was later pardoned.

arguing that they were a necessity in view of the extraordinary situation. With regard to the death penalty, the Court of Appeal in *Haaland* argued that 'for general-preventive reasons and for the purpose of promoting a legal reckoning on a legitimate basis without lynch justice, it was imperative that the King at that time imposed the death penalty for the most serious crimes committed by the traitors'.[43] This reflects a general assumption of a close connection between the death penalty and the success of the trials.[44] The courts were under enormous pressure to recognise the validity of the death penalty, and given the intensity of public opinion there was much concern that failure to do so would lead to vigilante justice. But the court did not address the death penalty in much detail from a *legal* perspective. Public attitudes therefore fed directly into the court reasoning of the day. In relation to loss of civil rights, some judges expressed their concern regarding its potential social ramifications. In the *Stephanson* case, Supreme Court Justice Edvin Alten argued against the use of loss of civil rights as a penalty, stating that it was a deeply unjust form of punishment, affecting individuals very differently depending on their professional and economic status.[45] The majority of the judges ruled in favour of this form of punishment, however.[46] The penalty of forced labour was deemed unproblematic, as it was considered the equivalent to a prison term, and was highly necessary given the limited prison resources in the country.

One of the most divisive issues decided by the courts early on – and which would define much of post-war debate – was the blanket punishment of NS membership. § 86 of the Norwegian Criminal Code became one of the central provisions in sentencing NS members (along with the provisional decree of 22 January 1942, which was only applicable to membership applied for or upheld after the date of its issuance, as well as the later 1944 Treason Decree, which replaced it). There were a number of problems surrounding § 86's direct application to party membership in the period between 8 April 1940 and 22 January 1942. The provision made criminally punishable an individual who 'illegally carries weapons against Norway or during a war in which Norway participates, or with the intention of such a war, provides the enemy assistance in word or deed or weakens the combative ability of Norway or one of her Allies'. This required the courts, first of all, to consider whether membership in itself

[43] Rt. 1945, pp. 13–26, at p. 25.

[44] Lars-Erik Vaale, *Dommen til døden: dødsstraffen i Norge 1945–50* (Oslo: Pax Forlag, 2004), p. 66.

[45] Rt. 1945, pp. 26–43, at p. 34.

[46] The vote was six to two in favour of the king's law-making powers to introduce loss of civil rights as a form of punishment in criminal law.

could amount to enemy 'assistance'. The Court of Appeal in *Haaland* stated that 'registration and membership of the NS after 8 April 1940 have to be characterised as providing the enemy assistance in word or deed'.[47] Citing the many functions and objectives of the NS, the Oslo Court argued that 'from being an ordinary political party, the NS turned to becoming an organisation that supported and cooperated with the enemy so that they could win the war'.[48] It added that any form of assistance to the enemy would be considered relevant under § 86, and it argued that membership in itself would amount to the crime of § 86 because it weakened the 'capacity for resistance' (*motstandsevnen*).

In addition, however, criminal liability also required *subjective* culpability. Responding to Haaland's line of defence that he was acting in good faith regarding his membership in the NS, and perhaps foreshadowing that many NS members would seek to rely on this argument, the Court of Appeal established that the element of subjective guilt would almost always be satisfied for NS members also when punished under § 86. The court stressed that '[t]hose who signed up to the NS had to understand that the NS was in support of German warfare and that each member's membership was of importance in this regard'.[49] The court therefore in effect made *mens rea* regarding *membership* sufficient, a leap from pre-war doctrine concerning the scope of the subjective element required to establish culpability.[50] However, the court did subsequently overturn a series of judgments from the lower courts where the subjective culpability was not addressed in sufficient detail, suggesting that it refined its position on this.[51] The court did not expressly address the question of whether Norway had been at war with Germany after the capitulation of Norwegian forces in North Norway in June 1940, as required by § 86. Norwegian authorities and courts deemed this self-evident.[52] But the court also emphasised that any claims by individuals that they had failed to recognise that the war had continued would not hold up in court: 'From the moment warlike operations began, Norway was at war with Germany.

47 Rt. 1945, pp. 13–26, at p. 21. 48 Ibid., p. 22. 49 Ibid.

50 Hans Petter Graver, *Dommernes krig: den tyske okkupasjonen 1940–1945 og den norske rettsstaten* (Oslo: Pax Forlag, 2015), pp. 166–167.

51 Rt. 1945, pp. 246–249; Rt. 1946, pp. 245–247.

52 This question is disputed – see Robert Bohn, *Reichskommissariat Norwegen* (Munich: Oldenbourg, 2000), p. 7; Hans Fredrik Dahl and Øystein Sørensen, 'Et parti av lovbrytere', in Hans Fredrik Dahl and Øystein Sørensen (eds.), *Et rettferdig oppgjør? Rettsoppgjøret i Norge etter 1945* (Oslo: Pax Forlag, 2004), pp. 113–116; Graver, *Dommernes krig*, pp. 167–168. The case did come up before the Supreme Court, where it held that there continued to be a war even after the capitulation: Rt. 1948, pp. 164–165.

The fact that the country troops eventually had to surrender and the entire land area became occupied did not end the war, as the King and the Government continued their struggle from their seat in London. This fact was widely known.'[53] That the defendant believed himself to be furthering Norwegian interests through his membership was also not accepted as legal exculpation.

When the *Haaland* case reached the Supreme Court, however, the judges were divided by a seven-four split on the question of whether NS membership could qualify as an offence under § 86. One of the dissenting judges, Judge Alten, argued that individual party membership was such a remote and insignificant factor in the enemy's war effort that it could not suffice to qualify as an offence under § 86.[54] Alten also pointed out that there was a paradox in that the wartime decrees had specifically criminalised NS membership as such. If this had already been covered by the offence of § 86, then there would have been no need to introduce these additional provisions. However, his remained a minority view, and the majority abstained from a strict legal-systematic interpretation. Two other dissenting judges differentiated between the NS and sub-organisations such as the *Hird*, arguing that due to its status as a 'combat organisation' (*kamporganisasjon*) only membership of the latter should qualify for criminal liability under § 86.[55] In the *Haaland* case, the question was not decisive, as Haaland had been a member of the *Hird*, which along with his other actions provided sufficient grounds for criminal liability under § 86. However, the court's decision that NS membership in and of itself qualified as an offence under § 86 became binding law.[56]

Further confusion arose because both the provisional decree of 22 January 1942 and the provisional decree of 15 December 1944 made NS membership punishable. More problematically, the later decree of 15 December 1944 made any period of NS membership *after 8 April 1940* punishable, whereas the earlier decree had established liability only after its issuance on 22 January 1942.[57] This unfortunate legal construct was a result of the complex dynamics between the exile government and the resistance during the law-making process. The overlap between the different provisions on NS membership made it necessary for the courts to explicitly state whether NS membership was punished under § 86 or either

[53] Rt. 1945, pp. 13–26, at p. 22. [54] Ibid., pp. 17–18. [55] Ibid., pp. 18–19.

[56] The judiciary did not distinguish between direct assistance to the German enemy and assistance that only benefited the NS as a party, neither in this nor in any future court decision; Andenæs, *Det vanskelige oppgjøret*, p. 109.

[57] Note that the earlier decree was formally replaced by the Treason Decree of 15 December 1944.

of the provisional decrees, and to arrive at a consistent interpretation. The courts gradually established that NS membership under the provisional decrees was only punishable from the date of issuing of the decree on 22 January 1942. The criminal nature of NS membership under the decree of 22 January 1942 and 15 December 1944 were deemed to be the same.[58] But membership prior to this date could, as we have seen, also be punishable under § 86 of the Criminal Code, if the conditions of those provisions were met. The complex relationship between the criminal law code and the provisional decrees nevertheless led one jurist to conclude that 'it would have been an advantage if the Treason Decree [of 1944] had never been adopted'.[59]

With the *Haaland* and *Stephanson* cases handed down, the foundations for the treason trials had been laid. After receiving a death penalty verdict, Haaland sought to be pardoned. An extraordinary cabinet meeting was held on 14 August 1945, which dismissed Haaland's request by a majority vote.[60] While the minutes from this meeting do not reveal the motivations behind the dismissal of Haaland's request, the pressure of public opinion is likely to have been the overwhelming factor, in addition to the significance of these trials' symbolism at the start of the broader reckoning.[61] Notably, however, Finance Minister Gunnar Jahn and Justice Minister Johan Cappelen initially opposed the government's refusal to pardon Haaland, but Cappelen changed his mind during the cabinet meeting.[62] Gerhardsen, handling the requests for death penalty pardons in lieu of Cappelen, received a visit from Haaland's sister, who pleaded that Haaland be pardoned. In his memoirs, Gerhardsen recalled how burdensome he had found the situation personally, but nevertheless felt he had no choice but to decline the request, telling Haaland's sister that a pardon would not be possible, 'given what the situation was in our country'.[63]

Given the intensity of public pressure, it is unsurprising that the courts approved the legal bases for the trials. But the lengthy deliberations and the dissenting judgments still demonstrate a fundamental wish to ground the trials in legal doctrine. Under no circumstances would the courts have

[58] Rt. 1945, pp. 304–307. [59] Andenæs, *Det vanskelige oppgjøret*, p. 120.

[60] RA/S-1005/A/Aa/L0004: 'Referat fra regjeringskonferanse', sak nr. 3, 'Fra Reider Haaland, som er dømt til døden ved enstemmig dom av Eidsiva lagmannsrett 16. juli, stadfestet med 9 mot 2 stemmer av Høyesterett 9. aug., forelå benådningsandragende', 14 August 1945.

[61] Vaale, *Dommen til døden*, pp. 69–70.

[62] RA/S-1005/A/Aa/L0004: 'Referat fra regjeringskonferanse', sak nr. 3, 'Fra Reider Haaland, som er dømt til døden ved enstemmig dom av Eidsiva lagmannsrett 16. juli, stadfestet med 9 mot 2 stemmer av Høyesterett 9. aug., forelå benådningsandragende', 14 August 1945.

[63] Gerhardsen, *Fellesskap i krig og fred*, pp. 234–237.

jeopardised the trials. But they were sceptical of some provisions, in particular the 1944 Treason Decree. There were a number of judges, first and foremost Justices Edvin Alten and Einar Hanssen, who in the early period issued dissenting judgments strongly opposing the premises and principles upon which the trials were being built.[64] We see in these early judgments the difficult balancing act between legal doctrine and the political and public pressure on the courts. What this demonstrates is the recognition of legal principle in peacetime, accompanied by a readiness to modify them so as to make them workable in the specific context of the occupation and the treason trials. Where legal doctrine proved challenging, it was frequently set aside by referring to the allegedly self-evident context of the occupation. The reason this would later spark protest is that what may have appeared self-evident to policy makers was much more contested and uncertain from the citizen's viewpoint. Throughout the treason trials, the government authorities emphasised the independence of the judiciary. But there were also questions of bias within the judiciary, with many Home Front members sitting in senior judicial positions.[65] And while formally the courts may have been independent, the overwhelming political importance of the trials had in many ways predetermined the outcome of the first court verdicts.

3.3 Quisling on Trial

Overall, it was a difficult climate in which to discuss critically Norway's reckoning with collaborators. Many central figures in the trials would later point out that this was not a time for nuance. In their memoirs, Einar Gerhardsen and Johannes Andenæs respectively remembered that 'in 1945, it was a common belief that all traitors should be punished, not just the big ones' and that 'anyone who advocated moderation in the reckoning at this time faced headwinds'.[66] The early period was marked by triumphalism and heightened expectations for a full reckoning with all 'unpatriotic' Norwegians. It was a patriotic narrative that was both one of the central aims and an outcome of the trials. The condemnation of 'traitors' furthered the myth that all others were 'good Norwegians' who had collectively resisted the enemy. The national orientation of the

[64] Lars-Erik Vaale, 'Høyesterett, Grunnloven og oppgjøret i Norge 1945–1965: rett og politikk i landets øverste domstol under rettsoppgjøret' (unpublished manuscript).

[65] This issue was raised for example in the case of Reidar Haaland, Rt. 1945, pp. 13–26.

[66] Einar Gerhardsen, *Samarbeid og strid: erindringer 1945–55* (Oslo: Tiden Norsk Forlag, 1971), p. 57; Andenæs, *Det vanskelige oppgjøret*, p. 71.

discourse also meant that the crimes against others than the country's majority played next to no role in it. Being on the right side of history was vital at this time, and those who could opt into the narrative of collective Norwegian resistance against a small group of traitors often did so, both demonstrably and vocally. The binary categories of guilt and innocence, NS members and non-NS members, thus allowed for the greyscales and complexities of the occupation to be eclipsed and provided a simple formula of identification with the patriotic community.[67] When disagreement arose regarding the implementation of the trials, it soon drifted away from factual discourse and became a question of national allegiance, often expressed in polemical wording. This climate of triumphalism and expectation exerted pressure on the authorities to keep their wartime promises and they monitored any changes in public attitudes towards the trials closely.

Once the *Haaland* and *Stephanson* verdicts had been handed down and passive membership in the NS formally classified as treason, newspapers widely saw their early, broad-sweep conceptions of treason confirmed.[68] As a legal category, the term 'treason' (*landssvik*) held various meanings across time, and – crucially – it was interpreted and applied by courts to the individual case. In public discourse, it took on a life of its own, and became a central component in narrations of the war more generally. The 'treason-stamp' was both broad and inclusive, constructed to apply to everyone who had in some way acted 'unpatriotically'. The nation's newspapers were quick during the first months following the liberation to characterise and condemn as 'traitors' anyone who had shown some form of involvement with the NS or the Germans. In their triumphant coverage of the early liberation months, newspapers delineated a broad dividing line between 'traitors' and 'good Norwegians'. Soon, those who had joined the NS, had fought for the Germans or had worked in the SS or other German organisations, had become marked as outcasts, as traitors of a society in which the majority had known how to be a 'good' Norwegian. The fact that the criminal nature of NS membership had been decided in a case against a major torturer cast an unfavourable light on NS membership as a whole.[69] Throughout June and July of 1945, there was a buzzing sense of satisfaction in relation to having all 'traitors' put on trial, with very little

67 This was a common dynamic also in other newly liberated countries – see Chapter 7.

68 See for example 'Effektivt rettsoppgjør', *Friheten*, 23 May 1945.

69 During the early stages of the trials, in the autumn of 1945, it was particularly cases against frontfighters, members of NS organisations as well as the NS leadership itself that were brought before the courts.

concern for variations in culpability or the broader implications for the individuals involved, their families, and society at large.

One of the most important sets of trials in terms of their symbolism for the post-war government, for the formation of a collective post-war narrative of resistance and betrayal, and as an authoritative verdict on wartime history, were those against high-ranking NS officials, including the trial of Vidkun Quisling himself.[70] The trial against Quisling opened on 20 August 1945 at the Oslo Court of Appeal, and lasted for three weeks. The DPP had deemed it important that this be one of the first cases to be brought to trial.[71] It was followed closely by the Norwegian and international press, and representatives of the chief Allied prosecutor of the Nuremberg Trials were present.[72] The presiding judge of the case was Erik Solem, a leading member of the Home Front and one of the authors of the Treason Decree. His prominent role in the trial led to objections of partiality from Quisling's defence team. His wartime activities aside, Solem had also published a three-piece series in *Verdens Gang* in June 1945 on the legal basis of the trials, in which he had used one-sided language against Quisling. This could easily have been interpreted as an a priori judgment.[73] However, the Supreme Court quickly dismissed this objection, and Solem kept his position. But during the trial, the notion of judicial impartiality was stretched, with Solem frequently going beyond the role of judge and launching 'aggressive' verbal attacks on Quisling.[74] This meant that the legal, the political and the personal interacted strongly in this key trial.

Quisling was indicted and sentenced on the basis of both the military and civilian criminal codes and the 1941–1942 provisional decrees concerning the death penalty.[75] He was accused of committing high treason and of seeking to overturn the constitutional order (based on his conduct ahead of the invasion and the attempted coup on 9 April 1940), of aiding the enemy in leading the collaborationist party NS and of calling for Norwegians to fight for the Germans. In addition, he was accused of the murder of Viggo Hansteen, who had been executed during the state of

[70] Hans Fredrik Dahl, *Quisling: A Study in Treachery* (Cambridge: Cambridge University Press, 2007 [1999]), p. 378.
[71] Ibid.
[72] Arne W. Brøgger to James B. Donovan, accompanied by diary notes, 4 September 1945, in 'The War Crimes Trials at Nuremberg', Archives of Harry S. Truman.
[73] On the discussion of judicial partiality during the trials, see in particular Borge and Vaale, *Grunnlovens største prøve*, pp. 178–182.
[74] Dahl, *Quisling*, p. 385. [75] RA/S-3138-01/D/Da/L0003: Dnr. 29, 1945, pp. 1522–1523.

exception in 1941, and fifteen other individuals who had been executed during the course of the war. The crimes against Norway's Jews also formed part of the indictment, with Quisling accused of being an accessory to their murder. Finally, he was accused of various counts of theft and embezzlement. Having gathered information in a short time span of just weeks from within Norway as well as from Germany, France and Great Britain, in close cooperation with the Allies, the prosecution laid out in detail the many occasions in which Quisling had betrayed his country. The prosecution in particular did not let the argument count that Quisling had acted in Norwegian interests, with prosecutor Annæus Schjødt stating that Quisling's policy would have left Norway as nothing but a 'German colony'.[76]

Quisling's defence attorney Henrik Bergh, on the other hand, argued that Quisling was a complex character, fanatically convinced of his own 'ideology' and captured in his own parallel universe. He also stressed that Quisling was convinced that he had acted in the Norwegian interest, both in defending it from Bolshevism and in seeking to secure the nation's independence. Quisling elaborated on his position that he deemed the exile government illegitimate, that the NS had been a *legal* party and that he had stepped in out of an emergency after the government had effectively stepped down. He was of the opinion that he was being blamed for the actions of the Germans on Norwegian soil. Among the fifty-one witnesses who were called were NS ministers, including Ministry of the Interior Albert Viljam Hagelin, civil servants from the *Reichskommissariat*, Wilhelm Wagner, Knut Rød, senior political and military figures from the pre-war era, as well as victims of the NS regime's actions, including teachers and two Jewish witnesses, Leo Eitinger and Asriel Hirsch. Their accounts provided insights into Quisling's actions and behaviours both before and during the war, as well as harrowing details of the horrors Norway's Jews had been subjected to during the war. And yet, many of the witnesses who had known Quisling in the 1920s and 1930s also stated positive things about younger Quisling, and suggested that the man they saw in front of them in court seemed like a different person. Based on these witness testimonies on Quisling's character, the court suspected a mental illness and briefly suspended proceedings to have Quisling neurologically examined. The examination was demanding and took its toll on his health. Quisling was therefore severely weakened when he gave a long, confused

[76] *Straffesak mot Vidkun Abraham Lauritz Jonssøn Quisling* (Oslo: Grøndahl, 1946), p. 257.

Figure 3.1 The verdict is handed down in the trial of Vidkun Quisling at the Oslo Court of Appeal (*Eidsivating Lagmannsrett*), 10 September 1945.
Source: Aktuell/NTB.

and often-fantastical defence speech, in which he talked about many aspects of his life, his ideology and objectives, but most of all defended his role as a 'buffer between the occupation power and the people'.[77]

Predictably, his defence was not accepted. On 10 September, the Oslo Court of Appeal sentenced Quisling to death (Figure 3.1). The court largely accepted the line of reasoning presented by the prosecution and found him guilty of harming the country by promoting Norwegians to take up arms for Germany (§ 80 of the Military Criminal Code), by attempting to bring Norway under a foreign power (§ 83 of the Civilian Criminal Code) and to overturn the country's constitutional order (§ 98 of the Civilian Criminal Code). He was also found guilty of the murder of Viggo Hansteen. With regard to the deportation of the Jews and the other murders, the court ultimately accepted Quisling's argument that he did not know what fait awaited them and sentenced him for negligent

[77] Dahl, *Quisling*, p. 404; citing *Verdens Gang* of 8 September 1945; *Straffesak mot Vidkun Abraham Lauritz Jonssøn Quisling*, pp. 326–366.

homicide rather than murder.[78] He was, in addition, sentenced for issuing the law concerning the confiscation of Jewish assets.

There was no doubt politically that this long catalogue of crimes of which the NS leader had been found guilty would result in a death penalty. However, one of the key *legal* questions of the case in fact concerned the death penalty and the legitimacy of its use in Quisling's case. Quisling's defence had argued that the death penalty could not be used because the indictment concerned in particular Quisling's actions leading up to 9 April 1940. However, the post-war use of the death penalty had only been introduced by way of the decree of 3 October 1941. The key events had taken place before the adoption of the relevant decrees, when the death penalty did exist in military law, but the Military Criminal Code stated that the death penalty could not be carried out after the war had ended. Quisling therefore appealed to the Supreme Court. The court, however, dismissed the defence's arguments and made a distinction with regard to the principle of retroactivity, arguing that a mere change to the *implementation* of punishment could not fall within the remit of the constitutional provisions protecting against retroactivity.[79]

In confirming the death penalty verdict, the Supreme Court, presided over by no other than Paal Berg, stated: 'During a nation's most fateful hour chaos must not prevail . . . and he who at such a crucial moment for his country sets himself above its constitutional authorities and thereby betrays his country, has no place within it.'[80] After Quisling had been sentenced to death, his wife Maria launched a tireless campaign to have her husband released.[81] She sent numerous letters to former friends and colleagues from his time as Minister of Defence for the Centre Party in the 1930s. One of them was the former Norwegian commander-in-chief, Otto Ruge, who had known Quisling closely at the time and had also testified in court. Maria Quisling begged him to support her plea that Quisling be pardoned. In his reply, Ruge expressed his sympathies, but regretted that there was nothing he could do. He had known Quisling well in the past, and respected him. But Quisling had been a 'political sleep-walker', obsessed by his political visions for Norway, and gone down a path that to him was both inexplicable and inexcusable.[82] Some prominent figures, meanwhile, opposed Quisling's execution, including Bishop Berggrav, who in a letter to the Prime Minister stated that Quisling had

[78] Rt. 1945, pp. 109–142. [79] *Straffesak mot Vidkun Abraham Lauritz Jonssøn Quisling*, p. 465.
[80] Ibid. [81] Dahl, *Quisling*, p. 412.
[82] RA/S-1005/D/Db/L0131: Letter from Otto Ruge to Maria Quisling, 5 October 1945.

acted in 'good faith', and had not been a 'raw criminal', but such appeals fell on deaf ears.[83] The king and cabinet refused to pardon Quisling and he was executed in the early hours of 24 October 1945.[84]

The trial of Vidkun Quisling had an enormous symbolic significance, both nationally and internationally.[85] Nationally, it constituted the trial with the most central symbolic meaning concerning the place of the NS and the occupation period in Norwegian history. It created the narrative that would underlie the reckoning as a whole. But the trial was also seen as symbolising the victory over Nazism on the international stage. In his letter to the Prime Minister following Quisling's death penalty verdict, Berggrav referred to the international expectation that Quisling be executed – and unsuccessfully implored the government to ignore these. But a pardon was, at this time, highly unrealistic. As the first leader of a National Socialist party to be tried, the world looked to Norway in October of 1945. His sentence symbolised the triumph of Allied cooperation and victory and the re-establishment of the rule of law in Western Europe.

3.4 Protest Gathers

From early August onwards, in the shadows of the more high-profile cases, a growing level of public dissatisfaction with the treason trials could be detected. Of particular concern was how the tens of thousands of impending cases would unfold. Despite the precedent established, the treason trials were proceeding more slowly than anticipated due to the overwhelming number of cases. This raised concerns in the wider public that many collaborators might evade trial. Furthermore, the fact that treason suspects were often not held in detention caused so much frustration in some communities that National Police Chief Andreas Aulie found it necessary to state in the press that people could be outside prison walls and still be under investigation for treason, and that it was merely a matter of time before their case was brought to court.[86] But there was also a

83 RA/PA-0320/2/H/L0017: Letter from Eivind Berggrav to Einar Gerhardsen, 19 October 1945.

84 RA/S-1005/A/Aa/L0004: Referat fra regjeringskonferanse, sak nr. 4, 'Quisling-saken', 16 October 1945.

85 Other ministers of Quisling's cabinet and senior officials, too, faced trial. Albert Viljam Hagelin, the Minister of the Interior, and Ragnar Skancke, the Minister for Education and Church Affairs, were sentenced to death. Six ministers, including the general secretary of the NS and Culture Minister Rolf Jørgen Fuglesang, were sentenced to lifetime imprisonment, and a number of others to prison terms of between fifteen and twenty years. Justice Minister Sverre Riisnæs, meanwhile, was declared insane and was not tried.

86 National Police Chief Andreas Aulie in a press conference, cited in '16,714 landssvikere er arrestert', *Arbeiderbladet* (9 August 1945).

growing scepticism about the impact of the trials on society. The slow progress therefore spurred criticism from both the 'ice front' and the 'silk front'. The former feared that the high number of pending cases would result in a delay, and ultimately a much more lenient reckoning than that conveyed by wartime promises.[87] The latter meanwhile warned of the social impact of the extended proceedings and increasingly voiced its concerns over the trials' legality and the social condemnation suspects faced.

These tensions were exacerbated when on 3 August the government decided that a first series of modifications to the treason decrees had become necessary. These would mean a softening and overall reduction of the scope of the reckoning. The impetus for this change was a letter sent by the Norwegian Women's Council (*Norske Kvinners Nasjonalråd*) to the government on 25 June 1945. In its letter, the Council protested against the sweeping provisions of the 1944 Treason Decree with regard to the economic compensation to be paid by NS members *and their families*. It argued that women would be hard hit if the husband and breadwinner of a family had been a member of the NS, even if the woman had not.[88] As the usual case was for the man to be the breadwinner, the letter argued, women would be punished economically and socially by their partner's culpability. The letter in particular opposed the provisions of the 1944 decree that made spouses economically liable if they had shared a household during the occupation. It argued that many women opposed divorce on religious grounds or in the interest of their children. During the uncertainty of war, more than at any other time, it would have been a challenge for a woman to seek a divorce. The letter concluded that there were therefore many possible reasons as to why a woman might have chosen to stay with her NS husband, and that this was not necessarily an indication of an unpatriotic attitude on her behalf.[89]

The Ministry of Justice took this matter seriously and conducted an internal assessment of the provision in question.[90] But when Johan Cappelen took the initiative and presented his proposal for a change to the treason provisions at such an early stage of the reckoning, he was confronted with significant opposition, in particular by the Compensation Directorate, which feared that spouses would be used to embezzle

[87] See for example 'Dommer', *Verdens Gang* (20 August 1945).

[88] All assets of NS members had been frozen immediately following the liberation: Svein Bue, 'Det økonomiske oppgjøret', in Dahl and Sørensen, *Et rettferdig oppgjør?*, pp. 160–192, at p. 179.

[89] RA/S-3212/D/De/L0300: Letter to the Norwegian government by *Norske Kvinners Nasjonalråd* (25 June 1945).

[90] RA/S-3212/D/De/L0301: Untitled memo of the Ministry of Justice, 26 July 1945.

money.[91] But Cappelen had Johannes Andenæs, a recognised legal expert, on his side. Andenæs had been asked to draft a legal assessment of the provisions, and came to the conclusion that they were problematic both from a legal and sociopolitical perspective. For all his support of the reckoning in general, Andenæs was, in fact, highly sceptical of the compensation principle. In legal terms there was no 'adequate causation', and he did not see how 'every little NS-member in the most remote parts of the country' could have been responsible for the course of the occupation.[92] In his report, he noted:

> Liability is established on the premise that it was the joining of ordinary members that enabled the party leaders to pursue their aims. Without a certain body of members, the party would not have reached the status with the occupier which allowed for it to seize governing power, the argument goes. Already here, there are many uncertain factors. An organised party was no precondition for enabling those who partook in the administration of the country to cause damage – they could have done it in practically the same way directly in the name of the occupier.[93]

Andenæs also pointed towards the sociopolitical dimension, and criticised that the impact these provisions had on the dependants of NS members led to punishment in absence of culpability. But Andenæs was equally aware of the unforgiving social forces advocating a strong punishment for collaborators, and concluded that 'such purely humane arguments are so easily dismissed by way of the new buzzword "campaign of pity"'.[94]

Despite the expected criticism, the Minister of Justice still managed to convince the cabinet to implement a series of changes to the 1944 Treason Decree.[95] In response to the criticism put forward by the Norwegian Women's Council, the new provisions rendered the compensation provisions of NS members more flexible, and gave uncompromised spouses of NS members greater economic protection in the context of compensation payments. The decree also loosened the previous requirement that anyone sentenced to more than six months in prison for treason would automatically lose their full set of civil rights. This was a fundamental change, and, ultimately, the courts only rarely handed down a penalty of full loss of civil

[91] RA/S-1005/A/Aa/L0004: Referat fra regjeringskonferanse, sak nr. 3, 'Endringer i landssvikanordningen', 31 July 1945; RA/S-3212/D/De/L0301: Letter from *Erstatningsdirektoratet* to the Ministry of Justice, 25 July 1945; the *Erstatningsdirektorat* argued that instead, authorities would take individual circumstances into close consideration.

[92] RA/S-3212/D/De/L0301: Undated memo entitled 'Erstatningsansvaret for N.S. medlemmer' by Johannes Andenæs.

[93] Ibid. [94] Ibid. [95] Ot.prp. nr. 92 (1945–1946), pp. 83–96.

rights, preferring instead to withdraw selective rights only.[96] The Ministry's official argument for the changes was that courts should not be prevented from handing down the judgments they felt appropriate in each individual case. But secretly, the Ministry was concerned that some of the provisions contained in the 1944 Treason Decree could be deemed retroactive.[97] The modifications significantly changed the course of the treason trials, and in particular spared many of the smaller 'traitors' and their spouses and families the harsher consequences of the 1944 decree. Moreover, the changes came at a time when, due to the unexpectedly broad scope of the reckoning, the Ministry of Justice had internally begun to turn its attention to the more long-term social consequences of the trials.[98]

Reactions to the changes to the treason decree in the capital's newspapers were mostly sceptical. The majority argued that the original – harsher – provisions had been appropriate and fully in line with Norwegian law. The amended provisions, they claimed, would ultimately lead to a weaker reckoning. The dividing line came to lie between *Aftenposten* and *Nationen* on the one hand, and *Arbeiderbladet*, *Friheten* and *Dagbladet* on the other.[99] In an editorial entitled 'Was this necessary?', *Arbeiderbladet* accused the 'campaign of pity' – 'which has already been set in motion' – of being behind the changes and concluded that 'in terms of collective psychology, this revision made no good impression'.[100] The newspaper wrote that the changes called for increased scrutiny of authorities on behalf of the public.[101] *Dagbladet*, too, strongly opposed the modifications and stated that the changes 'increased legal uncertainty'.[102] *Morgenbladet* and *Verdens Gang* were more conciliatory, with the latter praising the government's openness to modifications and stating that the changes made to the earlier provision 'must not be seen as a distancing

96 Anika Seemann, 'The Penalty of "Loss of Civil Rights" during the Norwegian Treason Trials, 1945–1953', *Scandinavian Journal of History*, 45 (2020) 3, pp. 360–383.

97 RA/S-1042/D/Dh/L0010: 'Notat for Statsråd Gundersen' from J. Chr Mellbye to Justice Minister Gundersen, January 1946.

98 RA/S-1005/D/Db/L0131: 'Landssvikerne som samfundsproblem', memo, Jens Chr. Hauge, 31 July 1945; 'Landssvikerne som sosialt problem', memo, Jens Chr. Hauge, 4 September 1945; Hauge suggested that an expert committee be formed on the long-term social effects of the trials. Other memos too discuss the long-term prospects of *landssvik* prisoners. This signals that early on, there was an awareness of the sociopolitical dimension to the trials.

99 'Var den nødvendig?', *Arbeiderbladet* (6 August 1945); 'Landssvikanordningen mer elastisk', *Dagbladet* (4 August 1945); 'Gråtekonenes seir', *Dagbladet* (6 August 1945); 'Oppgjøret med landssvikerne og deres hjelpere', *Friheten* (14 August 1945).

100 'Var den nødvendig?', *Arbeiderbladet* (6 August 1945). 101 Ibid.

102 'Gråtekonenes seir', *Dagbladet* (6 August 1945).

from the Treason Decree as such'.[103] At this stage we see a growing polarisation among newspapers, and growing scepticism towards authorities and jurists, in particular on the part of the 'ice front' press.[104]

A series of court sentences further contributed to the frustration and disappointment of many newspapers and citizens. Unlike some of the high-profile cases, whose culmination in the death penalty had been openly celebrated by the media, some verdicts against NS members and frontfighters were deemed to be too lenient. The trials against Hans Birger Egeberg, Arne Braa Saatvedt and Per Oppegard are examples of the strong responses individual cases could provoke from the media and the wider public during this period.[105] During the war, Egeberg had been a member of the infamous *Sonderabteilung Lola*, a special division within the German Security Service (*Sicherheitsdienst*) renowned for its violence, and Saatvedt and Oppegard had worked for the Gestapo. *Sonderabteilung Lola* had consisted of roughly 60–70 Norwegian citizens, operating primarily in Trondheim under their leader Henry Rinnan, a Norwegian citizen. The 'Rinnan group' – as it was widely referred to after the war – had primarily targeted resistance fighters, whom they lured into a relationship of trust in order to receive information on resistance activity. From 1943 onwards, the group had become more violent, subjecting several resistance members to acts of extreme violence and torture, resulting in numerous deaths. All three defendants had been involved in grave mistreatment of resistance members during interrogations, with Egeberg for example branding a swastika on a prisoner's back. Saatvedt had also committed a murder.

The prosecution had applied for a death penalty sentence in all three cases. The courts, however, only handed down a death penalty verdict against Saatvedt, with both Egeberg and Oppegard being sentenced to lifetime imprisonment instead. This sparked immediate responses from the 'ice front' papers, which demanded death penalty sentences for Egeberg and Oppegard.[106] Under the ominous heading 'Let the storm come', *Friheten* stated that the public had had enough of the leniency against 'traitors' and was preparing to take justice into its own hands.[107] A number of external contributors, too, voiced their disapproval, arguing that the

[103] 'Andres Mening', *Friheten* (7 August 1945). [104] 'Oppgjøret', *Dagbladet* (25 August 1945).

[105] The judgment of Arne Braa Saatvedt and Per Oppegaard is published in Rt. 1945, pp. 96–104.

[106] Rt. 1945, pp. 96–104. On the trials and their broader resonance, see Vaale, *Dommen til døden*, pp. 74–77.

[107] 'La stormen komme', *Friheten* (17 August 1945); 'Lov og dom', *Dagbladet* (17 August 1945); 'Dødsstraff eneste naturlige reaksjon mot landsforrædernes tortur', *Verdens Gang* (17 August 1945).

decisional practice demonstrated in the Egeberg and Oppegard cases could lead to public unrest.[108] The prosecution appealed both cases to the Supreme Court. It is not unlikely that it was, at least in part, the public responses to the judgments of the Court of Appeal that led to a revision of the judgment for Egeberg before the Supreme Court, resulting in a death penalty verdict.[109]

The reversal of the verdict in the Egeberg case could not, however, curb the larger dissatisfaction with the progress of the trials. Not only were the courts applying the death penalty more restrictively than many of its advocates had hoped, many also deemed the sentences against frontfighters and NS members too lenient. In the *Storting*, attitudes towards frontfighters were divided, and the question of whether the death penalty was appropriate to the crimes committed by frontfighters discussed intensely.[110] Many pointed to the idealism and young age of many who had enlisted, as well as the significant anti-Bolshevik propaganda of the interwar years. Others emphasised the severity of treason and the crimes committed. But the general public attitude during this time remained unforgiving. While coverage of these two categories of defendants was a lot more civilised than that of high-profile cases against torturers, we thus begin to see fundamental disagreement with regard to the handling of the occupation legacy.[111] *Friheten* warned of the possible consequences of a lenient reckoning, stating that 'people's trust and respect for the law and its practitioners are weakened, resulting in a danger to society'.[112] A few days later, *Dagbladet* complained that one had 'the impression that the courts have in many cases applied mitigating circumstances'.[113] Later, in an almost threatening manner, it referred to the possible consequences should the trials become too lenient, warning that the population would 'rise again and strike with the violent power of the healthy instinct and just resentment'.[114] By late August, in the view of the 'ice front' newspapers, authorities had already fallen short of their wartime promises. The initial anticipation and triumphalism was beginning to give way to a bitterness that would define the tone in the treason trials for many years to come.

[108] For a fuller account of the trials against Egeberg, Saatvedt and Oppegaard, see Vaale, *Dommen til døden*, pp. 74–77.

[109] Rt. 1945, pp. 75–82. [110] O.tid. (1945), pp. 14–35.

[111] '6 måneders fengsel for menige medlemmer i NS?', *Verdens Gang* (21 July 1945); 'Ømhet', *Dagbladet* (28 August 1945).

[112] 'Oppgjøret med landssvikerne og deres hjelpere', *Friheten* (14 August 1945).

[113] 'Lov og dom', *Dagbladet* (17 August 1945).

[114] 'Alvorlig advarsel', *Dagbladet* (20 December 1945).

Criticism soon became more vocal in the streets, too. Wider public debate began to revolve around three core criticisms: that the trials were progressing too slowly, that the judgments were too lenient and that their scope was not encompassing enough.[115] Several political and industry organisations wrote to the Ministry of Justice to demand consequential punishment.[116] Industry representatives and trade unions soon became involved in the debate as well. They urged the government to proceed more swiftly with the trials. On factory floors, they noted, the trials were causing much conflict, with many workers refusing to work alongside suspected 'traitors'.[117] At the Thune Works (*Thunes Mekaniske Værksted*) in Skøyen, just outside Oslo, workers refused to work after three officials were allowed to continue in their positions despite previous collaborative involvement with the occupier. Factories across the country expressed their solidarity with the Thune workers. The strike at Thune lasted for weeks, and it was only after the Ministry of Social Affairs mediated between the parties that it was formally brought to an end. But the tensions were far from resolved. By August, the situation across the country had intensified, and several formal appeals from trade unions, industry representatives and party organisations were directed to the government, all calling for a swift and encompassing implementation of the wartime promises.[118] One of them read: 'The Norwegian people, which in this battle of fate showed composure and honour under the regime of horrors of traitors and their henchmen, demand that the reckoning with society's rotten animals be seen to consistently and swiftly. All unnecessary procedure must be set aside, their crimes do not deserve mitigating circumstances.'[119]

[115] Johannes Andenæs, 'Rettsoppgjøret I', *Arbeiderbladet* (15 October 1945).

[116] RA/S-3212/D/De/L0300: Various letters.

[117] 'Sit-down streik på Thunes mek. verksted: arbeiderne nekter å arbeide fordi tre funksjonærer ikke er blitt fjernet', *Aftenposten* (3 August 1945); 'Gjenopptas arbeidet ved Thune i dag?', *Morgenbladet* (6 August 1945); 'Avblåses sit-down-streiken på Thune i dag?', *Aftenposten* (7 August 1945); 'Thune-arbeiderne fortsetter den ulovlige streik: den gjeder nu "samfunnsforholdene i sin alminnelighet i dag"', *Aftenposten* (8 August 1945); 'Thunestreik og trusler', *Morgenbladet* (10 August 1945); 'Thune-konflikten: nytt utvidet møte på sosialministerens initiativ', *Aftenposten* (17 August 1945); 'Arbeidet gjenopptas på Thune i morgen', *Morgenbladet* (20 August 1945); *Morgenbladet*, 'Oslo og Åkershus samorganisasjon slutter på om den ulovlige Thunekonflikten' (21 August 1945).

[118] 'En veldig vekst i landets fagbevegelse: en strøm av uttalelser om regjeringsspørsmålet og samlingen', *Friheten* (18 June 1945); 'Arbeiderne har en mening', *Friheten* (20 June 1945); RA/S-3212/D/De/L0300: Letter from *Norges Kommunistiske Ungdomsforbund* to the Ministry of Justice, 13 August 1945; letter from *Oslo og Akershus faglige samorganisasjon* to the Norwegian government, 15 August 1945; letter from Mil.Org. to Minister Cappelen, 20 August 1945; letter from *Norsk Formerforbund* to the Ministry of Justice, 21 August 1945.

[119] 'Landsforræderne må uskadeliggjøres straks!', *Friheten* (6 June 1945); 'Aktuelle vedtak i fagforeningene om samlingen og regjeringspolitikken', *Friheten* (27 June 1945).

Figure 3.2 Public protest in Youngstorget, Oslo, in connection with the treason trials, 20 August 1945.
Source: *Arbeiderbladet*/The Norwegian Labour Movement Archives and Library.

On 20 August, the strikes culminated in a large protest in Youngstorget, a major square in the centre of Oslo, where around 30,000 workers demonstrated against what they perceived as a lenient implementation of the treason trials (Figure 3.2).[120] They were dissatisfied with what they felt was slow progress and demanded a speedy and encompassing reckoning, threatening the authorities that extra-judicial justice would be the

[120] 'Rettsapparatet må løsrives fra reaksjonens agenter', *Friheten* (20 August 1945); 'Protest mot silkefronten', *Dagbladet* (21 August 1945).

consequence if their demands were not met.[121] The workers presented a resolution, which they delivered to the government later that day, demanding a swifter and more efficient handling of the trials.[122] Many also called for a broader use of the death penalty. A large protest by any standards, this one is all the more remarkable because so many workers took to the streets not to fight for better work conditions in a narrower sense, but for what they deemed a more 'patriotic workplace'. Several other protests also took place across the country.[123] Justice Minister Cappelen quickly called a press conference, in which he sought to reassure the public that the trials were being seen through according to previous promises. He also stated that calls for summary executions were a reflection of a Nazi mentality 'that should be banned from any discussion in our country'.[124] These were words which at that time 'irritated many ears'.[125] The press did not take long to respond: *Arbeiderbladet* re-emphasised the requirement that the 'people's opinion' be a central component in the administration of the trials and stressed the importance of the public staying alert and closely monitoring court practice.[126] *Dagbladet* argued that protest was necessary to counter the efforts of the 'pity campaign' and its influence on the courts.[127] *Friheten* wrote: 'It appears to us that Justice Minister Cappelen's words at yesterday's conference are a crass expression of how far the sense of justice of a government member can be removed from society's healthy legal instinct and demand for an efficient reckoning with the traitors.'[128] Both government representatives and the courts understood the consequences if public dissatisfaction grew further.[129]

3.5 Criticism and Caution

Attitudes towards the trials were far from unidirectional, however. The impatience expressed in newspapers and through protests was criticised by those advocating a more measured response to wartime acts. In autumn 1945, legal experts in particular became more outspoken on the central legal questions the trials were posing, the a priori judgements of the public

[121] 'Folkets krav: Døm fort og hardt!', *Friheten* (21 August 1945).
[122] RA/S-1005/A/Aa/L0004: Referat fra regjeringskonferanse, sak nr. 17, 'Resolusjon fra Oslo-arbeiderne om rettsoppgjøret', 21 August 1945.
[123] Vaale, *Dommen til døden*, p. 72. [124] Andenæs, *Det vanskelige oppgjøret*, p. 62. [125] Ibid.
[126] 'Rettsoppgjøret', *Arbeiderbladet* (27 August 1945).
[127] 'Oppgjøret', *Dagbladet* (25 August 1945). [128] 'Rettsoppgjøret', *Friheten* (25 August 1945).
[129] RA/S-1005/A/Aa/L0004: Referat fra regjeringskonferanse, sak nr. 5, 'Oppsigelse fra 800 politifolk, tilsluttet Oslo og Aker nye Politiforening', 20 December 1945.

and the growing protests and threats of vigilante justice.[130] The calls for harsher punishment that could be heard at Youngstorget prompted jurists both inside and outside the legal apparatus to emphasise the absolute requirement for due process. Independent jurists warned early on that public sentiment should not prevail over legal principle. The tensions that had emerged since late summer and the uncompromising accompanying rhetoric led to a number of influential publications and speeches on the part of legal experts. And the state authorities, recognising the social ramifications of the trials, also began to be more concerned about their long-term effects. They began to liaise with jurists on how best to restrict the reckoning and thus some of the long-term adverse effects they might have on society.

Johannes Andenæs published an influential and highly critical series of opinion pieces on the trials in *Arbeiderbladet* in October 1945. Andenæs was often consulted by the Ministry of Justice on the trials' central legal questions, and also – perhaps problematically – assumed many different roles throughout their duration, including as judge, legal adviser, and member of various government committees. However, he also publicly voiced a number of critical opinions. In his October 1945 article series, Andenæs criticised both the official handling of the trials as well as the responses and actions of the wider public. He was particularly concerned about the departure from established legal principles that he observed in court practice during the trials' early months. He also sought to counter the calls for harsh punishment and warned of a conflation of legal doctrine and 'the opinion of the people'. As a jurist, Andenæs viewed the protests and organised calls for harsher sentences with deep suspicion and an infringement upon judicial independence. He considered it a step away from Norway's legal culture that 'some groups at protests, in public gatherings and through threats of vigilante justice try to influence the courts to make decisions that do not correspond to the court's own conclusions'.[131]

In a manner that was unusually harsh for him, Andenæs attacked the 'small people who, during the war, remained silent as mice . . . and now rush forward demanding punishment against all who have not been as infallible as themselves'.[132] He criticised the public's habit of judging court

[130] For a thorough examination of the criticism of the reckoning from within the legal profession, see: Borge and Vaale, *Grunnlovens største prøve*, pp. 130–150.

[131] Andenæs, 'Rettsoppgjøret II', *Arbeiderbladet* (16 October 1945).

[132] Andenæs, 'Rettsoppgjøret III', *Arbeiderbladet* (17 October 1945).

verdicts based on sensationalist and one-sided press coverage. Both in social and juridical terms, he thus deemed the trials deeply problematic. While he accepted that the trials were necessary, he characterised them early on as a tragedy, 'an image of human weakness and delusion'.[133] He repeatedly reiterated his criticisms of the scope the trials had reached. For this he blamed the government-in-exile and 'Home Front propaganda' during the war, which, in his view, had been motivated by the wish to generate a deterrent effect and further opposition against the Nazi occupiers. This kind of rhetoric, Andenæs argued, had generated a culture of hatred and suspicion among the population that was difficult to transcend following the liberation. Moreover, the trials had allowed for an easy identification with the resistance and had fostered a myth that a majority of Norwegians had been active opponents of the occupation.[134]

In many ways this series of articles, written less than six months after the liberation, foreshadowed the social problems that lay ahead and that would haunt Norwegian society for decades. And Andenæs was far from the only critic to come forward. Jon Skeie, a professor of criminal law at the University in Oslo, published a pamphlet on the treason decrees and criticised many aspects of them, in particular the law-making powers claimed by the exile government, which he deemed unconstitutional.[135] He argued that the pre-war Criminal Code would have sufficed for the reckoning and provided a much higher degree of legal certainty. Justice Bjarne Didriksen, a judge at the Oslo District Court, likewise published a pamphlet on the legal and social challenges of the reckoning, criticising in particular its broad scope.[136] Given the emphasis on legal form that the government sought to convey during the reckoning, it had to take such criticisms seriously. From late 1945 onwards, we can observe a more deliberate presentation of the trials as in alignment with the rule of law. Legal principles also came to significantly shape official decision-making in the trials' administration.

As it turned its attention more to the legal-technical representation of the trials, the government also grew increasingly concerned over the hostile climate NS members were facing in society. The liberation period was, for many reasons, socially traumatic. NS members faced exclusion at work and

[133] Andenæs, 'Rettsoppgjøret I', *Arbeiderbladet* (15 October 1945).
[134] Andenæs, 'Rettsoppgjøret III', *Arbeiderbladet* (17 October 1945).
[135] Jon Skeie, *Landssvik* (Oslo: Norli, 1945).
[136] Bjarne Didriksen, *Gjenopprettelsen av landssvikerne: et aktuelt sosialt spørsmål*, Sosiale Småskrifter (Oslo: Norli, 1945).

in their private lives.[137] The strikes across the country were one of the most acute reflections of this, where '[i]f an employer wanted to keep an NS-man, he usually had to choose between him and the rest of his work-force'.[138] But these animosities affected all aspects of public life. The families of NS members were frequently frozen out of their social environments.[139] On one occasion, a housing company sent a request to the Ministry of Social Affairs insisting that it was necessary that 'treacherous' tenants be removed from its properties in the interest of all other tenants and inquiring what provisions could serve as a legal basis for such a measure.[140] Business relations with individuals and companies accused of treason were frequently severed.[141] Across businesses and organisations, private purges were held in an ad hoc matter and with hardly any governmental oversight.

The government soon launched a number of initiatives to counter the long-term collateral damage to society. In particular, it intensified its focus on the long-term reintegration of NS prisoners into society. On 16 October 1945, it established a 'Study and Work Committee for the Traitor Problem'.[142] The Committee held meetings throughout the autumn and investigated the socio-economic and professional backgrounds as well as the mental state of individuals under investigation for treason, before proposing a variety of measures for their successful reintegration into the workforce.[143] The fact that the government formed such a

[137] Baard Herman Borge, 'Forsoningen som uteble. Norges oppgjør med landssvikerne', in Bård-Anders Andreassen and Elin Skaar, *Forsoning eller rettferdighet?* (Oslo: Cappelen, 1998), pp. 204–234.

[138] Andenæs, *Det vanskelige oppgjøret*, p. 64. [139] Ibid.

[140] RA/S-3212/D/De/L0302: Letter by residents to ..., 14 June 1945; letter from ... to the Ministry of Justice, 10 July 1945; both referenced in undated departmental memo 'Landssvikfamilier i leigårde'.

[141] See for example RA/S-3212/D/De/L0302: Letter from ... to the Ministry of Justice, 10 January 1947, and letter from the Ministry of Justice to ..., 16 April 1947; the *Statens Kornforretning* had inquired about the legal right to sever business relations with millers investigated for treason; in its response, the Ministry of Justice stated that a treason conviction could not be a decisive element in terminating a contract, unless there were significant circumstances such as a prison term that rendered the miller unable to fulfil his contractual obligations. Such reservations towards sentenced 'traitors' would continue to be widespread throughout the following years.

[142] Officially appointed on 16 October 1945; RA/S-1005/D/Db/L0131: Note to the Foreign Ministry, 16 October 1945.

[143] RA/S-1005/D/Db/L0131: 'Landssvikerne som sosialt problem', memo, Jens Chr. Hauge, 4 September 1945; RA/S-1005/D/Db/L0131: Informal meeting notes of meeting on 1 October 1945; 'Referat fra møte i "Koordinasjonsutvalget"', 15 October 1945; letter from the Committee to the Ministry of Justice, 16 October 1945; letter from Prime Minister's Office to the Ministry of Justice, 16 October 1945 entitled 'Ad: Mentalundersøkelse av landssvikere i fengsel'; see also report by ... of 15 January 1946 on 'Landssvikerutvalget'.

committee within six months of the liberation, and listened to experts on the topic, shows that it recognised the problems the large scope of the trials might result in. It also shows that, far from cracking down on everyone accused of collaboration, it sought to carefully balance competing interests within society. Unlike some perceptions that reigned during the first year of the liberation, the government was therefore not engaged in unreflective retribution, but sought to bring into an equilibrium competing social interests without making itself vulnerable.

In order to pre-empt some of the adverse effects of the trials on society, but also to ensure that institutions would not be overburdened and the reckoning could be seen through, the DPP and Ministry of Justice in November 1945 announced that cases would not be brought against a number of individuals who had been involved only in lesser offences. This included individuals who had been under the age of 18 at the time of the offence, 'passive' NS members who during the war had conducted acts to the benefit of the nation, and members of the NS youth organisations.[144] The necessary legal bases to limit the scope of prosecutions in this way had already been included in the 1944 Treason Decree, but it was unclear up until this point whether the DPP would make use of them. Most importantly, the DPP stated that passive NS members who had signed up 'out of weakness or foolishness' and who had left the party before the issuing of the 'Quisling Decree' on 22 January 1942 would also not be prosecuted.[145] With regard to culpability, NS members with good education and in higher positions within the party would ultimately end up receiving higher sentences than those with less privileged backgrounds.[146] The prosecution of 'Germany workers' was largely reduced to those who had engaged in activities important for warfare, those who sought profit, including so-called *fem-mannslag*: workers who had collectively offered themselves to work for the Germans.[147] The actions of the hundreds of thousands of individuals who had carried out work for the German

[144] RA/S-1043_1/J/Jb/Jba/L0003: Copy of 'Rundskriv L. nr. 50 fra Riksadvokaten' on organisations 'Sol og Arbeidet' and membership in 'N.S.U.F', 15 November 1945; Lars-Erik Vaale, 'Myndighetene og NS-barnene i Norge etter 1945', Report, Ministry of Labour and Social Inclusion, 16 February 2023.

[145] RA/S-1043_1/J/Jb/Jba/L0003: Copy of 'Rundskriv L. nr. 52 fra Riksadvokaten' on passive NS membership, 19 November 1945. It is important to note that while these cases would probably not have led to a court ruling anyhow, the very state of being under investigation for treason could have such grave consequences for individuals that this was a significant measure in reducing the social ramifications of the treason trials.

[146] RA/S-1042/D/Dh/L0010: 'Notat for Statsråd Gundersen' by J. Chr Mellbye to Justice Minister Gundersen, January 1946.

[147] Justis- og Politidepartementet, *Om landssvikoppgjøret*, pp. 369–370.

occupiers, on the other hand, were not considered sufficiently reprehensible to warrant prosecution.

Overall, we see a shift from triumphalist coverage towards scepticism in the opinions voiced on the trials from August 1945 onwards. Jurists in particular started contributing to the public debate. And the tension between the 'ice front' and those taking a more cautious stance deepened throughout the autumn. To the Ministry of Justice and the DPP, this posed a dilemma. They took the objections made by jurists seriously, and began to engage more deeply with the social consequences of the reckoning. But at the same time, the strikes and protests of summer 1945 had visibly affirmed the social expectations that the trials be carried out in accordance with the wartime framework. To rebut such calls for violence, the state institutions had to emphasise that the state at all times held the prerogative over punishment. To this end they repeatedly emphasised that the reckoning was being carried out in accordance with the law and with wartime promises. But this in turn meant that they had to take seriously the criticism of expert jurists that the legal bases did not satisfy demands for the rule of law. This fundamental tension between the demands of the law and broader political and societal demands would occupy the institutions in charge of the trials for the remainder of their duration.

3.6 A New Parliament Is Elected

On 8 October 1945, elections for the new *Storting* were held, the first in liberated Norway. Those charged with treason had been stripped of their right to vote in these elections.[148] The parties had run their election campaigns on the basis of the Joint Party Programme (*Fellesprogrammet*), which emphasised unity and focused on the particular tasks of rebuilding the country. The treason trials did not feature as a central topic in the election campaign – possibly because they were not a matter of much dispute at that time. Instead, party programmes were concerned primarily with the nation's rebuilding. The modifications made on 3 August 1945 aside, all of the leading parties had every intent to carry out the trials in accordance with the wartime provisions. While the communist NKP pushed hardest for a speedy implementation of the trials, there was never really any political competition on the matter. There was also no immediate need to appeal to suspected collaborators as a constituency, as they were ineligible to vote.[149]

[148] 'Anordning av 4. Mai 1945' and 'Tillegg til Lov om suspensjon av 4. Mai 1945'.

[149] Stortingets Kontor, *Stortingsvalget 1945, Norges Offisielle Statistikk X 132* (Oslo: Aschehoug, 1947), p. iv.

In the elections, the Labour Party won an absolute majority, securing 76 of the 150 seats in the *Storting*.[150] This cemented the position of Gerhardsen, who set out to build a Labour-only government. Oscar Christian Gundersen replaced Johan Cappelen as Minister of Justice, bringing with him a stricter attitude towards the trials than his predecessor had shown. Gundersen had spent most of the war in exile in Sweden and London. He would remain in office until 1952, overseeing much of the remainder of the treason trials. The communist NKP jumped from 0.3 per cent of votes in 1936 to 11.9 per cent in 1945, securing 11 seats, more than ever before. At that time, it was considered almost a mainstream party, and there was talk at the time of the 'two Labour Parties'.[151] *Høyre* suffered significant losses and secured 25 seats (down from 36), *Venstre* 20 (down from 23) and the Centre Party 10 (down from 18). The Christian Democratic Party saw a considerable rise and secured 8 seats (up from 2). There was a profound change in the composition of the *Storting*, with ninety-nine – two- thirds – of the *Storting*'s MPs being new to parliament.[152] Many of the new parliamentarians had served in the resistance.[153] This significantly changed body was subsequently able to neutralise the reservations of the public towards the previous *Storting*.

Gerhardsen's government put forward its declaration on 11 December.[154] In front of the *Storting*, Gerhardsen confirmed his government's plans for the treason trials, stating that they would be carried through swiftly and in accordance with 'the Norwegian people's legal consciousness and legal traditions' – a seemingly straightforward policy.[155] Notably, he added that

> The objective [of the reckoning] must be to protect society from the real enemies of the state among the traitors, and to win back all the others as useful citizens. Prison sentences and forced labour must be administrated in accordance with their core purposes, and there is to be the least possible loss of useful labour.[156]

This differentiation had become necessary, given the broad scale the reckoning had, by this point, assumed. The government had understood

[150] Ibid. [151] Reference in Edvard Bull, *Norge i den rike verden* (Oslo: Cappelen, 1979), p. 82.

[152] Tim Greve, *Det Norske storting gjennom 150 år*, Vol. 3 (Oslo: I kommisjon hos Gyldendal, 1964), p. 389.

[153] Vaale, *Dommen til døden*, p. 85.

[154] There had been significant disagreement as to when the *Storting* could be reopened: Referat fra Regjeringskonferanse 23 October 1945, where Gerhardsen stated that, if necessary, the government would form without the participation of the *Storting*, as it was of the utmost importance that the government could form.

[155] S.tid. (1945–1946), pp. 23–24. [156] Ibid.

that it could have an adverse effect on the nation's reconciliation process if the majority of sentenced collaborators were not reintegrated. The economic arguments put forward in this context can also be seen as a convenient new narrative to justify limitations to the reckoning and promote social reintegration while attempting to limit the potential public backlash this could generate.

The government's position on the trials was challenged in the 'throne speech debate' (*trontaledebatten*), the traditional opposition response to the king's speech, which was held on 14 December 1945.[157] This was the first real political test of treason trial policies for the new government. Carl Joachim Hambro of *Høyre* in particular criticised that the government plans were not sufficiently precise. His party also attacked the lack of opportunities for a formalised political debate on the trials in parliament.[158] *Høyre* was soon to become a central critic in the context of the treason trials and an advocate for adhering to the rule of law with regard to all measures. John Lyng, a representative for *Høyre* who was new to the *Storting*, became an influential figure in the post-war era. As a jurist, he had led a resistance group in Trondheim. He later fled to Sweden and was then chosen to work for the exile government in London.[159] There, he had worked for the Justice Ministry and was able to make important connections. In the new *Storting*, he was a member of the Justice Committee and he in particular became a central voice in relation to the trials, opposing the political mainstream from the outset and frequently questioning their legitimacy and purposes.[160]

Political criticisms were voiced from a range of perspectives. In the debate in December 1945, a communist representative criticised the 'lenient treatment traitors had received', adding that it had 'caused annoyance among many good Norwegians'.[161] The communists bemoaned the so-called 'campaign of pity'.[162] On the other hand, Nils Trædal, the leader of the Centre Party, expressed his scepticism from a different angle. Trædal argued against equating the actions of '15–16 year olds' to the likes of Quisling and pleaded that they be given a chance by society.[163] Nils Lavik of the *Kristelig Folkeparti*, meanwhile, cautioned that the aim of the trials should be to turn sentenced collaborators into 'good Norwegians' for the benefit of Norwegian society rather than marking them with a 'stamp of inhumanness'.[164] But even within the Labour Party, the burden of the treason trials was beginning to divide attitudes. While Justice Minister

157 Ibid., pp. 27–88. 158 Ibid., pp. 28–35, at p. 35.
159 Roar Langslet, *John Lyng: samarbeidets arkitekt* (Oslo: Cappelen, 1989), pp. 50–51.
160 Ibid., p. 68. 161 S.tid., (1945–1946), p. 38. 162 Ibid., p. 39. 163 Ibid., p. 51.
164 Ibid., p. 54.

Gundersen sought to mediate between different positions, Sverre Løberg – a Labour Party hardliner on the treason trials – criticised the courts' handling of economic collaboration, which he labelled 'the most disgusting type' of treason, concluding that 'faith in our legal apparatus is weakened when one sees verdicts that decidedly torpedo the people's legal attitudes, which should instead form the basis of the entire reckoning'.[165] He also attacked some of his fellow parliamentarians harshly, arguing that a mild line would make the treason trials 'assume the character of a pure parody'.[166] Such statements point to the way in which the debate around the trials was becoming increasingly polarised.

Different party positions were thus becoming more apparent by the end of 1945, as well as differences within parties. Pressure on the government was mounting from all across the political spectrum. This, in combination with the growing differentiation of debate in wider society, made it increasingly difficult to manoeuvre the trials. Justice Minister Gundersen addressed the various criticisms during the December 1945 debate, stating that 'the government obviously understands that the treason trials need to be made the topic of a broad and in-depth debate in the *Storting*'. He reiterated that 'the enormous restructuration process we are facing can only be solved if its broader direction is firmly anchored in the legal attitudes of the people, and this connection will have to be made by the *Storting*'.[167] In a desperate attempt to convey a sense of political cohesion, Gundersen argued that there was probably a degree of misunderstanding among the members of the *Storting* and that, in reality, the trials rested on a profound political consensus.[168] He then urged the chamber not to create 'unnecessary unrest' around the topic and stated that 'a broad debate at this time would be more incoherent and arbitrary than defensible'.[169]

But deep down, Gundersen was beginning to sense that the fraught debate, in combination with the distinct institutional challenges the trials presented, posed a far-reaching challenge to the state authorities. The government could not afford a full debate on the trials within the *Storting* if this would risk exposing fundamental disagreement among politicians on the matter. The optimism that a swift reckoning would lead to a 'return to normality' and unite the nation had begun to fade. By 1 January 1946, only 8 per cent of cases against collaborators had been decided on by the courts. The trials were beginning to feel like a burden rather than a symbol of liberation, misplaced in scope and time as the distance to the occupation period grew.

[165] Ibid., p. 84. [166] Ibid., p. 85. [167] Ibid., p. 62. [168] Ibid. [169] Ibid.

CHAPTER 4

Adjudication

Bringing Collaborators to Justice, 1946–1947

This chapter analyses the ways in which the government sought to respond to the mounting administrative and political pressures on the treason trials in 1946 and 1947 and how the courts adjudicated in a wide range of offences, gradually producing a vast corpus of verdicts against the backdrop of a rapidly changing political climate. By this stage, the legal apparatus was struggling with the workload and the trials were being subjected to increasing social and political scrutiny, with many groups now cautioning that the trials were too harsh. But these pressures, coupled with the need for legal consistency, produced an enormous dilemma. While the government proposed various ad hoc measures to accelerate the trials and limit the scope of individuals liable for prosecution, it was reluctant to change the parameters of the trials through a larger legislative measure. The reasons for this were twofold: firstly, the Ministry of Justice and the Director of Public Prosecutions (DPP) had a genuine concern for legal principle and believed that the law should be applied equally throughout the treason trials. But secondly, the trials had also become closely linked to the authorities behind them, and any changes to existing policies could have formed the basis for political attacks. In this context, the invocation of the 'equality principle' also became a helpful shield against criticism of existing policies. When a series of publications began to challenge the official handling of the occupation legacy, the DPP and the Ministry of Justice closely monitored their authors in an attempt to contain criticism, highlighting the perceived threat from such publications. The overall policy in 1946 and 1947 therefore became concerned with prolonging the use of the original legal framework of the trials and presenting the trials as a success, despite increasing opposition to the original legal framework both in parliament and among the wider public. At the same time, the courts adjudicated the main bulk of the cases, and sought to develop a coherent sentencing practice. The complex balancing act between legal consistency and political and societal change, this chapter argues, reflected how the initial consensus around the trials was beginning to collapse.

4.1 Limited Resources

Six months on from the liberation, on 8 November 1945, DPP Sven Arntzen gave a speech on Norwegian radio regarding the status of the treason trials. Arntzen expressed some new estimates for when the trials might be concluded, stating that

> If we continue to work for another six months the way we have worked for the past two months … I believe that we will have come far enough to be able to see the end. … This is also necessary. For the treason trials are a matter we need to bring to a conclusion. They are not an end in themselves, but a necessary cleansing process before Norwegian society can return to a state of normality.[1]

The speech was an attempt to ease intensifying criticism of the trials, in particular of what was felt by many to be their frustratingly slow progress. Once the Supreme Court had approved the wartime decrees that formed the legal basis of the trials in August and September that year, the legal and administrative apparatus had begun working at full capacity to investigate and bring to trial those accused of collaborating with the enemy. Optimistic estimates on behalf of the government had been that the trials would be over within a year of the liberation.[2] However, it had soon become clear that the decrees would encompass many more individuals than the resistance and exile government had envisaged. Over the course of 1945 and 1946, the authorities therefore repeatedly had to modify their estimates as to when the trials would be brought to a close.

In seeking to address the backlog of pending cases, the Ministry of Justice, on the suggestion of the DPP, proposed an accelerated sentencing procedure in November 1945, which would allow prison sentences of up to one year to be handed down by executive decree rather than through a court verdict.[3] The DPP estimated that the bulk of cases would, in fact, receive a prison sentence of less than a year, meaning that this measure could lead to a considerable acceleration of the trials 'as a whole'.[4] In a letter sent to the Ministry on 26 October 1945, the DPP stressed that this would be in the best interest of those awaiting trial, as 'on a daily basis

[1] RA/S-1558/D/L0020: 'Rettsoppgjøret inntil nå', undated manuscript for DPP's speech on the status of the treason trials.

[2] Justis- og Politidepartementet, *Om landssvikoppgjøret* (Gjøvik: Mariendal, 1962), p. 454.

[3] Ot.prp. nr. 1 (1945–1946).

[4] Letter printed in Ot.prp. nr. 1 (1945–1946), p. 2.

messages [were being] sent to the prosecution authorities describing how crushing the long period of uncertainty and the waiting time for a trial were'.[5] Executive decrees (*forelegg*) issued by the administration were already common practice in the context of lesser offences which involved a monetary fine only. In relation to prison sentences, however, they were a novelty and a decided departure from the principle that only a judicial verdict could form the basis for imprisonment. The exile government's law committee had opposed a similar proposal by the Home Front during the occupation.[6] The right to be heard by a judge in court had up until that point – as in most Western legal cultures – been a fundamental principle of Norway's legal tradition and enshrined in § 96 of its Constitution.

But despite previous concerns, the Ministry of Justice managed to secure full cabinet support for the proposal.[7] On 30 November 1945, the Ministry put forward its proposal for a change to procedural law in criminal cases. One of its central justifications for the accelerated procedures bill was that sufficient judicial precedent now existed to ensure a consistent application of the law even without a court trial – an entirely different situation, the Ministry argued, to that immediately following the liberation.[8] Because many cases were so similar in nature, there was little risk of legal uncertainty. In the bill, the government also emphasised the detrimental effect that delayed trials had on prisoners and their families. A prolonged waiting period, the Ministry argued, ultimately jeopardised the long-term aim of the social and economic reintegration of collaborators into society.[9] Primarily, however, the accelerated procedures bill was guided by the overwhelming need to bring the trials to a swift conclusion.[10] By this time, the *speed* with which the trials would be implemented had become the

[5] Letter from the DPP to the Ministry of Justice, 26 October 1945; printed in Ot.prp. nr. 1 (1945–1946), p. 2.

[6] The report by the Schjødt Committee had during the occupation proposed that a maximum of *three* months' imprisonment should be handed down by executive decree: RA/S-3212/D/De/L0299: Report delivered to the Ministry of Justice by the Committee appointed on 8 September 1944, 26 September 1944. The main objection at the time was, however, that it was not necessary.

[7] RA/S-1005/A/Aa/L0004: Referat fra regjeringskonferanse, sak nr. 1, 'Ot.prp. om vedtagelse av frihetsstraff ved forelegg', 27 November 1945.

[8] Ot.prp. nr. 1 (1945–1946), p. 2. [9] Ibid.

[10] The Ministry was of course aware of the constitutional problems surrounding the bill, but justified these on the basis of the extraordinary circumstances the treason trials constituted and the relatively mild sentences that could be expected in the cases in question; RA/S-3212/B/Ba/L0046: 'Ot.prp. nr.1 (1945–46) og grunnlovens § 96', memo, Legal Department of the Ministry of Justice, 10 January 1946 (presumably wrongly dated as 1945); it is interesting to note that Gundersen estimated that there would be opposition to the bill, and therefore asked other cabinet members to join the meeting; RA/S-1005/A/Aa/L0004: Referat fra regjeringskonferanse, sak nr. 6, 'Proposisjon om frihetsstraff ved forelegg', 17 January 1946.

overwhelming concern of authorities: if they fell short, a significant loss in political popularity and arguably even political upheaval could be the consequence. The Ministry was aware of the constitutional concerns, but in an internal memo had concluded:

> It is not possible to determine an absolute defining line for that which is justifiable from a constitutional perspective. In making an assessment, the following will have to be prioritised: that due to the actions of traitors, our society today faces a legal reckoning of a dimension that is unprecedented in our history.[11]

By early 1946, attitudes towards the trials had become increasingly polarised, making it almost impossible for the government to secure the near-universal support for which it had hoped after the liberation. The fact that the trials could not be brought to completion within the original time frame led to frustration and suspicion in many camps. In the print media, attacks were hurled at the authorities regarding their handling of the trials.[12] Those favouring a harsh reckoning – in particular the 'ice front' press – feared that the trials would be watered down as the distance to the occupation period grew. Those in favour of a more lenient reckoning pointed to the social and economic implications for treason suspects who had spent months awaiting their trial, and cautioned that the trials 'should not be made permanent'.[13] All participants in this debate perceived time to be of the essence. What purpose did the trials serve if they did not follow immediately after the collapse of the occupying regime, allowing society to move on after their completion? What would be gained, others asked, by keeping treason suspects out of the workforce for so long, challenging their social reintegration? Although there were select calls to cut back significantly on the scope of the trials, such proposals were not given much attention by the wider press or the authorities in charge. Following the strikes and protests of the previous summer, the Ministry of Justice knew that any 'softening' of the trials could leave them politically damaged. The emphasis was therefore placed on increasing the speed of the trials, without reducing their overall scope and ambition.

11 Ibid., 'Ot.prp. nr. 1 (1945–46) og grunnlovens § 96'.

12 See for example 'Landssvikoppgjøret – noen tall', *Morgenbladet* (28 January 1946); 'Rettsoppgjøret', *Arbeiderbladet* (9 February 1946); 'Landssvikerne skal inn i produktivt arbeid', *Arbeiderbladet* (16 March 1946); 'Tilbake til samfunnet', *Aftenposten* (17 January 1946).

13 'Landssvikerproblemet', *Aftenposten* (19 March 1946).

At the same time, the government had an increasing regard for the social impact of the process.[14] The Working Committee formed in November 1945 on the long-term reintegration of sentenced collaborators presented its first reports to the government in January 1946. Some parts of these reports painted a bleak picture. In particular, the extended periods that many collaborators spent outside their communities, in combination with the stigmatisation they often faced upon their release, made successful reintegration challenging. The Ministry of Justice argued that the majority of collaborators were comparably high skilled and thus valuable to the workforce and society. It therefore proposed a number of measures to be adopted in work camps – such as vocational training sessions and educational measures – that would ease the return of convicts into society. Sentenced collaborators were to be separated from 'ordinary' criminals, and collaborators themselves were to be divided according to the gravity of their crimes. For those deemed to be 'smaller criminals', this was intended to prevent an 'unfortunate influence' by 'more dangerous prisoners'.[15] But critics were becoming suspicious of the beneficial treatment that they felt many sentenced collaborators were receiving.[16] Further strikes and threats of strikes in January 1946 signalled how reluctant large segments of the workforce were to receive investigated or sentenced collaborators back into their communities. If the authorities wanted to avoid further criticism,

[14] As we have seen, the first committees had formed as early as 1945 to look at the challenges of reintegration into the workforce. The Ministry of Work (*Arbeidsdirektoratet*) had long been monitoring the transition of sentenced *landssvikers* back into society and liaised with a number of employment and industry organisations on the matter; see RA/S-1005/D/Db/L0131: Letter from *Arbeidsdirektoratet*, 22 November 1945; RA/S-1042/D/Dh/L0009: Letter from *Arbeidsdirektoratet* to the Ministry of Justice, 7 January 1946. In April 1946, an agreement was reached between the Norwegian Employers' Association (*Norsk Arbeidsgiverforening*) and the Norwegian Confederation of Trade Unions (*Arbeidernes faglige Landsorganisasjon*) on the recommendation of the Ministry of Social Affairs on guidelines concerning the reinclusion of sentenced collaborators into the workforce: RA/S-1042/D/Dh/L0004: 'Pressemelding av 11 april 1946 fra Sosialdepartementet: Tidligere N.S. medlemmer og arbeidslivet', 11 April 1946; this was later (autumn 1946) expanded so as to include all professional societies: RA/S-1042/D/Dh/L0009, 'Landssvikernes sosiale gjeninnpasning', Ministry of Justice, February 1947; RA/S-1042/D/Dh/L0009: Untitled memo, Ministry of Justice, 12 January 1946; RA/S-1042/D/Dh/L0009: 'Hva skal følge etter domstolenes oppgjør med landssvikerne?', Memo, Ministry of Justice, 4 February 1947; RA/S-1042/D/Dh/L0009, 'Arbeidsformidlig og forsorgeunderstøttelse av tidligere N.S.-medlemmer', memo, Department of Labour (*Arbeidsdirektoratet*), 2 December 1946; in October 1948, the Ministry of Labour came to the conclusion that, statistically, the majority of sentenced collaborators succeeded in returning into the workforce: Ot.prp. nr. 14 (1949), p. 3.

[15] RA/S-1042/D/Dh/L0009: Untitled memo, Ministry of Justice, 12 January 1946.

[16] RA/S-1042/D/Dh/L0010: 'Oversikt over planleggingen av arbeidet med landssvikfangene', memo, Johannes Halvorsen, 12 July 1946; RA/S-1042/D/Dh/L0009: Untitled memo, Ministry of Justice, 12 January 1946; RA/S-1042/D/Dh/L0009: 'Om fullbyrdelsen av frihetsstraff i landssviksaker', memo 1 February 1949.

much therefore rested on the *Storting* passing the bill on accelerated sentencing procedures.

4.2 Parliamentary Opposition

It took until 7 February 1946 for the accelerated procedures bill to reach parliament. By that time, Minister of Justice Oscar Gundersen had to concede that the progress made in the trials was not what authorities had expected at the end of 1945.[17] In his speech before parliament, Gundersen pointed out that the legal and administrative apparatus had to handle around six to seven times the pre-war average of cases and was working at full capacity. He admitted that he could no longer provide a specific date for when the trials would be concluded, but added that it would certainly not happen by the end of the current year; more likely sometime in 1947.[18] Gundersen knew that this admission was going to be widely criticised. The bottleneck of the legal system was beginning to pose a serious threat to the political success of trials, the implementation of which was so closely tied to the momentum and consensus of the liberation.

Despite its aim of addressing some of the criticisms waged against the treason trials, the Ministerial proposition had come under sustained attack in the press. Some of the more moderate 'silk front' newspapers pointed out that the proposed accelerated sentencing procedures constituted an encroachment upon constitutional rights, first and foremost § 96, which stipulated that no one could be sentenced without a judgment.[19] On the other hand, sections of the 'ice front' press were critical of the proposal on the suspicion that treason detainees would benefit from the secrecy of administrative procedures, as in the absence of a trial there would be no broader forum of social condemnation of their actions. Reducing the trials to a mere administrative procedure would remove from the wider reckoning one of its core elements: that it be conducted *publicly*. Gundersen went to some length to address these criticisms. The constitutional objections were invalid, he reasoned, for the legal principle, 'which is meant to offer protection, in reality leads to unnecessary suffering for those whom it is meant to protect'.[20] In addition, individuals would still be able to *request* a court procedure.[21] However, Gundersen also stressed that

[17] O.tid (1946), p. 44. [18] Ibid., pp. 44–45.

[19] See for example 'Fengselstraff uten dom?', *Adresseavisen* (13 December 1945); 'Oppgjør i løndom?', *Friheten* (11 January 1946); 'Forenkler rettsopgjør', *Aftenposten* (16 January 1946).

[20] O.tid. (1946), p. 46. [21] Ot.prp. nr. 1 (1945–1946), p. 2.

under no circumstances would the proposed measures lead to a milder treatment of suspected collaborators and that their names would still be disclosed to the press.[22] Gundersen argued that at all times the treason trials would be carried out in close proximity to the demands of the wider population, and that there would be no departure from the fundamental principles of the trials as agreed during the occupation. But it was clear that the widespread support Gundersen alluded to in his statements no longer existed.

The *Storting*'s new Justice Committee was deeply divided on the accelerated procedures bill. Its eight members represented a broad spectrum of attitudes. The four Labour Party representatives were Magnus Johansen, Aani Rysstadt, Leif Granli and Einar Magnus Stavang, all of whom represented a mild to moderate line.[23] In line with his party, Communist Party (NKP) deputy Kittil Berg advocated a strict line. Meanwhile, the Liberal (*Venstre*) Party representatives Ketil Skogen and Lars Ramndal were soft and moderate respectively, and the conservative *Høyre*'s John Lyng also took up a moderate position. While the majority of members voted in favour of the proposal, 'due to the extraordinary work burden that has been imposed upon the prosecution and courts in the context of the treason trials', three committee members opposed it.[24] Lyng and Stavang cautioned that 'the government bill marks such a fundamental departure from established Norwegian legal principles' that they could not grant it their assent.[25] In line with the communist press, Berg on the other hand argued that the bill would make the trials less efficient due to an absence of public scrutiny. His remarks must be seen as part of his more general protest against the official administration of the trials and what his party perceived as a softening of the overall reckoning.[26]

The split within the Justice Committee also ran through parliament more generally. Unlike previous government proposals on the trials, the accelerated procedures bill was met with considerable opposition. But criticism was not limited to the bill itself; the debate also came to revolve around the broader status of the treason trials as they stood in early 1946. Many lamented the fact that the specialised context of the bills put forward to date had made an encompassing discussion of the issues impossible; a

22 O.tid (1946), p. 46.

23 Nikolai Brandal, '"En rettsstat verdig": oppgjøret i Stortinget 1945–50', in Hans Fredrik Dahl and Øystein Sørensen (eds.), *Et rettferdig oppgjør? Rettsoppgjøret i Norge etter 1945* (Oslo: Pax Forlag, 2004), p. 82.

24 Innst. O. nr. 24 (Ot.prp. nr. 1 – 1945–1946), p. 18.

25 Ibid.

26 Brandal, '"En rettsstat verdig"', p. 55.

full debate on the trials, they insisted, was still urgently needed.[27] Justice Minister Gundersen reassured MPs that they would be given this opportunity as soon as the government presented its bill for a Treason Act.[28] In the meantime, many MPs took advantage of the accelerated procedures bill debate to reflect on the broader meaning of the trials, presenting a range of legal, pragmatic, political and ideological standpoints. The debate on the bill therefore offers an insight into wider political attitudes towards the treason trials in early 1946, nine months on from the liberation.

The accelerated procedures bill received widespread support from Labour Party and *Venstre* Party representatives, who referred to the unprecedented scope of the trials and the interests of defendants in arguing for an accelerated sentencing practice.[29] While the NKP, following Berg's argument, generally opposed the bill on the basis that it proposed advantages which would benefit treason suspects, *Høyre*, along with members of the Christian Democratic Party (*Kristelig Folkeparti*) and the Centre Party, opposed the bill on grounds of constitutional principle.[30] Because the bill would dramatically strengthen the powers of the administration, they argued, it risked jeopardising the separation of powers. Furthermore, they opposed the idea of prison sentences being handed down 'in bulk' without an ordinary court procedure.[31] John Lyng, spokesperson of the Justice Committee and a rising star in the conservative *Høyre*, was particularly outspoken about the constitutional problems the bill raised. In what was to become a first act of party opposition in a matter relating to the treason trials, he succeeded in persuading most of his party fellows to oppose Gundersen's proposal.[32] A number of MPs argued that undermining the constitution could, in turn, undermine public trust in the treason trials as such, highlighting once again the central role that broader attitudes towards the trials played in political decision-making.[33]

Labour Party delegates rushed to support the proposal, with Magnus Johansen citing Jon Skeie, Norway's leading legal authority on criminal law, to the effect that there was no explicit constitutional provision that prevented prison sentences from being handed down by administrative

27 O.tid (1946), pp. 33, 47.

28 Ibid., p. 44; in fact, it was not until February 1947 that the promised debate was actually held.

29 Ibid., pp. 38–39.

30 However, there were hardliners and soft-liners in all of the major parties, and the opinions represented were often primarily personal ones.

31 O.tid. (1946), p. 52.

32 Hanne Marthe Narud, Knut Heidar and Tore Grønlie (eds.), *Stortingets historie 1964–2014* (Bergen: Fagbokforlaget, 2014), p. 44.

33 In particular John Lyng (*Høyre*) and Gabriel Moseid (Centre Party).

decree.[34] Rather than engaging with legal doctrine, however, most MPs rebutted the constitutional objections raised by *Høyre* by referring to the uniqueness of the treason trials and the demands and expectations of the people that they be carried through swiftly.[35] In line with this, they repeatedly cited 'practical considerations' as the primary argument for why the bill should be passed and why a loosening of ordinary criminal procedure was justified.[36] Lyng in particular opposed this pragmatic approach to the law and warned that the bill could form the basis for circumventing legal principle on a more long-term basis, creating a precedent for legal exceptions whenever the government deemed them convenient.[37] As in previous debates, this central point of disagreement was, in essence, one of conflicting temporal assumptions pertaining to the law: the question dividing parliamentarians was whether the trials should mark a return to 'ordinary' principles of constitutional law, thereby leaving the occupation years firmly behind, or whether they in fact represented a continued state of exception, thus justifying a corresponding deviation from the ordinary requirements of the rule of law. In a telling passage of his speech, Lyng argued that the treason trials were 'not the last act of the warfare which we have just brought to a conclusion, but the first act of the resurrection process in which we are now engaged'.[38] As we shall see, however, not all were convinced.

In addition to practical advantages, a core factor MPs invoked as a justification for the bill was the by-now familiar reference to the 'will of the people' and the people's 'legal attitudes'.[39] The majority's argument was that it was a collective demand of the population that the bill be implemented so that the trials could be seen through swiftly, justifying slight deviations from ordinary constitutional convention.[40] Frequent accusations of 'constitutional opportunism' or of 'firing with big cannons' were hurled at those who raised legal objections against the bill.[41] Theodor Broch, a Labour Party representative, called for 'a bit of audacity' in curtailing constitutional doctrine so that the trials could reflect the 'true' will of the people.[42] And in a more generalised attack, Sverre Løberg, a Labour Party hardliner, stated it was not the fault of the government but

[34] As Borge and Vaale have demonstrated, this rested on a selective interpretation of Skeie's arguments: Baard Herman Borge and Lars-Erik Vaale, *Grunnlovens største prøve: rettsoppgjøret etter 1945* (Oslo: Scandinavian Academic Press, 2018), pp. 209, 214.

[35] As in 1945, MPs continued to pay close attention to the press and broader attitudes towards the trials: O.tid. (1946), pp. 40, 48, 58, 62.

[36] Ibid., p. 40. [37] Ibid., p. 57. [38] Ibid. [39] Ibid., p. 62. [40] Ibid., p. 55.

[41] Ibid., pp. 41, 55, 59. [42] Ibid., p. 55.

that of 'jurists and the [silk front] press' that the trials had 'proven so disappointing'.[43] A deep scepticism of 'paragraphs' thus ran through the debate. While some criticism concerned the state of the legal apparatus and its capacity to handle the workload, most was aimed at the law as such and its shortcomings in seeing through the 'will of the people'. Undergirding these criticisms was the assumption that any reckoning is, by its very nature, political, and therefore must not be constrained too much by the law.[44]

More generally, the debate signalled a further diversification of attitudes towards the trials. By early 1946, *Nasjonal Samling* (NS) members had become more recognised as a group of fellow citizens and their ambivalent social status was both mentioned in the government bill and discussed more generally during the debate. Many of the more moderate MPs referred to the social stigma of punishment, both on suspected collaborators and their families, as well as on broader communities. Gundersen and his followers repeatedly referred to the treason 'stamp' and the harsh social condemnation many individuals had experienced.[45] The government emphasised that there were various forms and degrees of treason, a differentiation noticeably absent in earlier debates.[46] While the debates during the summer of 1945 had been guided by the trials' objective of keeping violence off the streets, now they were increasingly centred on the phases of reintegration of 'collaborators' into society once justice had been served. However, there was also significant opposition to the softening and diversification of debate on the trials. Members of the NKP in particular found the reference to detainees' welfare entirely inappropriate.[47]

As in previous debates on the trials, MPs largely followed their own consciences and attitudes, which in many cases were shaped by their own personal wartime allegiances and experiences. In early 1946 the most vocal MPs were still those on the outer ends of the opinion spectrum. The advocates of a strict reckoning continued to engage in a loaded rhetorical exchange with those in favour of a more lenient reckoning, frequently accusing them of being NS members or of having initiated a 'propaganda' machinery with the purpose of undermining the trials.[48] But, beyond this noise, moderate voices were beginning to build a platform within the political sphere on which the more binary attitudes of the immediate post-war period could be left behind.[49] The parliamentary debate on accelerated sentencing in February 1946 was the first sign that most MPs of the new

[43] Ibid., p. 47. [44] The NKP was the most outgoing on this, see for example Ibid., p. 59.
[45] Ibid., p. 46. [46] Ibid., p. 42. [47] Ibid., p. 58. [48] Ibid., pp. 37, 38, 41, 59.
[49] Ibid., p. 54.

Storting were beginning to advocate a middle-ground approach and increasingly saw the trials as a burdensome necessity to be brought to a conclusion with the fewest possible losses to the political establishment or society at large. With the notable exception of the NKP, these moderate voices could be detected in all parties, and as the distance to the occupation period grew, they gained in prominence and conferred a degree of nuance upon the debate that was previously absent.

4.3 The Limits of Free Speech

In early 1946, Jens Chr. Mellbye, a civil servant in the Ministry of Justice, noted in a memo to the Minister of Justice:

> The treason trials are followed with great interest by the entire population, and there is no shortage of criticism. On the one hand there are a large number of people who – based on the short statements in the press on verdicts in treason cases – argue that the sentencing practice is much too mild. On the other hand there is a not entirely insignificant number who believe that the practice is much too harsh, in particular against passive and minor NS-members.[50]

The tendencies that Mellbye had identified would remain true for the duration of the treason trials. Since the liberation, attitudes had diversified to a degree that almost ruled out the possibility that the government could satisfy all demands. At a time when the bulk of trials against collaborators still lay ahead, this diversification of attitudes towards the trials posed a significant threat to the public image of the project as a whole. Pressure on the Labour government was mounting not only from various political parties, but also from the wider public. Public intellectuals began to come forward, and more voices questioned whether the trials as a whole really rested on popular support. The government received an increasing number of protest letters from citizens regarding various policies of the trials.[51] At the same time, sceptics repeatedly warned of a softening. This development came at a difficult point in the treason trials: by 1 April 1946, only around 20 per cent of cases had been decided.[52] For the next eighteen months, therefore, authorities worked intensely on bring the trials to a conclusion, while hoping that their chosen course would continue to be carried by public support.

[50] RA/S-1042/D/Dh/L0010: 'Notat for Statsråd Gundersen' from J. Chr Mellbye to Justice Minister Gundersen, January 1946.

[51] See for example RA/S-1005/D/Db/L0131: Letter by . . ., 25 April 1946.

[52] Justis- og Politidepartementet, *Om landssvikoppgjøret*, p. 441.

While in 1945 criticism had mainly been restricted to legal experts, and only a select number of intellectuals had voiced their concerns publicly, in 1946 criticism of the trials became more widespread and influential. Throughout the spring of 1946, the trials came under increasing attack in a number of influential publications produced by prominent public figures. One such publication was the author Marta Steinsvik's 'Frank Statements' (*Frimodige Ytringer*), which resulted in the first major public scandal involving the trials.[53] Steinsvik's motivations for criticising the trials were manifold. They were guided in part by her Christian thinking as well as by a conviction that a failure to treat those accused of treason humanely would lead to social conflict in future.[54] However, her political position – including her proximity to radical-conservative and antisemitic circles – were further factors. Steinsvik was never a member of the NS, but close to the Christian-corporatist 'Society Party' (*Samfundspartiet*) and as we have seen, she had frequently voiced antisemitic ideas ahead of the war. Steinsvik had been contacted by a number of prisoners and their relatives, who reported that various forms of maltreatment had taken place in detention camps for those accused of collaboration in the summer of 1945. *Frimodige Ytringer* contained a long list of accusations of inhumane prison conditions and the mistreatment of suspected collaborators during the early months of the liberation.[55] At that time, prisons had lacked basic resources and prisoners' calorie intake was well below subsistence levels. This in itself was no surprise. Having just come out of the German occupation, the country had undergone significant administrative reorganisation and the occupation period had left prisons in a desolate condition. Upon liberation, these prisons were filled to many times their ordinary capacity with treason suspects.

But Steinsvik was also able to draw more widespread attention to the direct maltreatment of prisoners by prison guards that had occurred in the summer of 1945.[56] Select reports on this topic had already been published in the press during the summer months of 1945, but at the time they had

[53] Marta Steinsvik, *Frimodige Ytringer* (Oslo: Private Publisher, 1946); the term roughly translates as 'frank statements' and is a term from § 100 of the Norwegian Constitution (Freedom of Expression); the term literally means 'free and courageous statements', and refers to statements that are deemed to be controversial.

[54] Ingerid Hagen, *Oppgjørets time* (Oslo: Spartacus, 2009), p. 23.

[55] Hardly any publishing house at the time would have published such a book, the risk being deemed too high: Henrik G. Bastiansen and Hans Fredrik Dahl, *Ytringsfriheten i Norge i det 20. århundre* (Ytringsfrihetskommisjonen, 1999), p. 70.

[56] On the treatment of prisoners following the liberation, see Trond Risto Nilssen and Jon Reitan, *Legacies of the Nazi Camps in Norway: Falstad 1941–49* (Vienna: LIT Verlag, 2020), pp. 157–187, 199–207.

failed to attract much interest.[57] Few at the time considered the welfare of treason prisoners a subject of much importance, and detainees and their support groups lacked any meaningful platform on which to express their protest.[58] By 1946, however, this had changed. Steinsvik's book was discussed extensively in the spring of 1946 and sold around 2,000 copies. Not all celebrated her revelations. The political climate remained hostile to anyone who dared to call the trials into question, and in the 'ice front' press Steinsvik's publication was initially brushed away as the utterings of a 'hysterical' or 'insane and paranoid' woman.[59] But Steinsvik continued to confront politicians on the matter and distributed her book to MPs and select officials, including the DPP. Some of the instances of maltreatment she outlined were in fact so horrific that authorities could not ignore them. Fearing that Steinsvik's revelations might jeopardise the perception of the trials as a whole, the government resolved to launch an investigation.[60] While the investigation found many of Steinsvik's claims to be true, the Ministry of Justice and the DPP sought to downplay its findings. The instances of maltreatment were explained on the basis that some prison guards – many of whom had been members of the resistance and had received only minimal training – would have had an understandable desire to retaliate against their former oppressors. The investigation did, however, lead to a number of court cases against former prison guards and an increased scrutiny of prison conditions.[61] The decision to review cases shows that the trials were coming under pressure. Citizens were beginning to hold authorities accountable for transgressions of prisoners' rights. And the official narrative that the trials centred on adherence to legal principles meant that official action was necessary.

Steinsvik was not the only critic to put public pressure on authorities. In 1947, Eystein Poulsen, a pastor who frequently criticised the trials in the press, published a pamphlet summarising his objections to the ways in which the trials were being carried out.[62] Odd Einarson, a well-known

[57] 'Rettsstaten på glid?', *Aftenposten* (2 July 1945) – a collaborationist police officer was placed under such severe exemplary punishment that he attempted suicide; 'Forholdene på Ilebu', *Abeiderbladet* (5 July 1945); Johan Scharffenberg, 'Rettsstatens prinsipper', *Arbeiderbladet* (25 August 1945).

[58] This would, in fact, remain the case throughout the trials: Bastiansen and Dahl, *Ytringsfriheten i Norge i det 20. århundre*, p. 72.

[59] 'Marta Steinsvik sinnssyk, mener Scharffenberg', *Verdens Gang* (18 September 1946); 'Dagens debatt', *Verdens Gang* (20 September 1946).

[60] RA/S-1005/A/Aa/L0004: Referat fra Regjeringskonferanse, sak nr. 6, 'Vanskeligheter på Ilebu', 28 May 1946.

[61] RA/S-1555/D/L0039: Folder 'Mishandling av landssvikfanger'.

[62] Eystein Poulsen, *Den nådeløse rettferdighet: betraktninger omkring rettsoppgjøret* (Oslo: Logos forlag, 1947).

caricaturist, was critical early on of what he deemed to be victor's justice, turning his attention in particular to the one-sided opinion represented by the 'ice front' press. He launched a magazine that ran by the name 'The Troll's Mirror' (*Trollspeilet*), which contained revealing caricatures on the broader political culture surrounding the trials, inspired in style by the French nineteenth-century caricaturist Honoré Daumier (see Figure 4.1). According to the cynical review of the NKP organ *Friheten*, this 'strange magazine' propagated 'mildness against traitors on the basis of Christian charity'. Einarson's publication, it concluded, was part of the 'campaign of pity', presenting the same old arguments in a 'clumsy and tasteless form'.[63] 'The Troll's Mirror', however, struck a nerve, and soon reached more than 20,000 issues, causing some unease among the authorities in charge of the trials.[64] When, for unknown reasons, the main Norwegian magazine distributor *Narvesen* abruptly stopped selling the magazine in spring 1946,[65] Einarson decided to launch a new magazine with the writer and activist Toralv Fanebust. Appearing in spring 1946, they called their magazine '§ 100': a reference to the constitutional guarantee of freedom of speech. Fanebust and Einarson were intent on criticising both the trials and the powerful men behind them, and often deployed a harsh and uncompromising rhetoric.[66] In September 1946, the DPP requested an investigation into both magazines, but the police concluded that it provided no basis for legal proceedings.[67] Nevertheless, a Labour Party organ concluded that 'the bell is tolling for "§ 100" and "Trollspeilet"'.[68] And indeed, typesetters soon refused to publish the magazine for fear of legal consequences.[69] But the public criticisms launched against the course of the trials by figures like Einarson nevertheless proved damaging for the authorities' image. In their wake, one newspaper even went as far as to proclaim that treason trials had reached their 'Stalingrad'.[70]

63 'I Damsleths fotefar', *Friheten* (4 September 1945).

64 Eldar Einarson and Beate Straume (eds.), *Karikaturtegneren Einarson: varmefront* (Oslo: Damm, 1988), p. 77.

65 Einarson accused Bishop Berggrav of having been behind this measure; Berggrav was widely criticised in *Trollspeilet*. It is more likely, however, that distributors did not want to risk becoming criminally liable for disseminating libellous publications.

66 Hagen, *Oppgjørets time*, pp. 74–75.

67 'Ingen påtale mit "Pgr. 100" og "Trollspeilet"', *Morgenbladet* (7 September 1946).

68 'Klokken klemter for "§ 100" og "Trollspeilet"', *Halden Arbeiderblad* (7 September 1946).

69 RA/S-3212/D/De/L0051/0001: 'Typografenes aksjon mot "Samfundsliv" og "§ 100"', Note to Minister Gundersen, 21 February 1947. The memo discussed the boycott in relation to freedom of speech and concluded that given the 'evidently' criminal nature of the magazines, the typesetters' actions were justified.

70 'Snyltere på pressefriheten', *Morgenbladet* (12 September 1945).

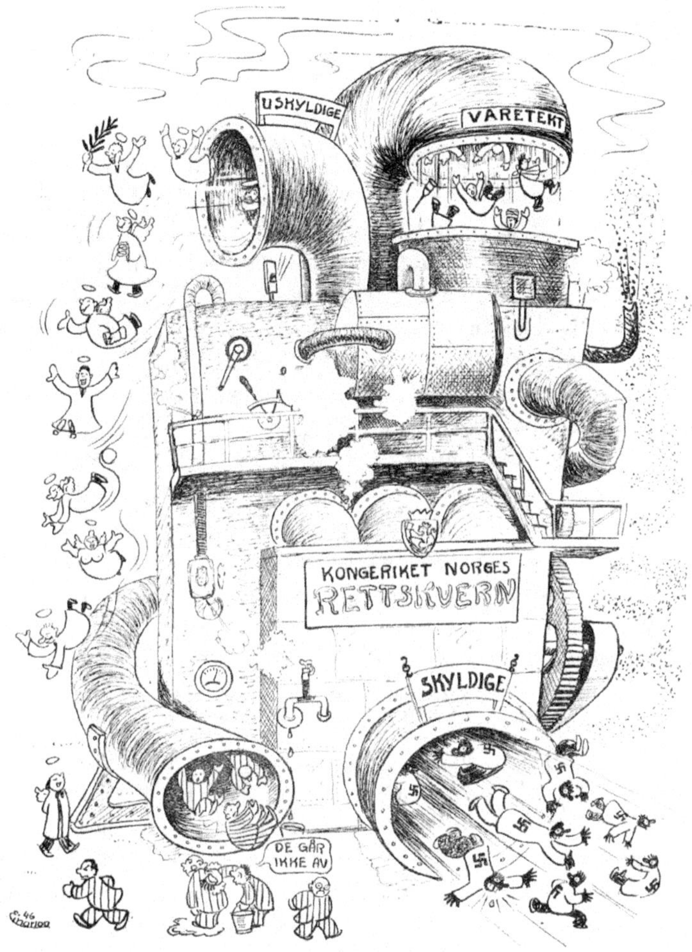

Figure 4.1 'Kongeriket Norges Rettskvern' (The Kingdom of Norway's legal mill), sketch by Odd Einarson, 1946.

The criticisms of the trials put forward by Einarson and Fanebust were often closely interwoven with personal attacks on the former Home Front leaders and members of the exile government who were now in charge of administering the trials.[71] Much criticism was one-sided and employed strong language. This provided the authorities with a ground for attack, because some of the statements could be deemed libellous under Norwegian criminal law. The DPP and the Justice Ministry closely monitored these publications, and in 1947 took actions against them, prosecuting Fanebust for libel after he had accused DPP Sven Arntzen of having acted as an informant during the occupation against an individual whom he failed to realise was a member of the resistance.[72] But it was not the reputation of individuals alone that provided the impetus for legal action in this case. Attacks on the trials were perceived by extension as attacks on the legitimacy of Norway's newly reformed political institutions. Political legitimacy rested as much on the implementation of wartime promises as it did on the immaculate pedigrees of those in power.[73] Any threats to the individuals in charge therefore threatened the project as a whole, and with it the very authority of the post-war government. The fact that the DPP was prepared to take legal action against critics of the trials highlights how closely they had become tied to the integrity and legitimacy of Norway's post-war leaders.

In parallel, calls for moderation continued to be mocked by 'ice front' representatives, who took great pleasure in attacking the 'campaign for pity' they accused their 'silk front' opponents of launching. While attitudes were diversifying, the 'ice front' remained hostile and sought to 'ridicule the spokespersons for moderation in the trials'.[74] In the early post-war period, the term 'silk front' in fact became such an integral part of political debate that it served as the basis for a popular sketch by comedian Leif Juster, in which he sang that 'Mr Silk is on the loose to have the traitors released'.[75] Public critics who called for leniency, such as Johan Scharffenberg, Marta Steinsvik and Odd Einarson, all faced significant

[71] Bishop Berggrav, too, came under frequent attack for his tendency to seek a central role in in the post-war era: Edwin Robertson, *Bishop of the Resistance: The Life of Eivind Berggrav* (Haddington: Handsel Press, 2001), p. 150.

[72] Fanebust had received a hint from a former *Sipo* member (Gard Holtskog); St.meld. nr. 64. (1950), p. 18.

[73] Arntzen stepped down as DPP on 1 September 1946. His official reason was that the position was much less profitable than his private law practice; RA/S-1005/A/Aa/L0004: Referat av Regjeringskonferanse, sak nr. 3, 'Riksadvokatembetet', 14 May 1946.

[74] Andenæs, *Det vanskelige oppgjøret*, p. 61.

[75] Leif Juster, 'Herr Silke': www.youtube.com/watch?v=PbAMF8NuOxs, last accessed 27 May 2022.

opposition from the 'ice front'. The editor of *Arbeiderbladet*, Martin Tranmæl, whose strong position on the trials was widely known, for example refused to allow Johan Scharffenberg to continue publishing in the Labour Party organ.[76] And when a number of bishops sent a letter to the Ministry of Justice in November 1946 demanding the release of treason prisoners on bail and advocating wider amnesties, they were mocked as 'silk bishops' by large parts of the Oslo press.[77] The 'ice front' papers thus continued their uncompromising stance towards advocates of a more lenient reckoning.

But it is important to understand that the measures taken against those advocating a more moderate line on the trials were impelled by a range of different motivations. While the 'ice front' had made it a political goal to call for the harshest punishment possible, the government rather feared for the success of the trials and the personal and political integrity of the individuals and bodies administrating them. Government policy, therefore, did not blindly follow the 'ice front'. In response to the 'ice front's calls, the authorities found it necessary to caution and call for moderation. This was highlighted for example by a debate on whether or not former NS members and their families who had been allowed to keep their radios during the occupation should have them confiscated, so that they could be given to 'patriotic Norwegians' instead. The idea carried significant popular support in both the press and the *Storting*, but in an internal memo of the Ministry of Justice a senior civil servant argued that 'regardless of whether there is a legal basis for such a measure, I believe that the actions in question are of such a nature that a society based on the rule of law cannot intervene without undermining its own worthiness'.[78]

The central government also alerted the lower levels of the administration to the one-sided coverage often found in the press. In January 1947, the DPP sent out a report to prosecutors across the country urging them to be vigilant regarding the information given to the press. In particular, he wrote, prosecutors should ensure that the press would present a bill as only an indictment, not as a final verdict. Moreover, prosecutors were to ensure that they communicated to the press the

[76] He was offered a column in *Morgenbladet*, however, and was able to continue his critical stance on the trials; Marie Josefine Kullerud, 'Tre kritikere, et rettsoppgjør' (Master's Dissertation, University of Oslo, 2016), p. 84.

[77] 'Silkebisper', *Dagbladet* (22 November 1946); *Neste fase i rettsoppgjøret – Biskopenes brev til Justisministeren, November 1946* (Oslo: Land og Kirke, 1946).

[78] RA/S-3212/D/De/L0302: 'N.S.-medlemmers radioapparater', memo, Ministry of Justice, 22 May 1946.

importance of not making predictions on the outcome of a court case.[79] If newspapers continued to publish material that was biased or factually wrong, then the DPP suggested that prosecutors should withhold information.[80] In a memo of July 1946, a senior civil servant within the Ministry of Justice considered various approaches to overcoming the polarity of the debate and preparing society for the successful reintegration of prisoners. He argued that the 'greatest possible openness' was required, and suggested that public statements should not be made only by authorities themselves, but also by 'prominent citizens'. He concluded that an open-format discussion on the national broadcaster could be a beneficial strategy.[81] These measures highlight how, for the authorities in charge, the aim was not the harsh punishment the 'ice front' propagated, but to safeguard the appearance of the trials and their own integrity and legitimacy. While public violence was no longer a concern, the popular support of the trials had come under threat. The libel case against Toralv Fanebust shows just how seriously the prosecution took criticism of the trials. In response to critics, the authorities sought to demonstrate that the trials were a success, even if it came at the cost of free speech.

Perhaps predictably, as the distance to the occupation period grew, attitudes on the punishment of collaborators began to change. There were a number of reasons for this: the treason trials had received so much attention that they became 'old news'. The distance in time also meant that the anger that large parts of the population had felt upon the liberation had receded into the background as people became more concerned with the present political context. But the public condemnation of NS members also meant that many began to question the approach taken. By early 1947, an increasing segment of the press argued that the treason trials, had, in fact, been too harsh. With scepticism of the trials increasing, and the distance to the occupation period growing, continued calls for a harsh reckoning were soon reduced to a small circle, mainly among communists and select interest groups. This led the DPP to review existing practices within the prosecution and to instruct prosecutors to apply for lesser sentences, consistent with the by now prevailing attitudes in society.[82] Such measures point towards a heightened public concern over the broader public image of the trials. For the remainder of the trials, it was the

[79] RA/S-1042/D/Dh/L0007: 'Rundskriv L. nr. 114', 16 January 1947. [80] Ibid.

[81] RA/S-1042/D/Dh/L0010: 'Oversikt over planleggingen av arbeidet med landssvikfangene', memo, Johannes Halvorsen, 12 July 1946.

[82] RA/S-1042/D/Dh/L0007: 'Rundskriv L. nr. 104', 24 October 1946.

tension between legal consistency and changing public attitudes that would define government policy and judicial practice.

4.4 Sentencing Practice

During the first two years of the trials, against the backdrop of the intense debates being held on the matter, the courts of the country worked continuously on developing a more or less consistent sentencing practice with regard to the crimes of the occupation period.[83] By 1946, it had become clear that the main corpus of cases would consist of those against NS members and individuals who had served in the various military and paramilitary organisations. In addition, the courts had gradually developed a practice concerning the question of which wartime actions would be punished under both the pre-war Criminal Code and the various new provisions introduced by the provisional decrees. As we have seen, the complex relationship between the Criminal Code and the Treason Decree had made this a difficult task for the courts at first. Beyond the questions of retroactivity that the relationship between the various legal bases raised,[84] the courts also had to decide whether the penalty should be meted out under the Criminal Code or the Treason Decree. Overall, sentences could vary significantly, depending on the nature of the crimes.[85] But what complicates the picture is that individuals had very often committed a number of offences, making it difficult to draw easy comparisons between cases. The most severe penalties were handed down for involvement in SS or NS organisations, in particular when combined with violence against Norwegian resistance members. In addition to prison terms or periods of forced labour, the courts typically imposed a fine relative to the income of the individual sentenced, and the loss of a range of civil rights.[86] In cases where an individual had been deemed to have aided the country, had acted under duress or the criminal nature of their actions, while satisfying the

83 The courts also worked under immense pressure. The Supreme Court's Chief Justice had in May 1946 described the reckoning as having caused a 'crisis-like situation' within the Supreme Court due to the additional workload. RA/S-3212/B/Ba/L0046: Referenced in a letter from the Minister of Justice to the Chief Justice of the Supreme Court, 25 May 1946.

84 See Chapter 1.

85 As we shall see in Chapter 5, the sentences also became more lenient over time. This separate issue will be discussed there. The present section discusses the overall average sentencing practice produced during the trials.

86 Fines were usually handed down in relation to an individual's income situation. For an analysis of the ways in which civil rights were withdrawn, see Anika Seemann, 'Citizen Outcasts: The Penalty of "Loss of Civil Rights" during the Norwegian Treason Trials, 1945–1953', *Scandinavian Journal of History* 45 (2020) 3, pp. 360–383.

decrees, had been only marginal, the courts could decide to acquit. This section accordingly charts the range of offences that came before the courts as well as mitigating or aggravating factors the courts factored in when sentencing.

In addition to the party leadership around Vidkun Quisling, most senior NS members received high penalties. Often, they were found guilty of having breached § 98 – an attempt to overturn the constitutional order – in addition to § 86 – aiding the enemy. This group included senior civil servants who had promoted the aims of the NS as well as certain groups of judges. The judges of the Acting Supreme Court (*Kommisarisk Høyesterett*), for example, were sentenced under both § 86 and § 98, typically to prison or forced labour ranging from six years to lifetime.[87] In their case, the courts deemed it particularly problematic that they had been mature men who had received the 'best education in the country': as jurists, indeed, they should have understood better than anyone else the nature of their crimes. The judges of the *Folkedomstolen* were also held criminally liable.[88] The county governors (*fylkesførere*), who had reported directly to Quisling and had been able to exercise a considerable degree of political influence, also received high penalties. County governor and former prime minister Jens Hundseid, for example, who had been a member of the NS and had persuaded his subordinates to join the party, was sentenced to ten years' forced labour. During his trial, he tried to argue that he had felt threatened by Quisling due to conflicts between the two going back to 1932–1933, when Quisling had served as defence minister in his cabinet. The court dismissed this due to a lack of evidence.[89]

The penalties handed down for lower positions in NS organisations varied significantly, reflecting the manifold roles individuals had assumed within the party organisations. Penalties at the higher end of the spectrum could run to ten, twelve or fifteen years in prison or forced labour. The harshest sentences frequently resulted from a long list of activities, such as in the case of a 36-year-old NS member, who had had various honorary roles within the NS, acted as an informant, initiated the compilation of lists of 'enemies of the state' and had also served as a frontfighter. He was sentenced to fifteen years in prison.[90] Those who had held more junior or limited roles in the party received lower sentences, but the ultimate

[87] Hans Petter Graver, *Okkupasjonstidens Høyesterett* (Oslo: Pax Forlag, 2019), pp. 148–152; Rt. 1946, pp. 1139–1167; Rt. 1946, pp. 1205–1235; Rt. 1946, pp. 1268–1280.

[88] Hans Peter Graver, *Dommernes krig: den tyske okkupasjonen 1940–1945 og den norske rettsstaten* (Oslo: Pax Forlag, 2015), pp. 170–172, 176–179.

[89] Rt. 1946, pp. 1043–1051.

[90] Rt. 1946, pp. 946–950.

sentence depended on the precise nature of their activities. To take a small handful of examples: A 57-year-old farmer who had been a member of the NS and the *Hird*, and who as a local mayor had approved funds to the NS and had supported an appeal for military mobilisation, was sentenced to four years of forced labour.[91] A 52-year old teacher who had been a local press officer of the NS and who had been local head of the party's teachers' association was also sentenced to four years of forced labour.[92] And the liaison person of the NS labour union NSFO at Tønsberg Brewery, who had also held a range of other honorary positions in the party, received a two-and-a-half-year forced labour sentence.[93]

With regard to the various suborganisations of the NS, the defence at times tried to argue that membership could not be penalised under the treason provision § 86 of the Criminal Code because membership could not be said to amount to 'aiding the enemy'. However, the Supreme Court gradually established that activities in the entire spectrum of NS organisations did in fact qualify as an offence under the provision. The court's reasoning was that they all supported the overall ideology and aims of the party. Service in the *Førergarden*, the personal guard of Quisling, was for example considered akin to 'other support of N.S. and Quisling'.[94] The same was true for various 'aid organisations', including the social welfare organisation *NS Hjelpeorganisasjon* (NSH), which the court deemed a 'Nazi-informed organisation'.[95] Membership of the NS youth organisation *Ungdomsfylkning* (NSUF) could also fall under § 86, as could its suborganisation *Unghirden*.[96] However, in all these cases, punishment under § 86 still required a subjective awareness on the part of the defendant that the organisation in question had also promoted the NS as such.[97] But in most cases, the court argued that such an awareness had been present.

The production and dissemination of NS propaganda was deemed to fall under § 86 and was typically sentenced harshly.[98] Halldis Neegård Østbye, a leading member of the *Nasjonal Samling* Women's Organisation, had been a highly aggressive propagandist during the war and was sentenced to seven years' forced labour – a comparatively high penalty for a woman, who on average received lower sentences than

91 Rt. 1946, pp. 250–253. 92 Rt. 1946, pp. 263–266.

93 Rt. 1946, pp. 601–603; RA/S-3138-17/D/Da/L0015/0124, 62/47, Helge Morten Ulf Larsen.

94 Rt. 1946, pp. 852–853. 95 Rt. 1946, pp. 606–613. 96 Rt. 1945, pp. 180–183.

97 This was not always established. In a case against a 67-year-old farmer and former member of NSH, the court accepted the defence's reasoning that the defendant had assumed it was an exclusively humanitarian organisation: Rt. 1946, pp. 353–356.

98 Rt. 1946, pp. 834–837.

men.[99] But even at a less extreme level, charges of propaganda dissemination were treated seriously. A 27-year-old woman who had been county leader for the Women's *Hird* was sentenced to two years for the propaganda she had produced to recruit new members.[100] The actor and war correspondent Karl Holter, who had been a member of the NS and written several propaganda pieces for *Fritt Folk*, had his sentence increased from three years and three months to five years of forced labour by the Supreme Court in September 1946.[101] The lower court had argued that '[in] modern warfare, where all means are used, the war correspondent's efforts are no less significant than armed combat, and there is no reason to believe that the accused did not understand this'.[102] Based on similar reasoning, acting as a photographer on the front was seen as even more severe than frontfighter activity.[103]

Participation in military and paramilitary activity typically attracted harsh sentences, but there were also significant variations in how the courts assessed the gravity of these actions. Those who had taken up arms for the German military, or their Norwegian counterparts, had served in varying roles and for different durations. At the same time, they were at various stages of life and had been driven by differing motivations. This was reflected in the wide range of penalties they received. Activity in the *Hird* was generally deemed a serious offence. One 36-year-old man who had served in the *Hird* and participated in a number of 'missions' against the resistance for example was sentenced to ten years' forced labour.[104] A 25-year-old, having served in the *Hird*, *Germanske SS* and as a personal guard for Quisling, received eight years of forced labour.[105] However, penalties for military service could vary significantly depending on organisational affiliation and individual attitude. In one case, a 31-year-old who had been a member of the NS and had partaken in a German weapons course in Holmestrand, south of Oslo, but who had *not* been a member of the *Hird* and indeed had provided some aid to the resistance, had his sentence reduced from two years' forced labour to one year by the Supreme Court.[106]

99 Women were sentenced under the provisions of the Criminal Code much more rarely than men: Norges Offisielle Statistikk XI 179, *Statistikk over landssvik 1940–1945* (Oslo: Statistisk Sentralbyrå, 1954), p. 30. For an analysis of gender during the treason trials, see Christina Holzmann, 'Geschlecht vor Gericht. Kollaborationsprozesse und Geschlechterordnung nach dem Zweiten Weltkrieg', *L'HOMME. Europäische Zeitschrift für feministische Geschichtswissenschaft* 35 (2024) 2 (forthcoming).

100 Rt. 1946, pp. 367–369.

101 Rt. 1946, pp. 932–935.

102 Rt. 1946, pp. 932–935, at p. 934.

103 Rt. 1946, pp. 471–472.

104 Rt. 1946, pp. 153–157.

105 Rt. 1945, pp. 367–369.

106 Rt. 1945, pp. 337–339, 337; RA/S-3138-13/D/Dc/L0023/0008. Lnr. 158/45 Øverby, Petter.

One group of individuals who received a great deal of public attention were the 'frontfighters': individuals who had joined SS divisions such as the *Norske legion* or *Regiment Nordland* and served on the Eastern Front. As with all groups of offenders, there was considerable heterogeneity when it came to frontfighters and the penalties they received. But overall, their actions were punished harshly. Frontfighters on the younger end of the age spectrum could still easily face four or five years' forced labour.[107] Even in the case of a young man, who – the court recognised – had received misleading information when he was recruited, the Supreme Court went no lower than three years of forced labour.[108] A 40-year-old man who had served in a number of military divisions was sentenced to seven years.[109] These cases illustrate the ways in which the court saw military service for the enemy as one of the most significant acts of treason[110] and one which, 'out of concern for the future, meaning for general-preventive reasons' it was necessary to punish with the greatest severity.[111] At the same time, it is important to note that frontfighter cases centrally revolved around 'treason' rather than the humanitarian crimes they had committed. In particular, crimes committed outside Norway's borders played next to no role.[112]

Besides treason, provisions concerning crimes against bodily integrity also played a central role in the trials. These cases typically involved individuals who had been NS members and who had held party positions as well as military or police roles in the German *Sipo* or Norwegian *Stapo* throughout the occupation. Such acts of violence were deemed particularly reprehensible when they concerned 'Norwegian patriots' – often meaning resistance members.

Norwegians who had worked or acted as informants for *Sipo* or *Stapo* also attracted harsh punishment. Acting as an informant was described by the Supreme Court as 'the enemy's best and most dangerous weapon'[113] and it was punished under § 86. The severity of the sentences depended on the number of occasions in which an individual had informed and the importance of the information they had provided. Unlike many other offences, including military activity, these cases regularly involved women.[114] This included the Norwegian lover of Siegfried Fehmer, the

[107] Rt. 1945, pp. 166–170; Rt. 1945, pp. 297–301. [108] Rt. 1945, pp. 159–164.
[109] Rt. 1945, pp. 173–179. [110] Rt. 1945, pp. 173–179.
[111] Rt. 1946, pp. 854–859, at p. 855.
[112] Terje Emberland and Matthew Kott, *Himmlers Norge: nordmenn i det storgermanske prosjekt* (Oslo: Aschehoug, 2012), p. 20.
[113] Rt. 1945, pp. 339–342, at p. 342.
[114] In the case of a woman who had had a paid position with the Gestapo, the Oslo Court of Appeal had originally handed down a death penalty verdict: Rt. 1946, pp. 619–624.

head of the Gestapo in Oslo. This woman was accused of delivering to Fehmer intelligence from an Oslo-based resistance group, leading to the imprisonment and mistreatment of some of its members. She was sentenced to fifteen years of forced labour.[115] In November 1945, the Supreme Court sentenced an NS official who had informed the Germans on several occasions to eight years of forced labour.[116] In the same month, a chauffeur who had informed to the *Stapo* on two occasions, in addition to embezzling money seized from people in hiding, was sentenced to twelve years' forced labour.[117] A woman who had informed on a couple to the Gestapo for distributing illegal newspapers was sentenced to six years' forced labour.[118] However, the courts also carefully distinguished individual motives when it came to punishing these kinds of action under § 86. In one case, a 52-year-old widow had reported to the police that a neighbour and her son illegally held dynamite and guns in their possession. During the trial it emerged, however, that her intent was not at all to 'aid the enemy' by passing on this information, but that it could exclusively be explained by a 'longstanding, bitter personal animosity' with her neighbours.[119] Hers was one of the relatively few cases of the trials which led to a conditional sentence.

The degree to which carrying out work for the Germans was punished depended on the military significance of the activity.[120] The court only included activities that were particularly 'reprehensible or indecent' under § 86 of the Criminal Code or the decrees.[121] Ordinary workers, who entered the Germans' employ, were typically not sentenced. Individual work for the Germans was only punished when it was of military importance and an individual had given up a secure and well-paid Norwegian position to do so.[122] The DPP issued a circular letter on 10 February 1946 stating that 'it will typically only be a matter of punishing those who have performed work of direct military importance despite previously having well-paid and permanent Norwegian work'.[123] Correspondingly, in 1946, for example, the Supreme Court held that a 35-year-old construction worker and father of four with no means could not be held criminally liable for working as a chauffeur for the German *Organisation Todt* and *Transportkorps Speer*, after having unsuccessfully tried to find 'Norwegian work', and given that the salary he received was not above average.[124]

115 Rt. 1946, pp. 577–579. 116 Rt. 1945, pp. 257–263. 117 Rt. 1945, pp. 225–228.
118 Rt. 1946, pp. 34–35. 119 Rt. 1946, pp. 964–968.
120 The treatment of businesses, as opposed to individual workers, is discussed separately in Chapter 5.
121 Rt. 1945, pp. 154–159. 122 Referenced in Rt. 1946, pp. 1263–1266, at p. 1265.
123 Ibid. 124 Rt. 1946, pp. 135–137, at pp. 135–136.

In general terms, the courts considered a range of mitigating and aggravating circumstances. Young age was deemed a particularly important mitigating factor,[125] as was a childhood in NS milieus.[126] Exposure to German culture at young age,[127] or a conflict or loyalty due to dual citizenship and family ties, were also given weight.[128] Support of 'patriotic' individuals, most significantly the resistance[129] and hiding those searched by the Gestapo, was also an important argument in having one's sentence reduced. In addition, the courts would usually take into account whether an individual had ended their NS membership *during* the war.[130] In one case, meanwhile, the Supreme Court recognised the obligation of a man to care for his dying wife as a central motive in his NS membership, by which he had hoped to secure his job and source of income.[131] Other factors included the seniority an individual held within the party[132] and invalidity resulting from war service.[133] The post-war circumstances individuals found themselves in could also become relevant, such as in the case of a woman whose husband had already been sentenced. Due to the hardship her imprisonment would have meant for her family, her penalty was made conditional.[134] Conversely, social status, too, could count to the disadvantage of the accused, such as in the case of a 64-year-old woman who had held a certain 'social position' based on her wealth and was therefore deemed to be a person who would have had a certain influence on her community.[135]

The courts also at times considered the long-term effects of penalties for individuals. They would, for example, look at an individual's motives and personal circumstances to determine their prospects of economic and professional resocialisation after they had served their sentences. For a senior member of the NS, the court found it appropriate that the individual would have to live a 'more modest' life after serving in prison.[136] But in the case of a group of frontfighters the court stated that they should retain the possibility 'to feed themselves and their relatives in their field of work'.[137] And in a 1946 case concerning a railway clerk, the court argued that the individual in question 'had neither been aggressive nor malicious' and that there should remain 'the possibility that he, after serving his sentence can be re-employed by the railway or in another capacity in the

[125] Rt. 1945, pp. 166–170; Rt. 1945, pp. 249–252; Rt. 1945, pp. 365–367.
[126] Rt. 1945, pp. 173–179, at p. 179. [127] Rt. 1945, pp. 221–225.
[128] Rt. 1946, pp. 1185–1190. [129] Rt. 1945, pp. 337–339; Rt. 1946, pp. 590–596.
[130] Rt. 1946, pp. 543–546. [131] Rt. 1946, pp. 376–384.
[132] Rt. 1946, pp. 1244–1247, at p. 1245. [133] Rt. 1946, pp. 789–791.
[134] Rt. 1946, pp. 237–239. [135] Rt. 1946, pp. 1244–1247, at p. 1245.
[136] Rt. 1946, pp. 1258–1263. [137] Rt. 1945, pp. 371–373.

public service'.[138] Such reasoning signals that even early on, the social reintegration of sentenced collaborators was also a concern of the courts.

The picture that emerges from these cases is one in which crimes against the nation played the decisive role. This was the same across other European countries, because the construction of a patriotic narrative was one of the central implied purposes of post-war trials. As elsewhere in Europe, the crimes against the Jewish minority as such did not play a central role. Though there were select cases of prosecution (which I will discuss), typically, antisemitic crimes were not attributed much weight in determining the penalty.[139] As regards the bulk of the cases that were brought, the majority of cases concerned NS members. Of those who had committed other offences, the vast majority were sentenced for their membership and other offences, first and foremost serving in NS organisations or the military and paramilitary organisations.[140] But what this wide range of cases also highlights are the many ways in which individuals were deemed to have collaborated during the trials, and the vastly differing degrees of involvement with NS and German organisations. Individual circumstances and motivations were complex, something which was easily sidelined in the post-war discourse, in which there was both little understanding and little differentiation when it came to 'collaborators'.

4.5 Justifications and Perceptions

The vast range of offences adjudicated upon over the course of the trials was mirrored in the widely differing justifications and experiences of those who were sentenced. As we have seen, the courts considered a number of arguments brought forward by those accused of wartime offences. However, there were some key arguments that ran through the trials which the courts did not accept, and which would later form a core narrative of those who rejected the trials as unjust. To understand the trials also from the perspective of the defendants, and why they rejected the reckoning as a deeply unfair process, it is therefore worth examining some of these arguments. While personal experiences of the trials naturally varied greatly, and individuals tried to justify their actions in different ways, critiques converged on the notion that the reckoning was unjust and

[138] Rt. 1946, pp. 488–492, at p. 489, similar reasoning in Rt. 1946, pp. 866–870.

[139] Graver, *Dommernes krig*, p. 177.

[140] For a full overview of the cumulative presence of several offences, see Justis- og politidepartementet, *Om landssvikoppgjøret*, pp. 116–119.

unconstitutional. During the trials, the lines of defence and grounds for appeal most frequently concerned the question of what would have been in Norway's best interests, the relationship between Norwegian and international law, and the violation of constitutional principles.

One line of defence advanced by those accused, but which was rarely successful, was that wartime actions had been taken in the best interests of Norwegian society. Strengthening the NS, so the argument went, would strengthen Norway's position vis-à-vis the Germans.[141] One NS member argued that he had taken the decision 'to support NS, as it was our only way to freedom'.[142] In the case of a 60-year-old engineer and NS press official, the Supreme Court concluded that

> despite his good abilities and his many prerequisites for judging the situation, his view ... was blinded and removed in that he had already for many years before the occupation been and still was strongly concerned with certain economic theories and that he now in N.S.'s program found a position that matched his views on these issues. The defendant then saw it such that N.S. had committed to the program to carry out the same economic line as the defendant advocated, and this has probably weighed so strongly on him that this monomaniacal attitude to the particular problem must be considered to have been the main reason for his failing national attitude.[143]

In this rare context, emphasising the long-held beliefs of the defendant, the court accepted mitigating circumstances when handing down the sentence. Overall, however, the court tended to reject arguments about acting in the 'country's best interest', especially when it concerned the joining of NS or military divisions.

Throughout the trials, there was a great deal of uncertainty surrounding the scope of the Hague Conventions of 1907, in particular concerning the permissible actions of the occupying power.[144] Those who stood accused regularly brought forward the defence that their actions had been covered by the legitimate rights of the occupier under international law. In many cases, this line of defence was unsuccessful, with the court arguing that individuals had done more than was permissible or necessary under international law to maintain public order. However, the dividing line would be difficult for the courts to draw. In a case concerning beer supplies

[141] See for example Rt. 1945, pp. 13–26, at p. 21; Rt. 1945, pp. 43–51, at p. 50; Rt. 1945, pp. 75–82, at p. 78.

[142] RA/S-3138-17/D/Da/L0015/L0124: 62/47 Larsen, Helge Morten Ulf, Rapport til Politimesteren i Tønsberg, 1 October 1945.

[143] Rt. 1946, pp. 995–998, at p. 997; RA/S-3138-17/D/Da/L0029b/0209.

[144] See §§ 42–56, Hague Convention of 1907.

for the German military, the Supreme Court was divided on the question of whether a Norwegian citizen's arrangements of beer supplies to the German military had been done in an improper (*utilbørlig*) manner because the initiative he had shown in doing so had gone beyond that which was strictly necessary.[145] In many cases of economic collaboration, this line of defence indeed proved successful.[146] An argument that NS members would later put forward was that if even the courts were not agreed on such questions, it was unreasonable to expect individuals to have understood the dividing line during the war.

Another line of justification frequently invoked, but never successful, was that Norway had not, in fact, been at war after the capitulation agreement had been signed on 10 June 1940. The reason this was such a central question was that a state of war was a prerequisite for punishing individuals under § 86 of the Criminal Code. The Supreme Court had already rejected the idea that Norway had not been at war in the *Haaland* case. This corresponded with the official government position. However, this interpretation continued to be challenged in court. In a case that came before the Oslo Court of Appeal in 1947, for example, the defendant sought to argue that 'he cannot be convicted of a crime against section 86 of the Criminal Code, because in his view there was no state of war between Norway and Germany after June 10, 1940'.[147] This case led to a full investigation of the facts of the capitulation. However, again, the court reaffirmed the line of previous judgments, as too did the Supreme Court upon appeal in 1948. The courts also had to establish the subjective element of culpability in this regard, meaning that the individual had to have understood that Norway was at war. However, while the courts typically found that such an awareness had been present, NS circles would maintain that the reckoning had been unjust because Norway's status as a belligerent state had not been clear to them during the war.

A further argument put forward by those who stood trial was that the overall situation *in hindsight* appeared much clearer than it had been at the time of the war. This pertained to the criminal nature of certain offences, the assessment of international law, as well as the situation on the ground. There was considerable uncertainty even among defence lawyers of front-fighters, for example, concerning the question of when the Soviet Union became an ally of Norway and when diplomatic relations to Finland were

[145] Rt. 1947, pp. 49–54. [146] Rt. 1948, pp. 470–480.

[147] Rt. 1948, pp. 164–165; see also RA/S-3138-06/Da/L004/0001: Rapport til politimesteren i Follo of 3 August 1945.

cut off, as fighting against the Soviet Union was only an offence under § 86 if the Soviet Union was in fact an 'allied state of Norway'.[148] In a letter to the Ministry of Foreign Affairs, one defence attorney wrote that his defendants – a group of frontfighters – 'have stated that they were not aware that Norway was allied with Russia'.[149]

As the trials unfolded, more and more aggrieved former NS members arrived at the view that the whole undertaking was not only unjust, but illegitimate, based on unconstitutional laws and a misinterpretation of the status Norway had held during the war in international law. In the immediate post-war period, those accused of treason found it difficult to make their perspective heard in public outlets. But as they began to become more organised in the late 1940s, they formed a number of associations to further their interpretation of the war and the reckoning. These included the *Forbundet for Sosial Oppreisning*, later in part carried on as the *Institutt for Norsk Okkupasjonshistorie*, as well as an association specifically for former frontfighters. In addition, they distributed their own newspaper, *Folk og Land*, which was widely read in former NS circles.

Many of the offenders also produced letters to public figures, in which they repeated the arguments they tried to also convey in court, seeking to explain their wartime behaviour. Bishop Berggav, for example, received numerous communications, some of which criticised his strong stance on punishing NS members, and pointed to his own ambiguous behaviour in the summer of 1940.[150] As one former NS member stated in a letter to Berggrav:

> I was of the opinion that, as NS member, I would have better possibilities to protest against the possible mobilisation of Norwegian boys for Germany. In the event of a mobilisation, my two adult sons would have been among the first to go to war for Germany. If the NS did not exercise the right to take over the government there would have been a German military government (German protectorate). This was, so to speak, the reason I pro forma signed up for the NS.[151]

In a similar manner, another letter writer argued:

> A large part of the passive members joined the party to help defend Norway's independence, if Germany were to win. [T]hey believed that it was only with the help of the NS that there could be an opportunity to save

148 RA/S-3212/D/De/L0302: Correspondence between Høyesterettsadvokat J. B. Hjort [and several other defence attorneys] and the Ministry of Justice, June 1945–March 1946.

149 Letter by Øivind Aasland to the Ministry of the Exterior, 31 October 1945, in RA/S-3212/D/De/L0302.

150 One problem here was that collaborators in part relied on Nazi propaganda.

151 RA/PA-0320/2/H/L0017: Letter to Bishop Berggrav from . . ., 8 January 1950.

> the country's independence. They therefore considered the NS an insurance.[152]

The letters sent to Bishop Berggrav do not only show why some former NS members felt the trials to be unjust, but the force with which they had felt the social consequences that followed. One letter writer decided to stay anonymous, merely signing off the letter as 'Passive member of *Nasjonal Samling*'. The letter writer was responding to Berggrav's public statements that, while he felt the reckoning was needed, it should be conducted moderately. The reckoning was, however, not being conducted according to this moderate line. Instead, the author of the letter stated: 'The reality is that passive NS members are subject to severe penalties, namely the loss of civil rights and fines. These fines are pushed so high that the members who own something are threatened with financial ruin. This is in many cases worse than imprisonment.' The author contrasted this to the decision not to prosecute the Germany workers. Overall, he argued that it would be natural for NS members to feel 'hatred and bitterness' over the way in which the reckoning had been conducted. However, it is perhaps the conclusion of his letter which most directly conveys the writer's own feelings: 'It is embarrassing to write anonymously, but the conditions in the country unfortunately make this necessary for an N.S. member.'[153]

A representative perspective of how NS members perceived the trials is that of NS member Arne Bergsvik. Bergsvik, who had been the director of an artificial silk factory and mayor in Notodden, stood trial for having been an NS member and for having promoted the Nazification of the municipal administration in his time as mayor.[154] He was sentenced to four years' forced labour. In 1946/1947, in Ilebu prison, he wrote a memoir of the experience, intended mainly as a private note to future generations of his family.[155] He later had it printed and (because he believed his family might emigrate) translated into English. In it, he elaborated on the NS view of the war, and laid out many of the arguments individuals had presented in court, including that he believed the country had not been at war, and that he had acted in the country's best interest.[156] At a more fundamental level, Bergsvik criticised that he felt the exile government's actions were being evaluated from the wartime perspective, whereas those of NS members were being assessed from today's.[157] Personally, he experienced the trials as a farce, where 'judges act in part as prosecutors, scold the accused and

[152] RA/PA-0320/2/H/L0017: Letter to Bishop Berggrav from an anonymous writer, 3 January 1946.
[153] Ibid. [154] RA/S-3138-22/D/Da/L0001/0001, Anr. 1/45, Bergsvik, Arne. [155] Ibid.
[156] Arne Bergsvik, 'Vi er ikke noe forbrytere' (pamphlet, 1950), p. 117. [157] Ibid., p. 124.

ridicule their arguments and motives, the defenders find it difficult to speak, because they do not dare to "annoy" the judge'.[158] This reflects many of the positions that first came to the fore in letters and which would later become more vocalised through the organisations formed by former NS members.

4.6 Legislating the Treason Act

When the Treason Act was finally debated in parliament on 6 February 1947, and MPs received the opportunity to review the reckoning as a whole, the majority of MPs voted in favour of retaining the legal basis of the trials in its present form. The reason the bill was put before parliament so late was twofold: on the one hand, the wartime decrees had raised difficult legal questions, and various drafts were sent back and forth between departments for almost a year before the bill could be finalised. But a further reason for the delays was that the government was keen to avoid broader public uncertainty while the trials were ongoing. Throughout the preparations of the bill, the Ministry of Justice also followed the reckonings in other countries closely, including in the Danish press.[159] The government members knew that a broad debate on the trials would again lead to heightened scrutiny. There had been signs throughout autumn 1946 that the *Storting*'s Justice Committee in particular might oppose the bill.[160] In light of growing public pressure on the trials, the failure to have the bill passed by parliament could have been a fiasco for the government. But Gundersen need not have worried. As it turned out, even critics of the trials within parliament were reluctant to change the broader parameters of the trials at this late stage and the *Storting* passed the bill. Most MPs stated that any fundamental changes would lead to an unequal treatment of treason suspects, with sentences dependent on the time at which the individual case was processed.

But the debate became about more than passing the Treason Act. For parliament, it was an opportunity to reflect more broadly on the trials. For the government, it had become necessary to defend its policies. In his address to parliament, Gundersen expressed satisfaction with the trials and

[158] Ibid., p. 168.

[159] RA/S-3212/D/De/L0302: See mappe 'Danske Regeringsdokumenter'; RA/S-3212/D/De/L0302: 'Amnesti for de smaa Landssvigere', *Politiken* (26 October 1946), marked 'to be shown the Minister', and viewed by Gundersen on 7 November 1946.

[160] Brandal, '"En rettsstat verdig"', p. 57.

the progress that had been made.[161] He took his address to argue more generally that the chosen course had been both just and appropriate, and sought to counter both 'ice front' and 'silk front' criticisms by steering a decided middle ground. He emphasised in particular that, in his opinion, the scope of the trials had been appropriate in light of the strong public opinions present in society following the liberation. He added: 'Had the legal apparatus not intervened, then other forces in society would have done so, and if not through different means altogether, then certainly by way of an isolation process that perhaps for decades would have left a pariah caste composed of those who had not been punished.'[162] This statement placed the trials more firmly in the distinctive liberation setting. Such arguments would become a central part of government communication on the trials. The official logic now went that the trials had been an outflow of a historic anomaly – a burden but also a necessity on the government. But although the trials had served their original purpose, the government argued that legal consistency now demanded that the framework not be changed. This allowed the Ministry to operate on two temporal planes, and to reconcile the more problematic aspects of the trials with peacetime demands for the rule of law.

More than in previous debates, Gundersen emphasised the benefits for society in bringing the trials to a conclusion from an economic and social perspective. He pointed towards the large burden the trials meant for society and stated that a total of '45,000 prison years' had been handed down in the course of the reckoning. He highlighted that it was 'comparatively high-skilled workers that we are talking about'.[163] While prisoners did work in camps, it was almost impossible, Gundersen stated, to organise work placements efficiently across the country to ensure that prisoners worked closest to their expertise.[164] It was of the essence, therefore, that the trials be seen through quickly, so that those sentenced could return to society. At the same time, Gundersen stressed that there would be no amnesties in Norway, and that widespread pardons would also not be forthcoming. He argued that it would be 'an extremely problematic path to pursue if pardons bodies were to widely revise court decisions at this stage'.[165] But it was not just judicial independence that was of concern. The decision not to implement widespread amnesties was also related to the fact that the trials still served a demonstrative dimension to the

[161] O.tid. (1947), p. 13. At the time of the debate, around three-quarters (approx. 75,000) of cases had been investigated, and around 60 per cent of cases decided by the courts or by decree.
[162] Ibid., p. 13. [163] Ibid., p. 15. [164] Ibid., pp. 15–16. [165] Ibid., p. 17.

government. In fact, in light of mounting criticism of the trials, this demonstrative purpose of the trials even grew with the distance to the occupation.

An overwhelming majority of MPs voted in favour of the bill. But the debate on the bill exposed the problems that had accumulated around the trials. Within the Justice Committee, many were critical of the course the treason trials had taken. Some argued that the provisions in the pre-war criminal code would have sufficed to carry through the reckoning.[166] While the Committee realised that the provisional decrees of 3 October 1941 and 22 January 1942 had been meaningful from the perspective of deterring NS membership, it stated that it was unfortunate that the provisional decree of 15 December 1944 had not been announced publicly. The Committee did admit that this form of reasoning was based on 'wisdom in hindsight', however. But altogether, the Justice Committee decided to provide a full legal critique of the framework of the trials based on peacetime legal principles. This signals a desire within the Committee that the rules at the basis of the treason trials should be able to stand according to *ordinary* legal doctrine, and that reference to the extraordinary situation of the period no longer sufficed. But the principle of equality before the law had to prevail, the Committee argued, despite the flawed legal basis of the trials.[167] The Committee therefore supported the bill, as it agreed that the trials had, at this stage, advanced too far for their legal basis to be revised. Nevertheless, its deliberations signal that it closely monitored the government's adherence to rule of law standards.

Many MPs equally used the debate as an opportunity to criticise the wartime decrees. They gave voice to their dissatisfaction with the delay in the debate, arguing that it had caused the *Storting* to be sidelined from exerting a material influence on the course of the trials.[168] The *Storting* contained two extreme wings: on the one hand those dissatisfied with the reckoning for what they felt was its leniency, and on the other those deeming it to have been too broad and encompassing, with a moderate majority arguing that it had been in line with public demands. MPs across the party spectrum acknowledged that there was by now a wide range of opinions in society, and that the 'ice front' and 'silk front' reflected only the most extreme views.[169] The majority of politicians argued that while there was no consensus on the trials, the vast majority of the population nevertheless supported the trials in their present form.[170] But the frequent

[166] Innst. O.I. (1947), p. 1. [167] Ibid., p. 2. [168] O.tid. (1947), p. 25.
[169] Innst. O.I. (1947), p. 2. [170] O.tid. (1947), p. 30.

and generalised assertions that the continuation of the existing policies rested on popular support also signal that MPs were anxious, given the heated debate that had raged since the liberation and the perceptible changes the debate had undergone in recent months.

This middle course led to mixed responses among those who desired a fundamental change in how the trials were conducted. NKP members repeated their claim that the trials had failed to do justice and had not satisfied public demand.[171] The hard-line approach by the NKP and its strong opposition to the Labour government's policies reflect the general differences between the two parties, which were growing increasingly apart.[172] John Lyng of *Høyre*, on the other hand, repeated his argument made a year previously, and stated that it would have been more fortunate had the scope of the trials been more limited. But despite these protests, the vast majority of MPs supported the bill. While the political situation had changed and there was much more scope for nuance, the *Storting* found itself unable to depart from the rules as they had been adopted. Many MPs criticised the framework of the trials, but the logic that 'if one has said *a* one has to say *b*' prevailed at this point in time.[173] The argument weighed heavily that any major change to the trials at this stage could lead to significant individual injustices. But perhaps more importantly, major changes could have led to uncertainty and further dissatisfaction among the general public.

In early 1947, we thus find a parliament dominated by a more moderate tone and a desire to bring the trials to a swift conclusion while still maintaining their outward authority and inner cohesion. The distance to the occupation experience was beginning to show – both within the chamber and in the wider public. The complexity of implementing the trials had also drawn attention to the fact that it would be difficult to satisfy all in the process.[174] With its many references to the press and wider public opinion, the debate shows the continued – if not heightened – importance of the broader public attitudes towards them. MPs were acutely aware how disputed the trials were, and a continuation of previous practice was its safest option to avoid public criticism. But the *Storting* had also actively been prevented from changing the contours of the trials due to the late timing of the debate. Any changes would have been difficult for parliamentarians to justify at a time when roughly 50 per cent of cases had been decided. Gundersen and his government could now rest assured that the trials would not undergo any dramatic changes. But at the same time,

[171] Ibid., pp. 22–23. [172] Ibid., p. 23. [173] Ibid., pp. 7, 30. [174] Ibid., pp. 30–31.

the debate indicated that broader public attitudes had softened considerably since 1945, and would presumably continue to do so. While this dilemma seemed manageable with regard to the provisions of the Treason Act, it proved more difficult with a topic of such gravity as the death penalty.

4.7 The Death Penalty Dilemma

Already in early 1946, there had been signs of widespread scepticism in wider society towards the death penalty.[175] The first opinion survey on the treason trials was published in March 1946, and it confirmed that attitudes towards the death penalty were diverse.[176] The *Fakta* institute had surveyed 3,000 members of the public and found that only 60 per cent of Norwegians favoured the death penalty – a result that, according to Johannes Andenæs, 'goes decidedly against the overall assumption that there is near-universal support for the death penalty'.[177] In some districts, indeed, a majority opposed the death penalty. At the time, however, it was unlikely that any opinion poll would provoke changes to the legal and political framework of the trials at this point. Not only did authorities strive for legal consistency, some of the most prominent cases of the treason trials still lay ahead. The trials against the core members of the by now infamous *Sonderabteilung Lola*, also known as the 'Rinnan group', were yet to take place, including the case against its leader, Henry Rinnan (see Figure 4.2). Given the grave nature of the crimes committed by this group, it was no surprise that the case against Rinnan and his close accomplices was met with great interest and anticipation. The trials began on 30 April 1946 and lasted for around five months.[178] They were celebrated by the press, providing 'ice front' papers in particular with ghastly stories to support their broader arguments for a harsh reckoning and the continued use of the death penalty.[179]

Several high-profile cases against former NS 'ministers' were also scheduled to take place that spring. Following the trial against Quisling in autumn 1945, the cases against former Minister of Domestic Affairs

175 The government received protest letters from opponents. See for example: RA/S-1005//Db/L0131: Telegrams to the Norwegian Government (3 and 4 May 1946); RA/S-3212/D/De/L0301: Binder 'Henstillinger om avskaffelse av dødsstraffen'.

176 'Faktas Meningsmålinger: Landssvikoppgjøret – Folkedommen strengere enn domstolene', *Verdens Gang* (9 March 1946).

177 Johannes Andenæs, 'Folkedommen og landssvikoppgjøret', *Verdens Gang* (13 March 1946).

178 John Lyng, *Forræderiets epoke* (Oslo: Gyldendal Norsk Forlag, 1979), pp. 185–186.

179 Aage Georg Sivertsen, *Rinnan: et nærbilde* (Oslo: Universitetsforlaget, 1995), pp. 101–133; Aage Georg Sivertsen, *Rinnanbanden. Infiltrasjonen. Torturen. Oppgjøret* (Oslo: Kagge, 2022).

Figure 4.2 Members of the Rinnan group on trial.
Source: Schrøderarkivet/Sverresborg.

Albert Viljam Hagelin and Minister of Church and Education Ragnar Skancke were followed closely by the press. A close ally of Quisling, Hagelin had played a central role in the Nazification of the country after 1940. The Oslo Court of Appeal unanimously sentenced him to death on 4 December 1945. He appealed the case to the Supreme Court, which unanimously dismissed the appeal on 3 May 1946. Hagelin was executed on 25 May 1946. Skancke had been responsible among other things for sacking most of Norway's bishops and for ordering teachers to join NS organisations. He had not, however, initiated the violent deportation of teachers to Finnmark in winter 1942,[180] and on several occasions he had in fact opposed orders from the *Reichskommissariat*. Many deemed him to be of a different category of culpability to Quisling and Hagelin. When on 21 May 1946, the Oslo Court of Appeal handed down a death sentence (by a 4–1 majority), this came as a great surprise to many public figures and large parts of the 'silk front' press.[181] The response to the Skancke

180 Nicola Karcher, *Kampen om skolen: nazifisering og lærernes motstand i det okkuperte Norge* (Oslo: Dreyers Forlag, 2018), p. 158.
181 'Minister Skancke dømt til døden', *Morgenbladet* (22 May 1946).

judgment signalled a further shift away from undifferentiated condemnation of key NS figures.

The death penalty was debated a second time by the *Storting* in December 1946. A renewed debate was necessary given the limited period of validity of the wartime decree.[182] It had been clear to the Ministry of Justice as early as January 1946 that an extension of the death penalty laws would be necessary because of the many cases still pending. However, Gundersen had cautioned against scheduling the debate prematurely, referring to the potential public uncertainty a new debate might foster in relation to the trials.[183] The second debate on the death penalty was therefore not put on the agenda until the autumn.[184] The government was aware that public attitudes towards the death penalty were diversifying, but having its use prevented by the *Storting* would have been a significant defeat for the government. In fact, there was so much unease within the Ministry of Justice concerning the death penalty that it even considered a number of options for avoiding a full parliamentary debate on the matter. Ultimately, however, the Ministry deemed it too problematic legally and politically to avoid a full debate within the *Storting*.[185]

The government's bill did not contain a set time frame for the use of the death penalty, as the DPP had stated that it was unclear when the final cases that might result in a death penalty verdict would be brought to trial. It was important, therefore, to avoid a 'battle against time'.[186] In its bill of 24 October 1946, the government therefore proposed an indefinite extension of the use of the death penalty for the context of the treason trials. The bill did not go into much detail on the death penalty as such, but argued that the 'internal equality' of the trials was by now the primary concern. By this it meant that the same legal framework should be applied to the trials throughout their duration.[187] The bill argued that anything else would go against the general sense of justice in the wider population, in particular if some were spared the death penalty only for the reason that

182 The act passed by the *Storting* on 6 July 1945 had merely confirmed that the death penalty could be applied for as long as the corresponding wartime decree remained valid.

183 RA/S-1005/A/Aa/L0004: Referat fra regjeringskonferanse, sak nr. 3, 'Lovbestemmelser om dødsstraff', 10 January 1946; the prosecution was at this time considering applying for a death penalty sentence in more than 200 cases.

184 Lars-Erik Vaale, *Dommen til døden: dødsstraffen i Norge 1945–50* (Oslo: Pax Forlag, 2004), p. 97.

185 RA/S-3212/D/De/L0301: Departmental memo 'Loven om dødsstraff. Mulige alternativer til regjeringsforslaget i Ot.prp. nr. 141 (1945/46)', 20 November 1946.

186 RA/S-3212/D/De/L0301: Letter from DPP Sven Arntzen to the Ministry of Justice, 18 July 1946.

187 Ot.prp. nr. 141 (1945–1946), pp. 5–6.

their case had been brought to trial later on.[188] As of 1 October 1946, the prosecuting authorities expected the death penalty to be applied for in a further 148 cases to the 60 cases already decided upon.[189]

However, the bill sat uneasily with the *Storting*'s Justice Committee, which debated the matter on 2 December 1946.[190] The Committee was torn between a continued use of the 'exceptional' laws defined by the occupation period, or a return to 'ordinary' constitutional doctrine. Two of the Committee's eight members opposed the bill altogether, advocating instead an abolition of the death penalty. While the majority of MPs ultimately voted in favour of the bill, there was considerably more unease about the death penalty than there had been during the debate in the previous *Storting* in June 1945. Compared to this debate, the main justification employed by MPs for the death penalty had also changed: rather than invoking the 'will of the people', the majority of MPs sided with the government's reasoning that the 'inner consistency' of the trials demanded it.[191] But this rationale faced significant opposition. Gabriel Moseid of the Centre Party argued that wrongful punishment of one should not serve as a justification for the wrongful treatment of another, and that the government's references to the 'inner justice' of the trials were irresponsible. And indeed, true opposition to the death penalty within parliament is likely to have been much higher, with some MPs stating that they voted in favour of the bill only 'with a bleeding heart'.[192]

The reluctance of both the government and the *Storting* to abolish the death penalty must be seen in relation to broader press coverage of the time.[193] In January 1947, judicial independence came under significant pressure in the 'ice front' press following the verdict against a German executioner. *Hauptsturmführer* Oscar Hans had led an 'SS-Sonderkommando' and overseen the execution of more than 268 people during the occupation. The Oslo Court of Appeal sentenced Hans to

188 Nineteen executions had been carried out by this point. It is important to remember that at this stage, several high-profile cases were still pending, including the application for clemency by Skancke. Any changes to the law would therefore directly affect pending cases.

189 Ot.prp. nr. 141 (1945–1946), pp. 8–13.

190 Gundersen had predicted this; see Referat fra Regjeringskonferanse, sak nr. 3, 'Lovforslag om rettsoppgjøret', 12 November 1946.

191 Ibid., pp. 56–57; this reasoning in many ways corresponds to the logic applied to the Treason Act, which took place just months later.

192 O.tid (1946), p. 725.

193 It was the familiar spectrum, with some newspapers arguing that the judgments were too lenient: for example, 'Omkring dommen', *Arbeiderbladet* (10 January 1947); 'En utfordring mot rettsbevistheten', *Friheten* (9 January 1947); Untitled, *Nationen* (3 February 1947); 'Grini-bødlene', *Morgenbladet*, 9 January 1947.

death by a 5–2 majority on 17 January 1947. The decisive question in the case had not been whether or not Hans had performed the executions, but whether or not he *had known* that he was carrying them out in the absence of valid legal judgments. The two dissenting judges concluded that they could not find that Hans had known that he had executed the individuals in question in absence of a valid judgment. They consequently applied for acquittal.[194] The press response to these dissenting verdicts was fierce, with the Labour Party organ *Arbeiderbladet* among others demanding that the dissenting judges be removed from any further cases.[195] However, several of the more moderate newspapers, including *Aftenposten* and *Morgenbladet*, responded by condemning the proposal that authorities interfere with judicial independence.[196] Justice Minister Gundersen emphasised publicly that the judges in question would under no circumstances be removed, and that the government respected judicial independence.[197] While this case concerned a German war criminal rather than a Norwegian collaborator, the episode signalled how much attention select cases still drew, and how quickly the legal apparatus and the broader handling of the post-war trials could come under attack.

Hans was not the only high-profile case to stir debate during the first months of 1947. In March 1947, the Supreme Court sentenced 'Minister' Ragnar Skancke to death after he had appealed his case. Almost a year had passed since the initial death sentence – a delay caused by an unsuccessful attempt by Skancke's legal team to admit new evidence to the case. Yet by now there was significantly more opposition to Skancke's execution. The protests were directed both at the death penalty in the specific case and its more general use. Many argued that Skancke had not driven the campaigns of his ministry, but largely followed orders. In no way, their argument ran, was he comparable to a Quisling or a Hagelin. Former colleagues and relatives of Skancke came forward and applied for a pardon on Skancke's behalf, arguing that he was a 'naïve' and submissive individual who was not at all suited to politics: a follower rather than a leader.[198]

194 Berit Nøkleby, *Krigsforbrytelser: brudd på krigens lov i Norge 1940–45* (Oslo: Pax Forlag, 2004), pp. 49–51; Lars-Erik Vaale and Baard Herman Borge, 'Caught between International Law and National Constitution: The Legal Reckoning with Foreign War Criminals in Norway after 1945', in *Max Planck Institute for Legal History and Legal Theory Research Paper Series*, No. 1, 2022, p. 22.

195 'Dønnum & Co', *Arbeiderbladet* (21 January 1947); editorial, *Arbeiderbladet* (3 February 1947).

196 'Hans', *Aftenposten* (7 February 1947); 'Uvettige angret', *Morgenbladet* (24 January 1947); Jens Schulz, 'Hvor går anstendighetens grense?', *Verdens Gang* (14 January 1947); defence attorneys, too, came under frequent attack.

197 'Dissensen blant dommerne i rettssaken mot Oscar Hans', *Arbeiderbladet* (29 January 1947).

198 Vaale, *Dommen til døden*, pp. 112–113.

Predictably, this prompted heated and critical responses from 'ice front' papers. However, there was by now significant and widespread unease about the death penalty, which made a continuation with the present course difficult. A total of 656 pastors signed a joint letter to the Ministry of Justice asking for Skancke's execution to be prevented.[199] They argued that the Norwegian people were 'beginning to be liberated from the mentality of war', and that the death penalty was inhibiting the process of reconciliation in wider society.[200] A group of public intellectuals appealed to the government in an open letter on 24 May 1947, similarly referring to a change in attitudes and arguing for a return to 'normality'.[201]

The controversy surrounding the *Skancke* trial placed the government and the judiciary in a difficult position. While there was an increasing number of voices urging caution and advocating a return to 'normality', the heated debate on the treason trials as a whole made it a risky climate in which to propose changes to their broader framework or to grant pardons. The *Hans* case had revealed the public pressures being placed on courts. But broader public unease surrounding the death penalty continued to increase. In early 1947, the Supreme Court handed down two death penalty verdicts by the slim margin of 3–2.[202] This sparked a debate surrounding the question of whether such a narrow margin made the use of the death penalty defensible. The uncertainty expressed by many experts and a large portion of the press prompted the Ministry of Justice to propose a change to the majority of judges required in the Supreme Court to hand down a death penalty verdict. Up until that point, the vast majority of death penalties had been decided by a chamber of five Supreme Court judges. The government proposed that instead, death penalty cases should be decided upon by a nine-member chamber and that a qualified majority of six judges would be needed to sentence an individual to death. If death penalties continued to be handed down with a 3–2 majority, it could, in the words of Gundersen, prove a 'severe strain on the wider population's sense of right and wrong and attitudes towards the treason trials as a whole'.[203]

[199] Ibid. [200] 'Biskopen om dødsdommen over Skancke', *Dagbladet* (18 April 1947).

[201] 'Dødsstraff', *Verdens Gang* (24 April 1947); 'Et varsko', *Arbeiderbladet* (23 April 1947); 'Skancke-saken', *Dagbladet* (25 April 1948); 'Respekt for menneskeliv', *Verdens Gang* (27 May 1947); Steinar Stokstadt, 'Dødsstraff og benådning', *Verdens Gang* (30 May 1947); Jakob Naadland, 'Tvilen kring dødsstraffen', *Verdens Gang* (13 June 1947); 'Vakling og usikkerhet', *Arbeiderbladet* (19 May 1947); Knut Johannessen, 'Dødsdommene i Høyesterett', *Verdens Gang* (12 May 1947); 'Dødsdom', *Dagbladet* (24 May 1947).

[202] Ot.prp. nr. 84 (1947), p. 1. [203] Ibid.

The Justice Committee agreed with the government's proposition. The Committee did, however, estimate that the changes would slow down the treason trials by six months. The bill was put before parliament in June 1947, where it caused significant debate. MPs overwhelmingly agreed that attitudes towards the death penalty had changed. However, responses to what this meant in practice were mixed. A considerable number of MPs opposed the proposed changes, arguing that the majority that would become necessary would cause further delays to the trials, something that was deemed highly problematic. Across all parties, there was agreement that the emphasis should by now be on closure, not on a further extension of the already lengthy trials, for 'the people are tired of the death penalty'.[204] An educational dimension also suffused the debate, with some MPs arguing that it was time to prepare the population for a return to 'normality'.[205] This stands in marked contrast to previous debates, where the people's wishes and expectations had been considered authoritative on their own accord. Some MPs argued that it might affect the way the trials were perceived if changes were made at this stage, forfeiting the very purposes of the bill.[206] However, the majority of MPs argued that attitudes in wider society had changed so much that modifications had to be made to bring the law into harmony with social expectations and introduce a new threshold of legal certainty.[207] The bill was therefore passed.[208]

The debate on death penalty verdicts in the Supreme Court confirms that the death penalty was seen as only a provisional measure and that it was tied closely to the treason trials. It was part of an overall framework which, with growing distance to the liberation, increasingly seemed like an anomaly. To many MPs, the treason trials as a whole marked a curious extension of wartime thinking, and one that seemed increasingly alien as time progressed. To the government, the modification of the Supreme Court's rules was a significant advantage: the new majority required in the Supreme Court made it highly likely that fewer death sentences would be handed down. At the same time, it spared the government the potential controversies of proposing an abolition of the death penalty or an extensive use of pardons, both of which could easily have made the government appear soft or – worse – inconsistent.[209] Yet, the modification also sent a

[204] O.tid (1947), p. 351. [205] Ibid., p. 353. [206] Ibid., pp. 349–350.

[207] Ibid., pp. 335, 351.

[208] Ibid., pp. 355–357; L.tid. (1947), p. 144. Kaas and Brænd were pardoned, and their sentence converted to life imprisonment: RA/S-1005/A/Aa/L0005, Referat fra Regjeringskonferanse, sak nr. 1, 'Benådningsandragende – Finn K. Kaas og Arne Brænd', 18 September 1947.

[209] RA/S-1005/A/Aa/L0022: 'Konferanse 18 November 1947 Protokoll for hemmelige saker'.

strong political signal to the courts, in contrast to the government's previous emphasis on judicial independence. The government's proposal to change the Supreme Court's composition in death penalty cases reflected its desire that a reduction in death penalty cases align court practice with changed public attitudes. At the same time, the government was unwilling to propose an abolition of the death penalty due to the criticism this could prompt. The strategy pursued by the government therefore highlights the complexity of anchoring the treason trials in public attitudes while at the same time ensuring their legal consistency.

4.8 Conclusion

Throughout 1946 and 1947, there was an overwhelming pressure to bring the treason trials to a close. Yet, state authorities were also reluctant to change their larger framework. Despite the accelerated sentencing procedure adopted in February 1946, the trials continued to prove a significant burden on the legal and administrative apparatus. Towards the end of 1947, the bulk of cases – more than 80 per cent – had been processed, but a conclusion before the end of 1947 still seemed out of reach.[210] The DPP estimated that some cases before the Courts of Appeal would not be concluded until the turn of the year 1948/1949. The reason was that some of the latest cases to be brought to trial were also some of the most complex.[211] The Supreme Court, in turn, would be occupied with the treason trials for an 'additional number of years'.[212] Yet the DPP introduced some slight modifications to curb the scope of the trials in late 1947. In a letter to the Ministry of Justice, he pointed out that now – '2 ½ years after the liberation' – a slight softening of policies could be justified, and that the authorities would not prosecute individuals who had only committed 'trivial' acts of treason and who had been in permanent employment since the liberation. These individuals, he reasoned, would suffer much more from a trial at this stage than if they had been prosecuted immediately. In the eyes of the DPP, the overall benefits of reintegrating collaborators into the workforce also justified these restrictions.[213] By late 1947, such measures were not as likely to encounter the responses they would have faced in 1945 and 1946. On the contrary: harsh policies in the context of the treason trials could now provoke a public backlash.

[210] RA/S-1558/D/L0020: Letter from DPP Andreas Aulie to the Ministry of Justice entitled 'Avviklingen av rettsoppgjøret', 25 November 1947.
[211] Ibid. [212] Ibid. [213] Ibid.

Despite these differences in attitudes, however, several factors limited the changes that could be made to the legal framework of the trials. First, the implementation of the trials was closely linked to the government's larger political credibility. Any changes to the legal framework of the trials carried the risk of weakening the institutions behind it. Second, the Ministry of Justice had a strong regard for equality of law application. It sought to present the trials as a *legal* rather than a political process. Therefore, any changes prompted by a change in public attitudes alone could undermine the Ministry's integrity. But what the benchmark of the law actually *was* remained undefined in this period. As we have seen, debates surrounding the death penalty in particular were defined by a tension between 'wartime' and 'peacetime' mentalities. The difficult balancing act faced by the Ministry of Justice and the DPP in particular during 1946 and 1947 reflects the distinct challenges the law encounters in phases of rapid political transition. And the government knew that the challenge of reconciling legal principle with an extraordinary legal undertaking such as the treason trials would only increase as time went on.

CHAPTER 5

Limitation

Pragmatism and Political Promises, 1948–1949

By 1948, the trials had far exceeded estimates for their original time frame. This chapter looks at the effects the growing distance from the occupation had on court practice and the broader administration of the trials. It highlights how the unexpectedly long duration of the trials confronted the Ministry of Justice and the Director of Public Prosecutions (DPP) with two specific challenges: first, statistics were beginning to show that court judgments handed down in 1945 and early 1946 had been much more severe than later court practice. This posed a problem for the larger public 'image' of the trials, which by now relied strongly on the argument that like cases should be treated alike. Second, broader attitudes towards the trials in civil society had by now changed perceptibly, as the anger of the liberation moment had receded into the background and public attention had turned towards the new world order that was forming. This allowed for and necessitated an acceleration of release procedures. But this change in mood, and desire for reconciliation, also meant that many crimes would not be prosecuted in full. By 1948, there was a pragmatic argument to be made that the reckoning with *economic* collaborators would be conducted on a much smaller scale than had been promised upon the liberation. In addition, the court judgment against Knut Rød, the wartime head of the Oslo-Aker department of *Stapo* responsible for the deportation of the Jews, confirmed that the Holocaust would play only a limited role in the reckoning. With regard to the pre-existing legal framework, meanwhile, Justice Minister Gundersen had a number of reservations against changing the legal parameters of the trials, as he was concerned for their long-term legacy and the ways in which the trials might be challenged more fundamentally if they were to be softened. This fundamental tension, along with the decision not to prosecute a number of wartime crimes, defined the later stages of the trials. More generally, this chapter therefore highlights what a complex and time-sensitive instrument the law was within the broader political and social process of the treason trials.

5.1 Unequal Verdicts

Already in 1946 and 1947, there had been a high number of requests for pardons. Yet for prisoners, these had rarely been successful.[1] Only a total of seventy-two prisoners were pardoned during these years.[2] Pardons were only granted in exceptional circumstances, either in relation to the death penalty or where specific circumstances rendered the punishment particularly severe. Difficult family circumstances, in addition to illness or invalidity, were the most common grounds for pardons during this early period.[3] The government in particular looked to cases where the war or unusual circumstances had led to severe hardship. In July 1947, the cabinet had for example pardoned two brothers who had been sentenced to five and four years' imprisonment respectively for fighting on the Eastern Front, but whose father had spent several years in a German concentration camp before being killed in a plane crash in December 1945. Gundersen reported to the cabinet that the man's widow was in a serious nervous condition and the cabinet approved his recommendation for both her sons to be pardoned.[4] Yet such cases remained exceptions during the early period, and were decided on a case-by-case basis. While the reckoning was still ongoing, authorities were reluctant to overturn court judgments. Gundersen also repeatedly ruled out amnesties for specific groups of prisoners, as this 'would appear as a weakening of the reckoning in its entirety'.[5]

However, in the course of 1947, the government began to realise that many pardon requests were based on the argument that early sentences had been significantly harsher than later ones.[6] And indeed, sentences handed down in 1947 differed significantly from those handed down in 1945, with the latter at times being as much as two to three times as severe. During the debate on the Treason Act in February 1947, Gundersen had still categorically denied that there was an imbalance in sentencing practice. But he was forced to modify this statement later that year, as it emerged

[1] On 1 January 1947 authorities were able to report that there were approx. 450 unprocessed pardon requests; Justis- og Politidepartementet, *Om landssvikoppgjøret* (Gjøvik: Mariendal, 1962), p. 410.

[2] Ibid., p. 413. [3] Ibid., p. 417.

[4] RA/S-1005/A/Aa/L0005: Referat fra Regjeringskonferanse, sak nr. 1, 'Benådningsandragende', 24 July 1947.

[5] RA/S-1042/D/Dh/L0009: 'Landssvikernes sosiale gjeninnpasning?', memo, Ministry of Justice, February 1947.

[6] On inequality in frontfighter verdicts see RA/S-1043_1/J/Jb/Jba/L0002: Untitled memo, 3 February 1947; memo: 'Benådning – løslatelse på prøve' by byråsjef August Breder, 9 September 1947; speech by Erik Solem, *Dommerforeningens møte*, 5 September 1947.

that there were, in fact, huge discrepancies between earlier and later judgments. Certain groups, such as frontfighters, were particularly affected by this. The Ministry of Justice soon recognised the problem, in particular as 'equality before the law' was such a core principle underlying the trials. It was important to the government that the trials could be justified from a legal perspective, and that they underscored the authorities' prerogative on punishment as well as their institutional integrity. While the treason trials were coming to an end, with less than 10 per cent of cases still to be decided by early January 1948, action was necessary so that the trials remained credible. This meant that it would be impossible to let verdicts stand that were completely out of line with the court practice developed during 1946 and 1947. The question, then, became how to address the problem of sentencing inconsistencies.

Throughout 1947, the Ministry of Justice had considered a number of different strategies to even out the variations in prison sentences. In September 1947, the cabinet approved the most severe cases for pardons.[7] However, this procedure soon turned out to be insufficient in levelling court verdicts, as several hundred cases handed down in 1945 and early 1946 had to be rectified. The Ministry initially considered releasing on parole those prisoners who had received a disproportionately harsh sentence, which would have been possible through a relatively straightforward change to the Prisons Act of 1903. The DPP had originally taken the initiative for such a measure, arguing that the alternative – an individual review through the court system or through central authorities – would result in significant added costs to the treasury.[8]

However, the Ministry of Justice opposed any change to the Prisons Act. A new rule allowing treason prisoners to be released on parole would have meant that *all* sentenced collaborators would fall within its remit. This, in turn, would have placed significant authority into the hands of individual prison directors, who according to the Prisons Act would be in charge of deciding upon the granting of parole. On such a politically sensitive topic as the treason trials, the Ministry was reluctant to place authority over this corrective measure with individual prison directors. It also cautioned that such a practice could again lead to uneven release practices across the country. The Ministry agreed with the DPP that an

[7] RA/S-1005/A/Aa/L0005: Referat fra Regjeringskonferanse, sak nr. 1, 'Dommer i saker mot unge frontkjempere avsagt på tidlig tidspunkt av landssvikoppgjøret', 11 September 1947.

[8] Statements made by the DPP in letter to the Ministry of Justice of 12 June 1947, referenced in RA/S-1043_1/J/Jb/Jba/L0002: 'Benådning – løslatelse på prøve', memo, byråsjef August Breder, 9 September 1947.

appeals procedure would pose significant challenges to the already burdened court system. Instead, it therefore proposed to form an advisory appeals committee, which would consider each case and aid the Ministry's decision whether or not to pardon an individual.[9] While any such body appointed by the Ministry in order to overturn or change court verdicts raised questions of the separation of powers and judicial independence, a civil servant from the Ministry of Justice concluded that, in light of the widespread demands for closure and the overwhelming need to correction unequal verdicts, 'concerns of [constitutional] principle ought presumably to be set aside'.[10]

On 19 January 1948 the Ministry of Justice instituted a Pardons Committee. As members it appointed Justice Erik Solem, DPP Andreas Aulie and law professor Johannes Andenæs. The work of the Pardons Committee was complex and time-consuming. Its task was, first and foremost, to review the cases of frontfighters and *Hird* members, which showed the widest discrepancies between sentences passed early and late. By summer 1948, the Committee had reviewed more than 384 such cases, the vast majority of which resulted in a considerable change of the verdict.[11] Once the Committee had reviewed all frontfighter and *Hird* cases, it continued with a review of the judgments handed down in 1945 and 1946, and reviewed all cases that had led to a prison term of more than eight years.[12] In addition to notable deviations from established court practice, the Committee in its reviews of cases also took into consideration cases of personal hardship. Death penalty verdicts, however, continued to be considered by the cabinet.

The Minister's own explanation for why judgments had been uneven was that the courts had lacked experience in applying the complex and new legal provisions at the heart of the reckoning.[13] But public sentiment in the early post-liberation period had also influenced the courts and led to harsher judgments. As we have seen, however, such influences could never have been openly recognised by the Ministry, which placed a great emphasis on the centrality of the rule of law and judicial independence in the process. The specific pardons system adopted had the advantage that the gravest cases could be overturned in relative silence while the overall legal framework of the reckoning remained unchanged. The superimposition of the new body on the old judicial structure meant that the authorities now operated on two temporal planes. While the Treason

[9] Ibid. [10] Ibid. [11] Justis- og Politidepartementet, *Om landssvikoppgjøret*, p. 418.
[12] Ibid., p. 419. [13] Speech by Minister of Justice Gundersen, *Juristforeningen*, 20 February 1948.

Act of 1947 had confirmed the legal principles that had been adopted during and immediately after the war, the review practice adjusted sentences to the status quo of 1947 onwards.

5.2 Early Release

From late 1947, the Ministry of Justice and the DPP had also begun to focus more acutely on how the treason trials could be brought to a conclusion. As we have seen, the DPP increasingly chose not to prosecute lesser crimes. This led to 5,231 cases of prosecutorial waivers, each of which had been approved by the DPP himself. The vast majority of these concerned passive *Nasjonal Samling* (NS) members. The DPP considered whether further reductions could be achieved, for example by excluding certain criminal offences from criminal prosecution altogether. However, the DPP cautioned in a letter to Minister of Justice Gundersen in September 1947 that any such measure would 'very quickly be commented upon in the press and lead to troublesome and in any case useless discussions'.[14] This highlights the continued centrality of public attitudes on any administrative measures relating to the trials. The main question troubling the DPP and the Minister of Justice was how a gradual reduction of the trials could be reconciled with the broader symbolic messages they were still meant to convey. Instead, the DPP proposed a more subtle review of pending cases through members of his own central authority with a view to halting procedures. This, he hoped, could 'stop a number of less important cases from being brought to court and at the same time prevent new ones from being taken up based on the exceedingly eager initiative of younger policemen'.[15]

The administrative conclusion of the trials from an institutional perspective was just one dimension of government policy at this time. Equally central was the reintegration of sentenced collaborators into society, and in particular into the workforce.[16] It had been a key promise of the Gerhardsen government that the treason trials would be carried out with the fewest possible losses to the workforce.[17] However, the authorities had realised early on that reintegration would be a difficult 'two-way

[14] RA/S-1558/D/L0020: 'Avslutningen av rettsoppgjøret', letter by DPP Andreas Aulie to Justice Minister Gundersen, 26 September 1947.

[15] Ibid.

[16] RA/S-1042/D/Dh/L0009: 'Hva skal følge etter domstolenes oppgjør med landssvikerne?', memo, Ministry of Justice, 4 February 1947.

[17] S.tid. (1945–1946), pp. 23–24.

process'.[18] The impetus for an accelerated release procedure had been given by a group of church representatives in November 1946. They had written to the Ministry of Justice, requesting a more expansive use of release on parole given the 'slowness' of the reckoning.[19] An accelerated release was to signal to sentenced collaborators that society was willing to welcome them back. This, the church representatives argued, was necessary in order to overcome the deep rifts that the trials had brought upon society.[20] But at the time, the government had been cautious not to interfere too severely with the ongoing reckoning. In responding to a letter from Bishop Berggrav on the matter, Minister of Justice Gundersen wrote in November 1946 that he would not want to put a proposal before the *Storting* until such time that he could be certain it would be approved. He added that

> The climate surrounding the treason trials is ever so volatile and people's legal attitudes do manifest in strong ways in both directions. . . . One can of course say that our task is to guide ordinary legal consciousness, and that we shall not be bound by it. But we cannot walk too far ahead. It is a heavy load that we have to pull forward. There is no point in whipping the horse to make it run faster, if that means that it loses its load. For it is the load that has to move forward.[21]

Despite Gundersen's reluctance, the Ministry of Justice had begun early on to differentiate among the prison population, with a clear separation being drawn between 'hardened and aggressive' individuals and those with value for the workforce.[22] Reintegration and re-education became central concerns for the Ministry.[23] On 1 January 1948, approximately 4,500 individuals remained in prison on counts of treason.[24] In addition to the case-by-case decisions of the Pardons Committee, the authorities deemed the time ripe to gradually pass a number of legal acts to the effect of accelerating the release of treason convicts back into society. There were a

18 RA/S-1042/D/Dh/L0009: 'Hva skal følge etter domstolenes oppgjør med landssvikerne?', memo, Ministry of Justice, 4 February 1947.

19 *Neste fase i rettsoppgjøret – Biskopenes Brev til Justisministeren, November 1946* (Oslo: Land og Kirke, 1946).

20 Ibid., p. 11.

21 RA/PA-0320/2/H/L0017: Confidential letter from Justice Minister Gundersen to Bishop Berggrav, 20 November 1946.

22 RA/S-1042/D/Dh/L0009: 'Hva skal følge etter domstolenes oppgjør med landssvikerne?', memo, Ministry of Justice, 4 February 1947.

23 See for example Ibid.; RA/S-1042/D/Dh/L0010: 'Oversikt over planleggingen av arbeidet med landssvikfangene', memo, Johannes Halvorsen, 12 July 1946.

24 Justis- og Politidepartementet, *Om landssvikoppgjøret*, p. 412.

number of rationales behind these measures. Statistics were beginning to show that these prisoners were mostly first-time offenders and unlikely to reoffend. The government had also gained a better understanding of the grave social ramifications of extended imprisonment, not only on prisoners themselves, but also on their families and local communities. Moreover, treason convicts were often high-skilled workers, who were at risk of being permanently excluded from their respective professions. By 1948, the job market had become very competitive, which would make it more challenging for sentenced collaborators to secure employment, in turn exacerbating the 'social problem' this group represented.[25] It was therefore desirable to reintegrate them into society rather than turn them into outcasts who might pose a social and political threat.[26] But at all stages, this process was limited by the importance of safeguarding the overall authority of the trials, and the degree to which wider society would accept such a change in policy.

Formally, the same sentencing rules applied to treason prisoners that applied to ordinary prisoners. The ordinary provisions on prison parole, as laid down in the Prisons Act of 1903, consequently applied also to treason prisoners.[27] According to these rules, prisoners could be released on parole once they had served two-thirds of their prison sentence and spent a period of at least six months in prison. However, according to this rule, the period a prisoner had spent in custody was entirely irrelevant.[28] This caused significant delays in the release of treason prisoners, as many of them had spent disproportionately long periods awaiting their trial and the commencement of their prison term, compared to in the pre-war legal system. The main reasons for these delays were institutional limitations. But the Ministry of Justice was initially reluctant to grant treason prisoners 'special treatment'. The Ministry had been subjected to much criticism due to the separation between 'treason' prisoners and ordinary prisoners, and what many perceived as a more lenient treatment of 'treason' prisoners in working camps. In any proposals for accelerated release procedures, the Ministry took into close consideration the attitudes of 'the general public' on the matter.[29] After careful consideration, two sets of provisions were

[25] RA/S-1042/D/Dh/L0009: P.M. 'Spörsmål om visse endringer i reglene for fullbyrdelse av straff for personer straffet for landssvik' by Justice Minister Gundersen, 11 May 1948.

[26] RA/S-1042/D/Dh/L0009: 'Hva skal følge etter domstolenes oppgjør med landssvikerne?', memo, Ministry of Justice, 4 February 1947; the memo had already warned of the 'bitterness' that many collaborators felt towards society, and that this severely jeopardised their reintegration.

[27] Fengselsloven av 12 December 1903. [28] § 21, Fengselsloven av 12 December 1903.

[29] RA/S-1043_1/J/Jb/Jba/L0002: 'Om löslatelse på pröve av landssvikfanger'; memo, Ole Bäröe, 21 January 1946.

passed by parliament in May 1946 and March 1947 respectively, which allowed periods of custody in excess of ninety days to be taken into account, and created the possibility that prisoners could be released early if the entirety of the prison term amounted to less than five months.[30] But the reluctance within the Ministry to propose any changes to the existing framework for fears of public backlash highlights how much it still focused its attention on the broader public image of the trials.

5.3 The Halftime Act

In January 1948, a cross-party group of parliamentarians agitated for a further acceleration of release procedures.[31] The background for this was that the DPP had had to make renewed corrections regarding the conclusion of the trials, arguing that they would last until at least 1949. The MPs brought forward their initiative in particular due to the burden that the 'treason stamp' meant for prisoners and their families, and the 'damaging effects' that they feared for society if a more radical change were not adopted.[32] The group of MPs proposed releasing prisoners who had not previously been convicted of crimes after they had served *half* of their prison sentence, rather than two-thirds as required under the Prisons Act. The Ministry of Justice was initially sceptical of any such change, fearing it could make the trials 'lopsided' and that the broader authoritative message of the treason trials would be undermined. It is interesting to note, however, that in 1946, the Ministry had in fact considered such a change itself.[33] In a letter to Bishop Berggrav in November 1946, Gundersen had even suggested that he personally would like to see a rule introduced whereby prisoners could be released after just *one-third* of their sentence had been served.[34] But by 1948, he had changed his mind.

It is worth reflecting for a moment on the more underlying reasons for the change in Gundersen's attitudes on early release procedures. The fact that he had considered a release of prisoners after just one-third of a prison

[30] Justis- og Politidepartementet, *Om landssvikoppgjøret*, p. 413; these provisions applied to both *landssvik* prisoners and ordinary prisoners and were abandoned again in 1950.

[31] The group consisted of three MPs respectively of Labour and *Høyre*, and one of *Venstre*, the Centre Party and the Christian Democratic Party respectively.

[32] Draft proposal 'lovforslag av de 9 stortingsmenn Einar Stavang, Henrik Robberstad, Anders Noddeland, L. Grønland, Lars Breie, Nils Trædal, Gudbr. B. Tandberg, Erling Wikborg og E. Fredriksfryd, 21. Januar 1948', printed in Ot.prp. nr. 72 (1948), p 1.

[33] RA/S-1042/D/Dh/L0009: Untitled memo, Ministry of Justice, 12 January 1946.

[34] RA/PA-0320/2/H/L0017: Confidential letter from Justice Minister Gundersen to Bishop Berggrav, 20 November 1946.

sentence indicates that he was concerned for prisoners' prospects for reintegration. His statements of November 1946 are a clear indication that we should not think of the authorities in Norway as having been guided by a desire for vengeance after 1945, which then gradually declined. As Gundersen's change of heart shows, the process was, in fact, significantly more complex. The reason why Gundersen no longer favoured an accelerated release was that the trials had come under so much pressure. The contested nature of the trials meant that any departure from previous practice could have been perceived as a concession to political opponents. This indicates how much the Ministry of Justice was guided by ideas of the overall status and authority of the trials, regardless of whether the measure was meaningful from an institutional or socio-economic perspective. To the Ministry, the argument of 'equality before the law' also remained a central concern. It would be unfortunate, the Ministry concluded, if some prisoners were to benefit from such a rule while those who had already served their entire term could not. But internal notes suggest that the Ministry was, most of all, wary of implementing any changes that could lead the public to challenge the legal quality of the trials. As one senior civil servant pointed out, it was 'not easy to find a right and appropriate solution'.[35]

Given the pressure from MPs and the overwhelming need to bring the trials to a conclusion, however, the Ministry of Justice was increasingly prepared to make concessions.[36] It eventually agreed to propose a law that would enable the release of treason convicts with a sentence of no more than eight years after they had served half their prison sentence.[37] The Ministry also proposed that all prison terms of six months or below be turned into 'parole sentences'. In line with its internal deliberations, the Ministry openly acknowledged the challenges to successful resocialisation that had resulted from the lengthy reckoning and the delayed commencement of prison terms.[38] However, in its proposal for the bill, the Ministry of Justice sought to emphasise the 'firmness and consequentiality' with which it had carried through the trials.[39] Gundersen made sure to emphasise that

[35] RA/S-1042/D/Dh/L0009: 'Hva skal følge etter domstolenes oppgjør med landssvikerne?', memo, Ministry of Justice, 4 February 1947.

[36] RA/S-1042/D/Dh/L0009: P.M. 'Spörsmål om visse endringer i reglene for fullbyrdelse av straff for personer straffet for landssvik' by Justice Minister Gundersen, 11 May 1948.

[37] Ot.prp. nr. 72 (1948), p. 2; this did not apply to economic collaborators (discussed later in the chapter) and those who had attempted to flee or in any other way avoid prison.

[38] Ibid. [39] Ibid.

> A more elastic release provision does not shake the core of the treason trials; the sentences handed down have established once and for all the attitude of society on the crime of treason, and neither the general legal consciousness nor the general-preventive effect can suffer if small changes are made to accommodate for the particular difficulties of the legal reckoning with the traitors.[40]

This signals the emphasis the Ministry wanted to place on the symbolism of the trials, even while they were in their administrative phase-out. We can also discern a subtle change in rationale of the trials. The previous debates had centred around the individual-preventive effects of punishment, as sentenced collaborators were regarded during the early stages as a potential threat to society.[41] But by 1948, most 'treason' prisoners had been recognised as integral members of the workforce and unlikely to reoffend.[42] However, punishment still served the 'general-preventive' effect of acting as a deterrent against potential future acts of treason. As such, it was to convey a broader message to society about the requirement of loyalty towards the state. At this point in time, in the early stages of the Cold War, this message became of ever-increasing importance.[43]

During the debate on the Halftime Act, the *Storting* was divided according to by now familiar lines. Within the Justice Committee, NKP member Berg predictably opposed any softening of provisions, arguing that the trials had taken much too long and that the government had failed in its promise.[44] Lyng (*Høyre*), Ramndal and Skogen (both Liberal) opposed the limitation that the provision excluded certain groups of prisoners and thereby led to unequal treatment. In doing so, they again sought to demonstrate the importance of following ordinary legal rules even in the context of the treason trials – whether this worked to the benefit or the detriment of treason convicts. But the majority of the Justice Committee nevertheless agreed to the provisions.[45] Within parliament itself, the measure was so contested that it took a second round of debates before it was eventually passed. Many MPs indeed wanted to go further in softening the trials.

40 Ibid., pp. 2–3. 41 Ibid., p. 3.

42 On 1 April 1948 3,801 individuals were still in custody, 882 of them were farmers or were farm or forest workers, for whom there was a great demand; RA/PA-1261/D/L0001/0001: 'Spørsmål om visse endringer i reglene for fullbyrdelse av straff for personer straffet for landssvik', memo, Ministry of Justice, 7 March 1948.

43 The context of the Cold War is discussed in more detail in Chapter 6.

44 Innst. O. nr. 112 (1948), p. 162. 45 Ibid.

The debate concerning the Halftime Act once again showed the growing pressure on the authorities to allow for the smooth integration of sentenced collaborators into society. At the same time, as in many previous debates, objections were raised both by hardliners and more moderate voices. The motivations were different for these two groups, however. While NKP and hard-line Labour representatives insisted on a harsh reckoning, as one might expect of people whose identity was defined around the resistance and the memory of political persecution under the occupation, more moderate voices sought to reconcile legal principle with institutional limitations and sociopolitical rationales. The Ministry was concerned that the bill might be interpreted as displaying weakness and, during the debate, Gundersen repeatedly stressed that it was not an amnesty provision.[46] But in the end, the Halftime Act was passed, and upon its implementation, 1,163 of the 3,200 individuals in prison at the time were released with immediate effect.[47] Another 724 prisoners were released throughout the remainder of 1948, a further 887 were released in 1949, and upon the turn of the year 1949/1950, there remained practically no treason prisoners with sentences of less than two years.[48]

5.4 Escape to Argentina

The introduction of changes aimed at a gradual release of short-term prisoners should not be mistaken for an overall 'softening' of the trials. Rather, the focus of the trials shifted towards those who were deemed the most serious offenders and whose conviction carried a central meaning for the trials as a whole. For those who could be reintegrated swiftly, there was the concern that every month spent in prison might jeopardise their successful return to their professions and social communities. While the bulk of prisoners had been released by the late 1940s, however, the authorities were intent on not appearing weak. Successful law enforcement remained a central concern. And the flight of a group of collaborators in 1947 showed just how far the DPP was prepared to go to ensure that the law was enforced against suspected and sentenced collaborators.

On 3 July 1947, a group of ten former NS members set sail for Argentina aboard the motor ship *Solbris*, triggering the largest international manhunt of the treason trials. Four of the men aboard the *Solbris* had

[46] Ot.prp. nr. 72 (1948), p. 5; O.tid. (1948), p. 345.
[47] Justis- og Politidepartementet, *Om landssvikoppgjøret*, p. 413.
[48] RA/S-1043_1/J/Jb/Jba/L0002: Memo 'Benådning av "korttidsfanger"', 31 January 1950.

received prison terms for treason and had managed to escape Espeland prison close to Bergen, while the six others were still awaiting trial, some for senior activities in the NS as well as the SS. The group managed to sail from Bergen aboard a ship which had been prepared by the six still awaiting trial. When the Norwegian authorities heard about the flight, they exchanged countless messages with overseas embassies and ports in the hope of locating the vessel. The affair was covered widely by the Norwegian press, but for several weeks, the authorities failed to determine the ship's location.[49] The press speculated intensely on its whereabouts, with initial guesses including Ireland and Sweden. Soon, rumours were in circulation that the successful escape was an indication that powerful NS networks were still operating throughout the country. This, of course, was exactly the kind of speculation that cast an unfavourable light on the Gerhardsen government's handling of the occupation legacy.

Via the British Foreign Office it emerged that the *Solbris* had first sailed to Weymouth on 5 July, and from there had travelled to Vigo in Spain. The Norwegian embassy in Spain was able to locate the ship in Vigo, where the prisoners had the ship repainted and refuelled before continuing their voyage to Tenerife, where they arrived on 30 July 1947. While Norway pressed the Spanish government to detain the ship, the men aboard the *Solbris* were in luck: a series of communication issues between officials in Tenerife and the Spanish mainland meant that they could depart the island unnoticed. Although Spanish orders to detain the *Solbris* did eventually come through, the ship had by that point managed to reach a smaller island in the Canaries, whose harbour authorities had not yet been alerted. There, the *Solbris* refuelled and loaded up on food and water before setting sail for Argentina. At this point, the Norwegian Foreign Ministry had already liaised with British authorities, who via the Colonial Office had made sure to 'notify the authorities in the British territories at which the "Solbris" might call with a view to any possible action they may be able to take to detain the ship and the crew'.[50] The Norwegian Foreign Office in addition called for all Norwegian vessels to look out for the *Solbris* and to detain it if found.

By August 1947, *all* ports on the coastlines of Western Africa, the Eastern Coast of South America and the Caribbean had been informed via the Norwegian embassies to notify the Norwegian Foreign Office

[49] News first broke as early as 9 July 1947, and reporting continued for weeks.

[50] RA/S-1558/D/L0014: Letter from the British Foreign Office to the Norwegian Embassy, 29 July 1947.

immediately if the ship was seen. Meanwhile, the DPP via the Norwegian Foreign Office liaised with a number of foreign governments to ensure that, once found, the escapees could be formally extradited to Norway. Given the enormous machinery that the DPP had set in motion, it seemed unlikely that the runaways would succeed. And even if they had still held hopes of reaching a remote harbour unnoticed, those hopes soon faded when, after an engine failure, they landed on a prison island in the Brazilian Fernando de Noronha archipelago in the Atlantic Ocean.[51] The men were transferred to the Brazilian mainland and the Norwegian government filed a formal extradition request to the Brazilian state.[52] The DPP and the Foreign Office were meticulous in producing the documents required, doing everything they could to ensure that the capture of the escaped 'traitors' would be presented as a success. The Ministry of Justice had planned to return the prisoners swiftly, even inquiring as to the cost of chartering an airplane in which to transport the fugitives.[53] In the end, however, the Norwegian authorities failed. On 12 May 1948, the Supreme Court of Brazil turned down Norway's extradition request, stating that there was no obligation under international law to extradite political prisoners: as the crimes committed by the individuals in question 'neither affect man's natural rights, nor interfere with international (universal) security', they were deemed an entirely domestic affair.[54] This was, of course, because the crimes in question concerned acts of treason. More generally, this episode therefore mirrors the way the treason trials had been framed. The men from the *Solbris* ultimately reached Argentina and, like many other European Nazis, built a new life there.[55] The Norwegian government decided not to submit a new extradition request.[56] The case was but one instance of coordinated efforts by NS networks to evade

[51] 'Ten Hunted Men Land on Jail Isle – From Weymouth to Brazil', *Daily Express* (30 August 1947); Astrup Nielsen, *Eventyret på Solbris* (Bergen: Martinussen, 1952).

[52] DPP Andreas Aulie had previously raised concerns over an extradition request: RA/S-1051/D/L0063/0003, Letter from DPP Andreas Aulie to the Ministry of Justice, 2 August 1947. He argued that it could both set a dangerous precedent with regard to the extradition of political prisoners, and 'the potential negative effects that a rejected Norwegian request could have on the general opinion around the reckoning here at home'.

[53] RA/S-1051/D/L0063/0003: Letter from Thos. Cook & Son to Ministry of Justice, 23 March 1948.

[54] RA/S-1558/D/L0014: Translation of Judgment of Brazilian Supreme Court of 12 May 1948; see also Hersch Lauterpacht and Elihu Lauterpacht, *International Law Reports* 18 (1951), Case number 99, pp. 301–302.

[55] Anne Kristin Furuseth, *Norske nazister på flukt: jakten på et nytt hjemland i Argentina* (Oslo: Schibsted, 2013), pp. 159–164, 177–216.

[56] RA/S-1051/D/L0063/0003: Letter from the Norwegian Foreign Office to the Ministry of Justice, 3 June 1948.

justice. During the early post-war period, at least forty-two individuals evaded punishment by fleeing to Argentina, Brazil and Spain, among other countries.[57]

5.5 The Last Execution

In 1947/1948, the application of the death penalty in treason cases continued to stir mixed feelings. For the government, it was almost impossible to steer a middle ground. It received increasing numbers of letters from citizens and intellectuals requesting that the death penalty be abolished or its implementation stopped.[58] But when the government had first pardoned two death penalty convicts in September 1947, this had led to increased scrutiny by the 'ice front' press and advocates of a harsh and consequential reckoning.[59] In December 1947, the government pardoned a third individual, Olaf Gamborg-Nilsen, who had been sentenced to death for murder. In its reasoning, the Ministry argued that

> We are now approaching the final stages of the reckoning and the death penalty has not been introduced as a permanent element of our criminal justice system. Even though no changes have been made – or will be made – to the criminal nature of the offence of treason, one dares acknowledge that a change in attitudes has manifested itself in wide circles of our population with regard to the necessity of executing death penalty verdicts. Deep societal considerations and moral and ethical factors are at the basis of any assessment of this question and particular weight is given to the general legal attitudes of the people. The Ministry recognises the change in general attitudes that so clearly has taken place.[60]

Several opponents of the death penalty took this growing uncertainty as an opportunity to call for its abolition. In January 1948, fourteen prominent Norwegian women sent an appeal to the government that the death penalty be abolished.[61] On 26 February 1948, Gabriel Moseid of the Centre Party and Haldor Haldorsen of the Liberal Party presented to the government a formal proposal to abolish the death penalty and urged the Ministry of Justice to take the matter under renewed consideration. In a

[57] Furuseth, *Norske nazister på flukt*, p. 42 (endnote 30).

[58] RA/S-1005/A/Aa/L0005: Referat fra Regjeringskonferanse, sak nr. 2, 'Statsministeren refererte: ... 2. skriv fra Norges Fredslag om dødsstraffen. T.E.', 7 August 1947); RA/S-1005/D/Da/L0040: Letter from Minister of State to the Ministry of Justice, 21 January 1948.

[59] Lars-Erik Vaale, *Dommen til døden: dødsstraffen i Norge 1945–50* (Oslo: Pax Forlag, 2004), p. 131.

[60] 'Kgl. res. av 5. December 1947', Justis- og Politidepartementet, *Om landssvikoppgjøret*, p. 411.

[61] 'Dødsstraffen. Kjente kvinner vil ha den avskaffet', *Verdens Gang* (16 January 1948); 'Dødsstraffen', *Arbeiderbladet* (17 January 1948); 'Dødsstraffen', *Verdens Gang* (19 January 1948).

series of memos, the Ministry weighed up the pros and cons of an abolition at this stage of the trials.[62] In spring 1948, fifteen cases in which the prosecution had applied for a death penalty verdict were still pending before court, and the prosecution was considering applying for a death penalty in another two cases. The prosecution believed that only a few of these cases would lead to a death penalty verdict in court, however. The DPP argued that there were significant arguments against the continued use of the death penalty, given the time that had passed since the liberation and the fact that collaborators no longer posed a security threat to the nation. The general-preventive purposes had also been fulfilled, he argued, in that the death penalty had been implemented in a sufficient number of cases for authorities to have made an example that 'treason is a crime of a distinct category and is punished by death'.[63] Moreover, the DPP argued that

> The death penalty is not a part of the Norwegian legal system. This has long since been expressed in the law-making of this country, which followed a natural course [in abolishing it]. This conviction is deeply rooted in the people's sense of justice. But experience has taught us that this form of punishment is necessary when the nation is at peril during a war, enemy occupation and presumably also during any attempt to overthrow the state with violent means.[64]

But there were also a number of powerful arguments against changing the legal framework as such. The most significant of these was that like cases would be treated differently. A change in the law would also make impossible the execution of death penalty verdicts already handed down, which was a particularly important argument, given that several high-profile death sentences had not yet been executed. Ultimately, the DPP and the Ministry of Justice therefore decided that it was best to uphold the penalty, and the Ministry of Justice drafted a corresponding report to be presented to the government and the *Storting*.[65]

The *Storting*'s Justice Committee was divided on the question of whether to uphold the death penalty. Four MPs went against it, stating that the long distance in time since the liberation warranted a return to 'the legal and moral standards of peace time'.[66] This was the same argument

[62] RA/S-1558/D/L0020: 'Ang. spørsmålet om å oppheve dødsstraffloven av 13 December 1946', memo, DPP Andreas Aulie, 1 May 1948.

[63] Ibid. [64] Ibid.

[65] At the time the matter was debated in the *Storting*, thirty-five death penalty verdicts had been executed, twenty-three against Norwegian citizens, eleven against German citizens and one against a Danish citizen.

[66] Innst. O. nr. 119 (1948), p. 173.

that had been in circulation during the previous debate: that the long-term effects were detrimental to society, and that the general-preventive effects of the trials declined as the distance to the occupation grew. Those in favour, by contrast, argued that there might still be cases so serious that they deserved a death penalty verdict. In the *Storting*, the majority of MPs voted to keep the death penalty. But 40 per cent of MPs were opposed, a decided increase from the debate eighteen months earlier.[67] In addition, the argumentative patterns of MPs suggest that true opposition to the death penalty was much higher at this point.[68] However, conveniently perhaps, the rationale that had guided most recent debates was that of the 'inner coherence' of the reckoning and equality before the law, and so this argument prevailed. A majority of sixty-two over forty-three voted in favour of the government's proposal, ensuring the continued availability of the death penalty.[69]

Much of the debate on abolishing the death penalty revolved around the question of how relevant the Cold War context had become.[70] The debate became a competition between mentalities of war and peace, between optimists and pessimists. Some argued that the threat of the Cold War necessitated the continued availability of the death penalty as a warning sign to potential future traitors. Others wished for the nation to return to a mentality of peace.[71] But in the end, this was a debate that revolved as much around the Cold War, legitimacy and the post-war nation as it did around the fate of one individual: Ragnar Skancke, Quisling's Minister for Church and Education, was still in prison awaiting his execution, after succeeding in having his case reassessed on the grounds of new evidence, but failing to overturn the death penalty verdict in December 1947. The case against Skancke carried a central symbolic meaning for the treason trials as a whole. As the Minister for Church and Education during the occupation, he was a living symbol of the pain and suffering that had been inflicted upon teachers and pastors. On 27 August 1948, the government rejected Skancke's appeal to be pardoned. He was executed on 28 August 1948. It was the last time the death penalty was used in Norway.

[67] NKP, predictably, voted to keep it, as did a majority of the Labour Party. The Christian Democratic Party and the Centre Party were united against it. The Conservative *Høyre* and the Liberal *Venstre* were divided, with the latter being almost entirely against it.

[68] Nikolai Brandal, '"En rettsstat verdig": oppgjøret i Stortinget 1945–50', in Hans Fredrik Dahl and Øystein Sørensen (eds.), *Et rettferdig oppgjør? Rettsoppgjøret i Norge etter 1945* (Oslo: Pax Forlag, 2004), p. 61.

[69] O.tid. (1948), p. 381.

[70] The role of the Cold War in the administration of the treason trials is explored more fully in Chapter 6.

[71] O.tid. (1948), pp. 362–381.

5.6 Economic Collaboration

In many ways, the Norwegian treason trials were a reckoning of multiple speeds. This was not just signalled by what many perceived as the unreasonably late and unnecessary execution of Ragnar Skancke. While the Pardons Committee was reviewing judgments, the Halftime Act was releasing prisoners back into society and a growing uncertainty surrounded the use of the death penalty, around 70 per cent of the reckoning with economic collaborators still lay ahead. The earliest years of the reckoning had in particular been focused on *political* collaborators. Only select groups of economic collaborators, chosen primarily on the basis of the comparative simplicity with which they could be prosecuted, had been brought to trial.

In early 1947, almost all juridical questions regarding economic collaboration remained unresolved. It was particularly the larger cases, involving major Norwegian corporations, that had not yet reached the courts. While in November 1947 the DPP was able to report that 9,636 cases against economic collaboration had been decided and 3,900 remained, he stated that it was impossible to predict how long the conclusion of these cases would take.[72] Most of the cases that were tried late in the process required complex investigations. Economic cases depended on a multitude of documents, such as company records and correspondences with business partners, some of them held in German archives, and many of them lost. From a juridical perspective, these cases were therefore significantly more complex than proving cases of NS membership or those of the various military divisions. Often, they took several months to investigate.[73] The time-consuming nature of these cases, the DPP stressed in a correspondence with the Ministry of Justice, had to be borne in mind for any overall plans to bring the trials to a swift conclusion.[74]

For the courts, the dividing lines within the complex of 'economic treason' were significantly more difficult to draw than had been the case in relation to individual party membership or physical violence. § 2 of the Treason Decree of 1944 and § 86 were sufficiently vague for almost any contact with the occupier to fall within their scope. But limits had to be drawn both for legal and for practical reasons. The Hague Conventions of 1907 permitted some forms of interaction between the local economy and

[72] RA/S-1558/D/L0020: Letter from DPP Andreas Aulie to the Ministry of Justice entitled 'Avviklingen av rettsoppgjøret', 25 November 1947.
[73] Ibid. [74] Ibid.

the occupier, and this meant that the courts did not want to punish Norwegians for collaborating within the scope of permissibility as laid out by these conventions. But more importantly, practical and economic considerations were at the heart of the prosecution's broader policy towards economic collaborationism. The prosecution sought in particular to limit the number of cases brought to trial. As we have seen, the authors of the Treason Decree of 1944 had decided during the occupation that – for practical reasons – Germany workers would not be prosecuted. DPP Sven Arntzen reconfirmed this policy in autumn 1945. But there remained thousands of cases of companies that in some form had interacted with the occupier. During the early period of the treason trials, the prosecution authority tried to assess what the situation had been in various parts of the country and across different sectors of the economy to define more clearly the offence of economic collaboration. It turned out to be a difficult task. In January 1946, Jens Chr. Mellbye – a senior civil servant – in a memo to Gundersen summed up the situation as such: 'One has to remember that the occupation lasted for five years. The Germans got full power over the entire Norwegian industry. One has to look the truth in the eyes that practically speaking the entire population worked for German interests.'[75]

To the prosecution, a key consideration in deciding whether or not to bring cases to trial was that of coercion. Some professions, the authorities concluded, had been more vulnerable to direct influence by the Germans. The key question was therefore which directives had been given 'from above', either from the NS or directly from Terboven. Wherever individuals or businesses had been forced to work for German interests, either through direct coercion or because they would not have had another option to ensure their financial survival, they would not be held to account. However, it would be almost impossible to determine where to draw the line.[76] While the prosecution was trying to narrow down the scope of the economic reckoning, some senior advisors cautioned that too lenient a stance against economic collaborators would raise widespread dissatisfaction in the wider population, which 'do not have the necessary insights to understand and assess the difficulties that present themselves'.[77] For the prosecution authorities, it became a challenging balancing act to determine what degree of punishment was sensible at this stage of the

75 RA/S-1042/D/Dh/L0010: 'Notat for Statsråd Gundersen' from J. Chr. Mellbye to Justice Minister Gundersen, January 1946.

76 Ibid.

77 RA/S-1042/D/Dh/L0010: 'Ervervsvirksomhet for fienden', memo, Johannes Andenæs, 11 November 1945.

reckoning, and to assess the demands the population still had that the economic collaborators would be brought to justice. Many conflicts within the workforce during the early period of the trials had, after all, only been kept at bay through the promise of a reckoning with economic collaborators.

DPP Andreas Aulie gradually developed a minimum threshold to make the prosecution of the offence of economic collaboration workable and through his communications sought to achieve a similar legal interpretation by prosecutors across the country.[78] In line with the term 'improper' in § 2 section 3 of the Treason Decree, he argued that not any contribution to the wartime economy would suffice. Rather, it had to be 'reprehensible or blameworthy'.[79] It was with this threshold criterion that the prosecution brought cases to trial. However, perhaps envisaging similar lines of excuse to those offered in court by NS members, Aulie emphasised that the criterion could not be what individuals had personally deemed to be acceptable. Rather, there had to be an *objective* standard of behaviour. Even if an entire county had believed that collaborative engagement with the enemy was in Norway's best interests, this could not avoid criminal culpability, for 'one should not mistake defeatism for what we call legal opinion'.[80] However, if an individual was genuinely confused as to the situation, they should be able to have this count as an *excuse*. In particular, the uncertain situation in the summer of 1940, the DPP suggested, should potentially offer an excuse for what would otherwise have been collaborative behaviour.[81] Similarly, having acted on orders from senior officials should count to the benefit of the accused.[82] In order for cases to be fully reviewed by higher courts in the case of an appeal, the DPP encouraged prosecutors to list as many details as possible in the respective bill of indictment.[83]

As the trials progressed, the prosecution sought to further reduce the number of cases brought to trial. As with other cases of collaboration, the DPP realised that cases brought late would affect individuals more severely. Businesses were strongly affected by being under investigation for treason and many lost business partners and customers. Aulie also recognised that the occupation had brought individuals into a difficult situation. He therefore chose not to bring to court many cases 'in which the evidence

[78] RA/S-1042/D/Dh/L0007: 'Rundskriv L nr. 106', 26 November 1946.

[79] RA/S-1042/D/Dh/L0010: 'Rettsstridig og utilbörlig bistand til fienden', memo, DPP Andreas Aulie, 14 January 1947.

[80] Ibid. [81] Ibid.

[82] The Prosecution and the Compensations Directorate therefore gathered material into a handbook as a guideline for local prosecution authorities and courts.

[83] RA/S-1042/D/Dh/L0007: 'Rundskriv L nr. 106', 26 November 1946.

was unclear'.[84] By July 1950, of 16,378 recorded cases of economic collaboration, Aulie had opted to halt proceedings 'on grounds of evidence' in around 12,000 cases. This was widely criticised by those who argued that economic collaborators had been let off lightly, while small-scale 'political' collaborators had absorbed so much hatred. However, had one been more 'zealous', Aulie later concluded, the treason trials would have carried on for many more years and would have amounted to an 'irresponsible and impossible burden for the legal apparatus'.[85]

Gradually, the prosecution authorities began bringing cases of economic collaboration to trial. Throughout the trials, as many as 250 decisions on economic collaboration reached the Supreme Court, some of them as late as 1953.[86] The courts had to make difficult decisions. Largely, they followed the recommendations given by the prosecution. Rather than developing a set of categories, courts looked at cases in their individuality and took into account a wide range of circumstances to assess culpability. They confirmed that the time when the act of collaboration had occurred was of central importance, as was the scope of the collaborative activities. Courts distinguished in particular between existing firms and those founded during the occupation specifically with the aim of offering themselves to collaboration. In the case of firms already in existence before the war, courts considered a broader range of circumstances, such as whether it was a specialist industry which depended on interaction with the occupier, whether the company prioritised its relations with Norwegian or German business partners, and the political pressures that had been applied to the respective business sector.[87] A further factor was the strategic importance of certain businesses for the German war effort. But the courts also looked at the benefits the German occupation had brought to Norwegian companies, and whether or not the company had seized them for profit or expansion. These various considerations made it so much more challenging to determine the fault lines of economic collaboration than in cases of political collaboration.[88]

Some of the German investments in the Norwegian economy, had, in fact, brought significant advantages in the post-war period. This concerned in particular the aluminium and heavy water industries. Norsk Hydro is

[84] RA/S-1558/D/L0020: 'Min behandling av saken mot Fagernes', undated memo, DPP Andreas Aulie.

[85] Ibid. [86] Justis- og Politidepartementet, *Om landssvikoppgjøret*, p. 279.

[87] Ibid., pp. 279–280.

[88] Anette Storeide, *Norske krigsprofitører: Nazi-Tysklands velvillige medløpere* (Oslo: Gyldendal, 2014), pp. 354–359.

one example of a company that was significantly expanded by the Germans, but which post-war authorities deemed equally important for the rebuilding of the nation. Ultimately, some of the major corporations came out of the reckoning relatively unscathed, while small and middle-sized companies were punished comparatively harshly.[89] There were several reasons for this: smaller cases were brought earlier, as it was easier to investigate them. Moreover, large corporations benefited from the better legal expertise that their resources allowed for. But large corporations also benefited from close connections to legal and political elites. During the occupation, large corporations also had better information channels and ways of assessing the legality of their measures. Not least, smaller companies also had to make a greater, more active, effort to draw the attention of the German occupier, while Germans were largely familiar with the major corporations even before the invasion.[90] This meant that smaller companies often appeared to have collaborated much more eagerly than larger ones.

More than any other category of collaboration, the case of economic collaboration signifies the challenges faced by the law in dealing with such a complex social and economic situation as an enemy occupation. In total, only 777 economic collaborators received a prison term, making it much milder than the reckoning with political collaborators.[91] This is perhaps unsurprising, given that the trials in their earliest period had been about the victory over the NS and the German occupier, and relied on a simple punitive marker such as NS membership to generate an outgroup which was made responsible for the trauma of collaboration. By the time the economic cases reached the courts, the DPP deemed that there was hardly a good reason to prosecute this form of collaboration. This indicates that there were core pragmatic limits to the degree to which authorities would and could go against the interests of the economy and extend the reckoning. The case of economic collaboration therefore also shows that, by this stage, the main concern was to contain the total number of cases brought to trial. In post-war Norway, political and economic collaboration thus became two very separate categories of offence, with the latter managing to avoid the social stigma that had been attached to the former.

5.7 Knut Rød

Norway's post-war trials were also limited in significant other ways. They were built around crimes against the majority population rather than

[89] Dag Ellingsen, *Krigsprofitørene og rettsoppgjøret* (Oslo: Gyldendal, 1993), pp. 201–210. [90] Ibid.
[91] Ibid., pp. 130–131.

wartime crimes as such. This meant that the Holocaust played a marginal role. And no case better reflects the failure to prosecute Norwegians' contribution to the Holocaust than the trial of Chief Superintendent Knut Rød, who had been in charge of the deportation of the Jews in the greater Oslo region. Rød had first overseen the arrests of Jewish men, then meticulously drawn up lists and plans for a systematic arrest of Jewish women, children and the elderly in the early hours of 25 November 1942, so as to ensure that Jews could not alert one another about the impending deportations. Rød's plans even included Jewish patients at Oslo hospital, who were – often against the protest of their doctors – detained and brought to Oslo harbour for deportation to occupied Poland. The case against him had been protracted. He had initially stood trial in 1946 for his role in the deportation of Norway's Jews. The Court of Appeal had, however, acquitted him, after his defence team had successfully argued that Rød's behaviour had, in fact, been a 'camouflage' for his resistance activities, and that his involvement in the deportations had been the result of coercion from his superiors.[92] The case had then been appealed to the Supreme Court. The court argued that Rød's motivations could not be established and ordered a retrial. The case was then brought back to the Court of Appeal in 1948.

The case needs to be understood against the backdrop of Rød's longer career in the police and his actions during the war. Rød had been a member of the police since 1927, and had joined the NS in January 1941. Between July 1941 and September 1943, he served in the *Stapo*. During his retrial, the argument was again advanced that he had aided the resistance, although it remained somewhat unclear how. Yet, again he was acquitted by the Oslo Court of Appeal – and this time the case was not appealed to the Supreme Court. A number of theories have been proposed as to why he was acquitted. Some have referred to his long-standing connections in the police. A further reason why Rød may have been kept in his post-war position is that, by the time the case came up again in 1948, he was delivering intelligence on communist activity to the police. This highlights the changing priorities for the country's elite in light of the looming Cold War. At the same time, there was a considerable unwillingness to associate the Norwegian police force with complicity in the Holocaust. While it had been comparatively easy to single out and associate Quisling and his close Allies with the fate of Norway's Jews, the

[92] Oskar Mendelsohn, *Jødenes historie i Norge gjennom 300 år* (Oslo: Forlaget Press, 2019), p. 714; RA/S-3138-01/D/Da/L0969: Oslo politikammer, Dommer, nr. 969: Dnr. 4094 Knut Rød.

persecution of the Jews overall was framed as an 'unnorwegian' phenomenon: the deeper roots of antisemitism in Norway were left unaddressed during the trials.[93] As Synne Corell has shown, Rød's acquittal also meant that the police chose to halt ongoing investigations into their own involvement in the crimes against the Jews.[94] The case against Knut Rød was therefore only the culmination of a wider absence of interest in the Holocaust and the killings of civilians and prisoners of war both in Norwegian camps and on the Eastern front.

More generally, the case of Knut Rød reveals the importance of an individual for the nation rather than their actions as such in the decision to prosecute. This was evident also in the trial of two border guards, Håkon Løvestad and Peder Pedersen, in autumn 1947. Løvestad and Pedersen were accused of having shot and killed the Jewish couple Jakob and Rakel Feldmann as they were trying to flee the country in autumn 1942.[95] Both of the accused had been resistance members, and the jury vote to acquit them was likely influenced by this fact.[96] In his bill of indictment, the prosecutor stressed that the jury could find that there had been a case of 'necessity' as the couple had put Løvestad and Pedersen in danger. However, this was a controversial conclusion, as there was some evidence to suggest that the two had *already* decided to murder the couple and steal their possessions. The Jewish communities in Norway were left in shock by these judgments, leading many to reflect that they were not considered 'real Norwegians' by their compatriots.[97]

There was similar disbelief in the Jewish community after the final verdict against *Hauptsturmführer* Wilhelm Wagner was handed down.[98] Wagner, a German citizen, had been responsible in the German *Sipo* for Jewish cases, and had ordered the arrest of the Jews to be taken on the German cargo ship *Donau*. As a witness during the Quisling trial, Wagner had attempted to shift responsibility onto Quisling and the NS. Nevertheless, he was initially sentenced to death as a foreign war criminal. The court established that Wagner had known what fate awaited the

[93] Jon Reitan, 'Møter med holocaust: Norske perspektiver på tilintetgjørelsens historiekultur' (PhD Dissertation, NTNU, 2015), pp. 119–120.
[94] Synne Corell, *Likvidasjonen: Historien om holocaust i Norge og jakten på jødenes ejendom* (Oslo: Gyldendal, 2021), p. 12.
[95] Baard Herman Borge and Lars-Erik Vaale, *Grunnlovens største prøve: rettsoppgjøret etter 1945* (Oslo: Spartacus, 2018), p. 192.
[96] Ibid.
[97] Irene Levin, *Vi snakket ikke om Holocaust: mor, jeg og tausheten* (Oslo: Gyldendal, 2020), pp. 155–161.
[98] Rt-1947, pp. 248–259; RA: L-dom Oslo 2479.

deported Jews, explicitly referencing Auschwitz in its reasoning. However, Wagner appealed to the Supreme Court, which reduced the sentence to twenty years' imprisonment, arguing that Wagner had only played an 'inferior' role in the crimes committed against the Jews and that he had been pressured to follow orders from his superiors.[99] Again, the Jewish population were at a loss to understand the reasoning, given that Wagner's very position had been created to solve the 'Jewish problem' in Norway.[100]

This is not to say that crimes against Jews were not prosecuted as such. However, it is important to reflect on the ways in which these crimes were framed. The involvement in the seizure of Jewish property, which was punished under the treason provision of § 86, is a case in point.[101] For one senior NS official sentenced, it was deemed to be of particular gravity that he had been so comprehensively involved with administering seized Jewish property. A woman who had worked as a secretary for the Liquidation Board was in May 1946 punished under § 86.[102] However, the judgment stressed that this case principally concerned the support that the accused had given to the NS and the Germans: the specific crimes against Jews were reduced to only a secondary consideration, because the cases were brought as cases of treason. The judgment highlighted that 'The Jews were considered enemies of the Germans and the new age and it must be assumed that it was in the German interest that the measures against them were implemented.'[103] In other cases, acts against Jews were equated with acts against resistance.[104] In the case of the actor Karl Holter, the court argued that the 'strong hatred of Jews' expressed in some of his writings had to be seen as 'a defence of the Germans' persecution of the Jews' and 'propaganda for the benefit of the enemy'.[105] This, too, highlights how antisemitism was seen as inherently *German* in nature: an alien body only imported into Norway with the occupying power.[106]

There were parallels when it came to the prosecution of crimes against prisoners of war. It had emerged in autumn 1945 that Norwegians serving in SS divisions and the *Hird* had mistreated prisoners in Norway's concentration camps. In January 1947, for example, a guard at Rognan prison camp was sentenced to death for the murder of a Serbian POW. The Supreme Court subsequently upheld the ruling, but during a retrial reduced the penalty to fourteen years' imprisonment. This was despite

[99] Rt. 1947, pp. 248–259, at p. 249. [100] Levin, *Vi snakket ikke om Holocaust*, pp. 156–157.
[101] Rt. 1946, pp. 1205–1235. [102] Rt. 1946, pp. 541–543. [103] Ibid., at p. 542.
[104] Rt. 1946, pp. 1205–1235, at p. 1230. [105] Rt. 1946, pp. 932–935, at p. 934.
[106] Christopher S. Harper, 'Rettsoppgjørets behandling av deportasjonen av jødene fra Norge under okkupasjonen 1940–1945' (HL-senterets temahefte nr. 16, 2012).

the fact that the lower court had acknowledged that the camps were 'pure extermination camps and that the purpose was to systematically kill all prisoners'.[107] According to estimates, around 360 Norwegians served as guards in these camps, 43 of whom were sentenced during the trials. However, many of the sentences were light in relation to the crimes committed, 27 of which concerned the death of prisoners. Moreover, estimates are that many more would have been sentenced had the cases been investigated fully.[108]

One reason for why no full investigation into crimes against POWs was ever carried out was the difficulty involved in establishing causation. The POWs who might have been able to serve as witnesses had been sent back to their home countries.[109] Investigating these actions therefore often required cooperation with the Soviet Union. And while a Norwegian-Soviet joint commission was set up to investigate the fate of Soviet POWs, this proved challenging due to competing interests over the purposes of its mandate, with the Norwegian authorities fearing it could lead to compensation requests and claims of ownership for sites built in Northern Norway.[110] Later, there was some concern that Soviets could use commemoration events for Soviet POWs in Norway for espionage, prompting the Norwegian authorities to move the graves to mass burial sites.[111] This also highlights the complex transnational dimension of post-war justice, as – particularly in light of the Cold War – Norwegians now had an interest in toning down the investigation into the fate of Russian POWs. At the same time, it seems that the select court cases against Norwegian citizens concerning the mistreatment of POWs were brought mainly to convey how foreign prisoners should or should not be treated under international law, also with reference to future wars.[112] Overall, individuals who had mistreated or killed POWs received comparatively light sentences. As with the crimes committed by Norwegian frontfighters on the Eastern front, the cases came to centre around duties towards the national community rather than the crimes against individuals. The systematic mistreatment of POWs by Norwegians, by contrast, did not feature prominently in the trials.

[107] Rt. 1947, pp. 368–378, at p. 376.

[108] Nils Christie, *Fangevoktere i konsentrasjonsleire: en sosiologisk undersøkelse av norske fangevoktere i 'serberleirene' i Nord-Norge i 1942–43* (Oslo: Pax Forlag, 1972), p. 63.

[109] Ibid., pp. 43–44.

[110] Bjørn Westlie, *Fangene som forsvant: NSB og slavearbeiderne på Nordlandsbanen* (Oslo: Spartacus, 2015), pp. 194–212.

[111] Ibid., pp. 213–218.

[112] Rt. 1947, pp. 368–378.

When it comes to the crimes against Norwegian Jews and prisoners of war, the post-war reckoning therefore failed to provide an opportunity for punishment and reconciliation. Instead, through its limited focus on crimes against the state and the construction of patriotic narratives, it facilitated a state of collective amnesia that would last for more than four decades. For the few Jews who were able to return home to Norway, this had immediate consequences. They were often met with little understanding for their fate and also faced significant challenges in reclaiming their property, often only receiving a fraction of their assets.[113] And at a more underlying level, they were not included in the patriotic post-war narrative. At the same time, the small group of Jews who remained in Norway were hesitant to make their voice heard, as they did not want to reinforce negative stereotypes that could hamper their integration into Norwegian society.[114] Decades would pass before the Norwegian state began to acknowledge its shortcomings in how it conducted the post-war reckoning in relation to Jews and prisoners of war.[115]

5.8 Citizens

Norway's pre-war political elites also got off lightly. The debate surrounding the pre-war elites' culpability concerned both their pre-war and wartime actions in relation to defence policy, the handling of the invasion and their participation in negotiations with the Germans during the summer of 1940. The focus was in particular on Johan Nygaardsvold himself, the ministers in Nygaardsvold's cabinet, the individuals who had taken part in the Realm Council negotiations, and the *Storting*'s Presideum. Nygaardsvold had stated repeatedly both during and after the occupation that he expected to be put before a court for his failure to establish sufficient defence ahead of the German invasion, and large parts of the population had shared this expectation.[116] Norwegian constitutional law knew a particular type of court procedure, the *Riksrett*, which dealt with cases of misconduct on the part of senior officials.[117] As a preparatory stage

113 Mendelsohn, *Jødenes historie i Norge*, pp. 725–728; Berit Reisel, *'Hvor ble det av alt sammen?': plyndringen av jødene i Norge* (Oslo: Forlaget Press, 2021), pp. 180–237.

114 Levin, *Vi snakket ikke om Holocaust*, pp. 155–156.

115 An investigation into the liquidation of Jewish assets during the war would only be made in the 1990s. Following a government investigation, compensation payments of 450 million NOK were made. See Norges offentlige utredninger: NOU 1997:22.

116 Harald Berntsen, *I malstrømmen: Johan Nygaardsvold 1979–1952* (Oslo: Aschehoug, 1991).

117 The provisions concern ministers, MPs and Supreme Court Justices: §§ 86, 87 *Grunnloven*.

of such a procedure, the actions of the pre-war elites had been investigated by an investigative committee appointed by the eighty-ninth *Storting* in August 1945.[118] The report the committee presented in 1946 was damning, and criticised many of the individuals who had played leading roles in the events of 1940. But in September 1948, the Parliamentary Review Committee (*Protokolkomiteen*) recommended that no action be taken.[119] In November 1948, the matter was put before the *Storting*, where it was debated at length.[120] But ultimately, after eight painful days of debate in parliament, the majority of MPs voted that no legal measures be taken against Nygaardsvold and his cabinet, nor against any of the other institutions or individuals who stood accused of their shortcomings in the fateful year of 1940.

It is likely that in this matter, too, time was once again a decisive factor. Calls for an impeachment procedure against Nygaardsvold and his cabinet had been almost *unisono* in 1945.[121] But by the time the 1,500-page report had been presented by the Investigative Committee and the Parliamentary Review Committee had made its assessment, the situation had changed. 1948 was not a year in which to show weak leadership. And the fact that Labour was still in power meant that an impeachment procedure was likely to result in negative consequences for the party. Moreover, given the already heated discussions surrounding the war and the treason trials, the political bodies wanted to avoid a large-scale investigation that would have antagonised debate further. While several military officials were brought to trial in the post-war period for their failure to secure Norwegian defence during the invasion,[122] the political elites walked free. But in the medium term, the decision not to launch impeachment proceedings proved to be one of the core factors that made the trials vulnerable to attack. As a consequence, criticism of the trials intensified in late 1948 and 1949.[123]

The decision not to have an impeachment procedure, and the correction of verdicts on the recommendation of the Pardons Committee, reignited debates in late 1948 on whether the trials as a whole had been too broad and how they should be brought to a conclusion. Former DPP Sven Arntzen, responding to an article by Conservative Party (*Høyre*) MP John Lyng in *Aftenposten*, stated that punishment had, in his opinion,

118 S.tid. (1945), p. 131. 119 Inns. O. IX A. (1948). 120 S.tid. (1948), pp. 416–736.

121 'Impeachment' is here understood in the sense of the *Riksrett* procedure in Norwegian Constitutional law.

122 Rt. 1948, pp. 503–517; Rt. 1948, pp. 168–180.

123 The specific nature of these debates is discussed in Chapter 6.

served its purposes, and that the situation was radically different from that in 1945. At the same time, he stressed that no concessions could be made under the pressure of agitation by members of the NS, for such a measure could – 'at this dangerous time' – undermine the entire purpose of the trials: 'to impose the duty of loyalty to the country's authorities during war'.[124] But efforts were soon under way to accelerate the release of prisoners. By late 1948, the Pardons Committee had begun to consider a wider range of cases. There was now a growing awareness that *all* early judgments had been disproportionately harsh in light of later court practice.[125]

The Ministry of Justice recognised the need to bring these judgments into greater alignment with later court practice. The Ministry was cautious not to appear as an '*über*-Supreme Court', but argued that if the courts were found to have changed their position significantly since the liberation, then a reversal of some of the harsher judgments was a 'requirement of justice'.[126] Around the same time, opinions were fast changing in favour of broader amnesties. The social consequences of the 'treason stamp' had led to such grave consequences for individuals after their release that many politicians deemed a broader review to be appropriate.[127] In a cabinet meeting on 16 December 1948, Gundersen reported that he had received a request from ten cross-party MPs for all sentenced collaborators who would have been released before 1 April 1949 to be granted an amnesty before Christmas 1948. Gundersen, however, did not recommend this, and the Cabinet opted instead to grant pardons only in individual cases, taking into consideration particular hardship.[128] Gundersen and the rest of the cabinet would remain reluctant to give in to too swift or generalised a release of prisoners.

Nevertheless, it was clear to all that the tide was turning and that the trend was towards accelerating the release of prisoners into society. In an article published in November 1948, law professor Johannes Andenæs was

124 John Lyng, 'Rettsoppgjøret i perspektiv', *Aftenposten* (18 December 1948); Sven Arntzen, 'Er rettsoppgjøret lagt for bredt an?', *Aftenposten* (24 December 1948); John Lyng, 'Er rettsoppgjøret lagt for bredt an?', *Aftenposten* (31 December 1948); Sven Arntzen, 'Bør det skje lempninger i oppgjøret?', *Aftenposten* (6 January 1949).

125 RA/PA-1261/D/DL0001/0001: 'Straffeutmålingen i visse grupper landssviksaker', memo, DPP Andreas Aulie, 8 December 1948.

126 RA/S-1043_1/J/Jb/Jba/L0002: 'Revisjon av landssvikdömmer ved benådning', memo, byråsjef August Breder, 27 October 1948.

127 Lars Roar Langslet, *John Lyng: samarbeidets arkitekt* (Oslo: Cappelen, 1989), p. 80.

128 RA/S-1005/A/Aa/L0005: Referat fra Regjeringskonferanse, sak nr. 4, 'Benådning', 16 December 1948.

able to identify a decided change in broader public attitudes, stating that while public opinion had originally been in favour of a harsh reckoning, many now accused authorities of having been too strict.[129] The prisoners' personal situation increasingly moved towards the centre of government policy. The Justice Ministry's Prison Division compiled lengthy reports on prisoners' conditions and welfare. Citizens' groups launched campaigns for the accelerated release of prisoners, in particular relatives. Requests for pardons soared. A number of church representatives too, increasingly pushed for the release of prisoners.[130] Bishop Berggrav in his annual report for 1948 to the Ministry of Church Affairs announced that the Church would begin to work towards generating a broader basis for unconditional forgiveness in society.[131] This, he argued, was in line with the by now dominant desire of the wider population. It was important to meet individuals with 'unexpected goodness' in order to overcome the social frictions the treason trials had generated.[132] In many ways, this was in line with the logic that had underlain Berggrav's famous pamphlet, written four years earlier.[133]

In several memos, the Ministry of Justice considered various options for a further softening of the trials and accelerated release procedures. For the Ministry, the central argument in favour of a further review was the time that had passed since the liberation.[134] Since the passing of the Halftime Act, the average age of prisoners had only gone up further, as had their propensity for illness. As a consequence, their ability to be reintegrated into society had fallen, and this at a time of increasing competition in the employment sector.[135] However, within the Ministry, the decisive counterargument to accelerated release procedures was that any modifications could easily appear as a reversal of previous practice. The Ministry was therefore particularly uneasy about any proposals suggesting further *legislative* changes. The Halftime Act had already caused much controversy. In a memo of 31 May 1949, the Ministry of Justice came to the conclusion that the Halftime Act had 'not led to the peace surrounding the treason

129 Johannes Andenæs, 'Rettsgrunnlaget for landssvikoppgjøret', *Aftenposten* (19 February 1949).

130 RA/S-1558/D/L0020: 'Om lempninger i landssvikoppgjøret', confidential memo, Ministry of Justice, 31 May 1949; RA/PA-0320/1/H/0031: 'Oslo biskops Årsmelding for 1948 til Kirkedepartementet'.

131 RA/PA-0320/1/H/0031: 'Oslo biskops Årsberetning til Det Kgl. Kirkedepartement for 1949'.

132 Ibid.

133 Eivind Berggrav, *Folkedommen over NS* (Oslo: Land og Kirke, 1945).

134 RA/S-1043_1/J/Jb/Jba/L0002: 'Lempninger i landssvikoppgjøret', memo, Johannes Halvorsen, 23 May 1949.

135 RA/S-1043_1/J/Jb/Jba/L0002: 'Om lettelser i fullbyrdelsen av frihetsstraff for landssvik', memo, Ministry of Justice, 20 May 1949.

trials or sentencing practice that one had expected'.[136] In fact, the Ministry believed that the Halftime Act had widely been perceived as a 'sign of weakness of the authorities' and an 'admission that [they] had gone too far and punished too severely during the treason trials'.[137] It therefore concluded that it would be 'most desirable now to avoid a debate in the *Storting* around the treason trials'.[138] From 1949 onwards, the Ministry thus sought to avoid any measure that could appear as a concession to 'those who scream loudest for amnesties' or that could appear as 'an unfortunate vacillation in the treason trials'.[139] The Ministry was also concerned that any measures that further changed the rules for sentencing practice might lead to inequalities by working to the advantage of those whose cases proceeded to court comparatively late. The most central concern of government policy, however, was the *appearance* of coherence and firmness. The challenge became to limit the social burden on society while nevertheless retaining the trials' symbolic meaning and deterrent effect.

Gundersen's ministry in particular did not want to appear to give in to the widespread calls for amnesties.[140] Amnesties were a topic of much anxiety within the Ministry of Justice, as it was believed that they could undermine the authoritative message of the trials. The Ministry looked closely to other countries and their respective amnesty practices.[141] In May 1949, the topic of softening the trials was controversial and was debated within the cabinet.[142] However, the government remained cautious about the advantages of amnesties. An expansion of the existing pardons practice was thus deemed the measure that would generate 'the least possible publicity both inside and outside of prison camps'.[143] In response to the rumours circulating about a wave of impending amnesties, Gundersen made a series of public rebuttals in January

[136] Ibid.; RA/S-1558/D/L0020: 'Om lempninger i landssvikoppgjøret', confidential memo, Ministry of Justice, 31 May 1949.

[137] RA/S-1043_1/J/Jb/Jba/L0002: 'Om lettelser i fullbyrdelsen av frihetsstraff for landssvik', memo, Ministry of Justice, 20 May 1949.

[138] Ibid.

[139] RA/S-1043_1/J/Jb/Jba/L0002: 'Lempninger i landssvikoppgjøret', memo, Johannes Halvorsen, 23 May 1949.

[140] RA/S-1558/D/L0020: 'Om lempninger i landssvikoppgjøret', confidential memo, Ministry of Justice, 31 May 1949.

[141] RA/S-1043_1/J/Jb/Jba/L0002: 'Amnestilover eller revisjon av pågående rettsoppgjør i andre land', undated memo.

[142] RA/S-1005/A/Aa/L0006: Referat fra regjeringskonferanse, sak nr. 3, 'Landssvikoppgjøret', 25 May 1949.

[143] RA/S-1043_1/J/Jb/Jba/L0002: 'Om lettelser i fullbyrdelsen av frihetsstraff for landssvik', memo, Ministry of Justice, 20 May 1949.

1949.[144] But the widespread pardons were in many ways an amnesty practice through the back door. And while the main guiding principle was that the trials should be conducted in close alignment with ordinary criminal procedure, the rationale of pardoning practice thereby reflected the distinct temporal cycle of the treason trials.[145]

5.9 Civil Rights

A gradual reduction of prison terms was not the only modification made by the Ministry of Justice to correct unequal verdicts and ensure a smooth return of sentenced 'traitors' into society. The two other forms of punishment widely handed down by courts during the treason trials were monetary fines and the partial or complete loss of civil rights. These, too, had been handed down unevenly over time and called for a review. Modifications with regard to fines were the least controversial. Where a fine was deemed too harsh in light of the overall statistics and later practice, authorities subsequently reduced it.[146] Likewise, reductions were made when it would mean disproportionate hardship to an individual and jeopardise their livelihood.

The topic of civil rights was significantly more complex.[147] While courts had only in exceptional situations handed down a loss of *all* civil rights, selective loss of these rights was very common. A total of 44,406 of the 46,085 individuals convicted for treason partially lost these rights.[148] During the preparations of the trials, this form of punishment had carried a strong symbolic meaning. It offered an opportunity to exclude from the national community those who were deemed unworthy of it. But in addition to the loss of a specific right, such as the right to vote or the right to join the army, this form of punishment also carried with it a number of additional legal consequences. The reason was that many statutes dating from the pre-war era linked specific changes in an individual's legal status to a loss of civil rights – a form of punishment that had

144 Oscar Christian Gundersen, 'Noen betraktninger omkring rettsoppgjøret med landssvikerne', Speech at the Oslo branch of the Norwegian Attorneys' Association (*Foredrag i Oslo Krets av den Norske Sakførerforening*), 18 January 1949 (Oslo: Aschehoug, 1949); 'Ikke amnesti sier statsråd Gundersen', *Dagbladet* (31 December 1947).

145 RA/S-1558/D/L0020: 'Om lempninger i landssvikoppgjøret', confidential memo, Ministry of Justice, 31 May 1949.

146 Justis- og Politidepartementet, *Om landssvikoppgjøret*, pp. 429–430.

147 RA/S-1043_1/J/Jb/Jba/L0003: 'Utgangspunktet for rettighetstap', memo, byråsjef August Breder, 31 January 1949.

148 Justis- og Politidepartementet, *Om landssvikoppgjøret*, p. 426.

never before been handed down to the extent that it was during the treason trials.[149] The authors of the 1944 Treason Decree had either overlooked or silently accepted these legal consequences, but they now seemed out of line with the purposes of the trials.

Losing civil rights meant losing access to public old-age pensions. Over the years, many elderly NS members had agreed to a sentence and loss of civil rights by executive degree (*forelegg*) – following the introduction of this procedure by the *Storting* in 1946 – without realising that this would entail the suspension of their pension payments. Many accordingly found themselves in severe financial hardship.[150] Another consequence was that students were automatically taken off the register at most Norwegian universities. But most consequentially of all, the loss of civil rights affected individuals' rights to work in certain professions, even when these professions had not been specifically targeted by the wartime provisions. The sub-laws governing certain professions had in the pre-war era ruled out access to occupational licences, including those for tradesmen and hoteliers. In the pre-war era, these would have been minor provisions, governing the few cases in which an individual lost their rights due to a criminal sentence. They had not been drafted with such widespread withdrawal of civil rights in mind as the nation came to experience after 1945. The Ministry of Justice concluded that with regard to loss of civil rights, authorities were widely considered to have 'overshot the mark'.[151]

As with all other forms of punishment, the work of the Pardons Committee had corrected those sentences of loss of civil rights displaying the greatest discrepancy to later practice on a case-by-case basis. However, given the thousands of cases that had resulted in a loss of civil rights, a review through the Pardons Committee alone was not practically possible in order to achieve the desired results. The Ministry therefore opted instead to propose a broader change through an act of legislation.[152] The main rationale was that the many thousands who were now excluded from their professions could return to the workforce. The government bill proposed that anyone with a fine of less than eight years regain their rights

[149] RA/S-1043_1/J/Jb/Jba/L0003: 'PM om gjernervervelse av rettigheter som er fradømt i henhold til landssvikloven', memo, byråsjef August Breder, 7 May 1948. Of 'ordinary criminals' who received a prison term, only around 5 per cent received a penalty of loss of civil rights.

[150] RA/S-3212/D/De/L0302: 'Landssviksak ... – Lov om alderstrygd av 16 juli 1936 § 3)', memo, 23 November 1946.

[151] RA/S-1043_1/J/Jb/Jba/L0002: 'Benådning – løslatelse på prøve', memo, byråsjef August Breder, 9 September 1947.

[152] RA/S-1005/A/Aa/L0006: Referat fra Regjeringskonferanse, sak nr. 3, 'Landssviklovens regler om rettighetstap', 10 February 1949.

relating to their profession. The exceptions were attorneys, doctors, vets, pharmacists, midwives, pastors, teachers and sea captains, as these professions were considered to demand a particular element of public trust.[153] The Pardons Committee supported this proposal. It stressed that the broad ramifications of loss of civil rights ultimately jeopardised the reintegration of sentenced collaborators into society.[154]

Upon being presented with the Ministry's proposal, the *Storting*'s Justice Committee cautioned that the proposal could introduce an element of injustice into the final phase of the treason trials. However, the majority of the Committee nevertheless voted in favour of the bill. The Committee touched upon many of the underlying tensions that had governed the trials, but argued that the overwhelming aim was now to return to 'normality'. The debate in the *Storting* on 22 July 1949 similarly signalled MPs' desire for normalisation. In fact, the *Storting* went beyond the proposal put forward and opted also to normalise the political status of sentenced collaborators with regard to voting rights and military law, in addition to advancing their prospects for workforce reintegration. The provision introduced by parliament enabled individuals with a prison sentence of no more than one year to regain the right to vote and to join the military from 9 May 1950, the fifth anniversary of the liberation. In other words, the majority of parliamentarians now deemed former treason convicts worthy of regaining the status of full citizens.

Late 1949 also saw a 'Christmas pardon': a larger number of individuals were released after a review by the Pardons Committee.[155] On 1 January 1950, there remained a total of only 570 treason prisoners, 160 of whom were classed as 'short-term' prisoners with sentences of under eight years.[156] The arguments in favour of pardons kept rising, in particular as so much time had now passed since the liberation.[157] A senior civil servant within the Ministry of Justice proposed a further softening of the half-time rule for the short-term prisoners by arguing for a release after *one-third* of the term had been served – the same idea that Minister Gundersen had harboured three years earlier, but since dismissed. This proposal was met with significant opposition both by the minister as well as the Pardons

[153] Ot.prp. nr. 14 (1949), p. 6.

[154] Internal memo, 'Forslag til lov om endringer i landssviklovgivningens regler om rettighetstap', by Johannes Andenæs and Andreas Aulie, 19 January 1949.

[155] RA/S-1043_1/J/Jb/Jba/L0002: Memo 'Julebenådning', 22 November 1949; RA/S-1043-1/J/Jb/Jba/L0002: Memo 'Benådning av "korttidsfanger"', 31 January 1950.

[156] RA/S-1043_1/J/Jb/Jba/L0002: Memo 'Benådning av "korttidsfanger"', 31 January 1950.

[157] Ibid.

Committee. Andenæs was sceptical of seeing a further change introduced and warned of 'an absence of principle'.[158] It would further widen the gap between the different groups of prisoners that the Pardons Committee had sought to overcome through its meticulous work. Not 'mathematics', but gradual pardons of both long- and short-term prisoners were the answer, Andenæs argued, and instead proposed the release of larger groups of prisoners throughout the year. Gundersen, however, opposed any such acceleration and insisted on the continuation of previous practice because the Committee's suggestion could be considered 'a type of amnesty'. The cabinet sided with Gundersen on the matter.[159]

5.10 Time and Time Again

Despite the emphasis placed on gradually releasing prisoners back into society, some of the more problematic cases would continue to occupy the authorities for several years. Prisoners with an original sentence of eight or more years – of which there were 558 – provided a separate category of individuals which caused the Ministry of Justice and the Pardons Committee much concern. From November 1949 onwards, the Pardons Committee began to review these more severe cases, which did not fall within the scope of the Halftime Act.[160] The rationale behind this opening was a perception that the eight-year mark constituted an arbitrary boundary. On the other hand, there was a good reason why this group of offenders – who had often committed serious crimes – had been excluded by the Halftime Act.

Rather than expanding the applicability of the Halftime Act, however, the Ministry of Justice proposed a more elaborate approach for the release of long-term prisoners. This included a psychological assessment, a decision by the respective prison directorate, an assessment by the Pardons Committee, a resolution by the Justice Ministry's prison directorate and a final decision by the cabinet. Such a resource-intense procedure was possible only because the number of prisoners in this category was relatively small. Aulie, Andenæs and Gundersen considered the reports both an interesting 'experiment of criminal policy' and, most importantly, a

[158] RA/S-1043_1/J/Jb/Jba/L0002: Report 'Benådning av korttidsfanger' by Johannes Andenæs, 30 January 1950.

[159] RA/S-1005/A/Aa/L0005: Regjeringskonferanse, sak nr. 11, 'Landssvikoppgjøret', 21 February 1950.

[160] RA/PA-1261/D/L0001/0001: 'Om benådningsutvalget og om løslatelse av langtidsfanger', memo, Ministry of Justice, September 1949.

method of reassuring the public that it was appropriate that most of these more serious offenders be released into society.[161] Prisoners who had received nine or ten years' imprisonment were thereby gradually released after they had served just over half their term.

Gundersen remained cautious throughout the trials not to agree to a more widespread release of prisoners through a generalised legislative change or amnesties.[162] The most important ambition in his ministry's policies was to avoid an escalation of debate, even though it took seriously the concerns of prisoners and their reintegration into society.[163] The deterrent function of the trials was attaining an ever-greater importance at a time in which national allegiance was of the utmost political significance.[164] Gradually, the speed of releases through pardons increased. On 9 May 1950, 6,343 individuals had signed a petition delivered to the *Storting* by 'wives and mothers of prisoners', arguing for a pardoning of those still in prison.[165] Prisoners themselves sent appeals to the government. In one letter, a treason convict emphasised that most prisoners had accepted their imprisonment and fate more generally. The prisoner cautioned that the heated debate on law, politics and justice that was raging outside of prison walls was of hardly any benefit to prisoners themselves.[166] But in each case, the decision remained a fine balancing act between prisoners' hopes and society's expectations.

5.11 Conclusion

As this chapter has shown, the administration of the trials became subject to fundamental tensions in the period between 1947 and 1949, all of which were the result of their unexpectedly long duration. The fact that court practice had changed over time indicates the strong influence of public pressure on judicial outcomes. As a consequence of the Pardon Committee's reviews, the trials began to operate on two temporal planes: while verdicts were being adjusted to later court practice, the original legal

161 RA/PA-1261/D/L0001/0001: 'Om benådningsutvalget og om løslatelse av langtidsfanger', memo, Ministry of Justice, September 1949.
162 RA/S-1005/A/Aa/L0005: Regjeringskonferanse, sak nr. 11, 'Landssvikoppgjøret', 21 February 1950; 'Ønsket om barmhjertighet må ikke føre ut i vilkårlighet – Justisministeren tar bestemt avstand fra det private lovforslag om amnesti', *Aftenposten* (6 March 1950).
163 RA/PA-0320/2/H/L0017: Letter from the Ministry of Justice to Bishop Berggrav, 3 June 1949.
164 Gundersen, 'Noen betraktninger omkring rettsoppgjøret med landssvikerne'.
165 S.tid. (1950), p. 919.
166 RA/S-1005/D/Da/L0040: Letter to the Norwegian Government from the Representative of Prisoners at Gulating Prison, 9 May 1949.

framework largely stayed in place. The social and economic need for their conclusion in particular remained a challenge from the perspective of the 'inner equality' of the trials. This was a matter that both the *Storting*'s representatives and the government recognised, and which led to difficult decisions during the final stages of the trials. At the same time, the argument provided a shield from attack in what had become a heated political debate culture. In particular the strong criticism of government policy had tied the trials closely to the government's authority. This made the Ministry of Justice wary of giving in to calls for fundamental changes to the framework of the trials, or to amnesties. Most of all, however, the adaptation of government policy on the trials to new political realities and economic rationales shows that the treason trials could never be just a matter of law, but always operated in a highly volatile political context.

CHAPTER 6

Interpretation
Competing Narrations of the Trials, 1948–1964

6.1 'A War before Our Eyes'

On 29 February 1948, Einar Gerhardsen stepped before a group of fellow Labour Party members at *Kulturhuset Folkvang* in Kråkerøy, just outside Fredrikstad on the South-Eastern coast of Norway, and gave one of the most influential speeches of his long political career. Within days of the Communist coup in Czechoslovakia, the Prime Minister declared that

> Events in Czechoslovakia have not only caused sorrow and outrage among most Norwegians – but also fear and a sinister atmosphere. The problem for Norway is, as far as I can see, most of all a domestic issue. It is the Norwegian Communist Party that perpetually threatens the freedom and democracy of the Norwegian people.[1]

This speech put an end to any ambivalence in the Labour Party's relationship towards the Communist Party and Communism as such. It was a watershed in the history of the Labour Party.[2] The days when politicians and journalists commented on 'the two labour parties' following the sweeping election result of the Communist Party in 1945, and conjured the spirit of the Joint Party Programme, were long gone.[3] In this speech, Gerhardsen not only brought to an end the close cooperation between the Labour Party and the Communist Party that had defined the period immediately following the occupation, he also defined a new internal enemy for the nation. It was a speech that made clear Norway's position in the world, not as a bridge between East and West, but as a firm part of the West.

1 'Friheten og demokratiet i fare', speech by Einar Gerhardsen, 29 February 1948, in Olaf Solumsmoen and Olav Larsen (eds.), *Med Einar Gerhardsen gjennom 20 år* (Oslo: Tiden Norsk Forlag, 1967), p. 61.

2 Eirik Wig Sundvall, *Gerhardsens valg: Arbeiderpartiets tunge avskjed med Sovjetunionen 1917–1949* (Oslo: Gyldendal, 2016), p. 15.

3 S.tid. (1945), p. 57.

This chapter looks at the ways how, from 1948 onwards, the meaning of the trials changed in light of the broader Cold War context internationally and intensifying criticism domestically. Administratively, the trials were coming to an end. They had, from the perspective of the public authorities, succeeded in their original purposes of securing inner peace and stability during the early months following the liberation, and of marking the victory over Nazism and German aggression. Yet, from 1948 onwards, they became acutely relevant in light of the new political threats and challenges the Norwegian state faced. Officials repeatedly sought to refashion the trials into a broader message addressed to citizens on the requirements of loyalty towards the state in times of conflict. The main backdrop for this refashioning was a series of scandals and controversies surrounding the trials between 1948 and 1950 that touched upon their broader legitimacy and legacy. One of these scandals, the so-called Somdalen affair, revolved around the use of both German and Norwegian Gestapo agents in investigations carried out by the Treason Police during the early period of the trials. Another concerned criticisms brought forward by a former member of the military resistance, Oliver Langeland, in two widely read books published in 1948 and 1949, which culminated in a libel case against him. But by extension, the strong response of the government was also the result of the ways in which opponents were exerting pressure on senior officials and the administration of the trials. Critics had begun to closely associate the administration of the trials with the integrity and moral authority of the key figures and institutions behind them. The reaction to critics of the trials from 1948 onwards, this chapter argues, can be explained by the political threat they posed to officials, but also to the broader legacy of the trials and their relevance in the political climate of the time. Moreover, the discursive climate surrounding the trials also directly affected the ways in which the final administrative stages of the trials were handled, and made the government wary of adopting any measures that could either spur strong public reactions, or look like an admission of errors or an appeasement of the critics. This chapter therefore argues that, in light of a tense political and social climate, the final stages of the trials assumed a renewed demonstrative dimension as the government sought to highlight its administrative and interpretative authority over the trials in a changed political context.

6.2 Criticisms and Scandals

In November 1949, news broke in the major Oslo newspapers that the Treason Police had used former Gestapo agents in its investigations during the early period of the trials.[4] The most prominent case was that of Bernt Somdalen, a Norwegian citizen who had been a member of the Gestapo division IV N, responsible in particular for brutally interrogating resistance members, and who had also acted as a denunciator. Like many leading officials, Somdalen had, upon the liberation, initially succeeded in evading capture by blending in with ordinary Wehrmacht soldiers. But within a few weeks he had been identified and taken to Akershus prison in Oslo. Somdalen was a charismatic and eloquent figure, with a talent for quick thinking and psychological manipulation. These skills had taken him far up the Nazi hierarchy. He soon realised that these talents might aid him in the post-war order, too. In particular, he hoped to avoid a death penalty verdict, which, given the grave crimes he had committed, he soon realised was highly likely. In August 1945, Somdalen penned a letter to the prison officials at Akershus and offered his services to the police in uncovering the Gestapo networks that had terrorised the country during the war. The Liaison Division (*Sambandsavdelingen*), the secret police division entrusted with investigating Nazi networks, and the Treason Police were quick to accept his offer, in particular out of fear that many leading criminals could flee the country and evade their trial, but even more so because they feared underground activity among these networks. Because he had been so well connected within the Gestapo, Somdalen's services were soon relied upon extensively, and Akershus prison 'lent' him to police departments across the country, where he operated under the name of 'Police Inspector Bang'.[5]

The case became publicly known because a defendant in a treason case, Gard Holtskog, had claimed that evidence provided in his case was invalid due to the illiberal methods employed in its investigation. Holtskog's defence attorney had addressed this issue in court.[6] After the scandal broke, the initial response by the Oslo authorities who were in charge of Akershus prison was to deny the allegations. Responding to an inquiry by

[4] The *Norwegian Journal of Commerce and Shipping* had first reported on the matter in September 1949, accusing authorities of having relied on violent and dangerous individuals to expose networks of traitors and Germans through illiberal methods: 'Rakner det i Landssvikavdelingens etterforskningsapparat?', *Norges Handels og Sjøfartstidende* (3 September 1949); see also 'Provokatører benyttet i landssvikoppgjøret', *Morgenposten* (25 November 1949); 'Dødsstraffkandidaten Somdalen ble lovet frihet', *Dagbladet* (25 November 1949); 'Provokatører og angivere i politiets tjeneste', *Friheten* (26 November 1949); 'Landssvikpolitiet brukte også Finn Kaas hevder Ragnvald Huse', *Dagbladet* (1 December 1949); 'Svineri', *Nationen* (2 December 1949); 'Skarp kritikk av politiet', *Aftenposten* (28 November 1949).

[5] RA/S-1555/D/L0052: Letter from the Oslo City Court to the prosecution authorities, 24 February 1948.

[6] Ibid.

Morgenposten, Lars L'Abée-Lund, the Police Chief of Oslo, declared: 'I categorically deny that the Treason Police has used provocateurs. . . . I can guarantee that the Treason Police in Oslo has a clean conscience.'[7] At this point in time, however, the affair was widely known within the Oslo police and an internal investigation had already been launched.[8] L'Abée-Lund had himself provided an overview of the instances in which Somdalen had been lent to other police departments on 1 March 1948.[9] His denial must therefore be seen as an indication of how troublesome the Oslo police believed the affair could become during the final stages of the trials. On the one hand, a formal revision procedure for all cases would have been close to impossible institutionally. On the other hand, L'Abée-Lund knew that unjust judgments could not stand if the broader reckoning was to retain its moral and political authority. Calls for a full investigation soon loudened in the press.[10] Andreas Aulie, the Director of Public Prosecutions (DPP), therefore decided to launch a number of review procedures into court cases.[11]

The claims that no one in the police knew of the affair soon became untenable. While L'Abbée-Lund continued to deny that he had had any knowledge of the affair, State Attorney of Oslo Lauritz Dorenfeldt quickly issued a statement in defence of the Oslo police authorities, pointing to the internal investigation that had been carried out, and referring to the 'extraordinary' situation after the liberation. He indicated that investigations conducted shortly after the liberation had revealed that *Stapo* and *Sipo* agents had 'established an undercover apparatus that was much larger and more dangerous than one had initially thought'.[12] He subsequently tried to counter criticism by claiming that while Somdalen had been helpful, his statements or actions had never been the decisive element in a conviction.

At this stage, however, the damage was done, and the affair could no longer be downplayed. The matter further spurred distrust in authorities, and by extension the treason trials more generally. The case of Somdalen was reported across all major newspapers and became inextricably linked

[7] 'Provokatører benyttet i landssvikoppgjøret', *Morgenposten* (25 November 1949).
[8] An internal investigation into the matter had taken place in 1947; see RA/S-1555/D/L0052.
[9] RA/S-1555/D/L0052: Letter from Lars L'Abée-Lund to Kriminalsjefen, 1 March 1948.
[10] 'Falske provokatørrapporter fra Somdalen?', *Morgenposten* (28 November 1949).
[11] RA/S-1555/D/L0052: 'Gard Holtskog m.fl. – beskyldninger rettet mot embets- og tjenestemenn ipolitiet, påtalemyndigheten, fengselstyret m.v.', memo, 21 April 1949.
[12] 'Landssvik-politiet og dets bruk av provokatører', *Morgenposten* (29 November 1949); 'Skarp kritikk av politiet', *Aftenposten* (28 November 1949).

with the broader legitimacy of the trials.[13] The timing could not have been more unfortunate, given that the Pardons Committee and the Ministry of Justice were in the process of pardoning individuals and bringing the trials to a close administratively, after they had been a strain on the resources of the legal apparatus for years. In addition, the authorities already had to investigate and prosecute dozens of cases concerning the maltreatment of prisoners in the immediate liberation period, several of which led to a court verdict.[14] The accusations threatened to delegitimise the trials as a whole.

The Somdalen affair was not the only matter putting pressure on officials. In 1948 and 1949 a number of books were published attacking the trials. These differed significantly from Marta Steinsvik's earlier publications outlining illiberal prison conditions. Rather, these books followed the line previously taken by Odd Einarson and Toralv Fanebust and criticised the inner logic of the trials as well as the powerful – mostly Home Front – men behind them. Some of these authors had a clear self-interest, in that they themselves had been sentenced for treason.[15] As we have seen, in the late 1940s, *Nasjonal Samling* (NS) groups were becoming more organised in articulating what they felt were the grave injustices of the trials, even though most contributions came from a select few but highly vocal individuals. But there were two prominent authors in particular who posed a challenge to the authorities: the Nobel Prize–winning author Knut Hamsun and the head of the military resistance in Oslo, Oliver Langeland.

In 1949, Hamsun published his work *On Overgrown Paths*, which constituted his personal reckoning with the trials.[16] The question of how to proceed in the case of Hamsun had been a challenging one for officials. Hamsun was a national hero, his works woven into Norway's cultural fabric. In addition, he was eighty-five years old and near-deaf at the time of the liberation. There seemed to be many reasons against subjecting this old and frail Norwegian treasure to a trial. Nonetheless, while Hamsun had not formally been a member of the NS, he had publicly voiced his support for National Socialism throughout the occupation. On Hitler's death, he

[13] Newspapers continued to cover the affair closely – see for example 'I et rettssamfunn', *Dagbladet* (5 December 1949); 'I hvor stor utstrekning nytter politiet amerikanske metoder i etterforskingen?', *Friheten* (6 December 1949); 'Grumsete kilder for angrepet på landssvikpolitiet', *Arbeiderbladet* (8 December 1949), 'Somdalen-metodene er sterkt forkastelige', *Morgenposten* (9 December 1949); 'Etterforskingsmetoder i strid med straffeloven', *Friheten* (9 December 1949); 'Et ekko', *Aftenposten* (12 December 1949); 'Stig ned, Gundersen', *Dagbladet* (15 December 1949).

[14] RA/S-1555/D/L0039: Files 'Mishandling av landssvikfanger'.

[15] Per Harsem, *Utrolig men sant!* (Oslo: Private publisher, 1948).

[16] Knut Hamsun, *Paa gjengrodde stier* (Oslo: Gyldendal, 1949).

had published an obituary in *Aftenposten*, describing him as 'a warrior for humankind and a preacher of the gospel of justice for all nations'.[17] His position was widely known nationally and internationally. It was eventually decided to declare him unfit to stand trial, while demanding that he pay financial compensation in an administrative procedure. But in 1949, Hamsun published his book on the trials, in which he attempted to prove his mental soundness.

On Overgrown Paths was a diary of his time spent in police custody, hospitals and mental institutions following the liberation. In it, Hamsun was unapologetic about his support of the Nazis and highly critical of the ways the assessments of his mental capacity were conducted.[18] Interest in the book was immense, but public reactions to it were mixed. While some found his vocal support for National Socialism reprehensible, others celebrated the wit and skill of this old man, who so clearly had proven the doctors and officials wrong about their assessment, and exposed some of the deep-seated dilemmas surrounding the treason trials. While the investigating doctor, Gabriel Langfeldt, had considered pressing charges for libel for the way Hamsun had depicted him, he decided not to do so. For officials, the book's publication was highly uncomfortable, but there was nothing much they could do in response. Overall, they considered the Hamsun case an anomaly, it being best not to heat up the debate even further.

The books published by Oliver Langeland were another matter. Langeland's books *Judge Not* and *That Ye Not Be Judged* would become the most controversial publications to do with the trials.[19] Langeland was all the more noteworthy as a critic because he had not been close either to the NS or the by now defunct Society Party (*Samfundspartiet*), as many earlier critics had.[20] He was a former general who had been head of the military resistance *Milorg* for greater Oslo from 1942 until 1944. This, the Ministry of Justice believed, made his criticism particularly 'dangerous' for the greater trust in and legacy of the trials.[21] Langeland was sixty-one years old at the time he published his book, and had served in the military for twenty-one years before the war. He had experienced the dissolution of the

[17] Knut Hamsun, 'Adolf Hitler', *Aftenposten* (7 May 1945).

[18] Hamsun, *Paa gjengrodde stier*; 'Renslighet', *Dagbladet* (24 December 1947).

[19] Oliver Langeland, *Dømmer ikke* (Oslo: Heim & Samfund, 1948); Oliver Langeland, *Forat I ikke skal dømmes* (Oslo: Heim & Samfund, 1949).

[20] He was, however, openly antisemitic and had repeatedly appeared in public to voice his opinions.

[21] RA/S-1042/D/Dh/L0005: Untitled memo, Ministry of Justice, 3 December 1948.

Union in 1905, and was concerned for Norway's status and role in the world. All of this played a central role in Langeland's thinking.[22]

Judge Not, published in September 1948, was a sweeping attack on the trials. Its timing was no coincidence. Langeland published his book as a direct response to the *Storting*'s Protocol Committee's proposal not to impeach the Nygaardsvold government.[23] He argued that the trials were an expression of 'victor's justice', targeted at members of the NS, while the true responsibility for the occupation and all its consequences lay with the Nygaardsvold government, which had failed to provide an adequate military defence in the 1930s.[24] To prove his point, he compared the actions of senior politicians and civil servants during the occupation to those of individuals sentenced for treason. He criticised in particular the actions of leading politicians during the summer months of 1940, as well as the many overlaps between industry and the German occupier, arguing that the direction of the trials and the focus on the NS had been unjust. His book also contained a condemnation of Bishop Berggrav's calls to a group of civilians in April 1940 to lay down their weapons. Langeland contrasted this to Berggrav's strongly worded pamphlet of 1945, so as to point out what he perceived as the hypocrisy of the Church. Langeland was particularly appalled that no member of the government or senior administration had been subjected to legal consequences. His overall verdict of the Norwegian people was damning. Almost all had collaborated, he argued, and the resistance narrative that had gradually formed after NS members had been brought to trial was little more than a myth.

Most of all, Langeland was a military thinker. One of his core arguments was that the treason trials had left the nation weakened and unfit for a future war, which he believed to be imminent.[25] He argued that the treason trials should have been centred around a few major cases which constituted clear acts of treason. Instead, the trials had been turned into a process that was enormously damaging to the nation and its unity due to their broad scope, and had ultimately produced an unnecessary split in society. Langeland argued that, rather than punishing those who truly carried responsibility for the occupation, NS members had disproportionately been made responsible for the situation. To highlight the plight of NS members, Langeland used the example of the fictional widow Olava. Olava had only been a member of the NS for two short weeks in the autumn of 1940 but was sentenced to a fine and loss of civil rights, the

[22] Langeland, *Forat I ikke skal dømmes*, p. 7. [23] Langeland, *Dømmer ikke*, pp. 7, 45–46.
[24] Ibid., pp. 6, 15–21. [25] Ibid., p. 5.

latter of which led to her pension being withdrawn.[26] To Langeland, the purposes of the treason trials ought to have been to unite the nation and to morally strengthen its inner bonds so as to prepare it for future conflict. But instead, the trials had singled out NS members for the benefit of a larger myth of resistance.[27] This, Langeland argued, concealed the true scope of collaborative behaviour in Norway and put the nation at significant risk of repetition. To him, the Germany workers and officials had been much more strategically important to the German war effort than passive NS members. In fact, the overriding focus on the NS had been a strategy to divert attention away from the shortcomings of officials and industry. Langeland wanted an open discussion about the mistakes that could be learnt from the previous war, so that the nation could stand prepared for the future.[28]

The handling of the trials, Langeland argued, had also furthered distrust in public institutions. And finally, the blanket indictment of NS members large and small according to the treason provisions had watered down the criminal offence of treason. This, he argued, had eliminated the deterrent effect the offence should have, at great danger to the nation in the case of future conflict. To demonstrate his point, Langeland pointed to the seemingly absurd fact that treason could now be established by way of administrative decree. In the pre-war period, treason had been one of the gravest offences to be found in the criminal code, whereas now: 'We put the treason stamp onto thousands of individuals who have committed such irrelevant crimes that the entire reckoning with them is done with a fine of 200 kroners. That is nonsense. For treason, people should pay with their lives, not a week's salary.'[29] But it was not too late, he argued, for institutions to regain public trust and morally strengthen the nation for future combat. He suggested that an honest response from officials could restore trust in public institutions. His criticism thus differed profoundly from that of those arguing forgiveness. Langeland defended the death penalty, and demanded a harsh reckoning with those whom he deemed responsible for Norway's wartime fate.[30] He argued that those responsible had to admit their own shortcomings and face trial. But most of all, Langeland wanted to make a strategic and military argument, because he feared a new war was coming. And to him, the risks of a new war lay far more in the failure of the elites than what he considered petty acts of collaboration and conformity.

[26] Langeland, *Dømmer ikke*, pp. 48–49. [27] Langeland, *Forat I ikke skal dømmes*, p. 7.
[28] Langeland, *Dømmer ikke*, p. 6. [29] Ibid., p. 7. [30] Ibid., p. 6.

Langeland's book struck a nerve. His employment of many of the criticisms put forward against the trials made him a celebrated figure among NS members and those who had pointed out the flaws of the trials before. The book was widely discussed in the press, and attracted much comment and criticism from leading figures of the trials as well as from the wider public.[31] It sparked a broad debate that soon went to the core of the trials' legitimacy. Over the course of just a few months, it sold 25,000 copies.[32] Langeland had given voice to the criticisms that NS members and their families had long harboured against authorities. What made his book so powerful was the way in which it picked up on lingering criticism of the trials, and turned it into a damning report on Norway's past *and* future. He embraced many of the criticisms previously put forward by critics of the trials, such as the question of whether Norway had, in fact, been at war. He argued that, even after 25 September 1940, the situation had been far from clear to those who fought on the ground. As a resistance fighter, Langeland felt contempt for the exiles who had governed Norway from their neat offices in London.[33]

But nuance was not Langeland's strength. Moreover, as Langeland himself admitted, his book was a 'work in haste'.[34] It contained many contradictions that indicated that Langeland had used his critique of the trials principally to make a military argument. Langeland based much of his criticism on the fact that the authors of the 1944 Treason Decree had insisted on punishing anyone who had been a member of the NS after 8 April 1940. His juridical critique was often superficial, however, and his analysis omitted how the courts had used the wartime decrees, as well as the key changes that had been implemented to the Treason Decree, such as the amendments of 3 August 1945. Stylistically, Langeland employed a list of documents from the occupation period, which to him exemplified the close interaction between Norwegian officials and industry representatives and the German occupier. He argued that many of these figures, despite not being members of the NS, had shown much more questionable behaviour than 'Olava'. What Langeland ignored, however, is that a case

[31] See the exchange between Langeland and Andenæs in *Aftenposten*: Johannes Andenæs, 'Oppgjør med oppgjøret', *Aftenposten* (27 November 1948); Oliver Langeland, 'Oppgjør med oppgjøret', *Aftenposten* (4 December 1948); Johannes Andenæs, 'Hr. Langeland og sannheten', *Aftenposten* (11 December 1948); Oliver Langeland, 'Likhet for loven', *Aftenposten* (18 December 1948); Johannes Andenæs, 'Major Langeland – professor Andenæs', *Nationen* (6 January 1949).

[32] SAO/A-10085c/J/Jc/Jca/Jcac/3215: Letter from Roar Fjeld to Oslo Criminal Police, 2 September 1950.

[33] Langeland, *Dømmer ikke*, p. 16.

[34] Ibid., p. 8.

such as 'Olava''s would have been extremely rare to occur, if it had occurred at all, as the DPP had declared as early as in November 1945 that no cases would be brought against entirely passive NS members who had left the party before 1942.[35] In addition, passive members were also eligible for acquittal under the Treason Decree itself. Most importantly, the fictional case against 'Olava' was therefore not, as Langeland expressly argued, a case typical of the treason trials.[36]

Despite its inconsistencies, Langeland's book deeply troubled the government. His attack on the trials came at an inconvenient time for Norway's political leadership. Administratively, the trials were drawing to a close. Politically, they were becoming increasingly remoulded into a moral compass for the future, rather than a reckoning with the past.[37] But the Ministry of Justice did not want to see the core principles of the trials called into question. As we have seen, its unofficial policy at this stage was to *avoid* any debate that could increase uncertainty. But given the widespread attention Langeland was receiving, it was unlikely that debate on the trials would subside. The one-sided presentation of argument in Langeland's books troubled officials, who for years had sought to convey the complexity of the treason trials and present them as a fair project. Now, they feared, Langeland's interventions were likely to reinfuse the debate with more misconceptions, leading to ever-greater polarisation. The leading authorities therefore soon considered measures be taken to curb their influence.

6.3 Struggle for Authority

DPP Aulie had first proposed a formal investigation into Langeland's book *Judge Not* on 3 November 1948.[38] On 19 November, Aulie sent a letter to the Ministry of Justice, arguing that he would like the investigation into

[35] RA/S-1043_1/J/Jb/Jba/L0003: 'Riksadvokatens Rundskriv L. nr. 52' (19 November 1945).

[36] Langeland, *Dømmer ikke*, p. 48. The court files reveal that there indeed seems to have been one case, which resembles the case of 'Olava'. Here, a widow had agreed to a loss of civil rights by administrative decree based on her – false – statement that she had been an NS member through to the end of the occupation. When it emerged that she had, in fact, left the party much earlier, the case was overturned: SAO/A-10085c/J/Jc/Jca/Jcac/3210, Document 43.

[37] See Oscar Christian Gundersen, *Noen betraktninger omkring rettsoppgjøret med landssvikerne: foredrag i Oslo krets av den Norske sakførerforening, 18 January 1949* (Oslo: Aschehoug, 1949).

[38] SAO/A-10085c/J/Jc/Jca/Jcac/L3206: Document 1, letter from DPP Aulie, 3 November 1948, cited in Memo Jnr. 4283/48-S; the Church Ministry had previously written to the Ministry of Justice concerning Langeland's depictions of Bishop Berggrav's actions following the invasion. Bishop Berggrav had written to the Church Ministry on 1 November 1948: SAO/A-10085c/J/Jc/Jca/Jcac/L3206, Document 1.

Langeland's books to be expanded, as he had come across a further manuscript containing strong criticism of the treason trials and the key figures behind it. He urged for an investigation to be conducted into these writings, as he began to see a 'collective offensive against the treason trials' and expected 'that further books, newspaper articles etc. of a similar nature would be published'.[39] Aulie declared himself prejudiced, as some of the core criticisms of the book were directed against him personally, and instead suggested that a special investigator be entrusted with the investigation of the book. On 7 December 1948, the cabinet discussed Langeland's first book and appointed Øystein Thommessen, a senior Supreme Court advocate and former member of the Home Front leadership as a 'substitute DPP' to investigate his writings. He was asked to assess what legal measures could be taken against Langeland and to produce a comprehensive report on the validity of his claims.[40] The choice of a Home Front member to conduct the investigation was not uncontested.[41] When Langeland published his second book, containing similar allegations and arguments, in June 1949, the investigation was expanded to include it as well.[42]

The Somdalen Affair, too, became the subject of an investigation by the prosecution. Like Langeland's books, it had been seized upon by the press, and offered a starting point for widespread criticism of the treason trials, both by individuals and a number of campaign groups.[43] In light of the criticisms of the police methods employed during the trials, pressure on the legal enforcement apparatus grew in the first few months of 1950. An increasing number of treason prisoners had started to come forward during this time, criticising the treatment in prisons or the investigative measures employed. In order to appease criticism of the trials, Gundersen promised that a thorough investigation would be carried out, and that a corresponding White Paper would be put before parliament in order to offer transparency on the matter. Where there were miscarriages of justice, cases would be opened up again. Gundersen stressed, however, that insofar

[39] Ibid.; the fact that Einarson and Fanebust relaunched their magazine in March 1949 confirms this fact.

[40] RA/S-1005/A/Aa/L0005: Referat fra Regjeringskonferanse, sak nr. 2, 'Oppnevning av setteriksadvokat'.

[41] Lorentz Vogt, 'Påfallende uforsiktighet', *Nationen* (14 December 1948).

[42] St.meld. nr. 64. (1950), pp. 1–2.

[43] RA/S-3212/D/De/L0306: Letter by *Forbundet for Social Oppreisning*, sent to the *Storting* via the Ministry of Justice, 20 March 1950. The group had been formed in Sweden in October 1949 and aimed to rehabilitate NS members and discredit the trials.

as select cases of miscarriage were concerned, these could not be utilised in an attempt to undermine the trials as a whole.[44]

The second report, covering the Somdalen Affair, was drafted under the authority of DPP Aulie himself.[45] The investigation resulted in two detailed reports, delivered to the Ministry of Justice in August 1950 by Thommessen and the DPP respectively. Together, they totalled more than 250 pages and were published as a White Paper by the Ministry of Justice. Both reports are interesting in that they address not only the matters at the heart of the Somdalen and Langeland scandals, but they also contain lengthy sections about the larger wartime and post-war context, the nature and complexities of social and political transition, and on the various shortcomings and achievements of the post-war authorities.[46] As much as to offer their version of the truth of past events, the reports were drafted with a potential future military conflict in mind, and sought to highlight the relative achievements of the authorities that had overseen Norway's transition from war to peace. But both the DPP and the Ministry of Justice were also hopeful that an authoritative verdict after a full public investigation could put an end to the heated debate surrounding the trials.

The report which the DPP's office delivered to the Ministry of Justice on 1 August 1950 on the Somdalen Affair was more than one hundred pages long and contained an evaluation of a range of topics, including the accusations of maltreatment of prisoners and illiberal investigative measures such as those employed in the case of Somdalen. DPP Aulie emphasised that in order for a just assessment of any allegations of police misconduct to take place, the evaluation had to acknowledge that the treason trials were an outflow of a 'serious societal crisis' and that 'peace norms' could not be applied. The administration of political power in summer 1945 simply could not be measured against 'normal circumstances'.[47] Police and prosecutorial activity had not been part of the 'ordinary administration of the law' but was 'first and foremost a gigantic

[44] S.tid. (1950), pp. 306–307.

[45] While Aulie realised that he was investigating actions that he would have had the oversight of in his capacity first as National Police Chief and then as DPP from October 1946 onwards, he was still chosen to draft the report.

[46] A further investigation was launched against Arne Bergsvik's pamphlet. Some historians have argued that this was to devalue Langeland's publications. However, the court files show that authorities were concerned that Bergsvik would publish his pamphlet abroad, as he had written it in English as well as Norwegian; SAO/A-10085c/J/Jc/Jca/Jcac/L3206: Memo Jnr. 4283/48-S, Document 1.

[47] St.meld. nr. 64 (1950), p. 2. and 'Beretning fra riksadvokaten om undersøkelser som er foretatt i anledning av beskyldninger mot politiet, vaktmannskaper ved fangeleirene m.v. for bruk av ulovlige metoder under rettsoppgjøret mot landssvikerne', printed in St.meld. nr. 64 (1950), p. 4.

military and police manoeuvre, a tactical operation'.[48] The report discussed extensively the structure of the police force following the liberation, pointing out in particular that the police had had to rely on many 'untrained and inexperienced' individuals during the early months of the trials, and that of course some 'unfortunate elements' had slipped in as well.[49]

A narrative of danger suffused the report, and the power struggles of the early period featured prominently. But the DPP defended the police, and concluded that in periods of transition, the police would always be criticised from all angles and ultimately become 'scapegoats'.[50] The DPP detailed the complex relationship between Home Front forces, the legitimate police, the many unskilled staff relied upon in the early months of the liberation, and the high pressure everyone was operating under in light of the intense public condemnation of NS members.[51] The DPP drew a clear line between the official police forces, who had undergone training before the war and abroad, and the Home Front forces. Drawing upon examples of the frictions between resistance forces and the ordinary police force from other countries, the DPP stressed that it was important at the time not to sideline the eager Home Front forces and semi-trained individuals engaged with arresting individuals and guarding prisons in spring and summer 1945, or else these forces might have chosen to disrespect police authority altogether and instead have conducted their own reckoning.

The report admitted that many 'unfortunate' episodes had taken place in treason prisons throughout 1945 and laid out in detail the cases of maltreatment that had taken place and the respective disciplinary responses to them. But given the circumstances, matters could hardly have been administered in a better way according to the DPP. The DPP stated that one purpose of the investigation had to be to assess what authorities could learn from events. This was an indication that the report had been written with the future in mind as well as the past. In highlighting the complexities of social and political transition, the DPP drew a number of alternative scenarios that could have materialised, had it not been for the work of authorities and their close observation of the power dynamics during the period of transition. Ultimately, therefore, the report had one core message: that during periods of social change, it was in the best interest of

[48] St.meld. nr. 64 (1950), p. 58. [49] Ibid., pp. 5, 11. [50] Ibid., p. 12.

[51] During the early weeks following the liberation, many NS members were held in custody for extended periods, sometimes for the individuals' own protection.

citizens to trust the (legitimate) authorities in charge. In light of the brooding Cold War context, this was more than merely an abstract point.

The report went as far as to state that it was 'public opinion' that had been the driving force behind the most central policy decisions. During the transition, the report concluded, the danger thus emanated not only from NS groups and underground activity, but from the public itself. Pointing to the protests throughout 1945, the DPP found that the authorities had had little to no scope for manoeuvre. In response to the question as to why the individuals who had – in some instances severely – maltreated individuals were not prosecuted, the DPP's response was that, at the time, few members of the wider public would have accepted such measures.[52] A further reason provided was that, from an investigative point of view, the cases reported on were challenging, with many investigations having to be stopped, due to a situation of 'argument against argument'.[53]

But in his report, the DPP also acknowledged the suffering through which society had put NS members.[54] Implicitly, the report revealed a dilemma for anyone affected by the maltreatment: in the early period, the prosecution would not have brought legal action due to heated public opinion and power struggles, with the DPP stating that most would have considered it 'ridiculous' if those who had maltreated prison inmates accused of serious wartime offences had been prosecuted.[55] Later, after the prosecution found out through Marta Steinsvik's writings that maltreatment had indeed taken place, the report claimed that many cases would have been subject to a statutory lapse of time.[56] The report also contained a long section on the Somdalen affair, detailing the occasions upon which Somdalen had been used as an interrogator. But the DPP stated that ultimately this was a special case, as many officials had fallen victim of Somdalen's considerable charisma, and that he had 'clearly managed to bluff the members of the police who had to deal with him'.[57] The report concluded that while the times had indeed been extraordinary, these measures were 'alien to and in contradiction with Norwegian criminal law procedure'.[58] What is interesting here is the justification upon which the DPP relied: the report signals that in fact, the police and prosecution had felt exposed to the intensity of public opinion. Through admitting failures, the DPP was able to show that his office's standards had, throughout the trials, always been those of the rule of law, but that circumstances had simply not allowed for a universal

[52] St.meld. nr. 64 (1950), p. 16. [53] Ibid. [54] Ibid., p. 58. [55] Ibid. [56] Ibid.
[57] Ibid., p. 22. [58] Ibid., p. 24.

adherence to them. Society had to be protected from itself, a situation that had required the authorities to lower their pre-war standards.

Finally, the report contained two lengthy sections on the 'criticism of authorities' and the 'slander campaign led from the prisons'. These sections, the DPP argued, had become necessary because it had emerged during investigations that a group of prisoners, 'both Gestapo men and their Norwegian helpers', had been part of a 'permanent conspiracy' to undermine the treason trials as a whole, and had brought into circulation false rumours of extensive maltreatment, and launched personal attacks on the individuals behind the trials.[59] Some of these allegations, the DPP found, were so 'dangerous' that they warranted an investigation for libel.

As we have seen, public attention was first brought to cases of maltreatment through Marta Steinsvik's books in 1946. When maltreatment of prisoners received wider attention in the press in 1947 and 1948, many prisoners – including war criminals from Germany – had come forward to complain about alleged misconduct at the hands of British and Norwegian police or prison guards in 1945.[60] These prisoners had their own interest in discrediting the criminal justice system, as many of them hoped to have their sentences reduced or overturned if they could claim that they had been victims of a miscarriage of justice. Soon, hundreds of prisoners were claiming to have been mistreated in prison. It soon turned out, however, that many complainants were connected and the origin of countless rumours could be traced back to a handful of former *Sipo* and Gestapo members. Gard Holtskog, who had first drawn the attention of authorities to the Somdalen affair, was the individual at the centre of this web. During the occupation, Holtskog had joined the NS and become Police President of Finnmark in Northern Norway. He had been involved in several acts of terrorism and torture, and on one occasion had handed down a death penalty verdict at a Nazi Special Court. After the war, he had been sentenced to lifetime imprisonment.

In his report, the DPP drew upon a large set of examples to argue that there were various groups and organisations that posed a significant threat to the treason trials – and by extension to the rule of law itself. The DPP's office argued that Holtskog was a deeply manipulative individual who had decided to undermine the authority of the trials and the bodies entrusted with their administration. And indeed, some of the accusations that

[59] Ibid., p. 4.

[60] RA/S-1555/D/L0052: 'Gard Holtskog m.fl. – beskyldninger rettet mot embets- og tjenestemenn i politiet, påtalemyndigheten, fengselstyret m.v.', memo, 21 April 1949.

Holtskog made and the sheer expanse of stories that he put forward suggest that he actively sought a platform to obstruct authorities. This may have been out of personal conviction, psychological disorder or simply to rile those who held him in prison. The gravest and potentially most threatening claim that Holtskog had put forward was that former DPP Sven Arntzen had been an informant for the Gestapo.[61] In August 1948, Holtskog had approached prison authorities and claimed that he was in the possession of original documents to prove the affair.[62] The claim was taken so seriously that his successor, Andreas Aulie, launched a large-scale investigation, having the letters provided by Holtskog examined in a crime laboratory. His office went as far as to contact the British occupying forces in Hamburg to interrogate several German war criminals in prison and to assess the authenticity of the documents. All of them independently identified formal inaccuracies demonstrating that these documents were not genuine.[63]

The way in which the affair was handled by the DPP's office casts some light on the broader purposes of the report. While its initial aim had been to clarify the accusations of misconduct within prisons, it ultimately went much further. The DPP's report was written with an awareness that the investigation concerned not simply select allegations, but the larger legitimacy of the trials and their standing in the wider population. The DPP could not have known to what extent treason prisoners might insist on having their cases reopened, or in what ways criticism of the implementation of the trials might continue, perhaps carrying with it the resignation of those behind them. That is why the report provided an opportunity to draw attention to the activities of those circles who were most critical of the trials and to discredit many of the allegations they had made. The report's reflections on periods of political transition in turn highlight its fundamental purpose of reinstilling faith in the state apparatus during times of crisis.

Øystein Thommessen presented his findings on Langeland's publications to the Ministry of Justice on 30 August 1950. His report expressly stated that the investigation had primarily concerned the 'attacks on the treason trials'. This speaks to the broader relevance of the investigation, beyond the accusations of libel against select individuals mentioned in

61 It was the same claim that Einarson and Fanebust had put forward several years before, where it was brushed aside by authorities as nonsense during the Fanebust trial. It turned out that Holtskog was the originator of the claims back then, too.

62 RA/S-1558/D/L0016: Report by Oslo Police Station, 26 August 1948.

63 RA/S-1558/D/L0016: Interrogation Report by British Intelligence Office, 31 December 1948.

Langeland's books. Early on in his report, Thommessen stressed that there were many aspects of the books that the investigation would not concern itself with. These included in particular Langeland's criticisms of the prewar government, the foreign and defence policy of the Nygaardsvold government, the Administration Council and the Realm Council negotiations. The reason was that these had already been authoritatively decided upon by the Investigative Committee of 1945, which the *Storting* had subsequently discussed in 1948.

The first twenty pages of the report contained a detailed summary of the official government position on the trials. Thommessen discussed in particular the claim, so widely relied upon by NS members, that Norway had not been at war, thus rendering § 86 of the Criminal Code inapplicable.[64] This point was so central to the trials, as not only did the applicability of § 86 depend upon it but the question also related to the larger continuity of state, embodied by the exile government.[65] The arguments Thommessen presented were somewhat circular, in that he drew extensively upon earlier court decisions of the treason trials to reaffirm his position. It was clear that he had no intention of introducing an element of uncertainty into a long and comprehensive reckoning that was only just coming to a conclusion. But luckily for him, it was easy to dispel some of the examples Langeland drew upon as exaggerated – or simply false. A case like that of 'Olava' appears to have occurred only in one case by error, despite Langeland claiming that there were 'countless cases that are not different in essence from this one'.[66] Indeed, during the investigation of the case, Langeland was forced to admit that he did not know of a case like that of 'Olava'.[67]

In response to Langeland's criticism that 'thousands of individuals have been sentenced for negligible affairs compared to those supportive actions of civil servants that did not lead to any measures', Thommessen drew a distinction. Any involvement of officials with the occupying authorities prior to 25 September 1940 had, in his view, been entirely unproblematic. The Administration Council had been designed to safeguard Norwegian interests.[68] And the decision to stay in place after 25 September 1940,

[64] This, to this day, is the unchallenged position in Norway, while German literature is more ambivalent on the matter.

[65] Even though the question had been decided as early as in the *Haaland* case, and reconfirmed in the Skancke Appeal case, Thommessen found it important to stress this.

[66] Langeland, *Dømmer ikke*, p. 48.

[67] SAO/A-10085c/J/Jc/Jca/Jcac/3210, Document 43.

[68] Brev til Det Kgl. Justis- og Politidepartement fra konstituert riksadvokat Ø. Thommessen, 30 August 1950, p. 20.

Thommessen argued – in line with the findings of the Investigative Committee of 1945 – was defensible, in that it would not have served the national interest if all 'patriotic' civil servants had stepped down immediately after Terboven had seized power. It was the period following 25 September 1940 that was the most complex. While some civil servants were sacked by the *Reichskommissariat*, others continued in office until the liberation. For leading civil servants, some form of contact with the occupier was inevitable, and many saw their position as a 'trench' from which they could continue in the national struggle.[69] The risk that for each resignation an NS member might take the position was what kept so many civil servants in office, Thommessen reasoned.[70] No general directives could be given at the time for civil servants to step down, as the line between legal and illegal action was always dependent on each particular case. Individuals therefore had to make difficult choices. They were also not able to directly confront the occupying regime, as otherwise they would have lost their position.[71] Many civil servants had, therefore, to a degree appeared to be acting in the interest of the occupier. But if these civil servants had not stayed in power, those 'damages that the occupation and Nazi-governance resulted in for our country could easily have reached an entirely different scale'.[72] This meant that many of the 'administrative decrees' issued by civil servants during this time looked problematic when taken out of context. At the time, however, it had been necessary to 'read between the lines', Thommessen argued.[73] This offered as much an instruction for citizens in the case of future conflict as an evaluation of past events.

Both reports served a number of purposes: they were aimed at opposition to the trials, but also at conveying a broader message on the role of public institutions in times of crisis. They were therefore both backward and forward looking. The trials had come under threat, on the grounds both of valid critique and widespread misrepresentations. In the toxic debate culture that surrounded the trials, however, the two were difficult to keep apart. Misrepresentations were so common that the Minister of Justice penned letters to newspapers correcting their false statements or responding to information requests.[74] The authorities had no interest in having either their own legitimacy or that of the trials called into question. There were several reasons for this: within the political sphere, criticism of

[69] Ibid. [70] Ibid., p. 21. [71] Ibid. [72] Ibid. [73] Ibid.

[74] RA/S-3212/D/De/L0306: Personal letter by Justice Minister Gundersen to *Verdens Gang*, 8 February 1949; personal letter by Justice Minister Gundersen to *Aftenposten*'s editorial board of 15 February 1949 – which, according to a handwritten note, was never sent for fear that this would intensify debate and polemics even further.

the trials – and the bodies behind them – provided grounds for opposition work. Moreover, any unresolved irregularities surrounding the trials could lead to demands that cases be reopened, with unpredictable administrative and legal consequences. Those who had been involved in the administration of the trials would have to fear for their political or professional status. The White Paper was therefore meant to be an authoritative assessment, not merely of the topics investigated, but also with regard to the trials as a whole and the integrity of the institutions that had administered them.

But more generally, the reports delivered by Aulie and Thommessen ultimately revolved around the role of state institutions in times of political and military conflict. They emphasised the requirement for public faith in authorities, and stressed the importance of government stability. This fit the broader turn that government communication on the trials had taken since 1948. The trials had always been justified in terms of a general societal prophylaxis, but the dominant mode of reasoning had focused on the need to punish and confine specific compromised individuals for the sake of the inner peace and security of the nation.[75] Now, by contrast, future conflict became the dominant focus in official reasoning on the trials. As we have seen, the Cold War context had a direct impact on the use of pardons and the decision not to grant amnesties in order to safeguard the deterrent message of the trials. But the authorities went further: they turned the trials into a political message for the new era. In a speech delivered in January 1949, Justice Minister Gundersen stated that in the event of a future conflict

> it appears to me that in particular for those who may feel tempted to join a treacherous organisation, for small advantages, out of personal fear, out of doubt regarding the outcome, to obtain security in both directions, or to further group interests or party purposes – precisely for those, the treason trials can serve as a moral and legal benchmark, an unshakeable starting point for the thought that precisely in such a situation, society demands at the very least discipline and unity.[76]

6.4 The Trial of Oliver Langeland

> If one should have pressed charges for libel in every case in which accusations had been made during the treason trials without the

[75] Gundersen stressed this point in several of his speeches, see for example Gundersen, *Noen betraktninger omkring rettsoppgjøret med landssvikerne*.

[76] Gundersen, *Noen betraktninger omkring rettsoppgjøret med landssvikerne*, p. 16. Underlining in the original.

> slanderer having his evidence straight, then we would have had to live through the treason trials again, this time in the form of libel cases.[77]

This was the conclusion the DPP reached in his report of 1950 on the overall 'smear campaign' against the treason trials. But, in reality, the DPP stated, the prosecution had abstained from its right to prosecute in most cases, even despite there having been grounds for indictment. The reason was that the treason trials were such a profound societal process that authorities had to grant a 'certain margin for exaggeration' in relation to the broader debates surrounding them. Reasons of 'procedural efficiency' also meant that proceedings could not be brought in all cases, as the burden on the legal system would have outweighed the public interest.[78] Yet some publications were so 'dangerous', the DPP argued, that it had become necessary to launch proceedings for libel. Aulie referred in particular to the case of Oliver Langeland, against whom one of the largest libel trials in Norwegian history had been initiated on 1 March 1950.[79]

The trial against Langeland was something of a public spectacle, lasting several weeks and followed closely by the press.[80] The press understood this as the authorities' 'battle against rumours'.[81] A total of 125 individuals were called to the witness stand, including high-profile figures such as Oslo police chief Kristian Welhaven and Bishop Berggrav.[82] The trial took place between 15 November and 9 December 1950. What was it about Langeland's books that was so dangerous to warrant such effort, especially as this involved putting so many high-profile witnesses on the stand? It is likely that Langeland's high profile rendered him such a threat in the eyes of the authorities. As a former resistance member, he was highly respected. His arguments had some cohesion and his motive was not his own absolution, but what he generally held to be in Norway's best interests. He thereby offered an alternative post-war narrative to the 'official' one. His books had been popular and influential, with the figure of 'Olava' in particular giving NS members a platform of identification, leading in turn

77 The DPP's letter of 1 August 1950 referred to libel cases and stated that the authorities could have started proceedings in a much broader scope than they had decided to do so; St.meld. nr. 64 (1950), p. 111.
78 Ibid., p. 2.
79 SAO/A-10085c/J/Jc/Jca/Jcac/L3210: Document 47, letter from Høyesterettsadvokat Rolf Arne Foss, 1 March 1950: during his investigation into Langeland's books, Thommessen had reached the conclusion that there were sufficient grounds to press charges against Langeland for libel.
80 'Fri kritikk av rettsoppgjøret', *Morgenposten* (16 November 1950) (see Figure 6.1).
81 'Myndighetene til aktiv kamp mot ryktene', *Dagbladet* (3 March 1950).
82 'Lagmannsrettssaken mot Langeland og Bergsvik begynt', *Aftenposten* (15 November 1950); '125 vitner, forhandlingene vil ta 2-3 uker', *Dagbladet* (15 November 1950).

Figure 6.1 Oliver Langeland (second from left), pictured with his defence attorney Rolf Foss (first from right) at court in Oslo.
Source: NTB.

to an intensification of debate. The report presented by Thommessen was thus likely to be contested, in particular in NS milieus, and would not be able to stop the spreading of Langeland's publications and ideas.

On 8 December 1950, the Oslo Court of Appeal handed down its verdict. The court acquitted Langeland, but declared twenty-three out of the thirty passages of his books null and void. Moreover, the court ordered that the books be confiscated.[83] Johannes Andenæs has argued that it was in particular Langeland's key role in the military resistance *Milorg* that led to his acquittal. It could have been too politically sensitive for a former member of the resistance to be sentenced to imprisonment for his version of wartime truths.[84] However, the verdict and confiscation of the books still produced an authoritative statement on the core elements of the trials, satisfying officials' aims. Thommessen subsequently deliberated whether the civil servants at the centre of the seven passages that had turned out to

[83] Høyesterettssak S. nr. 65/1951.
[84] Johannes Andenæs, *Det vanskelige oppgjøret* (Oslo: Tanum-Norli, 1979), p. 254.

be true should face disciplinary measures, but ultimately decided against it, as he found the events in question to be sufficiently ambivalent not to initiate proceedings.[85] The media response to the judgment was mixed. The newspapers closest to government policy found Langeland's acquittal generous.[86] On the other hand, *Nationen* – the Centre Party organ which had often taken a critical stance on the topic of the trials – celebrated it as a victory for NS members, and considered it a setback for the government's strategy.[87] Langeland appealed the confiscation order to the Supreme Court, which dismissed it in January 1952.[88] Nevertheless, a letter by the prosecution dated 1 July 1952 indicates that the actual confiscation was not seen through very efficiently and that the DPP's office had to remind local authorities several times to implement the court order.[89]

6.5 Debate

Langeland's trial coincided with a period of intensifying debate on Norway's role in the world, its defence policy and the potential threats of future conflict emanating from the USSR. For several years, the government had been planning the so-called Readiness Acts (*Beredskapslovene*), a set of laws to stipulate the scope of powers that lay with authorities in times of military conflict. During this time, the treason trials were refashioned so as to fit the broader justificatory narrative for the Act. In a speech in January 1949, Justice Minister Gundersen had expressly stated that a core consideration for authorities was to assess what lessons could be learnt from the treason trials with future conflict in mind.[90]

Norway's changing political constellations compounded the situation. The election of the *Storting* on 10 October 1949 had produced a result very dissimilar from that four years prior. The Labour Party gained nine seats, while the Communist Party lost a total of eleven seats and was no longer represented. The election had cemented the power of the Labour Party and especially of Prime Minister Gerhardsen, who formed his third

[85] RA/S-1042/D/Dh/L0004: Letter by Øystein Thommessen to the Ministry of Justice, 28 February 1951.
[86] 'Langeland frifunnet for straffbare ærekrænkelser', *Arbeiderbladet* (9 December 1950).
[87] 'Omkring Langeland-saken', *Nationen* (12 December 1950).
[88] 'Langelands og Bergsviks anke forkastet', *Aftenposten* (12 January 1952).
[89] SAO/A-10085c/J/Jc/Jca/Jcac/L3206, Document 3, Letter from Ryssdal to statsadvokat L. J. Dorenfeldt, 1 July 1952.
[90] Gundersen, 'Noen betraktninger omkring rettsoppgjøret med landssvikerne'.

government.[91] In August 1950, a confident government presented its proposal for the Readiness Acts, which would encompass a change to Chapters 8 and 9 of the Criminal Code. The Act in particular included a number of changes to § 86 of the Criminal Code, the treason provision so widely relied upon by authorities during the treason trials. It defined more clearly the scope of official powers and sought to generate a strong deterrent effect for any activity that could undermine state authority in times of crisis. But the Act was also the consequence of the painful process of modifying the treason provisions during and after the German occupation, and the strong reactions the previous legal uncertainty had caused. The authorities wanted to be prepared for the next state of conflict.

The proposal for the Act contained provisions that allowed authorities to detain an individual indefinitely without judicial oversight if that individual was thought to be in the process of threatening the 'security or safety of the state'.[92] The proposal also included provisions for a separate 'treason court' with wide authority and no appeals procedure.[93] Finally, it allowed for extended use of the death penalty. In its proposal, the Ministry of Justice drew extensively upon the experience of the occupation and the treason trials.[94] The bill was widely understood to be closely connected to the ongoing treason trials, as both concerned the question of loyalty to the state in times of war and conflict.[95] Parliament debated the bill in December 1950. The Justice Committee was critical of adopting such widespread measures in a legal act. In the end, the *Storting* rejected the provisions, and they became instead an 'Executive Order' (*fullmaktslov*). And while § 86 of the Criminal Code was expanded to include more specific instances of 'treason' – such as joining a 'treacherous party' or 'encouraging desolateness or defeatism' – there is little to suggest that they would have made the situation on the ground any clearer in the event of a foreign invasion or occupation.

Long before the last prisoners were released, the *Storting* had the opportunity to discuss the broader legacy of the treason trials. In 1952, the *Storting* finally held its debate on the White Paper of 1950. The

[91] Norges Offisielle Statistikk XI 13, *Stortingsvalget 1949* (Oslo: Stortingets Kontor and Aschehoug, 1950).
[92] Ot.prp. nr. 79 (1950).
[93] Hans Petter Graver, *Dommernes krig: den tyske okkupasjonen 1940–1945 og den norske rettsstaten* (Oslo: Pax Forlag, 2015), p. 209.
[94] Ot.prp. nr. 79 (1950), p. 4.
[95] 'Revisjon av forræderiloven og andre juridiske beredskapstiltak i emning', *Arbeiderbladet* (19 January 1949).

parliamentary exchange on the White Paper in the *Storting* had been delayed twice. The official reason was that the Ministry was too busy drafting the Readiness Acts.[96] But it is likely that fears of a renewed and controversial debate also made this delay highly desirable to authorities. Now, the debate presented an opportunity to reflect. The government was meticulous in preparing its statements to the *Storting* and eager to draw attention to the complexities of the occupation and the difficult positions civil servants in particular had found themselves in. The Ministry of Justice had gathered argumentative 'ammunition' – as Minister Gundersen called it – by monitoring in close detail the many critical newspaper articles on the trials.[97]

But at this stage, the trials had been widely accepted as a fact of political life in post-war Norway. Gundersen therefore faced only marginal opposition. The majority of the *Storting*'s Justice Committee approved of the report, but added that it did not deem either the report or the debate in the *Storting* an occasion to assess the broader legitimacy of the trials – something which, in their view, was only possible from a historical perspective.[98] By 1952, the *Storting* in general was more willing to discuss the fraught situation of spring 1945 and the ambivalences surrounding the trials than it had previously been. Labour Party MP Oskar Lindberget, the speaker of the Justice Committee, summarised the situation as follows: 'it is not right to argue on the assumption that there was war on 7 May and on 9 May there was peace'.[99] Lindberget argued against the claim – so popular among the critics of the trials – that authorities in 1945 had been swept away by vengeance, arguing that

> [i]f our legal system had sentenced according to the broader attitudes in the Norwegian population in 1945, many of those who have now gathered and who repeatedly attack the treason trials would be silent today. For they would be dead. I believe that many sentenced traitors can count their blessings that they were sentenced by a Norwegian court of law.[100]

The sharpness of this rhetoric introduced a new dimension to the debate on the trials in the *Storting*. But Linderberget also pointed to judicial independence, arguing that it was not the place of the *Storting* to demand a revision of court decisions. Finally – and many of the colleagues in the chamber agreed with him – he advocated that there finally be 'calm about the treason trials'.[101]

[96] Innst. S. nr. 232 (1950).
[97] RA/S-3212/D/De/L0306: Handwritten note, Justice Minister Gundersen, 16 February 1949.
[98] Innst. S. nr. 341 (1951), p. 658. [99] S.tid. (1952), p. 72. [100] Ibid., p. 77. [101] Ibid.

Bunkholt of the Centre Party on the other hand argued that ‘calm around the treason trials’ could only be achieved after a *full revision* of the trials. While no final verdict could be reached at this stage – this was to be left to history – it was necessary to admit mistakes, Bunkholt argued. A revision was necessary while there was still time for the victims of the trials to benefit from their legal rehabilitation.[102] He regretted that the *Storting* had not changed the fundamentals of the trials when it had had the opportunity in 1947. That way, he argued, the many social problems to which the trials had led could have been avoided. Bunkholt's contribution highlighted the many ‘what ifs’ of the debate. He argued that ‘the people's opinion’ had not been as violent and intense as the DPP and his followers now made it out to be. With a different kind of leadership, the waves of hatred could have been brought under control without the many compromises that had been made to the rule of law. But Bunkholt failed to gain much support for his views, with only seven MPs siding with him.[103]

Within the *Storting* as a whole, most MPs sided with the DPP's reports, but expressed regret for the transgressions of authorities and their aides during the transition. While the debate had originally been intended to only concern the specific scandals surrounding the trials in 1948, to many MPs it became a debate about the trials in their entirety. The press, too, perceived it as a broader verdict on the treason trials, and opinion ahead of the debate had been divided according to the familiar spectrum.[104] But the debate offered no new conclusions. Those who had previously criticised more fundamental aspects of the trials simply repeated their objections.[105] With the Communist NKP no longer represented in the *Storting*, Labour Party hardliner Sverre Løberg stood alone in arguing that the trials had been too mild.

While most MPs approved the White Paper of 1950, the debate in the *Storting* showed that emotions still ran high, and that many questions remained unsolved. John Lyng therefore proposed during the debate that an investigative committee be formed to fully work on the treason trials and gather all the relevant documents and statistics, so that they could provide an overview for future generations.[106] The idea as such was much

[102] Ibid., pp. 77–84. [103] Ibid., p. 160.

[104] ‘A-paktens og frontkjempernes mål på synspunkter de samme!’, *Friheten* (22 January 1952); ‘Et ekko fra Goebbels taler i Stortinget’, *Dagbladet* (22 January 1952); ‘Arbeidet som står igjen’, *Aftenposten* (23 January 1952); ‘Landssvikoppgjøret’, *Arbeiderbladet* (23 January 1952); ‘Siste ordet’, *Dagbladet* (27 January 1952); ‘Det siste ord?’, *Nationen* (27 January 1952); ‘Landssvikdebatten’, *Morgenbladet* (27 January 1952).

[105] S.tid. (1952), pp. 95–100.

[106] Lars Roar Langslet, *John Lyng: samarbeidets arkitekt* (Oslo: Cappelen, 1989), p. 81.

older. In 1949, Justice Minister Gundersen had drafted a proposal that would involve the collection of relevant material on the trials, so as to offer a full starting point for future investigations. Given the many controversies at the time, Gundersen feared that any future evaluation of the trials could be lopsided if material were lost. But his proposal also contained a decidedly educational component, in that he had wanted to demarcate the forms of behaviour acceptable 'if the country were hit anew by a tragedy of similar nature to that of the occupation'.[107] Lyng's proposal, by contrast, aimed at gathering material without a political message in mind.

The *Storting* voted in favour of Lyng's proposal and the government accordingly appointed a corresponding committee to investigate the trials. The committee itself appointed a smaller subcommittee in 1955, which it entrusted with drafting the report. Justice Minister Gundersen had initially argued that it would be desirable to find qualified individuals who would be 'sufficiently impartial to be able to give an account the objectivity of which could not be drawn into question', but soon realised that this would not be possible.[108] Everyone with sufficient knowledge of the trials had in some way been involved with or affected by them. However, Gundersen made sure to stress that the committee's task was to formulate only a 'representation' – not an evaluation – of the trials.[109] Yet he acknowledged that an investigation would never entirely be free of judgement.[110] The committee subdivided its report into nine sections, covering the prelude, legal foundations, administration, court decisions and the debate surrounding the trials. In addition to a summary of events, the committee report contained countless primary sources. After seven long years, the committee presented its report in 1962, in the hope that it could provide an end to a debate that had lasted almost two decades. But there was still many a painful debate to be held on the topic throughout the following decades.

6.6 Lifetime Prisoners

By the mid-1950s, the Pardons Committee and the Ministry of Justice had agreed that both the individual-preventive and general-preventive effects of

[107] RA/S-4250/F/L0009: 'Rettsoppgjøret med landssvikerne', memo written by Kristian Bloch after conferring with Justice Minister Gundersen, 23 December 1949.

[108] RA/S-1043_1/J/Jb/Jba/L0004: 'Landssvikoppgjøret. Instilling fra det av departementet oppnevnte utvalg med mandat å fremlegge en plan for arbeidet med å bearbeide det materialse og å vurdere de erfaringer som er samlet under landssvikoppgjøret', memo, Justice Minister Gundersen, 30 June 1955.

[109] Ibid. [110] Ibid.

imprisonment were no longer an argument in favour of continued imprisonment of sentenced collaborators. This applied in particular to those with a prison term of less than eight years. However, both institutions remained intent not to release prisoners too fast. They insisted that a continued regard had to be had to the relative gravity of an individual's crimes and the 'inner proportionality' in pardons practice.[111] But prisoners and their families, as well as many parts of society, increasingly pressed for their release. One senior prison official wrote in a letter to the Ministry of Justice that the mental state of many prisoners had deteriorated significantly in recent years, as they lived in a state of intense expectation, hoping that soon it would be their own turn.[112] The Ministry of Justice and the Pardons Committee eventually accepted that continued punishment was neither in the interest of prisoners nor of society, and reviewed all cases of imprisonment up to twenty years.[113] By March 1953, the vast majority of prisoners with original prison terms of up to twenty years had been released. Since its formation in 1948, the Pardons Committee had reviewed a total of 1,200 cases.[114]

Despite the general desire among the authorities to bring the trials to a conclusion, the release of *lifetime* prisoners proved to be significantly more complex from both a social and a political perspective.[115] In 1951, there remained seventy-six lifetime prisoners, four of whom had had a death sentence converted to one of lifetime imprisonment. These were released late, from 1951 onwards, with two female lifetime prisoners being released in November that year. The first male lifetime prisoners were not released before September 1952.[116] This was in part due to the high profiles of some of the individuals involved. Some had been senior NS ministers, others torturers or murderers. The release of these individuals therefore carried a central symbolism for the trials as a whole, but also posed a potential safety issue to society.

111 RA/S-1043_1/J/Jb/Jba/L0001: Memo 'Benådning av landssvikfangene' by byråsjef August Breder, 24 May 1952.

112 RA/PA-1261/D/L0001/0001: Note of 11 December 1951.

113 RA/S-1043_1/J/Jb/Jba/L0001: Memo 'Benådning av landssvikfangene' by byråsjef August Breder, 24 May 1952.

114 Justis- og Politidepartementet, *Om landssvikoppgjøret* (Gjøvik: Mariendal, 1962), p. 419.

115 RA/S-1043_1/J/Jb/Jba/L0002: 'Om benådning av landssvikfanger og krigsforbrytere', memo, Ministry of Justice, 1 September 1952.

116 Justis- og Politidepartementet, *Om landssvikoppgjøret*, p. 422. On 9 September 1952, Gundersen presented to the government a pardons plan for lifetime prisoners and war criminals; RA/S-1005/A/Aa/L0007: Referat fra regjeringskonferanse, sak nr. 3, 'Benådning av landssvikfanger og krigsforbrytere', 9 September 1952; RA/S-1005/A/Aa/L0007: Referat fra regjeringskonferanse, sak nr. 8, 'Benådning av livstidsfanger', regjeringskonferanse, 9 December 1952.

The treatment of the remaining lifetime prisoners led to some disagreement, especially between Justice Minister Gundersen and the cabinet on the one hand, and the Pardons Committee and the Ministry's Prisons Division on the other. The Pardons Committee presented a release plan for the remaining prisoners in June 1953, which the Ministry's Prison Division approved. In drawing up the plan, the Pardons Committee had assessed in detail the individual security threat posed by each prisoner. In most cases, it had reached the conclusion that the respective crimes had taken place in such a specific situation that a repetition was highly unlikely. There was therefore little point or justification in keeping individuals in prison, as this was unlikely to have any further beneficial effect on either society or the individuals themselves.[117] If the nation should end up in a situation similar to the occupation, then these individuals might potentially pose a threat. However, were such a situation to arise, the memo of the Pardons Committee continued, these individuals could be held in custody on grounds of being a security threat. This was a reference to the sweeping powers now provided by the Readiness Acts.[118] Inner coherence was another central argument in the pardoning practice. The Pardons Committee and Prisons Division therefore proposed a release plan that took into account the relative gravity of the crimes committed. However, the suffering of prisoners' family was also an increasing concern.[119]

Both the Ministry and the Pardons Committee agreed that it was the general-preventive effect that had been the most decisive element of the trials: demarcating which forms of behaviour would be acceptable in times of crisis and which would not. The majority of the population had, the authorities reckoned, by now been sufficiently deterred from committing any comparable acts to those for which the lifetime prisoners had been sentenced. It had been 'established for present and future times that the criminal provisions on treason are not just stated on paper, but are also applied in practice, and that they cover the most serious crimes known to our criminal law and are punished accordingly'.[120] Officials concluded that

[117] RA/S-1043_1/J/Jb/Jba/L0001: 'Benådning av landssvikfangene', memo, byråsjef August Breder, 24 May 1952.

[118] Ibid.

[119] RA/S-1043_1/J/Jb/Jba/L0001: 'Om løslatelse av livstidsfangene', undated memo, Ministry of Justice.

[120] RA/PA-1261/D/L0001: 'Om løslatelse av livstidsfangene', memo, Johannes Andenæs, 3 June 1953.

seven and a half years' imprisonment should have sufficient deterrent effect for most to be released, provided it was the less dangerous ones.[121]

But the release of the worst enemies to the nation, individuals who had only marginally escaped a death penalty execution, was, of course, much more than a mere administrative procedure. It was unsurprising, therefore, that the more serious offenders – in particular prisoners who had received a death penalty or had been high up in the NS hierarchy – were treated with particular caution. There was an enormous symbolic element in bringing the trials to a conclusion, but also a significant risk for the authorities of appearing weak. The government deemed that it was of the utmost importance for the overall success of the trials that even these last measures be carried by popular support, or at least accepted by the wider population. The Ministry of Justice and the government vetoed the plan of the Pardons Committee with regard to the most serious offenders due to concerns that too swift a release of the prisoners could be challenged by 'public opinion both inside and outside the *Storting*'.[122] They instead demanded a slower release than the Pardons Committee and the Prisons Division had initially proposed.[123] Even though it only changed individual release dates by a few months, the government's decision and close monitoring of wider public responses signal the anxiety that still characterised the broader public climate of the trials.

Of course, the mere release of prisoners into society would not have sufficed to ensure that they could return to society as full citizens. The 1950s therefore also saw a removal of the civil disabilities attached to convicts due to the loss of civil rights. Unlike the changes made in 1949, most of these changes applied to *all* prisoners with a prison sentence of less than three years.[124] The provisions on regaining the right to vote were modified once more, in May 1953, when all individuals sentenced to less than three years' imprisonment regained full voting rights.[125] Those with a prison sentence of three years or more were to regain their right to vote five years after their release or pardon had been granted, but not before

[121] RA/S-1043_1/J/Jb/Jba/L0001: 'Benådning av landssvikfangene', memo, byråsjef August Breder, 24 May 1952.

[122] Justis- og Politidepartementet, *Om landssvikoppgjøret*, p. 423.

[123] RA/S-1043_1/J/Jb/Jba/L0001: 'Om benådning av de gjenværende landssvikfanger', memo, Gustav Sjåstad, 21 September 1954; RA/S-1043_1/J/Jb/Jba/L0001: 'Om benådning av de gjenværende landssvikfanger', memo, Prison Division of Ministry of Justice, 27 June 1953.

[124] RA/S-1005/A/Aa/L0007: Regjeringskonferanse, sak nr. 4, 'Straffelovsregler om rettighetstap', 6 March 1952.

[125] 'Lov nr. 3 av 22 Mai 1953 om endringer i lovgivningen om rettighetstap', Justis- og Politidepartementet, *Om landssvikoppgjøret*, p. 428.

8 May 1955 – the tenth anniversary of the liberation – for those with a prison sentence of five or more years. The 1953 provision also led to an almost entire normalisation of access to professions. Within the Ministry of Justice, the treason provisions were increasingly seen as an anomaly, and as an outflow of a time of intense pressure on authorities, a 'state of crisis'.[126] But the Ministry of Justice decided to retain the treason provisions, in particular due to the simpler procedural rules (administrative decrees) that they offered. Even though the provisions had originally only been applicable to events during the German occupation, the courts had since expanded their applicability to the Cold War context. The Ministry considered the treason provisions 'more of a beauty spot than a melanoma' for the rule of law and argued for their continued availability.[127]

By November 1954, only eleven prisoners remained.[128] The last prisoners had such high profiles that their release was discussed in great secrecy. They included, for example, Quisling's Minister of Cultural Affairs Rolf Jørgen Fuglesang and his Minister of Social Affairs Johan Andreas Lippestad, but also a number of denunciators, torturers and murderers.[129] After careful consideration, the Pardons Committee concluded that most of these individuals no longer posed any danger. However, some posed significant problems, including Somdalen, who had been at the heart of the scandal within the Treason Police some years earlier. On 12 June 1953, Aulie noted on Somdalen's file: 'I consider Somdalen to be particularly lacking in conscience, a calculating and dangerous individual who ought to have received the death penalty.'[130] Gard Holtskog was another of the remaining eleven prisoners. Aulie described him as 'a scheming, nagging prisoner, who was the most eager and criminal individual during the slander campaign and probably its initiator'.[131] Aulie and Andenæs placed him at the bottom of the release order.[132] Finn Knutinge Kaas, whose controversial death penalty had led to a change in the Supreme Court composition in death penalty cases in 1948 was equally considered 'scheming' and 'dangerous'.[133] The topic of

[126] RA/S-3212/D/De/L0307: 'Spørsmål om å søke opphevet landssvikloven, landssvikrettergangsloven og utrenskingsloven', memo, Ministry of Justice, 30 July 1954.

[127] RA/S-3212/D/De/L0307: 'Spørsmål om å søke opphevet landssvikloven, landssvikrettergangsloven og utrenskingsloven', memo, Ministry of Justice, 1 February 1955.

[128] RA/S-1043_1/J/Jb/Jba/L0001: 'Om benådning av de resterende 11 landssvikfanger med livstidsstraff', memo, Prison Division of Ministry of Justice, 26 November 1955.

[129] RA/S-1043_1/J/Jb/Jba/L0002: Undated memo marked 'strictly confindential', 'Oversikt over dommene, det straffbare forhold samt benådningsutvalgets bemerkninger vedrørende 11 livstidsfanger', Ministry of Justice.

[130] Ibid. [131] Ibid. [132] Ibid. [133] Ibid.

release of some of the 'last eleven' was so contested that Andenæs held a meeting with all party leaders on the subject on 3 December 1955.[134] They were cautious, and asked for the decision to be made by the king. Ultimately, all party heads and the king argued that release should be made within the next year or two. The first to be released were the former NS ministers, who had not been involved in murders. In October 1956, the DPP and the Pardons Committee proposed that the final six be released relatively swiftly, as there were no grounds to justify their prolonged imprisonment.[135] The release of the final prisoners was unaccompanied by any major controversies. The last four lifetime prisoners were released in November 1957, bringing to an administrative conclusion Norway's long and difficult reckoning with its occupation past.

[134] RA/S-1043_1/J/Jb/Jba/L0002: Confidential letter from Johannes Andenæs to Johannes Halvorsen, 5 December 1955.

[135] RA/S-1043_1/J/Jb/Jba/L0003: Letter from DPP Andreas Aulie to Johannes Andenæs, 1 October 1956.

CHAPTER 7

Correlation
The Norwegian Treason Trials in European Perspective

7.1 Reckonings

The Norwegian treason trials were but one of many 'reckonings' with collaborators that took place in Europe during and in the immediate aftermath of the Second World War. Alongside international efforts to prosecute war criminals, all countries liberated from German occupation set out to bring a range of their own citizens to justice over their wartime actions. These trials and administrative procedures centred on those who were deemed to have forfeited their right to a place in the national community by collaborating with, or in other ways aiding, the German enemy. The first such trials were those held in the liberated territories of the Soviet Union at Krymskaia and Krasnodar in May and July 1943.[1] Across the continent, hundreds of thousands of individuals would be investigated for collaboration or treason following the war.[2] They faced penalties ranging from the loss of civil rights to death. Much later, after the official procedures had been concluded, many of those labelled 'collaborators' in the process faced a lifetime of social ostracism.

The national trials of wartime collaborators that took place across Europe between 1943 and the mid-1950s had a number of things in common. Most significantly, they were largely inward-looking processes, aimed at restoring social cohesion and processing the national trauma and humiliation of occupation. The trials commenced in the immensely volatile political and social climates that reigned during the final phase of the war and the months immediately following liberation. They were mostly

[1] Alexander V. Prusin, 'Traitors of War Criminals: Collaboration on Trial in Soviet Courts in the 1940s', in David M. Crowe (ed.), *Stalin's Soviet Justice* (London: Bloomsbury, 2019), pp. 79–103; Tanja Penter, 'Local Collaborators on Trial: Soviet War Crimes Trials under Stalin (1943–1953)', *Cahiers du Monde russe* 49 (2008) 2–3, pp. 341–364.

[2] István Deák estimates that across Europe, one in every twenty adults was investigated for treason, war crimes or collaboration; see István Deák, *Europe on Trial: The Story of Collaboration, Resistance, and Retribution during World War II* (Boulder: Westview Press, 2015), p. 8.

intended to be a stabilising factor in this delicate period of political transition, aimed at bringing the threat of violence under control and neutralising tensions in societies that were only just emerging from enemy occupation and in which many scores remained unsettled. Not least, they also served as a means for new governments to generate legitimacy and authority. For the post-war governments of Europe, the trials of collaborators – along with the administrative purges that accompanied them – proved a remarkably useful tool in shutting down political opposition. For Europe's national populations, meanwhile, the trials served as a convenient process through which they could attribute blame for the plight of the occupation years to specific groups of individuals. This helped foster a number of convenient myths about the war – first and foremost that the majority of the population had resisted German occupation, leaving only a small collaborative minority. Although they largely took place in a legal form, the essence of the trials and purges remained deeply political.

Beyond these shared features, however, each reckoning unfolded in a distinct national setting. The intensity, scope, institutional form and ultimate aims of the legal procedures against collaborators were closely connected to the political power constellations in each individual country during the war and following liberation. During the war itself, the character of the occupation regime, and the locus of governing authority, proved to be decisive factors in how the trials were planned. The distinct nature of the occupying regime also had a strong bearing on the types of actions that exile and post-war governments chose to criminalise. The institutional setting of the trials, meanwhile, depended on the status enjoyed by legal institutions and political elites following the liberation. Of particular importance in this respect was the degree to which a return to pre-war 'rule of law' principles was deemed possible or even desirable. And finally, the long-term contours of the trials were deeply marked by the character of each nation's own unique political power struggles during the early months and years of the post-war period. At the macroregional level, one can also easily detect a number of fundamental differences in how the trials played out in Western and Eastern Europe respectively. The brutality of German occupation, post-war ambitions for ethnic cleansing, the rise of communist regimes and the powerful influence of the Soviet Union all meant that the trials of collaborators unfolded under specific preconditions in the East.

Structured chronologically, this chapter relates the Norwegian treason trials to comparable processes in both Eastern and Western Europe. In contextualising the Norwegian trials, the chapter looks in particular at events in Denmark, France, Belgium, the Netherlands, Czechoslovakia, Poland, Italy and Hungary.[3] This range of countries allows the chapter to highlight the distinctiveness of the Norwegian post-war reckoning, but at the same time to appreciate those aspects of the Norwegian trials that reflected more general trends throughout Europe. In its analysis, the chapter identifies four key aspects of the Norwegian trials that help mark them out as somewhat distinctive within a wider European context: 1) the considerable planning capacities enjoyed by the exile government; 2) the relative absence of extra-judicial violence upon liberation; 3) the unparalleled scope of the trials; and 4) the strong focus placed by the Norwegian authorities on the trials' legality. Focusing on these four factors will allow the chapter to reflect on the ways in which the nature, scope and form of the Norwegian post-war reckoning correlated with the political, social and institutional circumstances the country found itself in both during and after the war.

7.2 Anticipation

From its London offices, the Norwegian exile government began as early as 1941 to plan its post-war reckoning with collaborators.[4] It was surrounded by European exile governments engaged in similar efforts. During the early years of the war, several European governments found themselves exiled in the British capital, including those of Norway, Czechoslovakia, Belgium, the Netherlands, Poland and France. From an early stage of the war, plans to punish and purge collaborators formed a key part of these governments' political agendas.[5] But their political power was often weak, in particular when they first arrived in London, and their constitutional legitimacy was often disputed by the Allies, the populations in their homelands, or both. Within this context, Norway's exile government benefited from a comparative lack of friction among Norwegian state institutions. Significantly, it continued to enjoy the support of King Haakon VII, as well as being recognised by both the British government and a considerable faction of

[3] The cases of Italy and Hungary have been chosen given the distinct complexities their changing wartime allegiances present. While other countries could have been drawn in, including Greece, the Soviet Union and Yugoslavia, this would have gone beyond the scope of this chapter. It should be pointed out that legal retribution in Czechoslovakia was different for Slovakia than in Bohemia, Moravia and Silesia, although the differences would be too much to cover in the context of this chapter.

[4] Ot.prp. nr. 92 (1945–1946), p. 70.

[5] Benjamin Frommer, *National Cleansing: Retribution against Nazi Collaborators in Postwar Czechoslovakia* (Cambridge: Cambridge University Press, 2005), p. 65.

the Norwegian population. This was in contrast, for example, to Belgium, where King Leopold III did not support the exile government, and to Czechoslovakia, where Edvard Beneš' status as head of the exiled government was widely disputed following his association with the Munich Agreement of 1938. But ultimately, all exile governments had reason to fear for their legal and political recognition, in particular during the first years of exile.[6] They therefore sought to establish communication channels to the populations in their home territories through which they could assert some form of authority from faraway London.[7] Announcing that collaborators would be punished formed a key part of these efforts. In their broadcasts and written communications, the exiles stressed time and again that those who collaborated with the German occupier would be brought to trial. This, they hoped, would deter citizens from cooperating with the Nazis while at the same time boosting morale to oppose German oppression.[8] Not least, they also hoped that their proclamations could forestall a domestic shift in power that would undermine their claims to authority.

Following their announcements that collaborators would stand trial once the war was over, the exile governments all set out to draft and issue provisional laws and decrees which criminalised various forms of collaboration.[9] While the criminal codes of the pre-war era typically contained provisions on treason, these had not been drafted with the scope and complexities of a long-term enemy occupation in mind.[10] In light of the fact that hundreds of thousands of citizens had, in some form or another, showed an allegiance to the German occupying powers and domestic Nazi parties, the exiles quickly came to the conclusion that additional legal measures would be necessary in order to bring collaborators to justice.[11] The exiles thus placed a particular emphasis on the legal craftsmanship and

6 Pavol Jakubec, 'Together and Alone in Allied London: Czechoslovak, Norwegian and Polish Governments-in-Exile, 1940–1945', *The International History Review* 42 (2020), pp. 465–484, at p. 468.

7 Baard Herman Borge and Lars-Erik Vaale, 'Stretching the Rule of Law: How the Norwegian Resistance Movement Influenced the Provisional Treason Decrees of the Exile Government, 1944–1945', *Scandinavian Journal of History* 46 (2021) 1, pp. 105–124.

8 Tony Judt, *Postwar: A History of Europe since 1945* (London: Penguin Books, 2010), p. 45.

9 See for example Peter Romijn, *Snel, streng en rechtvaardig: politiek beleid inzake de bestraffing en reclassering van 'foute' Nederlands, 1945–1955* (Houten: De Haan, 1989), pp. 41–48.

10 The French Criminal Code posed a slight exception – conveniently, its treason provisions had been significantly expanded in 1939. Nevertheless, the provisions had to be stretched and supplemented so as to accommodate for wartime events; see Peter Novick, *The Resistance Versus Vichy: The Purge of Collaborators in Liberated France* (London: Chatto & Windus, 1968), p. 143.

11 Luc Huyse, 'The Criminal Justice System as a Political Actor in Regime Transitions: The Case of Belgium, 1944–50', in István Deák, Jan T. Gross and Tony Judt (eds.), *The Politics of Retribution in Europe: World War II and Its Aftermath* (Princeton: Princeton University Press, 2000),

coherence of their decrees, and appointed juridical committees to draft the necessary provisions. The exiles' focus on the thoroughly legal foundations for post-war justice in turn highlights the importance they attached to at least being seen to be acting in accordance with the rule of law. In all cases, the principle was more important than the actual implementation: in practice, core legal principles were often interpreted very differently from the pre-war era as they were adapted to the unprecedented context of German occupation.[12]

In drafting and issuing their provisional decrees, a central question faced by all exile governments was which actions to criminalise. This depended on the particular nature of the occupation regime, and the strategic interests the exile governments pursued through their legal measures. The Norwegian Provisional Decree of 22 January 1942 – the so-called Quisling Decree – stands out among the wartime decrees issued in London as the only legal measure to criminalise both active and passive membership of a domestic fascist party (in this case *Nasjonal Samling*, NS).[13] In no other country was membership of a fascist party as such criminalised, either during or after the war. This in part reflected the unique status enjoyed by Vidkun Quisling and the NS under occupation: in no other country was the national fascist party propped up to such a degree. The NS held governing powers from September 1940, and in February 1942 the Germans promoted Quisling to Minister-President. Although Quisling lacked any real support among the population and acted only under strict order from the German civilian administration (*Reichskommissariat*), he and his party represented a serious threat to the exile government, not least due to the comprehensive Nazification efforts undertaken by the Germans. By designating membership of the NS as a central criterion for criminal punishment, the exile government hoped that individuals could be deterred from joining the party and thus prevent a further Nazification of the country. It was also an important symbolic act in the growing ideological fight of the Norwegian people against Nazism.[14] Ultimately, the Quisling Decree was the principal reason why the Norwegian treason

pp. 157–172, at p. 162; Harald Fühner, *Nachspiel: die niederländische Politik und die Verfolgung von Kollaborateuren und NS-Verbrechern, 1945–1989* (Münster: Waxmann, 2005), pp. 32–35.

12 Novick, *The Resistance Versus Vichy*, pp. 209–210; Frommer, *National Cleansing*, pp. 83–84.

13 'Justisdepartementets tilrådning til provisorisk anordning om tillegg til straffelovgivningen om forrederi av 22. januar 1942', printed as Appendix 1 in Ot.prp. nr. 92 (1945–1946).

14 On resistance towards Nazification in Norway, see in particular Arne Hassing, *Church Resistance to Nazism in Norway 1940–1945* (Seattle: University of Washington Press, 2014).

trials later became significantly more encompassing than those in other countries.

Beyond the Quisling Decree, however, the offences that the exile governments condemned and criminalised were largely comparable.[15] Through radio broadcasts and pamphlets, exile governments announced their intentions to bring the 'traitors', 'collaborators' and 'war criminals' to trial – terms which were often used synonymously in the exiles' communications. The decrees typically criminalised such actions as political and economic collaboration, denunciation and German military service. The wording of the decrees was often vague, allowing them to capture a vast range of 'unpatriotic' behaviours. Moreover, in addition to introducing new crimes of collaboration, the wartime decrees also announced the introduction of new penalties, such as hard labour and the loss of civil rights. They also reintroduced the death penalty or, in cases where it had not been abolished, broadened the scope of its applicability. Perhaps surprisingly, these decrees were broadly similar in nature between Eastern and Western Europe, despite the fact that the respective preconditions for collaboration varied significantly between the two halves of the continent. Across Eastern Europe, and especially in Poland, the German occupation strategy had been centred on securing living space for the German people and destroying pre-existing societies. Here, individuals took especially high risks in opposing the occupying power.[16] While the occupation in Czechoslovakia was less violent by comparison, there were enormous social tensions with ethnic Germans here over the humiliating loss of sovereignty in 1938. Yet despite the very different German occupation strategies in East and West, collaboration was condemned in similar ways by the exiles. Collaborators were, quite simply, deemed to have forfeited their place in the national community.

As the war raged on and the inevitable German defeat drew closer, the political prospects for all of the exile governments became increasingly complex. Above all, with victory in sight, a wide range of new political interest groups formed within national territories which began asserting their own demands for the post-war order. From faraway London, some of the displaced European governments were left with no option but to assent to this shift in power. Most famously, the Polish exile government lost

[15] In addition to the Norwegian decrees discussed in Chapter 1, decrees issued in exile include the Belgian Decree of April 1941, the Dutch Decree of December 1943 and the French Decree of June 1944.

[16] Nevertheless, Poland would see the largest underground resistance movement in all of Europe.

much of its influence to the communist Polish Committee of National Liberation (*Polski Komitet Wyzwolenia Narodowego*, PKWN) in Lublin, which enjoyed the decisive support of the Soviet Union. It was the PKWN which would draft the decisive legal basis for the reckoning, the Decree of August 1944, leaving earlier drafts by the Polish exile government and the Polish Underground redundant.[17] The remaining exile governments were able to retain a comparably good degree of international recognition, but all of them were nevertheless forced to respond to different resistance groups and political movements whose power increased radically as the end of the war neared. As we saw in Chapter 1, the Norwegian resistance movement, the Home Front, assumed a central role in shaping the final planning stages of the post-war reckoning.[18] That such joint planning was possible was due not least to the particularly homogenous nature of the Norwegian resistance, the well-developed communication channels that had been established between London and Norway, and the exile government's willingness to cooperate with the resistance.[19] This is not to say that the relationship was completely lacking in tensions, however: the Home Front was more radical in its demands for bringing collaborators to justice than the exile government, and more inclined to sidestep established legal principles. And in the end, it succeeded in having almost all of its demands enshrined in the 1944 Treason Decree. In this sense, the influence that the Norwegian resistance had on the drafting of the decrees was unique.[20] Other exile governments had to engage with significantly more fragmented resistance movements, and also pushed back on a number of their demands. Both the Belgian and Dutch governments, for example, were hesitant to accept the demands of the resistance, and instead sought to unilaterally impose their own visions for the post-liberation period, leading to tensions further down the line.[21]

Preparation for the post-war trials of collaborators naturally took a different form in countries whose governments had not fled into exile.

[17] Andrew Kornbluth, *The August Trials: The Holocaust and Postwar Justice in Poland* (Cambridge, MA: Harvard University Press, 2021), p. 90.

[18] On the dynamic between the exile government and the Home Front, see also Borge and Vaale, 'Stretching the Rule of Law'.

[19] Martin Conway, 'Legacies of Exile: The Exile Governments in London during the Second World War and the Politics of Post-war Europe', in Martin Conway and José Gotovich (eds.), *Europe in Exile: European Exile Communities in Britain 1940–45* (New York: Berghahn, 2001), pp. 255–274, at p. 260.

[20] Borge and Vaale, 'Stretching the Rule of Law', pp. 10–13.

[21] Ibid., p. 10; Novick, *The Resistance Versus Vichy*, pp. 19, 140–151; David Barnouw, 'Dutch Exiles in London', in Conway and Gotovich (eds.), *Europe in Exile*, pp. 229–246, at p. 239.

In this respect, the peculiar situation in Denmark posed distinct challenges for those wishing to plan a post-war reckoning. The Danish government had, upon the German invasion of 9 April 1940, been pressured into agreeing to a 'friendly collaboration'.[22] This left the Danish state apparatus formally intact, but pressured into complying with German demands. By 1943, the relationship between the German occupier and the Danish population had deteriorated considerably, with strikes flaring up across the country to protest against the increasingly oppressive German policies. The German government declared a state of exception, disarmed the Danish military and ended the policy of cooperation on 29 August 1943. After this date, Denmark was run by the heads of the Danish civil service, and this makeshift arrangement remained in place until the end of the war. As such, it was the organised resistance that initiated plans to bring collaborators to trial.[23] In November 1943, the Danish Freedom Council (Danish: *Danmarks Frihedsraad*) began circulating a pamphlet entitled 'When Denmark Is Free Again' (Danish: *Naar Danmark atter er frit*), in which it demanded, among other things, that 'those who have drawn personal advantage from the unfreedom of the country' be punished following the war.[24] The resistance, along with a civil servant committee representing the traditional Danish elites, accordingly drafted the relevant provisions. Given that Denmark remained under German occupation, however, the government and legislature were unable to adopt any corresponding measures. It was clear, therefore, that the Danish laws would have to be adopted retroactively following the war.

The preparation of the trials of collaborators also took on its own distinctive dynamic in countries that had witnessed shifting wartime allegiances and shorter periods of German occupation. Admiral Miklós Horthy's Hungary had for years been a wavering ally of Hitler. In March 1944, however, Hitler deemed Horthy's rule too unpredictable and directly occupied the country. From October 1944 until the gradual Soviet liberation in the winter and spring of 1945, Hungary was governed under the brutal leadership of Ferenc Szálasi and his fascist Arrow Cross Movement. In those areas liberated by the Soviet Union, the Hungarian Liberation Front – a political alliance formed in December 1944 and composed of a range of antifascist and communist parties – began to

[22] Claus B. Christensen, *Danmark besat: krig og hverdag 1940–45* (Copenhagen: Høst & Søn, 2005), pp. 103–113.

[23] Ditlev Tamm, *Retsopgøret efter besættelsen* (Copenhagen: Jurist- og økonomforbundet, 1984), pp. 67–111.

[24] Danmarks Frihedsraad, *Naar Danmark atter er frit* (1943), p. 1.

rebuild the country's political institutions. There was a consensus among the newly formed National Assembly and the Council of Ministers that collaborators would be brought to trial: in fact, the promise to bring collaborators to justice was a precondition for the January 1945 ceasefire agreement between Hungary and the Soviet Union. However, the decrees ultimately issued by the Council of Ministers were vague and needed to be supplemented and refined later on. Moreover, different political parties had differing opinions as to how comprehensive the Hungarian purge should ultimately be.[25]

In Italy, a country which also shifted allegiances during the war, the situation was similarly convoluted. The country had fought on Germany's side until September 1943, when it became subject to a dual occupation, with Germany controlling the North and the Allies the South. During the dual occupation, Italy's social and political climate was extremely volatile, and the country was marred by a civil war driven by class and ideological conflicts. After Mussolini was ousted in July 1943, the Italian resistance, the *Resistenza*, attempted to push Pietro Badoglio's government to purge the country of fascists. But Badoglio's conservative alliance had no political interest in sweeping purges. The *Resistanza* still intended for a comprehensive reckoning to take place following a German defeat, and issued a corresponding decree to this effect in April 1945. But the *Resistenza* was a disparate group, and its plans were nowhere near as coordinated or developed as those that some of the exile governments had been able to make.

The counterexamples of Denmark, Hungary and Italy help to highlight the considerable planning capacities enjoyed by the Norwegian exile government and Home Front. Unlike in Denmark, the Norwegian government was able to formally issue the necessary legal bases for the trials of collaborators *during* the war. Norway's planning for a post-war reckoning was also not disrupted by the chaos of civil war or competing political factions pursuing different plans, as was the case in Hungary and Italy. But even among the various plans for post-war trials that the exile governments of London developed during the war, the Norwegian plans stand out. Nowhere was the agreement reached between the exile government and the resistance as strong as in the Norwegian case. Towards the end of the

[25] Margit Szöllösi-Janze, '"Pfeilkreuzler, Landesverräter und andere Volksfeinde" – Generalabrechnung in Ungarn', in Klaus-Dietmar Henke and Hans Woller (eds.), *Politische Säuberung in Europa: die Abrechnung mit Faschismus und Kollaboration nach dem Zweiten Weltkrieg* (Munich: DTV, 1991), pp. 311–357, at p. 320.

war, all exile governments began to focus increasingly on the transition from war to peace and their own eventual return to their homelands. The plans to punish collaborators formed a central part of this strategy.[26] But in countries such as France and Belgium, remaining disagreements between exile governments and local resistance forces complicated the situation.[27] In Norway, by contrast, the planning was particularly detailed, and most importantly, driven by a broad consensus among all relevant parties. Both the exile government and the Home Front shared a fundamental interest in preventing violence and building a unity government. This meant that both parties were committed to ensuring the greatest possible adherence to their plans, and an orderly transition from occupation to liberation. Not least, it also meant that they were able to communicate their prearranged plans to the public in a uniform and consistent manner.

Beyond the consensus attained among its institutions, Norway's planning ability also benefited from the country's comparatively late liberation. The timing of the liberation mattered immensely when it came to the preparatory measures that exile governments and political movements were able to make. Norway's late liberation on 8 May 1945 meant that the exile government and Home Front had sufficient time to have in place a comprehensive and consensual plan for the transition period. But the late liberation also meant that they could draw upon lessons from other countries. In preparing for the moment of liberation, the Norwegian authorities closely monitored the tragic consequences of the social animosities that followed the liberation of France in June 1944.[28] In their communications to the public, the Norwegian government and resistance drew extensively on the example of France to warn of the detrimental effects of extrajudicial violence.[29] These communications appealed to the proud legal traditions of Norway and implored the population not to take justice into their own hands. The promise of a reckoning was made in return for a political transition of power without extra-judicial violence. That such promises could seem credible was facilitated by the agreement the government and Home Front had reached during the war.

[26] Fühner, *Nachspiel*, p. 33.
[27] Peter Schrijvers, 'The Liberation: A Wild Picture of Emotions', in Wannes Devos and Kevin Gony (eds.), *War, Occupation, Liberation: Belgium 1940–1945* (Tielt: Lannoo, 2019), pp. 243–244.
[28] Reidar Omang (ed.), *Regjeringen og hjemmefronten under krigen: aktstykker utgitt av Stortinget* (Oslo: Stortinget, 1948), pp. 482–486.
[29] Ibid., p. 486.

7.3 Transition

The German retreat and ultimate capitulation in May 1945 led to political power contests across Europe. Allied and Soviet occupations of varying durations coincided with transitions of institutional power at the national level. In most countries that had been occupied, the wartime governments or Allies had reached some form of agreement with the organised resistance concerning the character of interim control before centralised governing authority could be re-established. The agreement that the exile government had reached with the Home Front made for a comparatively smooth transition in the Norwegian case. Similar agreements between governments and resistance movements had also been reached in Denmark and the Netherlands. Under these wartime agreements, interim military control was followed relatively swiftly by the full re-establishment of centralised governing authority. But the transition from occupation to a stable post-war order proved much more challenging elsewhere. In countries such as France and Italy, the liberation from German occupation sparked – or reinvigorated – a series of fundamental political and institutional conflicts. Where the liberation was protracted, this also presented a challenge to the re-establishment of authority throughout the country.[30] Despite the fact that de Gaulle had reached an agreement with most factions of the French resistance well in advance of the country's liberation, various resistance units and communist groups continued to compete for influence at the local level.[31] In Hungary, too, centralised authority was only established over the course of several months. In Poland, the pro-Soviet Lublin Committee lacked popular support in the wider population and was perceived as having 'no roots at all in the Polish people', as one observer noted.[32] For many countries, the liberation was therefore followed by a considerably more unstable governing setting than in Norway.

One of the most central responsibilities of Norway's interim governing forces was to oversee the internment of suspected collaborators and war criminals. The swift internments of alleged 'traitors' were meant, not least, to forestall extra-institutional violence. This is reflected in the fact that the Norwegian internment decrees allowed for the internment of a wide range

[30] Novick, *The Resistance Versus Vichy*, pp. 60–61.

[31] Ibid., pp. 64–70; Henry Rousso, 'L'Épuration – Die politische Säuberung in Frankreich', in Henke and Woller (eds.), *Politische Säuberung*, pp. 192–240, 200.

[32] Kornbluth, *The August Trials*, p. 85.

of individuals, and made it possible to place individuals in protective custody.[33] Similar plans had been adopted right across Europe.[34] During the war, most of the various exile governments and national underground resistance movements had compiled lists of those to be interned (or executed) upon liberation.[35] Such lists were typically based on information gathered in secret about individuals and their membership in National Socialist organisations or German military formations, their work for German intelligence units, or their collaborative actions as politicians, civil servants or business owners. But nowhere were the internments carried out as planned. Despite the agreement reached between the Norwegian exile government and the Home Front on how to conduct the internments, the scenes in Norway were chaotic. Individuals faced assault, humiliation and unfounded, often multiple arrests, later leading the Director of Public Prosecutions to refer to this as a 'semi illegal' period.[36] Similar scenes unfolded in Denmark, the Netherlands and Belgium. Due to the chaos that ensued, the number of arrests was ultimately much higher than anticipated and the conditions in the overcrowded internment camps became increasingly desolate, especially in the Netherlands, which had suffered significant food shortages towards the end of the war. Nevertheless, despite the turmoil, in all of these countries the internments – along with the political transition more generally – remained largely within an institutional form.

The internment of political collaborators unfolded in a much more lawless and violent manner in France, Italy and much of Eastern Europe. Here, the internments blended with political witch hunts and private vendettas that had begun during the war, but whose destructive force the Nazi defeat had now fully unleashed. In France, Italy and across Eastern Europe, thousands of individuals were killed both inside and outside internment camps, in what later became known as the 'wild purges'.[37] Here, it was much more difficult to distinguish between formalised internments and extra-institutional violence. In France, an estimated 9,000 individuals died shortly before or after the liberation.[38] In Italy, an

[33] See Chapter 2. [34] Führer, *Nachspiel*, p. 35.
[35] Novick, *The Resistance Versus Vichy*, pp. 25–30.
[36] Johannes Andenæs, *Det vanskelige oppgjøret* (Oslo: Tanum-Norli, 1979), p. 64; 'Rikspolitisjefens årsberetning', Justis- og Politidepartementet, *Om landssvikoppgjøret* (Gjøvik: Mariendal, 1962), p. 462.
[37] Novick, *The Resistance Versus Vichy*, pp. 71–76.
[38] The number of extra-legal executions following liberation is estimated to be around 1,000–2,000: Henry Rousso, 'The Purge in France', in Jon Elster (ed.), *Retribution and Reparation in the*

estimated 12,000 individuals perished between 1943 and 1946 in a liberation that was marked by civil war and a deep crisis of state. In Eastern Europe, it was particularly the German minorities that faced violence and death. But nobody who might conceivably present a threat to political (largely communist) goals could feel completely safe. In Hungary, communist 'National Committees', which assumed legislative and executive functions at the local level, oversaw a first wave of brutal purges of potential political opponents. They combed towns and villages for members of the old bourgeois elite whom they summarily executed, long before any centralised state power could be established.[39] Not even the victims of Nazi violence were spared the extreme bloodshed in Eastern Europe. In Poland, thousands of Jewish Holocaust survivors, seeking to return to what was left of their hometowns and villages, were murdered by individuals who had since taken over their properties, or who simply refused to accept their presence in their neighbourhoods.[40]

Norway's social and political transition was much less traumatic and brutal. There were, in fact, no officially reported killings either inside or outside internment camps. The level of violence was similarly low in Denmark, the Netherlands and Belgium: in Denmark, there were 25 reported killings, fewer than 100 were reported in the Netherlands, and in Belgium 265 perished during the transition.[41] Nevertheless, there was one particular manifestation of post-war violence in Norway that was in fact very similar to that witnessed all across Europe: the violence against women who had fraternised with the German occupier.[42] The treatment of '*tyskerjenter*' ('Germany girls') is a particularly dark chapter in Norway's transition from war to peace. It reflected a pan-European pattern that could be observed for example in France, Italy, the Czech Lands, Denmark and Italy.[43] Public shaming of these women took a markedly similar,

Transition to Democracy (Cambridge: Cambridge University Press, 2006), pp. 89–123, at pp. 93–97.

39 Szöllösi-Janze, 'Pfeilkreuzler, Landesverräter und andere Volksfeinde', pp. 321–324; Szabolcs Szita, 'Die Volksgerichtsbarkeit als Teil der politischen Säuberung in Ungarn, 1945–1946', in Claudia Kuretsidis-Haider and Winfried R. Garscha (eds.), *Keine "Abrechnung": NS-Verbrechen, Justiz, Gesellschaft in Europa nach 1945* (Leipzig: AVA, 1998), pp. 207–216.

40 Klaus Kellmann, *Dimensionen der Mittäterschaft: die europäische Kollaboration mit dem Dritten Reich* (Vienna: Böhlau, 2019), pp. 337–338.

41 On the period of transition in the Netherlands, see Fühner, *Nachspiel*, pp. 35–37.

42 Keith Lowe, *Savage Continent: Europe in the Aftermath of World War II* (London: Penguin, 2013), pp. 163–178.

43 Ute Frevert, *Die Politik der Demütigung: Schauplätze von Macht und Ohnmacht* (Frankfurt am Main: Fischer, 2017), pp. 71–73; citing Benjamin Frommer, 'Denouncers and Fraternizers: Gender, Collaboration, and Retribution in Bohemia and Moravia during World War II and

ritualistic form across the continent.[44] Women's heads were shorn, and in many countries made to run the gauntlet through their hometowns and villages. They were made to carry signs announcing their alleged crimes and were frequently spat at or humiliated in other ways. In most countries, these women were interned, but later released. As we have seen, Germany girls were interned for extended periods in Norway. Officially, this was presented as a protective measure, but it served also as a form of punishment.[45] As with the overall level of violence, however, the *tyskerjenter* of Norway were spared some of the brutality seen elsewhere.

Overall, Norway emerged comparatively unscathed from the liberation period. In explaining the relatively low degree of violence during and immediately following Norway's liberation, a number of factors can be put forward. The first, as we have seen, was timing: the Norwegian exile government and Home Front had had the chance to witness the violence that erupted across Europe as Germans forces withdrew and propped-up collaborative regimes crumbled. This facilitated a certain pragmatism in the joint planning efforts and also shaped the ways in which Norway's interim authorities communicated with the public ahead of the liberation. In the weeks following Norway's liberation, officials repeated almost like a mantra that collaborators would be punished harshly and that violence was to be prevented by all means. In doing so, officials even drew attention to the violence that had occurred elsewhere and warned that this could have the effect of generating pity for collaborators.[46] The second reason was the nature of the occupation regime itself. The Germans treated the Northern nations with much greater respect than other countries, seeing them as fellow 'Aryans' rather than a people to be enslaved or eliminated.[47] This meant that pre-war social norms managed to survive relatively intact, and that the threshold for violence remained higher than elsewhere in Europe. Thirdly, Norway's institutional framework was conducive to stability: the judicial apparatus had survived the war largely untainted. In combination with the fact that the exile government and resistance movement had agreed to form a unity government, this meant that public announcements

After', in Nancy M. Wingfield and Maria Bucur (eds.), *Gender and War in Twentieth-Century Eastern Europe* (Bloomington: Indiana University Press, 2006), pp. 111–132.

44 Fabrice Virgili, *La France 'virile': Des femmes tondues á la libération* (Paris: Payot, 2000); Anette Warring, *Tyskerpiger: under besættelse og retsopgør* (Copenhagen: Gyldendal, 2017); Rianne Oosterom, *Moffenmeiden: over soldatenliefjes, knippers en omstanders: een geschiedenis in verhalen* (Amsterdam: Meulenhoff, 2019).

45 Knut Papendorf, *Siktet som tyskertøs: rettsoppgjøret i videre forstand* (Oslo: Novus, 2015).

46 Omang (ed.), *Regjeringen og hjemmefronten under krigen*, p. 486.

47 This does not include the Jews in Norway, however, as well as other ethnic minorities.

that collaborators would be brought to justice were credible to the Norwegian population.[48] But it also meant that the legal system was forced to absorb expectations that it would ultimately struggle to meet.

7.4 Function

Throughout the spring and summer of 1945, the primary purpose of the trials from the perspective of the Norwegian unity government was to channel the resentment and bitterness that had grown during the occupation into an orderly legal process that could pacify social tensions. Similar rationales guided the trials of collaborators across most of the continent. In the weeks following the liberation, Norwegian officials made frequent announcements that the trials of collaborators would soon commence and that justice would be duly served. This in turn placed immense public expectations in the legal system. But despite the intermittent protests and strikes that flared up across the country in the summer of 1945, the promise of the trials largely succeeded in appeasing social tensions. Elsewhere, as we have seen, extra-judicial violence could not be averted. In Czechoslovakia, violence against the German minority of the Sudetenland was even encouraged. Here, the Beneš government calculated that 'wild retribution' against Germans would lead to fewer difficult deportations when the planned 'transfer' of the German minority was carried out.[49] But wherever wild purges raged, governments ultimately had a strong interest in bringing them to an end: reconstruction would be impossible if the state could not re-establish its monopoly of violence.[50] The trials provided an opportunity for the newly established governments – whatever their composition or aims – to shape social sentiments and assert their own authority. The Polish Lublin Committee (PKWN), for example, which was aware that it was perceived as illegitimate and more Soviet than Polish, was very keen to have the trials commence swiftly so as to boost its public support.[51] Not least, the trials presented post-war governments with the chance to place themselves on 'the right side of history', for the laws and court verdicts established a first binding interpretation of war-time events. The legitimacy of the post-1945 order would be largely founded on these wartime narratives.

48 Hans Woller, '"Ausgebliebene Säuberung?" Die Abrechnung mit dem Faschismus in Italien', in Henke and Woller (eds.), *Politische Säuberung in Europa*, (Munich: DTV, 1991) pp. 148–191, at p. 182.

49 Frommer, *National Cleansing*, pp. 33–62.

50 Judt, *Postwar*, pp. 43–44; Novick, *The Resistance Versus Vichy*, pp. 62–63.

51 Kornbluth, *The August Trials*, p. 88.

For the trials to succeed as a demonstration of power, they would need to summon widespread public support.[52] To this end, post-war authorities across Europe sought to act in line with national sentiments, or to construct narratives that would facilitate the public's backing. Rallying public support for the trials was rarely a difficult feat. The experience of occupation had been humiliating to the populations of Europe. Not only had they been unable to defend themselves militarily but the vast majority of Europeans had unheroically accommodated to life under Nazi occupation. Percentages vary somewhat, but it is broadly true across the continent that roughly the same small percentage of people had been involved in collaboration as had participated in the resistance.[53] Upon liberation, the populations in formerly occupied countries were now all too keen to point fingers at specific groups and accuse them of treason and collaboration. In this way, they could make select groups responsible for the general plight and humiliation of occupation. The groups that nations selected as their scapegoats differed from one country to another. In Norway, where the NS had gained particular prominence, it was not surprising that its members faced particular hostility. However, in countries possessing German minority populations, these groups became a particular focus of public scorn. In bringing proceedings against select groups or subjecting them to other forms of repression, the ambivalences of occupation, collaboration and accommodation could conveniently be eclipsed. Political gains could only be made by feeding into the idea that only specific minorities had collaborated and that the majority had heroically resisted the German enemy. Confronting the widespread everyday collaboration that had taken place during the war was simply not an option in the summer of 1945.

During the war, certain political circles had envisaged the trials of collaborators as part of a much more ambitious process of political renewal.[54] The wartime resistance movements and communist circles in particular intended for the reckoning with collaborators to bring about fundamental political change. They were disappointed with what they considered to be the failings of the pre-war political elites and particularly critical of interwar capitalism. Instead, they wished to draw up their own post-war orders, a necessary element of which was a reckoning with the perceived failings of past elites, which would demand a comprehensive purge of politicians and civil servants. In Norway, these calls for renewal swiftly subsided following the liberation. Many senior resistance members

[52] Fühner, *Nachspiel*, p. 45. [53] Judt, *Postwar*, p. 33.
[54] Novick, *The Resistance Versus Vichy*, pp. 35–40.

had secured leading positions within the government and were now mostly interested in consolidating their power rather than bringing about far-reaching changes to state structures. The trials became about restoring confidence in state authorities, and experienced career civil servants were needed to this end. The same was true in most other Western European countries. In France, where collaboration had been widespread and the legitimacy of the Vichy regime remained contested, the resistance continued for some time to push for an encompassing 'purge' of Vichyists. But the establishment of a 'Party of the Resistance' had failed already in summer 1945; the majority of the French population ultimately had no interest in any fundamental political change and remained reluctant to accept the resistance as France's new elite.[55] Across Western Europe, leading resistance figures were either absorbed into mainstream politics or became marginalised – particularly so if they belonged to the more extreme (in particular communist) fringes.[56] Before long, the idea that the trials should bring about fundamental political and institutional change disappeared entirely.

In Eastern Europe, meanwhile, the trials also became an instrument for consolidating communist rule. Especially in Hungary, this was seen almost immediately following the German defeat. Moscow took an immense interest in the Hungarian reckoning, and due to the terms of the ceasefire agreement reached between Hungary and the Soviet Union on 20 January 1945 was also able to exert some influence over the process. Communists also dominated the Hungarian National Independence Front and were therefore able to shape the reckoning in a 'revolutionary' spirit, directed towards consolidating communist power.[57] In Czechoslovakia and Poland, the collaborator trials were initially much more comparable to those in the West than is often assumed. In Poland, the Soviet-backed government had to rely on the traditional juridical elites to implement the trials, which meant that they were much less a set of top-down political show trials than a judicial process that faced the typical challenges encountered also in countries all across Europe. Similarly, in Czechoslovakia, the decrees issued by the exile government were adopted almost without any changes in the summer of 1945 and the trials initially unfolded in similar patterns as those

[55] Rousso, *The Vichy Syndrome*, p. 19.

[56] Fühner, *Nachspiel*, p. 76; Martin Conway, 'Justice in Postwar Belgium: Popular Passions and Political Realities', in Deák, Gross and Judt, *The Politics of Retribution in Europe*, pp. 133–156, at pp. 150–151.

[57] László Karsai, 'The People's Courts and Revolutionary Justice in Hungary, 1945–46', in Deák, Gross and Judt, *The Politics of Retribution in Europe*, pp. 233–251, at p. 237.

in the West. Here, the explicit refashioning of the trials towards communist and Soviet ends began only in the late 1940s, as Stalin intensified his grip on Poland and following the communist coup in Czechoslovakia in 1948.

The political ends pursued by way of the collaborator trials thus differed from one country to another. The most profound differences, perhaps unsurprisingly, could be found between Eastern and Western European countries. But the fundamental nature of the trials was everywhere political. This was very much the case in Norway too, despite the fact that officials tirelessly sought in every possible way to frame the trials in terms of laws and legal principles. The political nature of Europe's collaborator trials was reflected, not least, in the unusual ways in which their legal bases were adopted and applied. As we have seen, many governments issued decrees during the war, and these rested on the provisional, extraordinary and often disputed law-making powers of exile governments. After the liberation, the post-war governments resorted to keeping their wartime decrees in place for as long as possible, without the cumbersome and lengthy process of involving parliaments and (provisional) national assemblies. As we saw in Chapter 2, Norway's unity government deemed it too risky to subject the wartime decrees to lengthy parliamentary proceedings, lest this led to uncertainty about its promises for a tough stance against collaborators. However, there was one notable exception: the unity government found it too politically contentious to have courts hand down death penalty verdicts without a parliamentary mandate. The death penalty was thus legislated upon, although the parliamentary process was kept a secret from the public and carried out swiftly – a sign that this was not an ordinary instance of parliamentary scrutiny. Those countries that had not been able to issue decrees during the war adopted legal measures at haphazard speed and with minimal public or parliamentary scrutiny. Denmark, for example, passed all of its legislation within a week in late May 1945.[58] That the legal bases for the reckonings were not subjected to ordinary parliamentary proceedings highlights the extraordinary sense of political urgency that governments felt in commencing the trials.

The fact that the legal bases of the trials were either issued as extraordinary wartime decrees or hurried through newly reconvened parliaments

[58] Lov Nr. 259 af 1. Juni 1945 om Tillæg til Borgerlig Straffelov angaaende Forræderi og anden landsskadelig Virksomhed; Lov Nr. 260 af 1. Juni 1945 om Tillæg til Lov om Rettens Pleje vedrørende Behandling af Sager angaaende Forræderi og anden landsskadelig Virksomhed m. v.; Tamm, *Retsopgøret efter besættelsen*, pp. 113–157.

meant that they almost all suffered from technical shortcomings. Almost all decrees were inflexible, and ill-suited to cater for the complexity of the reckonings that lay ahead. Courts across Europe came to struggle with their vaguely worded provisions and their often rigid demands for high penalties.[59] Most problematically, the legal bases of the trials were frequently retroactive, violating one of the most central principles of the rule of law. Where governments had issued wartime decrees, they typically applied to the *entirety* of the occupation, not merely from the date of their issuing. Where laws were adopted only after the liberation, as in Denmark, they were necessarily entirely retroactive. These shortcomings gave rise to some debate within political and academic circles across Europe.[60] The return to established, pre-war legal principles was, after all, intended to be a core element of the re-establishment of post-war authority.[61] However, in all countries which aimed to reconstruct their state infrastructure on a 'rule of law' foundation, the shortcomings of the decrees and laws at the basis of the trials were generally accepted by post-war political elites as a limited exception to ordinary standards of the rule of law, made necessary by the distinct set of circumstances the occupation had brought about.

7.5 Prosecution

The varying degrees of destruction that the war had brought across Europe meant that the institutional preconditions for bringing collaborators to trial varied significantly from country to country. Norway's judicial system had remained largely intact and appeared remarkably uncompromised, mainly because the Germans had established a parallel court system to push through their ideological agenda. The Norwegian exile government and Home Front therefore decided that the trials would be conducted within the ordinary court apparatus. That the unity government could rely on fully functioning institutions was also an advantage regarding the speed at which proceedings could be brought (during the war, it also allowed officials to assert with some confidence that the trials would commence soon after the liberation). Although some judges were removed on account of their NS membership, public faith in the court system was re-

[59] Even in Czechoslovakia, where authorities took two months following liberation to promulgate the Great Decree, they did not use the time to make improvements to its London draft, which was issued under pressure over growing vigilante justice; Frommer, *National Cleansing*, pp. 63–65.

[60] This was also true in Eastern Europe, see for example for the case of Poland: Kornbluth, *The August Trials*, p. 129.

[61] Novick, *The Resistance Versus Vichy*, pp. 140–141.

established comparatively quickly and the first trials reached court in June 1945. In Denmark, too, the ordinary court system was used, despite the fact that the resistance had pushed for a special court system to be instituted.[62] As in Norway, the use of the ordinary court system was intended to signal a return to 'normality' – the idea of 'special courts' were simply too closely associated with Nazi rule. But in both countries, the procedural rules for treason cases were adapted to the distinct demands of the hour. This included a higher presence of lay judges, who were to represent 'the people', and eased procedural rules to allow for a swifter handling of the impending caseload.[63]

By contrast, most European countries held the trials of collaborators outside the ordinary civilian court systems. Instead, they either placed them within the military courts or created new judicial branches altogether. Some employed a combination of several systems. The Belgian exile government issued a decree in 1944 handing over responsibility for the trials of collaborators to military courts.[64] France used a combination of military courts and novel court structures, with lay judges for the newly created *Cours de Justice* recruited in particular from the *Résistance*.[65] The idea that it was 'the people' or 'the nation' who should cast their verdict was reflected in particular in the so-called People's Courts, in which 'patriotic citizens' rather than trained judges would adjudicate. Sometimes these courts operated as criminal courts, and sometimes as administrative bodies that functioned alongside the criminal justice system. In Czechoslovakia, twenty-four extraordinary People's Courts were established in June 1945.[66] Though they functioned as criminal courts, they were highly political in character, with lay judges chosen according to party affiliation. In the Netherlands, in addition to the formation of a special branch of the criminal justice system, nineteen 'People's Tribunals', composed of individuals with a 'patriotic' mindset, sanctioned people in administrative proceedings for 'unpatriotic' behaviour. Such behaviour could consist of anything from being a member of the fascist party *Nationaal Socialistische Beweging* (National Socialist

62 Tamm, *Retsopgøret efter besættelsen*, p. 71.

63 Legal Procedures Decree (*Rettergangsanordningen*) of 16 February 1945.

64 Luc Huyse, 'Belgian and Dutch Purges after World War II Compared', in Elster (ed.), *Retribution and Reparation in the Transition to Democracy*, pp. 164–178, at p. 166.

65 Rousso, 'The Purge in France', pp. 101–103; Novick, *The Resistance Versus Vichy*, pp. 149–156.

66 Frommer, *National Cleansing*, pp. 78, 127–132; see also The Great Decree (No. 16/1945), printed as Appendix 1 in Frommer, *National Cleansing*, pp. 348–363.

Movement, or NSB) to subscribing to a National Socialist newspaper.[67] Despite the fact that these were not criminal courts, the Dutch 'People's Tribunals' could hand down prison terms of up to ten years. In Poland, responsibility for handling the trials shifted through four different sets of courts.[68] In general terms, then, the institution of such a wide range of special judicial branches highlights the distinctly political nature of the trials of wartime collaborators. The Norwegian trials, by contrast, had the semblance of a more ordinary adjudication process. But they, too, had special procedural rules in place for cases concerning collaborators and were treated within the court system as a special category of trials.

The political nature of Europe's post-war reckonings, and in particular their focus on crimes against the nation or the state, were reflected also in the new penalties introduced. In particular, the penalty of loss of civil rights was a central element of all collaborator trials.[69] The penalty involved the loss of the right to vote, to join military service and to stand for election. It also barred individuals from a wide range of professions and withdrew their public pension rights. This type of penalty particularly reflected the desire to attribute guilt to specific groups and exclude them from the national community. The Norwegian wartime decrees had expanded the scope of the penalty so dramatically that the exile government considered it suitable to be used *in lieu of* prison sentences.[70] This was aimed at preventing an overcrowding of prisons. In France, the equivalent penalty, termed *degradation nationale* ('national degration'), was introduced for the new catch-all administrative offence of *indignité nationale* ('national unworthiness').[71]

An even more controversial penalty characteristic of the post-war purges was the death penalty. All across Europe, the death penalty was reintroduced or made more widely available for the most serious cases of collaboration or treason. Along with Norway, several countries that had previously abolished the death penalty reintroduced it strictly as punishment for

[67] Peter Romijn and Gerhard Hirschfeld, 'Die Ahndung der Kollaboration in den Niederlanden', in Henke and Woller (eds.), *Politische Säuberung in Europa*, pp. 281–310, at p. 293.

[68] Kornbluth, *The August Trials*, p. 10.

[69] Novick, *Resistance Versus Vichy*, pp. 148–149; Kornbluth, *The August Trials*, p. 91.

[70] Anika Seemann, 'Citizen Outcasts: The Penalty of "Loss of Civil Rights" during the Norwegian Treason Trials, 1945–1953', *Scandinavian Journal of History*, 45 (2020) 3, pp. 360–383.

[71] Anne Simonin, 'L'indignité nationale: un chatiment républicain', in Marc Olivier Baruch (ed.), *Une poignée de misérables l'épuration de la société française après la Seconde Guerre mondiale* (Paris: Fayard, 2003), pp. 37–60.

collaborators.[72] However, the decrees that allowed for the use of the death penalty tied its implementation closely to the post-war trials, and usually set a date after which it could no longer be used. At the time of liberation, expectations among politicians and the wider public were high that the death penalty would be used widely. But it was ultimately used much more sparingly by the courts than many had hoped (or feared), and across Europe only a fraction of death penalty verdicts were ultimately executed.[73] This was true also in much of Eastern Europe, despite the comparatively high number of death penalty verdicts handed down there. In Poland, the 'August Decree' had even stipulated a death penalty verdict for certain offences. This, however, led to judicial caution in the form of high numbers of acquittals, followed by an amendment of the corresponding provisions two years later. Ultimately, the actual figures on how many death sentences were handed down and executed across Eastern Europe are difficult to establish.[74] In addition, the political remoulding of the trials to serve communist aims meant that the death penalty came to be used more intensely again from the late 1940s, as opposed to the gradual tapering down that took place in the West.

The death penalty was introduced in particular with national collaborationist elites in mind, as well as those individuals who had committed particularly heinous crimes during the war.[75] In this respect, the trials and – usually – executions of National Socialist party leaders and the national representatives of collaboration regimes occupied a central symbolic place in all post-war reckonings. While few leaders of National Socialist parties attained a level of infamy comparable to Norway's Vidkun Quisling, the trials of national fascists and collaborators held immense symbolic power for post-war governments and were mostly brought very soon after the liberation. Quisling's trial opened on 20 August 1945, with his death sentence verdict being handed down on 13 October 1945. He was executed eleven days later.[76] In the Netherlands,

[72] It was reintroduced in the Netherlands (previously abolished in 1870), Norway (previously abolished in 1902) and Denmark (previously abolished in 1930).

[73] The only exception is Czechoslovakia, where a provision in the so-called Great Decree stipulated that executions be carried out within *two hours* of a verdict being handed down. For this reason, a much higher percentage of death penalty verdicts were executed than elsewhere in Europe; Frommer, *National Cleansing*, pp. 484–485.

[74] Kornbluth, *The August Trials*, p. 135.

[75] In Norway, it was particularly Gestapo agents of the Rinnan group who received death penalty verdicts, as seen in Chapter 4.

[76] Hans Fredrik Dahl, *Quisling: A Study in Treachery* (Cambridge: Cambridge University Press, 2007 [1999]), pp. 409–415; *Straffesak mot Vidkun Abraham Lauritz Jonssøn Quisling* (Oslo: Grøndahl, 1946).

head of the fascist party NSB, Anton Mussert, was tried in November 1945, received a death penalty verdict on 12 December 1945 and was executed on 7 May 1946. In Czechoslovakia, the infamous Decree 17/1945 served as the basis for punishing the members of the Czechoslovak wartime government and leaders of fascist parties, with a total of eighteen receiving a death sentence.[77] Many key protagonists of the Czech Protectorate Government, however, managed to evade the death penalty. Things looked different in Slovakia: Jozef Tiso, the Slovak fascist leader, had fled to a Bavarian monastery following the war, before being extradited to his homeland, where his trial began on 2 December 1946. He was sentenced to death by the Slovak National Court on 15 April 1947 and hanged three days later. In Hungary, although post-war prosecutions of collaborators were somewhat patchy, it was particularly the fascist Arrow Cross movement that became the symbolic centre point of the trials of collaborators in the immediate post-war period, with its leader Ferenc Szálasi being executed on 12 March 1946.[78] The line of defence relied upon in court by former Nazi leaders was usually of a similar nature: they argued that they had tried to secure their nation's interests within the pan-Germanic order, and had therefore acted so as to safeguard the interests of the nation.[79] Predictably, the post-war courts across Europe rejected such arguments.

The question of how to punish collaborationist elites was considerably more complex in regard to governments that had entered into a *collaboration d'Etat* with Germany. In Denmark, the collaborationist elites largely remained in power following the liberation, and, unsurprisingly, they were not particularly inclined to attribute blame to themselves. While the Danish parliament instituted an investigatory commission into Denmark's *collaboration d'Etat* with Germany, it arrived at the unsurprising conclusion in 1947 that Denmark's state institutions had done nothing wrong. Conveniently, responsibility could instead be attributed to the leaders of the National Socialist Workers' Party of Denmark (*Danmarks Nationalsocialistiske Arbejderparti* – DNSAP) and the German minority's own National Socialist German Workers' Party of North Schleswig (*Nationalsozialistische Deutsche Arbeiterpartei-Nordschleswig* – NSDAP-N), although neither had exercised any real influence on the course of the

[77] The National Court Decree (No. 17/1945), printed as Appendix 2 in Frommer, *National Cleansing*, pp. 364–370.

[78] Szöllösi-Janze, 'Pfeilkreuzler, Landesverräter und andere Volksfeinde'.

[79] István Deák, 'Political Justice in Austria and Hungary after World War II', in Elster (ed.), *Retribution and Reparation in the Transition to Democracy*, pp. 124–146, at pp. 135–136.

German occupation.[80] The Hungarian regent Miklós Horthy, who had oscillated between supporting and opposing Hitler's cause for four years, did not face trial after the war; he was simply deemed too popular for a trial to be a political success. In France, the leading Vichyist collaborators Philippe Pétain and Pierre Laval stood trial in August and October 1945 respectively. Other leading Vichyists, however, were spared prosecution and were able to continue their careers in the civil service of the Fourth Republic. The question of which prominent figures should be summoned to stand trial was therefore not as straightforward a question as it had been in Norway, where Quisling had so overwhelmingly become the symbol of collaboration.

Along with the party leaders, members and supporters of the various National Socialist parties became central figures in the post-war trials. This was of course nowhere as explicit as in Norway, where membership of the NS had been criminalised by way of the exile government's 1942 Decree. But while party membership was not formally made a crime outside of Norway, parallel processes of attributing guilt to the members of National Socialist parties could nevertheless be observed. In the Netherlands, membership of the NSB was of relevance in the People's Tribunals, where NSB members were by default deemed to have been 'unpatriotic' and received administrative sanctions.[81] In France, membership of any kind of collaborationist organisation was not criminalised in and of itself, but was nevertheless punishable with 'national degradation' – a criminal sanction in all but name.[82] And in trials across the continent, membership of a fascist party could tip the balance against a defendant if they were on trial over their wartime actions. This was especially the case in the trials of public intellectuals and other prominent figures, whose support of the Nazi parties was deemed particularly reprehensible. But for all members of fascist parties, there was a strong presumption of culpability – something that those on trial felt also outside the court room, and for much longer than the duration of the trials themselves.

In addition to the leaders and supporters of fascist parties and collaborationist regimes, those who had joined various German intelligence and military formations took up a central place in the post-war reckonings. At the gravest end of this spectrum, agents of the German Security Police

[80] Christensen, *Danmark besat*, pp. 145–151, 417–422.

[81] Membership in collaborationist organisations was also a key criterion for the purges of state administrations, although these are not discussed here: Novick, *The Resistance Versus Vichy*, p. 87.

[82] Ibid., p. 148.

(*Sicherheitspolizei*) and informants working for the German military intelligence (*Abwehr*), many of whom had tortured and killed fellow citizens in their work, were prosecuted. Some of these trials had a particularly wide public resonance, such as the six-month-long trial of the infamous 'Rinnan group' in Norway, which to many Norwegians came to embody the horrors of Nazi occupation. These cases were limited in number, however. A much larger group was composed of volunteers to the Waffen-SS and the Wehrmacht. In Norway, around 5,000 individuals stood trial for having signed up to the Waffen-SS.[83] Across Europe, hundreds of thousands had joined the ranks of the Waffen-SS and (to a lesser extent) the Wehrmacht, often following aggressive German recruitment campaigns. But in the post-war period, attitudes toward Waffen-SS volunteers changed perceptibly over time. Especially in the immediate post-war era, their decision to fight for the German cause was strongly condemned, and they faced high penalties: as much as eight to ten years in the Netherlands, six to seven years in Norway and around four years in Denmark.[84] However, mitigating circumstances were soon put forward, and penalties were reduced significantly upon appeal. In Norway, as we have seen, the defence often cited the difficult social backgrounds as well as the impressionability of young recruits, and following this, public attitudes became somewhat milder. In Denmark, membership of the German minority of North Schleswig, and the conflicting national loyalties that this brought for individuals, were cited as additional grounds for leniency.[85] And with the Cold War taking shape at the end of the 1940s, public attitudes began to shift even further: now, Waffen-SS volunteers were increasingly seen simply as young and opportunistic anti-Bolsheviks who deserved a second chance in life. Their crimes against civilian populations and prisoners of war played next to no role in the early post-war period.

A common dimension of European post-war reckonings not found in Norway concerned the treatment of German national minorities. German minorities had been willing collaborators across Europe, often hoping for their 'return to the Reich' or political autonomy. In Denmark the members of the German minority in North Schleswig assumed a prominent place in the treason trials. The minority had – in vain – hoped that by

[83] Justis- og Politidepartementet, *Om landssvikoppgjøret*, pp. 192–194.

[84] Ibid., p. 195; Tamm, *Retsopgøret efter besættelsen*, p. 236.

[85] Anika Seemann, 'On War, Loyalty and Reconciliation: The German Minority in North Schleswig during the Second World War and the Post-war Reckoning', in Peter Thaler (ed.), *Like Snow in the Sun? The German Minority in Denmark in Historical Perspective* (Berlin: De Gruyter, 2022), pp. 91–114.

demonstrating its loyalty towards Nazi Germany, Hitler would reverse the hated Versailles border and reincorporate North Schleswig into the Reich.[86] A quarter of those sentenced in the Danish post-war trials belonged to the minority, although it counted only 30,000 individuals out of Denmark's population of almost 4 million.[87] However, during the post-war reckoning, the German minority in Denmark was treated comparatively mildly, as indeed was the German minority in Belgium, if we compare their treatment to that of German minorities in Eastern Europe.[88] Here, the minorities were subjected to ambitious – and brutal – national cleansing projects. The Polish and Czech exile governments had already decided during the occupation that the German minorities would be driven out of their territories.[89] The Czech exile government exerted pressure on Hungary to adopt similar plans, the aim being to then extradite the Hungarian minority in Czechoslovakia to Hungary.[90] But even prior to the expulsions, many minority members faced prosecution and expropriation. While it may seem paradoxical that minority members were prosecuted ahead of their expulsions, it was, in fact, a deliberate strategy: the narratives produced in court cases against minority members were used to publicly justify the impending expulsions.[91] With the aim of ethnic cleansing so closely tied to the trials in the East, a comparison between Eastern and Western Europe is particularly challenging in this regard. But even among Western European countries, Norway's ethnic composition stands out as one that was particularly homogenous, leaving its post-war reckoning largely unconcerned with questions of ethnicity.[92]

86 Johan Peter Noack, *Det tyske mindretal i Nordslesvig under besættelsen* (Copenhagen: Munksgaard, 1975), pp. 31–89.

87 On the German minority of North Schleswig during and after the Second World War, see Seemann, 'The German Minority of North Schleswig during the Second World War and the Postwar Reckoning'; Sabine Lorek, *Rechtsabrechnung-Retsopgør: politische Säuberung nach dem Zweiten Weltkrieg in Nordschleswig* (Neumünster: Wachholtz, 1998).

88 Ulrich Tiedau, 'Die Rechtslage der deutschsprachigen Bevölkerung in Belgien nach dem Zweiten Weltkrieg', in Manfred Kittel, Horst Möller, Jiri Pesek and Oldrich Tuma (eds.), *Deutschsprachige Minderheiten 1945: ein europäischer Vergleich* (Munich: Oldenbourg, 2007), pp. 435–487, at pp. 482–487; Jürgen Festersen, 'Dänemark und die deutsche Volksgruppe in Nordschleswig 1940–1955', in Kittel, Möller, Pesek and Tuma (eds.), *Deutschsprachige Minderheiten 1945* (Oldenbourg: De Gruyter, 2006), pp. 571–582, at pp. 581–582.

89 Francis Dostál Raska, 'The Czechoslovak Exile Government in London and the Sudeten German Issue' (Dissertation, Charles University in Prague, 2002); Bernadetta Nietschke, *Vertreibung und Aussiedlung der deutschen Bevölkerung aus Polen 1945 bis 1949* (Munich: Oldenbourg, 2003).

90 Szöllösi-Janze, 'Pfeilkreuzler, Landesverräter und andere Volksfeinde', p. 351.

91 Frommer, *National Cleansing*, pp. 228–243.

92 On the expulsion of Sudeten Germans more generally, see Detlef Brandes, *Der Weg zur Vertreibung 1938–1945: Pläne und Entscheidungen zum 'Transfer' der Deutschen aus der Tschechoslowakei und aus*

In comparison to ethnic minorities, fascist party members and volunteers to the Waffen-SS, economic collaborators were treated mildly.[93] During the war, the resistance movements in particular had produced ambitious plans to prosecute economic collaborators. In their view, it was deeply reprehensible that individuals had sided with the enemy for personal economic gain. However, as the trials of collaborators progressed, post-war authorities sought to reduce the number of cases against economic collaborators.[94] There were a number of reasons for this. In states with a *collaboration d'Etat*, economic collaboration had often been sanctioned by the collaborationist regime. But exile governments, too, had largely approved of 'keeping the wheels in motion', making it a thorny issue to punish after the war's end. Even more significantly, the post-war authorities recognised that the dividing line between opportunism and oppression was particularly difficult to draw in the case of economic collaboration, not least when taking into regard the fact that the populations of occupied territories still needed to be fed and clothed. But perhaps most important of all, businesses were central to post-war reconstruction: no post-war government had an interest in restricting the reconstruction of its core industries by placing them on trial. In practice, the element of time also worked in the favour of those under investigation for economic collaboration. The preparation of cases against economic collaboration was extremely complex and time-consuming. By the time the more central cases were brought, typically from 1947 onwards, other groups had borne the brunt of public scorn, and the punishment of economic collaborators no longer served any meaningful social purpose. By this point in time, the costs of reckoning with economic collaborators far outweighed the benefits.

For some countries, the picture just outlined needs to be qualified. Where there had been no collaborationist party or widespread organisational collaboration, the post-war fault lines were different. In Poland, ideological affinity with the German cause had been low and Polish-on-Polish crimes took place in a more ad hoc manner – as opposed to crimes

Polen (Munich: Oldenbourg, 2001); Norman Naimark, *Fires of Hatred: Ethnic Cleansing in Twentieth Century Europe* (Cambridge, MA: Harvard University Press, 2001); Joseph B. Schechtman, *Postwar Population Transfers in Europe, 1945–1955* (Philadelphia: University of Pennsylvania Press, 1962). As we have seen, the Norwegian treason trials were not concerned with the Holocaust or crimes against ethnic minorities.

93 Novick, *The Resistance Versus Vichy*, pp. 162–163.

94 In Norway, of around 16,400 cases initiated against economic collaborators, only 3,400 led to a court verdict; see Justis- og Politidepartementet, *Om landssvikoppgjøret*, p. 239.

against the Jewish minority. The crimes were not programmatic as in countries with organised National Socialist movements, collaborationist governments or large-scale industrial opportunism. Nevertheless, collaboration took a variety of forms, and during the post-war reckoning, individuals were sentenced for their roles in the police service, liaison roles, volunteering for the SS and other military divisions, economic collaboration and denunciations.

When it comes to collaborative participation in the crimes of the Holocaust, the trials across Europe are comparable in how little attention they paid to them. In many countries, there had been widespread, active participation in the deportation and killing of Jews. The overwhelming focus on crimes against the state rather than Jews during the post-war reckonings, however, furthered a narrative that participation in the crimes of the Holocaust had been limited to only a small group of individuals. This ignored the fact that the participation in crimes of the Holocaust had often been driven by pre-existing antisemitism. Questions of restitution were also left largely unaddressed in the immediate post-war period, and in some countries, antisemitism would persist and reignite over the following decades. In Norway, the Jewish population was much smaller than elsewhere in Europe. Nevertheless, Norway fits into the pan-European pattern: the number of cases brought after the liberation nowhere near reflected the actual number of Norwegian perpetrators or crimes.

Overall, then, the groups of individuals brought to trial in Norway, and those who went free, were comparable to those seen elsewhere across Europe. However, the scope of punishment varied considerably. Norway had by far the highest number of prison sentences in relation to its population.[95] For Western Europe, the figures are as follows: 633 out of every 100,000 Norwegians were sentenced to prison, compared to 596 out of every 100,000 in Belgium, 419 out of every 100,000 in the Netherlands, 374 out of every 100,000 in Denmark and 94 out of every 100,000 in France.[96] For Eastern Europe, the figures are more difficult to establish – not least because new categories of individuals, including political opponents and old elites, came within their remit. Here, the most reliable figures concern convictions. With around 69,000[97] convictions in the Czech lands and some 20,000[98] in Poland, even the most

[95] Novick, *The Resistance Versus Vichy*, pp. 186–187. For Eastern European trials, the figures are more difficult to read, especially as the trials also encompassed a range of political opponents.

[96] Ibid., p. 187. [97] Frommer, *National Cleansing*, p. 321.

[98] Kornbluth, *The August Trials*, p. 7.

comprehensive reckonings in Eastern Europe examined in this chapter pale in relation to their population when compared to the 44,000 in Norway.[99] The Norwegian figures therefore stand out as the highest in all of Europe.

Neither the extent of wartime collaboration nor the blanket criminalization of membership in the NS alone can explain these high figures. We must also, for example, factor in the different ways in which European countries handled the caseload following liberation. In Belgium and the Netherlands, many smaller cases were closed in 1945 and 1946 before they could proceed to trial.[100] The internment figures and number of impending cases were simply deemed too overwhelming for the authorities to handle. In Poland, too, the reckoning became less intensive than might have been, also in part because the figures were too overwhelming at the start, but also because the communist regime began to see a vigorous prosecution as inopportune. But the Norwegian case looks particularly extensive when compared with Italy and France. In Italy, the popular embrace of fascism since 1922/1923 posed a challenge to any widespread reckoning. Italy's Minister of Justice and Head of Communist Party Palmiro Togliatti held 'few illusions' about the possibilities of a comprehensive reckoning with fascists.[101] In France, meanwhile, the extent of support enjoyed by the Vichy regime during the war presented a similar challenge. With so many individuals compromised, comprehensive prosecution was simply not feasible from either a political or economic perspective. France and Italy therefore limited the numbers of prosecutions significantly in the immediate post-war period. But the scope of the trials in these two countries also needs to be seen in relation to the 'wild purges' that preceded them. Because both Italy and France had experienced severe outbreaks of spontaneous violence during their respective liberations, the very idea of a 'purge' lost political legitimacy. More generally, the 'wild purges' also meant that some of the public desires for vengeance had subsided.[102] Norway, by contrast, largely stuck to its wartime plans in bringing cases to trial. But here too, the trials eventually had to be adapted to the changing political needs of the post-war order. It is to these changing needs that the chapter now turns.

99 The figures would translate to around 784 convictions per 100,000 citizens in the Czech Lands, around 84 per 100,000 in Poland and 1,470 per 100,000 in Norway.

100 In Belgium, the basis for this was a decree of 25 May 1945.

101 Judt, *Postwar*, p. 48.

102 Novick, *The Resistance Versus Vichy*, p. 78.

7.6 Adaption

Europe's post-war reckonings faced criticism from the very outset. Across the continent, academic lawyers and public intellectuals had voiced concern over what they perceived as the trials' many legal and moral shortcomings. In Norway, as we have seen, the young law professor Johannes Andenæs took particular issue with some aspects of the wartime decrees. Along with a number of public intellectuals, including Bishop Eivind Berggrav and the doctor Johan Scharffenberg, Andenæs also raised his concern over the detrimental long-term social effects of the trials. He feared that the trials would produce a class of social outcasts and lead to a pointless split in society. Critics like Andenæs could be found all across Europe. In the Netherlands, Frans Duynstee, a law professor and adviser to the Dutch Ministry of Justice, warned early on that too comprehensive a reckoning would threaten social cohesion. In Poland, intellectuals criticised the fact that executions were carried out publicly, and also took issue with the vague wording of the reckoning's legal bases, which they argued led to legal uncertainty. In the immediate post-war period, such criticism was mostly limited to small groups of academics and humanitarians.[103] But as the distance to the occupation grew, criticism of the trials became more prevalent, even in places where they had initially enjoyed widespread public support.

During the war, the exile governments had largely underestimated the nature and extent of collaboration that was taking place within the occupied territories. This proved a problem after the liberation, when many more individuals fell within the scope of the wartime decrees than had been anticipated. As a result, prisons across the continent were overcrowded and the criminal justice systems did not have the capacity to deal with the caseloads. As we have seen, some countries, including the Netherlands and Belgium, sought to limit the scope of prosecution before the trials had fully begun. In contrast, Norway relied on an accelerated sentencing procedure, introduced in early 1946 in an attempt to handle the unexpectedly large caseload. But in all countries, the post-war trials ultimately took much longer than anticipated.[104] And the unexpected duration of Europe's post-war trials meant that the legal provisions that

[103] France is an exception. Here, intellectuals had strongly engaged in a debate over the Vichy legacy and debate was fierce from the outset.

[104] Most countries had estimated that the trials would be over by the end of 1945: Novick, *The Resistance Versus Vichy*, p. 158.

had been designed to cater only for the specific context of the liberation moment soon had to stand the test of time. Beginning in 1946, public moods began to shift from a desire for vengeance towards a desire for 'normalization'.[105] Public criticism of the trials intensified, as they began to be seen as a needless burden from the past. This shift in mood was also reflected in sentencing practice. Not immune to public sentiment, the courts increasingly began to hand down lower penalties as the distance from the occupation grew. Over time, this became a major problem for the legal consistency of the trials.[106]

As we saw in Chapters 5 and 6, the overall shift towards a desire for 'normalisation' and the gradual reduction in average sentences posed an enormous challenge to Norwegian officials, who in their public communications had presented the legality of the trials, and in particular the adherence to the rule of law, as key elements of post-war justice.[107] The administration of the trials in Norway had been guided by the fundamental principles of 'consistency' and 'equality before the law'. The Norwegian authorities genuinely intended to keep the trials as closely connected to the ordinary administration of the law as possible. This way, the considerable political criticisms they had begun to attract could be kept at a distance. But it also meant that the trials could not simply be phased out, as any changes made for political reasons could undermine their claims to legality. In order to ensure the consistency of the trials, the Norwegian Ministry of Justice therefore began to grant individual pardons so as to align earlier court cases with later practice. This was a time-consuming endeavour, but it was deemed preferable to introducing more widespread changes to the legal framework, such as amnesties.

Such efforts to maintain the trials' claim to legal coherence were particularly central in Norway. The authorities of some other countries were less concerned with the idea of 'legal consistency'. In particular in Italy, the trials were more easily accepted as fundamentally political processes and were quickly adapted to meet post-war needs. Not least, the wild purges had already discredited the idea that the transition could be administered by the law alone, and as a result, amnesties were less problematic: Minister of Justice Palmiro Togliatti granted a general amnesty as early as 31 July 1946. This generated the idea of an '*eupazione mancata*' – a

[105] This was also the case in Czechoslovakia; see Frommer, *National Cleansing*, p. 134.

[106] A change in public debate and a reduction of average verdicts could be seen across the continent, including in the East: Ibid., pp. 96, 106.

[107] This was less of a problem in the Netherlands; Romijn and Hirschfeld, 'Die Ahndung der Kollaboration in den Niederlanden', p. 296.

reckoning that never took place. But given the country's widespread and decades-long embrace of fascism, it is difficult to imagine what other course could have been taken. In France, meanwhile, the deep frictions generated by the Vichy legacy meant that the trials posed a considerable threat to social cohesion. Here, the issue of amnesties was more controversial than in Italy, and became part of a political battle between left and right. Ultimately, the right succeeded in its demands for widespread amnesties, which were granted successively from 1947 onwards. As in Italy, the 'wild purges' were used as an argument in favour of phasing out the reckoning.[108] French politicians also referred to the case of Italy in arguing for the advantages of embarking upon a course of reconciliation.[109]

Sweeping measures such as amnesties, used in order to adapt the contours of the reckoning to changing political demands, were more problematic in countries where the reckoning was constructed primarily as a legal process that stood above politics. By 1948, however, changing political circumstances prompted governments across Western Europe to begin phasing out the trials. As we saw in Chapter 6, the Norwegian treason trials attained a new political meaning at the dawn of the Cold War. Across Western Europe, political leaders began to focus on facilitating social reconciliation as the external threat of the Cold War grew. The communist parties, which continued to push for harsh punishment of collaborators, had largely become politically delegitimised. For the political centre, it was now important to prevent sentenced collaborators from becoming a marginalised and possibly radical group.[110] The trials were therefore gradually phased out – a process not free from frictions. In all countries, there were vocal groups beyond communist circles which criticised the trials for having been too lenient – in particular victims of the collaboration regime and the extreme fringes of resistance groups.[111] Moreover, phasing out could undermine the claim to the legitimacy of the trials as such, with the potential of unleashing new social and political conflicts. Governments therefore had to limit the detrimental social effects of the trials without attracting too much criticism or undermining the political authority that the trials had helped generate. The governments of

108 Rousso, *The Vichy Syndrome*, p. 51.

109 Ibid.; Amnesty law of 5 January 1951, followed by a law concerning total amnesty on 24 July 1953.

110 Huyse, 'Belgian and Dutch Purges after World War II Compared', p. 169.

111 Criticism also came from communists who had often been active members of the resistance, although their calls now lost political legitimacy in the West.

Norway, Belgium and the Netherlands continued to focus on not allowing the legal legitimacy of the trials to be questioned. This was reflected in the fact that they insisted on granting pardons rather than amnesties. Although the difference between pardons and amnesties may appear a legal technicality, it was a very deliberate choice: by granting pardons, governments could avoid calling the reckoning as such into question.[112]

The release of prisoners into society, however, did not guarantee their social reintegration. In fact, all across Europe, sentenced collaborators faced considerable challenges upon their release from prison. Beyond the social ostracism they encountered, the social reintegration of collaborators was hampered in particular by the penalty of loss of civil rights, which had in some cases been handed down *for life*, typically as a mandatory addition to prison penalties. This sanction had profound consequences for individuals, leaving them not only unable to vote or join military service, but also barring them from a wide range of professions and stripping them of their public pension rights. This penalty provided some of the most long-term detrimental effects to sentenced collaborators. Within a few years, as governments across Western Europe began to recognise the social consequences of this penalty, some of its conditions were overturned. In most countries, including Norway and Denmark, the vast majority of affected individuals regained their civil rights from the late 1940s, with more serious offenders gradually regaining these rights in the 1950s. At the other end of the spectrum we find Belgium, where some individuals never recovered their full civil rights.[113] Here, the regranting of voting rights became part of a power contest between political camps representing the Wallonian and the Flemish parts of the population.[114] In the absence of such ethnic struggles, and due to the overwhelming power of the Social Democrats following the war, the issue of full reintegration of sentenced collaborators did not mutate into a political contest in Norway.

As sentenced collaborators were being released and socially reintegrated across Western Europe, trials in Eastern Europe were increasingly being refashioned to serve the purposes of communism and Stalinisation. But the ways in which this process unfolded differed significantly from one country to another. In Hungary, the trials had been used from the very outset to purge political enemies and consolidate communist power. In 1946, a law was passed in Hungary that extended the criminal provisions used in the

[112] Führer, *Nachspiel*, pp. 170–176; O.tid. (1947), pp. 13–17.
[113] Huyse, 'Belgian and Dutch Purges after World War II Compared', p. 170.
[114] Ibid., pp. 174–175.

trials to encompass *all* political opponents. The situation was different in Czechoslovakia and Poland, where until 1948, the trials largely unfolded along the same patterns as in the West.[115] In Czechoslovakia, the Communist Coup in February 1948 resulted in a complete refashioning of the trials. As Stalin's grip on the country tightened, the trials of collaborators became used more widely as part of a 'revolutionary process' towards Soviet political ends. Soon, anyone on the wrong side of politics could face trial and execution. Where it was not already the case, legal obstacles were removed and the rule of law was largely set aside. The new government found the judgments handed down between 1945 and 1948 to be much too lenient and subsequently increased them or subjected political opponents to retrials. By the late 1940s, anyone deemed an obstacle to the new order could face trial and execution, even including some communists themselves. In a somewhat paradoxical twist, meanwhile, many former fascists were granted opportunities for rehabilitation by joining communist party organisations. By this stage, the trials no longer stood in any direct correlation with wartime events, but their entire purpose was simply to consolidate communist power.[116] When this had been achieved, in the mid-1950s, the trials were phased out.

The situation was slightly different in Poland. The Polish trials were not, in fact, an 'instrument of Soviet-style Stalinist justice',[117] as they are often misconstrued, but were limited by the legal, political and social constraints that all countries faced in their purges. In fact, during the early stages of the trials, communist officials expressed dissatisfaction with the judiciary's leniency towards collaborators and the fact that they tended to follow pre-war convictions and legal principles rather than moulding the trials to serve the new era. Overall, the Polish experience was in fact much more comparable to the experiences of the West than other Eastern European countries. This changed in 1948, as the judicial system was restructured to serve the ends of Stalinisation, while the trials of collaborators were still ongoing. At least for a short period in 1949 and 1950, there were attempts to make the trials more stringent so as to make them serve communist narratives. However, when it became clear this risked alienating both the judicial elites upon which the regime depended and the wider

[115] Frommer, *National Cleansing*, p. 134; Gabriel N. Finder and Alexander V. Prusin, *Justice behind the Iron Curtain* (Toronto: University of Toronto Press, 2018), p. 6.
[116] Deák, 'Political Justice in Austria and Hungary after World War II', p. 134.
[117] Kornbluth, *The August Trials*, p. 132. Cases against the political resistance were, however, brought separately in military tribunals.

population, the trials were gradually phased out. They effectively came to an end by way of an amnesty in 1956.

7.7 Memory

Across Europe, the post-war trials of collaborators helped lay the foundations for national memories of the occupation. As we have seen, one of the most central functions of the post-war trials of collaborators in Europe was to facilitate the idea of widespread, collective resistance. In this way, highly persistent myths of collective resistance were forged almost immediately following the liberation.[118] As it knew only the outcome of 'innocent' or 'guilty', the law turned out to be a useful tool to reinforce such one-sided narratives. In this way, the machinery of the law helped produce a black-and-white memory of the occupation. Over the course of the collaborator trials, the ambiguity of the occupation was sidelined, and the dividing line between the many 'good' and the few 'treacherous' citizens became absolute. Given the unprecedented nature of the widespread acts of collaboration that had taken place during the war, it was, of course, inevitable that some form of demarcation would be drawn between actions deemed to be acceptable and those deemed to be treasonous. But the effects of this legal process on memory cannot be overstated. It contributed to a form of collective amnesia around the ambivalences of the occupation that, in the long term, proved difficult to dispel.[119]

In fact, the myths that the trials helped forge remained in place for decades. It was particularly in those countries where collaboration had been most widespread that the amnesia was strongest. In France, memory of the wartime support for the Vichy regime and the German occupation remained one-sided until at least the 1970s. In Italy, addressing more than twenty years of fascist rule was always going to be socially and politically unfeasible; in the end, it was hardly attempted. The smaller European countries largely embraced a narrative of victimhood surrounding the German invasion, by which they could conveniently detract from their own wartime collaboration. Danish wartime memory, for example, focused overwhelmingly on the years 1943–1945 when its *collaboration*

[118] Arnd Bauerkämper, *Das umstrittene Gedächtnis: die Erinnerung an Nationalsozialismus, Faschismus und Krieg in Europe seit 1945* (Paderborn: Schönigh, 2012); Harald Welzer (ed.), *Der Krieg der Erinnerung: Holocaust, Kollaboration und Widerstand im europäischen Gedächtnis* (Frankfurt: Fischer, 2007).

[119] Rousso, *The Vichy Syndrome*, pp. 60–97.

d'Etat had ended.[120] The fact that the Danish state had collaborated with the Germans for a longer duration, even signing the Anti-Comintern Pact in 1941, was rarely spoken about. Norway, too, held onto a partisan memory of its wartime years. However, the fact that collaboration had taken place could not be ignored altogether. The notoriety of Vidkun Quisling and his party, as well as the sheer scope of the reckoning, meant that the collaboration era retained a prominent place in Norwegian public memory – even if this memory was one-sided. For Norwegians, it was not possible to eclipse this chapter as easily as it was for the Danes, but it was also not as necessary as it had been for the French and the Italians: Quisling and his followers could easily be branded as political outsiders who bore the primary responsibility for collaboration.

The forms that collaboration had assumed were thus acknowledged in different ways from one country to the next. But historical perceptions of Nazism, collaboration and victimhood were selective everywhere. From the outset, the trials had centred on reuniting national communities. In the immediate post-war period, it was therefore the 'nation' and the 'state' that were deemed to be the primary 'victims' of collaboration. It was only from the late 1960s onwards, when a new generation began to ask questions about the ambivalences of the occupation era, that a more critical public debate set in. Movies such as the French *Le Chagrin et la Pitié* (The Sorrow and the Pity, 1969) and *Lacombe, Lucien* (1974) helped stir fresh debates about the ambivalences of occupation.[121] And as international attention began to focus increasingly on the horrors of the Holocaust, the countries that had been occupied were forced to ask themselves in what ways they had contributed to Germany's efforts to exterminate Europe's Jews. As a consequence, France witnessed a new wave of indictments of Vichy officials for crimes against humanity in the 1980s and 1990s.[122] The French government subsequently recognised the Vichy regime's complicity in the deportation of the French Jews in an official apology in 1995. In the Netherlands, a series of movies throughout the 1960s, 1970s and 1980s

120 Nils A. Sørensen, 'Narrating the Second World War in Denmark since 1945', *Contemporary European History* 14 (2005) 3, pp. 295–315.

121 Susanne Dürr, *Strategien nationaler Vergangenheitsbewältigung: Die Zeit der 'Occupation' im französischen Film* (Tübingen: Stauffenburg, 2002); Richard J. Goslan, 'The Legacy of World War II in France: Mapping Discourses of Memory', in Richard Ned Lebow, Wulf Kansteiner and Claudio Fogu (eds.), *The Politics of Memory in Postwar Europe* (Durham and London: Duke University Press, 2006), pp. 73–101, at pp. 85–90.

122 In France, for example, the parliament adopted a law in 1964 which made it possible to prosecute individuals for crimes against humanity without a statute of limitations: Rousso, 'The Purge in France', p. 118.

similarly challenged prevailing resistance narratives and highlighted the occupation's antisemitic dimension. In Norway, nuanced reflections on the wartime deportation of the country's Jewish citizens occurred somewhat later, arguably because Norway's Jewish population had been much smaller than in France and the Netherlands. In the mid-1990s, intense debate ensued about the appropriate level of financial compensation to be issued to the Jewish community, with 450 million NOK (around 38 million GBP) being approved by the *Storting* in 1997.[123] On 27 January 2012, Prime Minister Jens Stoltenberg apologised publicly for Norway's participation in the Holocaust.[124] Gradually, the one-sided memories that the trials had facilitated were called into question across the continent, often leading to painful and controversial debates about the pan-European dimensions of fascism and antisemitism.

While it is possible to trace changes over time in public memories of the occupation in Norway, it is somewhat more difficult to assess the memory of the collaborator trials as such. In the first post-war decades, memories of the trials were closely interconnected with narratives of the occupation. While the trials were still under way, they occupied a prominent position in public discourse. But by the time the last prisoners were released in the mid-1950s, the trials had somewhat faded from public consciousness. Instead, and in harmony with wider post-war myths, the trials were thought of as an inevitable epilogue to the tyranny that German occupation had brought. This also meant that the trials as such were not called into question: it was the Germans and their henchmen who were responsible for the trials and, by extension, their shortcomings. The violence of the wild purges, the need for retroactive laws, the use of the death penalty and the stripping of civil rights were seen as inevitable outflows of the occupation. It was only in the 1970s, as critical voices began to question whether the trials had adequately addressed the crimes of the Holocaust, that the trials re-entered public debate. The emerging scholarly field of 'transitional justice' began to pay increased attention to the national reckonings with collaborators. In France, the trials of high-profile Vichyists brought the post-war reckoning back into public focus. But as the distance to the occupation grew further, interest outside scholarly

[123] Norges offentlige utredninger: NOU 1997:22; Berit Reisel, *Hvor ble det av alt sammen?': plyndringen av jødene i Norge* (Oslo: Forlaget Press, 2021).

[124] Prime Minister Jens Stoltenberg, Speech on the occasion of International Holocaust Remembrance Day (27 January 2012).

circles again subsided. Today, the complex and challenging efforts at post-war retribution have largely faded from public memory.

In Norway, public debate and memory concerning the post-war trials ran largely in parallel to the ebbs and flows of memories of the war itself. Here, too, the post-war trials were generally accepted as a process without which post-war reconstruction and reconciliation would have been impossible. But in Norway, public debate on the trials was more persistent than elsewhere, and it had its own distinct characteristics. Rather than being seen primarily through the prism of politics, debate centred to a considerable degree on the question of whether the trials were 'just', 'constitutional' or 'legal'.[125] These debates had begun while the trials were being carried out, and they continue to frame debate on the trials in the present day. Even in the twenty-first century, calls have been made to re-assess the legality of the trials. The trials also feature in works of popular history, which often claim to uncover scandals relating to the constitutional validity of the decrees or illegal methods employed during the trials.[126] This legal focus of the debate in Norway can best be explained by the fact that the Norwegian authorities intended – and managed – to contain the trials within a legal and institutional framework. In this way, the distinct contours of the Norwegian reckoning also shaped the way in which it was subsequently discussed and framed.

In Norway and across Europe, the individuals who had stood trial naturally had their own memories of the reckoning.[127] In the course of the trials, those interned, prosecuted and sentenced often formed tight bonds with one another, and collectively sought to challenge what they felt was a deeply unjust treatment. In parallel to the national myths of resistance, these prisoners forged their own narratives, according to which they had been selected as the scape-goats for their nation's shameful inability to defend itself militarily against the invading Germans. Everywhere in Europe, prisoners became well organised in groups and societies, establishing often highly vocal public platforms. They engaged in tireless campaigns to have the trials declared illegal, and to achieve some degree of public rehabilitation. Because the post-war trials had a range of legal shortcomings, these groups were equipped with a number of compelling lines of argument. They

[125] Hans Petter Graver, 'Rettsoppgjøret i Norge etter krigen – tid for et nytt juridisk blikk?', *Lov og Rett: Norsk Juridisk Tidsskrift*, 54 (2015) 2, pp. 65–68.

[126] See for example Ingerid Hagen, *Oppgjørets time: om landssvikoppgjørets skyggesider* (Oslo: Spartacus, 2009); Ingeborg Solbrekken, *Landssvikoppgjørets hemmelige historie: brukte norske rettsmyndigheter krigsforbrytere og nazi-metoder ved landssvikoppgjøret?* (Oslo: Tanum, 2015).

[127] Huyse, 'Belgian and Dutch Purges after World War II Compared', p. 177.

also typically succeeded in enlisting a number of public critics, including academic lawyers, in their campaigns. This was particularly the case in Norway, given the central focus on the trials in public debate both while they lasted and in the decades that followed.[128] But the approach of these groups was often too militant to facilitate constructive debate. Their overall social impact in challenging the powerful myths of the immediate post-war period was therefore limited – even in Norway, where the debate on the legality of the trials continued longer than in other Western European countries.

In Eastern Europe, memories of both the occupation and the trials of collaborators were consciously moulded according to the agendas of the ruling communist regimes. The idea of widespread wartime resistance against German oppression was of fundamental importance both to Eastern European nations themselves and to Soviet political goals. Eastern European nations preferred to see themselves as victims of 'fascist' aggression rather than acknowledging their own antisemitism and collaborationism. In this new political reality, there was no room to acknowledge the extent of wartime collaboration. In Poland, the 1956 amnesty – which was part of the broader process of de-Stalinisation and included both the treason trials and anti-State crimes of the post-war period – had effectively removed the idea of wartime wrongdoing from public consciousness. In combination with the high losses in fighting the Germans, the trials furthered a narrative of total Polish victimhood. In Hungary, where collaboration had been widespread, the memory of the war was moulded into a narrative of victimhood from German aggression. From 1948, a forty-year silence around both collaboration and the post-war reckonings settled on Eastern Europe.[129] In principle, 'glasnost' and the revolutions of 1989/1990 could have offered new opportunities to engage with collaboration and wartime actions. However, the legacies of Communism proved to be more than enough to deal with, without the additional burden of having to confront crimes and injustices from many decades past.[130] As post-communist Eastern European countries reasserted

[128] Susanne März, *Die langen Schatten der Besatzungszeit: 'Vergangenheitsbewältigung' in Norwegen als Identitätsdiskurs* (Berlin: Berliner Wissenschaftsverlag, 2008), p. 88.

[129] Tony Judt, 'The Past Is Another Country: Myth and Memory in Postwar Europe', in Deák, Gross and Judt, *The Politics of Retribution in Europe* (Princeton: Princeton University Press, 2000), pp. 293–323, at p. 308.

[130] Annamaria Orla-Bukowska, 'New Threads on an Old Loom: National Memory and Social Identity in Postwar and Post-Communist Poland', in Lebow, Kansteiner and Fogu, *The Politics of Memory in Postwar Europe* (Durham and London: Duke University Press, 2006), pp. 177–209; Carola Lau, *Erinnerungsverwaltung, Vergangenheitspolitik und Erinnerungskultur nach 1989: Institute für nationales Gedenken im östlichen Europa im Vergleich* (Göttingen: V & R, 2017).

their own national identities in a new world order, they had little interest in unheroic tales of collaboration, antisemitism and violent expulsions. The national and heroic tales of the Second World War were upheld by nationalistic regimes that to this day often evince little interest in critical introspection, concerning either the war or post-war retribution.

7.8 Conclusion

The Norwegian treason trials shared many features with the trials of collaborators that were held across Europe following the Second World War. However, as this chapter has demonstrated, the Norwegian trials also had their own specific characteristics, which correlated in different ways with the unique circumstances in which the country found itself both during and after the war. Facilitated by the comprehensive plans agreed by the exile government and the Home Front, the Norwegian liberation was remarkably bloodless. The punishment of collaborators was therefore able to be carried out in a much more institutionalised form than was the case in much of the rest of Europe. But as we have seen, the public pressure to punish collaborators was nevertheless immense. The scope of Norway's collaborator trials became considerable, due not least to the unique criminalisation of membership of its fascist party NS and the post-war authorities' decision to carry out the reckoning according to wartime plans. This delayed the conclusion of the trials and made it necessary to amend the framework of punishment when post-war political priorities changed.

The distinctive course taken by the Norwegian trials exposes some of the most fundamental challenges presented by the search for justice in post-war Europe more generally. Many collaborator trials have been criticised for being too lenient, in particular those of France and Italy. Such retrospective assessments, however, fail to take into account the social and political realities in which post-war justice unfolded. Post-war justice in Eastern Europe, meanwhile, is often regarded only through the lens of Soviet influence, overlooking the nuances of those countries' attempts at retributive justice, especially in the immediate post-war period. Everywhere in Europe, there were considerable political, social, institutional and economic constraints to the possibilities for a 'just' post-war retribution. And no case highlights this as clearly as the Norwegian one. Unlike the trials conducted in France and Italy, for example, those in Norway were ambitious in scope and thoroughly executed. They were by no means perfect, and left unaddressed many of the grey zones of wartime collaboration. But even in the form they took, they fell victim to their own ambitions. The punishment of such a large percentage of its population ultimately posed a threat to Norway's social cohesion and reconciliation. Denmark, Belgium and the Netherlands faced similar challenges in their post-war reckonings. As small European countries, there were limits to how deep a rift in their societies they could tolerate. And as the Cold War dawned, political arguments weighed most heavily in favour of bringing post-war retribution to an end.

In thinking about post-war retribution, much can therefore be learned by turning one's attention to smaller countries like Norway. These lessons have nothing to do with how other countries could have been more thorough, or how they could have implemented the trials better. But in historical terms, cases like the trials of Norwegian collaborators permit a more comprehensive view of the preconditions of – and also the limits to – the pursuit of justice in the aftermath of the Second World War. In recent years, much debate on post-war justice has assumed a moralising tone, and there has been an evident tendency to assess Europe's trials of collaborators from an abstract, ahistorical, often legalistic vantage point. But we cannot think about the post-war trials without factoring in the economic, social and political realities in which the countries found themselves, both during the war and after. There is little point in evaluating the trials against legal and moral standards developed much later, or in ignoring the historical context in which they unfolded. The case of Norway exposes the challenges in the immediate post-war era for the possibilities of what is now called 'transitional justice'. It also highlights the historical contingencies that shaped the transition of each European country as it emerged from the grip of German occupation and moved into the post-war order.

Conclusion

At the end of 1949, amid the heated debate on the treason trials and their broader legitimacy and legacy in Norwegian society, Justice Minister Oscar Gundersen came to the conclusion that there would 'never' be a 'last word' on the treason trials.[1] While the antagonised debate of the late 1940s had prompted the country's authorities to present an 'official' interpretation of the trials, it was clear to them that disagreement on the scope and form of the reckoning would continue. In 1962, the Treason Commission finally presented its report on the trials, ten years after the idea for the report had first been discussed in the *Storting*. As we have seen, this report was not designed to draw a final conclusion on the trials, but to gather material for the future on what had become a complex and painful process. In 1964, the report became the subject of a debate in the *Storting*. By this time, the trials and the form of their implementation had been accepted by most figures within the political establishment and there was hardly any disagreement. The trials now belonged to a time firmly fixed in the past, and the *Storting* had no interest in calling into question the ways in which the collaboration legacy had been handled after 1945. But in some parts of society, the treason trials would remain a strongly contested issue for many years to come.

Ahead of the debate in the *Storting*, the Ministry of Justice drafted an internal memo addressing the various points of criticism with which previous debates in the *Storting* had confronted the incumbent Minister of Justice. It was a memo that reflected more generally on the treason trials with the benefit of hindsight. In one passage, it asked:

> Did the treason trials become too large in scope? Should one have let the small ones walk free and possibly punished the bigger ones more severely?

[1] RA/S-4250/F/L0009: 'Rettsoppgjøret med landssvikerne', memo written by Kristian Bloch after conferring with Minister of Justice Gundersen, 23 December 1949.

> One thing that has to be clear [in any assessment of this question] is that a reckoning of this type will inevitably have to reflect the entire spectrum of wartime offences. Moreover, the administration of justice will always lead to discretionary dividing lines based on interpretation between those who walk freely and those who do not.[2]

With this passage, the Ministry gave expression to the fundamental dilemma of the law: that it is always open to interpretation, and that the dividing line between guilt and innocence can be blurry. In the case of the treason trials, this interpretative dimension of the law was of particular significance, as there was no precedent to rely on and the trials rested largely on novel legal provisions. This made the law especially ambiguous in a context in which the dividing line between guilt and innocence decided whether an individual was or was not qualified for association with the national community. In Norwegian society, and particularly during the early period of the trials, however, the ambiguities of the law were largely ignored and the dividing line between 'good' and 'treacherous' Norwegians became absolute.

Given the unprecedented nature of the acts of collaboration that had taken place during the war and the limited institutional resources available upon the liberation, it was inevitable that some form of demarcation would be drawn between actions deemed to be acceptable and those deemed to be treasonous. In planning and implementing the post-war reckoning, the Norwegian exile government had chosen a pragmatic response, designating membership of *Nasjonal Samling* (NS) as the central criterion for criminal punishment. There were a number of reasons for this. For one, membership was the most direct way of signalling support for a party whose mission it was to abolish the government which continued to cling to its thin thread of power from the desks of a few civil servants in London. But membership was also a straightforward category of culpability in legal terms: it was easy to identify members, and the party's membership catalogue provided clear evidence that could be used in court procedures.

This served to guarantee that NS members could be brought to trial and sentenced swiftly. As we have seen, the swiftness of the reckoning was a key concern in the early stages of the trials, when their primary purpose was that of preventing rampant violence in the streets. And the plans largely worked out. The promise that the reckoning would be handled by the

2 RA/S-1043_1/J/Jb/Jba/L0001: Memo on the scope of the trials and passive membership published ahead of *Stortingsdebatten*, 22 April 1964.

court system was accepted by the vast majority of the population. A strong contributing factor to this was that the rule of law had long enjoyed a strong status in Norway and was a central element of the nation's self-image. This permitted the anger that the liberation had unleashed to be channelled into legal form.

In planning the trials, the Norwegian authorities had looked to other countries, and had especially monitored the tragic consequences of social animosities following the liberation of France in June 1944.[3] The Norwegian exile government and Home Front were intent on preventing the open hostilities and mob justice that had swept many European countries, and which ultimately could have threatened the stability of their own rule. Any doctrinal shortcomings of the wartime decrees, or of the ways in which the courts interpreted the law to fit the unique set of circumstances that unfolded upon the liberation, should not be mistaken for a deliberate attempt by the Norwegian state to circumnavigate the rule of law as such, or to crack down harshly on a select group of individuals as an act of revenge. Rather, the decrees were an attempt to contain the reckoning in an official procedural and institutional form. The exile government in particular had a strong respect for the rule of law, and sought to reconcile pre-war legal doctrine with the distinct set of circumstances brought about by the occupation.

The trials largely fulfilled this core purpose of preventing violence. The process benefited from the relatively smooth transition of power and the largely consensus-driven politics of summer 1945, a situation markedly different from those of Belgium and France, for example. Compared to these two countries, the transition from war to peace in Norway took place in much a more institutionalised form. In France, even cautious estimates suggest that more than 1,000 individuals perished in extrajudicial purges following the liberation.[4] In Norway, there were cases of extralegal violence, too, most notably the assaults on prisoners and the 'Germany girls' (*tyskerjenter*). There was also the terror of social exclusion, with individual fates deeply marked by the experiences of the early post-war years. But as a whole, Norwegian society managed to avoid widespread violence. It also, significantly, had no German minority,

[3] RA/S-3212/D/De/L0299: various letters.

[4] Henry Rousso has suggested the figure of 1,259 individuals, although others consider the figure to be around 10,000; Henry Rousso, 'L'Epuration: die politische Säuberung in Frankreich', in Klaus-Dietmar Henke and Hans Woller (eds.), *Politische Säuberung in Europa* (Munich: DTV, 1991), pp. 192–234, at p. 202.

sparing it the violence encountered in Eastern Europe. The Norwegian post-war trials differed from the reckonings conducted in other countries not only in form but also in scale: the collective punishment of NS members presented a category of criminal liability unknown in other countries.

The emphasis on legal form and the vast scale of the trials carried with them a number of interrelated institutional, political and social complications. The legal apparatus had to process an unprecedented number of cases, far exceeding pre-war averages and wartime estimates. The trials therefore took much longer than anticipated. This in turn meant that the legal provisions that had been designed to cater for the specific context of the liberation moment soon had to stand the test of time. Predictably, public attitudes diversified as the distance from the occupation grew. The authorities began to be confronted with widespread criticism for the delays caused by the institutional limitations of the legal system. Soon, the trials had to straddle a middle ground in an ever more polarised debate on the handling of the difficult occupation legacy. The question became what degree of politicisation and change the legal basis of the trials could be subjected to, while still retaining its inherent qualities as law.

The reconciliation of political context and legal principle was one of the fundamental challenges of the post-war reckoning. The law is of course always shaped by political circumstances. But in times of scarce institutional resources, intense social pressure and political transition, legal norms are particularly fluid. As we have seen, the law and the institutions administrating the trials came under immense pressure during Norway's post-war reckoning. The government, the parliament and the courts departed on several occasions from pre-war legal doctrine. We saw this in the implementation of the death penalty, the widespread stripping of civil rights, and the handing down of prison sentences by executive decree. Courts in the early period following the liberation handed down sentences that were much harsher than later practice. As we have seen, there were instances where public pressure directly influenced legislative measures and court verdicts. It is important therefore to note that while the Norwegian reckoning largely took place in legal form, the law as such was malleable. The law was therefore subtly adapted to the circumstances and needs of the broader political context it encountered upon the liberation. Where a basis in pre-war legal doctrine could not be found, courts and senior politicians justified this by the 'exceptional circumstances' of the period.

But this is not to say that principles of law were deliberately sidelined in Norway after 1945. On the contrary, the fundamental principles guiding the administration of the trials from 1947 onwards were those of 'consistency' and 'equality before the law'. Officials clung to the rule of law as a guiding principle of the trials, and were hesitant to accept too many inroads into it. As the risk of public protest and unrest receded into the background, the focus for the government became to present the trials as an emblem of its own integrity and moral authority. Because the trials had been closely linked to Norway's legal traditions, this required at least some degree of adherence to the rule of law. While broader attitudes had changed, these principles meant that the government and parliament retained the core framework of the trials, even when the trials were no longer needed to prevent mass violence. In the final stages of the trials, this rationale in turn meant that the Ministry of Justice felt obliged to implement a pardons procedure by which it could painstakingly align earlier court cases with later practice. This measure reflected the government's strong regard for equality and the 'inner consistency' of the trials. But the necessity for this measure also points towards the complexities and limitations of relying on the law in the process of handling the occupation legacy in a climate of rapid social and political transition.

In the long term, the trials painted a one-sided historical picture of Norway during the occupation. While NS members were largely condemned, many other forms of collaboration were eclipsed from post-war consciousness. Thereby, the trials presented a version of the occupation to which the majority of the population was more than happy to subscribe. They drew a clear demarcation line between 'patriotic' and 'treacherous' Norwegians. As we have seen, the exile government and the Home Front had chosen not to criminalise 'Germany workers', even though formally and technically they might have fulfilled the criteria of the provisions in question every bit as much as NS members did. Many workers had to take up work with Germans to survive, although many more had voluntarily worked for Germans out of economic incentives. To draw a dividing line would have absorbed enormous resources and still have been impossible. While a comprehensive reckoning with collaborative business had been promised, it proved much more complex from a legal and institutional perspective than the simple reckoning with NS members. In the end, it lasted for a much longer time and was only carried through on a comparatively small scale.

Due to their long duration, the Norwegian treason trials came to concern not only the German occupation of Norway, but also the political climate in Norway during the early years of the Cold War. From preventing extrajudicial justice, the trials as they drew out in time gradually changed their meaning and focus: they came to stand for the authority of the institutions administrating them, and were refashioned into a 'moral guideline' for the degree of loyalty the state required from its citizens at the outset of the Cold War. Although the Norwegian authorities looked to other countries to see how they were handling their wartime legacies, the process of the treason trials as a whole was largely introspective. This was true of all countries which conducted such reckonings. For these were national reckonings with 'traitors', not a pan-European reckoning with fascism.[5] The most central idea to capture the public mind during the early post-war years was that of 'national betrayal'. Consequently, the actions of Norwegian citizens during the war attracted much more attention than those of Germans. It is perhaps not surprising, therefore, that in the trials there was less of a focus on Germany as a culprit, especially in the public debates and among critics: Norwegians had no interest in presenting themselves as victims of German aggression. By blaming the NS for the plight of the occupation, the idea of a strong nation, able to defend itself had it not been for this group of 'traitors', could be upheld in the post-war era. By the early 1950s, this had become increasingly important, especially given the emerging Cold War context.

Despite its high ambitions, Norway's reckoning with its collaborators became a messy affair. As this book has demonstrated, the law as a tool in handling the occupation legacy had its shortcomings and inconsistencies, in particular as the trials took so long to be concluded. Criticism of the trials increased over time, and became closely aligned with attacks on the government organs that administered them. While the government expended much effort in presenting the trials as a success, it knew that the trials as a societal process were unable to satisfy all expectations, and that continued criticism was inevitable. It is perhaps a fundamental fallacy in situations following a traumatic societal experience that the law can resolve them. For the law is tied to its own logic and cannot in and of itself heal a society from such a collective rupture as an enemy occupation. This,

[5] There was, however, considerable cooperation concerning the prosecution of German war criminals: Berit Nøkleby, *Krigsforbrytelser: brudd på krigens lov i Norge 1940–45* (Oslo: Pax Forlag, 2004), pp. 52–55.

then, points to the larger challenges following the occupation across European countries. All countries that had come out of German occupation experienced the subsequent course of punishment and reconciliation as a deeply painful process. The fact that Norway was able to rely more extensively on legal form than most other European countries did not make this process any more straightforward.

APPENDIX I

Numbers of Individuals Investigated in Norway during the Treason Trials and War Crimes Trials[1]

Norwegian citizens[2]	
Cases in total	92,805
Death penalty verdicts	30
Sentence of imprisonment	17,000
Sentence to other penalties (fines and/or loss of civil rights)	3,450
Executive decree leading to sentence of imprisonment	3,120
Executive decree leading to other penalties (fines and/or loss of civil rights)	25,180
Acquittals	1,375
Prosecutorial waiver	5,500
Case dismissed due to a lack of evidence	37,150
Foreign citizens	
Cases in total	347
Death penalty verdicts	15
Sentence of imprisonment	66
Acquittals	5
Case dismissed due to a lack of evidence	261

1. *Source*: Justis- og Politidepartementet, *Om landssvikoppgjøret* (Gjøvik: Mariendal, 1962), p. 110.
2. Note that these figures include some few foreign citizens who were prosecuted under the treason provisions due to their close relationship to the Norwegian state.

APPENDIX 2

The Key Legal Provisions of the Treason Trials

A.1 Pre-war Legal Provisions

Den borgerlige straffelov av 22. mai 1902 [*The Civilian Criminal Code of 22 May 1902*]

Den militære straffelov av 22. mai 1902 [*The Military Criminal Code of 22 May 1902*]

A.2 Provisional Decrees Issued during the War[1]

3 October 1941: Provisorisk anordning om tillegg til den alminnelige Borgerlige Straffelov av 22 mai 1902 [*Provisional decree amending the Civilian Criminal Code of 22 May 1902*]

3 October 1941: Provisorisk anordning om tillegg til den militær straffelov av 22. mai 1902 [*Provisional decree amending the Military Criminal Code of 22 May 1902*]

22 January 1942: Provisorisk anordning om tillegg til straffelovgivningen om forræderi [*Provisional decree amending the criminal law provisions on treason*] (The 'Quisling Decree')

22 January 1942: Provisorisk anordning om tillegg til den alminnelige borgerlige straffelovs kapitler 19, 21 og 22 [*Provisional decree amending chapters 19, 21 and 22 of the Civilian Criminal Code*]

26 February 1943: Provisorisk anordning om gjenoppretning av lovlige forhold i den offentlige tjeneste i Norge [*Provisional decree on the re-establishment of legal conditions in the public sector in Norway*]

[1] The legal measures issued by the exile government during the war (*provisoriske anordninger*) have been referred to as 'provisional decrees' throughout this manuscript. They are also sometimes referred to as 'provisional ordinances' or 'provisional laws' in English.

26 February 1943: Provisorisk anordning om rettergangsmåten i visse forræderisaker [*Provisional decree on legal procedures in specific treason cases*]

24 November 1944: Provisorisk anordning om endring i provisorisk anordning av 26 februar 1943 om gjenoppretting av lovlige forhold i den offentlige tjeneste i Norge [*Provisional decree on changes to the decree of 26 February 1943 on the re-establishment of legal conditions in the public sector in Norway*]

15 December 1944: Provisorisk anordning om tillegg til straffelovgivningen om forræderi [*Provisional decree amending the criminal law provisions on treason*] (The 'Treason Decree')

16 February 1945: Provisorisk anordning om rettergang i landssviksaker [*Provisional decree on legal procedures in treason cases*]

A.3 Decrees Issued and Legislation Passed after the War

6 July 1945: Midlertidig lov om bruk av dødsstraff [*Temporary Act on the use of the death penalty*]

3 August 1945: Provisorisk anordning om endring i landssvikanordningen av 15. desember 1944 [*Provisional decree on changes to the Treason Decree of 15 December 1944*]

22 February 1946: Lov om tillegg til straffeprosessloven av 1. juli 1887 [*Act amending the Criminal Procedures Act of 1 July 1887*]

13 December 1946: Midlertidig lov om bruk av dødsstraff [*Temporary Act on the use of the death penalty*]

21 February 1947: Lov um straff og økonomisk ansvar for landssvikarar (*Landssviklova*) [*Act on the punishment and economic liability of traitors*]

19 June 1947: Lov om tillegg til lovene om Høyesterett [*Act amending the laws of the Supreme Court*]

9 July 1948: Lov om endring i reglene om fullbyrdelse av frihetsstraff for landssvik [*Act on changes to the rules of imprisonment*]

28 July 1949: Lov om brigde i retts-tap reglane i landssviklovene [*Act amending the laws on loss of civil rights in the treason provisions*]

22 May 1953: Lov om endring i lovgivningen om rettighetstap [*Act amending the laws on loss of civil rights*]

Bibliography

Archives

I Riksarkivet (The National Archives of Norway)

Justisdepartementet

Justisdepartementet, 4. sivilkontor S – RA/S-1042

Series D/Dh: Landssviksaker Rettsoppgjøret

Justisdepartementet, 4. sivilkontor S – RA/S-1042/D/Dh/L0004.
Justisdepartementet, 4. sivilkontor S – RA/S-1042/D/Dh/L0005.
Justisdepartementet, 4. sivilkontor S – RA/S-1042/D/Dh/L0007.
Justisdepartementet, 4. sivilkontor S – RA/S-1042/D/Dh/L0009.
Justisdepartementet, 4. sivilkontor S – RA/S-1042/D/Dh/L0010.

Justisdepartementet, Fengselsstyret D del 1 – RA/S-1043

Series: J/Jb: Rettsoppgjøret med landssvikerne

Justisdepartementet, Fengselsstyret D del 2 – RA/S-1043_1/J/Jb/Jba/L0001.
Justisdepartementet, Fengselsstyret D del 2 – RA/S-1043_1/J/Jb/Jba/L0002.
Justisdepartementet, Fengselsstyret D del 2 – RA/S-1043_1/J/Jb/Jba/L0003.
Justisdepartementet, Fengselsstyret D del 2 – RA/S-1043_1/J/Jb/Jba/L0004.

Justisdepartementet, 4. politikontor P4 – RA/S-4242

Series D: Saksarkiv ordnet alfabetisk etter emne

Justisdepartementet, 4. politikontor P4 – RA/S-4242/D/L0100 (Landssvik).

Justisdepartementet, Den administrative avdeling – RA/S-4250

Series F: Byråsjef Beichmanns komitéarbeide

Justisdepartementet, Den administrative avdeling – RA/S-4250/F/L0009 (Landssvikutvalget).

Justisdepartementet, Lovavdelingen – RA/S-3212

Series B: Kopibøker
Arkivenhet RA/S-3212/B/Ba/L0046.

Series De: Strafferett. Prosess. Frigjøring og rettsoppgjør
Justisdepartementet, Lovavdelingen – RA/S-3212/D/De/L0051.
Justisdepartementet, Lovavdelingen – RA/S-3212/D/De/L0299.
Justisdepartementet, Lovavdelingen – RA/S-3212/D/De/L0300.
Justisdepartementet, Lovavdelingen – RA/S-3212/D/De/L0301.
Justisdepartementet, Lovavdelingen – RA/S-3212/D/De/L0302.
Justisdepartementet, Lovavdelingen – RA/S-3212/D/De/L0306.
Justisdepartementet, Lovavdelingen – RA/S-3212/D/De/L0307.

Riksadvokaten

Riksadvokaten Diverse Saker

Series D: Saksarkiv ordnet etter organets hovedsystem
Riksadvokaten, diverse saker – RA/S-1558/D/L0014 (Diverse).
Riksadvokaten, diverse saker – RA/S-1558/D/L0016 (Diverse).
Riksadvokaten, diverse saker – RA/S-1558/D/L0020 (Diverse).

Riksadvokatens Landssvikarkiv

Series D
Riksadvokatens landssvikarkiv – RA/S-1555/D/L0052.
Riksadvokatens landssvikarkiv – RA/S-1555/D/L0053.

Johannes Andenæs

RA/PA-1261/D/L0001.

Eivind Berggrav

RA/PA-0320/2/H/L0017.

Statsministerens Kontor

Series A/Aa: Referat fra regjeringskonferanser
RA/S-1005/A/Aa/L0004.
RA/S-1005/A/Aa/L0005.
RA/S-1005/A/Aa/L0006.
RA/S-1005/A/Aa/L0007.
RA/S-1005/A/Aa/L0022 (Protokoll for hemmelige saker).

Series D/Da: Notater til regjeringskonferanser

RA/S-1005/D/Da/L0040 (Regjeringene Gerhardsen og Torp. Notater til regjeringskonferanser. Justisdepartementet).

Series D/Db: Sakarkiv fra Statsministerens kontor

RA/S-1005/D/Db/L0131 (Landssvikutvalget).

Landssvikarkivet

II Statsarkivet i Oslo (Regional State Archives in Oslo)

SAO/A-10085c/J/Jc/Jca/Jcac/L3206-17 (Langeland Casefile).

III Online Archives

The Harry S. Truman Library and Museum, Online Collection: 'The War Crimes Trials at Nuremberg'.

Parliamentary Papers and Official Periodicals

Stortingsforhandlinger, 1942–1964.
Norsk Retstidende, 1942–1955.
Norsk Lovtidend, 1941–1955.
Norges Offisielle Statistikk IX. 107, *Stortingsvalget 1936* (Oslo: Stortingets Kontor and Aschehoug, 1937).
Norges Offisielle Statistikk X. 132, *Stortingsvalget 1945* (Oslo: Stortingets Kontor and Aschehoug, 1945).
Norges Offisielle Statistikk XI 13, *Stortingsvalget 1949* (Oslo: Stortingets Kontor and Aschehoug, 1950).
Norges Offisielle Statistikk XI 179, *Statistikk over landssvik 1940–1945* (Oslo: Statistisk Sentralbyrå, 1954).

Newspapers and Periodicals

Available via the Norwegian National Library

Aftenposten, Oslo (1945–1964).
Arbeiderbladet, Oslo (1945–1964).
Dagbladet, Oslo (1945–1964).
Friheten, Oslo (1945–1964).
Morgenbladet, Oslo (1945–1964).
Nationen, Oslo (1945–1964).
Oslo-Pressen, Oslo (1945).
Verdens Gang, Oslo (1945–1964).

Printed Primary Sources

Bastiansen, H., and Dahl, H. F., *Ytringsfriheten i Norge i det 20. århundre* (Ytringsfrihetskommisjonen, 1999).
Berggrav, E., *Folkedommen over NS* (Oslo: Land og Kirke, 1945).
Danmarks Frihedsraad, *Naar Danmark atter er frit* (1943).
Det norske arbeiderparti, *Landsmøtet, 31. august – 2. September 1945*, Referat ved Bjarne Jullum (Oslo: Arbeidernes Aktietrykkeri, 1947).
Didriksen, B., *Gjenopprettelsen av landssvikerne: et aktuelt sosialt spørsmål*, Sosiale Småskrifter (Oslo: Norli, 1945).
Didriksen, B., *Innstilling fra Undersøkelseskommisjonen av 1945* (Oslo: Familieforlaget, 2010).
Justis- og Politidepartementet, *Om landssvikoppgjøret* (Gjøvik: Mariendal, 1962).
Langeland, O., *Dømmer ikke* (Oslo: Heim & Samfund, 1948).
Forat I ikke skal dømmes (Oslo: Heim & Samfund, 1949).
Langeland, O., *Neste fase i rettsoppgjøret – Biskopenes Brev til Justisministeren, November 1946* (Oslo: Land og Kirke, 1946).
Langeland, O., *Norway's Schools in the Battle for Freedom* (Montreal: Royal Norwegian Government's Information Office, 1942).
Omang, R. (ed.), *Regjeringen og hjemmefronten under krigen: aktstykker utgitt av Stortinget* (Oslo: Aschehoug, 1948).
Poulsen, E., *Den nådeløse rettferdighet: betraktninger omkring rettsoppgjøret* (Oslo: Logos forlag, 1947).
Prime Minister Jens Stoltenberg, *Speech on the Occasion of International Holocaust Remembrance Day* (27 January 2012).
Skeie, J., *Landssvik* (Oslo: Norli, 1945).
Steinsvik, M., *Frimodige ytringer* (Oslo: Private publisher, 1946).
Stenografisk referat fra Riksadvokatens og Erstatningsdirektoratets kursus (Oslo: 4–8 June 1945).
Steinsvik, M., *Straffesak mot Vidkun Abraham Lauritz Jonssøn Quisling* (Oslo: Grøndahl, 1946).

Secondary Sources

Andenæs, J., *Det vanskelige oppgjøret* (Oslo: Tanum-Norli, 1979).
Austad, T., 'Berggrav, Hitler og Luther', in P. Voksø (ed.), *Eivind Berggrav, Brobygger og kirkeleder, 1884–1984* (Oslo: Gyldendal, 1984), pp. 88–103.
Bakken, B., Larsen, R., Jørgensen, A. and Fjeld, Å., *Død over de tyske okkupanter: de norske kommunistenes motstandskamp 1940–1945* (Moss: Informasjonsforlaget, 1998).
Barnouw, D., 'Dutch Exiles in London', in M. Conway and J. Gotovitch (eds.), *Europe in Exile: European Exile Communities in Britain 1940–45* (Oxford: Berghahn, 2001), pp. 229–246.
Bastiansen, H., and Dahl, H. F., *Norsk mediehistorie* (Oslo: Universitetsforlaget, 2019 [2003]).

Bauerkämper, A., *Das umstrittene Gedächtnis: die Erinnerung an Nationalsozialismus, Faschismus und Krieg in Europa seit 1945* (Paderborn: Schöningh, 2012).

Berg, P. A., *Kirke i krig* (Oslo: Genesis forlag, 1999).

Berntsen, H., *I malstrømmen: Johan Nygaardsvold 1979–1952* (Oslo: Aschehoug, 1991).

Bohn, R., *Reichskommissariat Norwegen* (Munich: Oldenbourg, 2000).

Bohn, R., and Elvert, J., *Kriegsende im Norden: vom heißen zum kalten Krieg* (Stuttgart: Steiner, 1995).

Borge, B. H., 'Forsoningen som uteble. Norges oppgjør med landssvikerne', in B.-A. Andreassen and E. Skaar (eds.), *Forsoning eller rettferdighet?* (Oslo: Cappelen, 1998), pp. 204–234.

Borge, B. H., and Vaale, L.-E., *Grunnlovens største prøve: rettsoppgjøret etter 1945* (Oslo: Scandinavian Academic Press, 2018).

'Stretching the Rule of Law: How the Norwegian Resistance Movement Influenced the Provisional Treason Decrees of the Exile Government, 1944–1945', *Scandinavian Journal of History* 46 (2021) 1, pp. 105–124.

Brandal, N., '"En rettsstat verdig": oppgjøret i Stortinget 1945–50', in H. F. Dahl and Ø. Sørensen (eds.), *Et rettferdig oppgjør? Rettsoppgjøret i Norge etter 1945* (Oslo: Pax Forlag, 2004), pp. 52–86.

Brandes, D., *Der Weg zur Vertreibung 1938–1945: Pläne und Entscheidungen zum 'Transfer' der Deutschen aus der Tschechoslowakei und aus Polen* (Munich: Oldenbourg, 2001).

Brathagen, K., 'Oppgjøret med NS-kvinnene', in H. F. Dahl and Ø. Sørensen (eds.), *Et rettferdig oppgjør? Rettsoppgjøret i Norge etter 1945* (Oslo: Pax Forlag, 2004), pp. 136–159.

Brevig, H. O., Hans, O. and de Figueiredo, I., *Den norske fascismen: Nasjonal Samling 1933–1940* (Oslo: Pax Forlag, 2002).

Bruland, B., *Holocaust i Norge. Registrering. Deportasjon. Tilintetgjørelse* (Oslo: Dreyers Forlag, 2017).

Bruland, B., Berggren, E. B. and Tangestuen, M., *Rapport frå ein gjennomgang av Hva visste hjemmefronten?* (Oslo: Dreyers Forlag, 2020).

Bue, S., 'Det økonomiske oppgjøret', in H. F. Dahl and Ø. Sørensen (eds.), *Et rettferdig oppgjør? Rettsoppgjøret i Norge etter 1945* (Oslo: Pax Forlag, 2004), pp. 160–192.

Bugge, H. O., Coward, K. and Rognlien, S. (eds.), *Festskrift Lovavdelingen 100 år 1885–1985* (Oslo: Universitetsforlaget, 1986).

Bull, E., *Norge i den rike verden* (Oslo: Cappelen, 1979).

Butler, R., *Legions of Death: The Nazi Enslavement of Europe* (Barnsley: Pen & Sword, 1983).

Christensen, C., *Danmark besat: krig og hverdag 1940–45* (Copenhagen: Høst & Søn, 2005).

Christie, N., *Fangevoktere i konsentrasjonsleire: en sosiologisk undersøkelse av norske fangevoktere i 'serberleirene' i Nord-Norge i 1942–43* (Oslo: Pax Forlag, 1972).

Clemmesen, M. H., and Faulkner, M. S., *Northern European Overture to War, 1939–1941* (Leiden: Brill, 2013).

Colla, M., 'The Spectre of the Present: Time, Presentism and the Writing of Contemporary History', *Contemporary European History*, 30 (2021) 1, pp. 124–135.

Conway, M., 'Justice in Postwar Belgium: Popular Passions and Political Realities', in I. Deák, J. T. Gross and T. Judt (eds.), *The Politics of Retribution in Europe: World War II and Its Aftermath* (Princeton: Princeton University Press, 2000), pp. 133–156.

'Legacies of Exile: The Exile Governments in London during the Second World War and the Politics of Post-war Europe', in M. Conway and J. Gotovich (eds.), *Europe in Exile: European Exile Communities in Britain 1940–45* (New York: Berghahn, 2001), pp. 255–274.

The Sorrows of Belgium: Liberation and Political Reconstruction, 1944–1947 (Oxford: Oxford University Press, 2012).

Conway, M., and Gotovitch, J., *Europe in Exile: European Exile Communities in Britain 1940–45* (Oxford: Berghahn, 2001).

Corell, S., *Krigens ettertid: okkupasjonshistorien i norske historiebøker* (Oslo: Scandinavian Academic Press, 2010).

'The Solidarity of a National Narrative: The German Occupation in Norwegian History Culture', in H. Stenius, M. Österberg and J. Östling (eds.), *Nordic Narratives of the Second World War: National Historiographies Revisited* (Lund: Nordic Academic Press, 2011), pp. 101–126.

Likvidasjonen: historien om holocaust i Norge og jakten på jødenes eiendom (Oslo: Gyldendal, 2021).

Dahl, H. F., *Fra klassekamp til nasjonal samling: Arbeiderpartiet og det nasjonale spørsmål i 30-årene* (Oslo: Pax Forlag, 1969).

'Dette er London', NRK i krig 1940–1945 (Oslo: Cappelen, 1978).

Norsk idéhistorie, Bind V: De store ideologienes tid: 1914–1955 (Oslo: Aschehoug, 2001).

'Innledning: Oppgjøret som rystet Norge', in H. F. Dahl and Ø. Sørensen (eds.), *Et rettferdig oppgjør? Rettsoppgjøret i Norge etter 1945* (Oslo: Pax Forlag, 2004), pp. 9–29.

'Dealing with the Past in Scandinavia: Legal Purges and Popular Memories', in Jon Elster (ed.), *Retribution and Reparation in the Transition to Democracy* (Cambridge: Cambridge University Press, 2006), pp. 147–163.

Quisling: A Study in Treachery (Cambridge: Cambridge University Press, 2007 [1999]).

Krigen som aldri tar slutt: en historie – mange fortellinger (Oslo: Aschehoug, 2017).

En kort historie om rettsoppgjøret etter krigen (Oslo: Pax Forlag, 2018).

Dahl, H. F., Hagtvet, B. and Hjeltnes, G., *Den norske nasjonalsosialismen: Nasjonal samling 1933–1945 i tekst og bilder* (Oslo: Pax Forlag, 2009).

Dahl, H. F., Hjeltnes, G., Nøkleby, B., Ringdal, N. J. and Sørensen, Ø., *Norsk krigsleksikon* (Oslo: Cappelen, 1995).

Dahl, H. F., Kirchhoff, H., Lund, J. and Vaale, L. E. (eds.), *Danske tilstande – norske tilstande: forskelle og ligheder under tysk besættelse 1940–45* (Copenhagen: Gyldendal, 2010).

Dahl, H. F., and Sørensen, Ø. (eds.), *Et rettferdig oppgjør? Rettsoppgjøret i Norge etter 1945* (Oslo: Pax Forlag, 2004).

Dahl, H. F., and Sørensen, O., 'Et parti av lovbrytere', in H. F. Dahl and Ø. Sørensen (eds.), *Et rettferdig oppgjør? Rettsoppgjøret i Norge etter 1945* (Oslo: Pax Forlag, 2004), pp. 100–107.

Deák, I., 'Political Justice in Austria and Hungary after World War II', in J. Elster (ed.), *Retribution and Reparation in the Transition to Democracy* (Cambridge: Cambridge University Press, 2006), pp. 124–146.

Europe on Trial: The Story of Collaboration, Resistance, and Retribution during World War II (Boulder: Westview Press, 2015).

Deák, I., Gross, J. T. and Judt, T. (eds.), *The Politics of Retribution in Europe: World War II and Its Aftermath* (Princeton: Princeton University Press, 2000).

Devos, W., and Gony, K. (eds.), *War, Occupation, Liberation: Belgium 1940–1945* (Tielt: Lannoo, 2019).

Drolshagen, E., *Der freundliche Feind: Wehrmachtssoldaten im besetzten Europa* (Munich: Droemer, 2009).

Dürr, S., *Strategien nationaler Vergangenheitsbewältigung: die Zeit der 'Occupation' im französischen Film* (Tübingen: Stauffenburg, 2002).

Eide, M., *Blod, sverte og gledestårer: VG, Verdens Gang 1945–95* (Oslo: Schibsted, 1995).

Einarson, E., and Straume, B. (eds.), *Karikaturtegneren Einarson: varmefront* (Oslo: Damm, 1988).

Ekman, S., and Grimnes, O. K., *Broderfolk i ufredstid: norsk-svenske forbindelser under annen verdenskrig* (Oslo: Universitetsforlage, 1991).

Ellingsen, D., *Krigsprofitørene og rettsoppgjøret* (Oslo: Gyldendal, 1993).

Elster, J. (ed.), *Retribution and Reparation in the Transition to Democracy* (Cambridge: Cambridge University Press, 2006).

Emberland, T., 'Antisemittisme i Norge 1900–1940', in T. B. Eriksen, H. Harket and E. Lorenz (eds.), *Jødehat: antisemittismens historie fra antikken til i dag* (Oslo: N.W. Damm & Søn, 2005), pp. 401–420.

Emberland, T., and Kott, M., *Himmlers Norge: nordmenn i det storgermanske prosjekt* (Oslo: Aschehoug, 2012).

Ericsson, K., and Simomen, E. (eds.), *Children of World War II: The Hidden Enemy Legacy* (Oxford: Berg, 2005).

Espeli, H., 'The Economic Effects of the German Occupation of Norway, 1940–1945', in J. Scherner and E. N. White (eds.), *Paying for Hitler's War: The Consequences of Nazi Hegemony for Europe* (Cambridge: Cambridge University Press, 2016), pp. 235–265.

Espeli, H., Næss, H. E. and Rinde, H. (eds.), *Våpendrager og veiviser: advokatenes historie i Norge* (Oslo: Universitetsforlaget, 2008).

Færøy, F., 'Hjelperne fra Norges Kommunistiske Parti', in Ø. Sørensen and K. B. Simonsen (eds.), *Historie og moral: nazismen, jødene og hjemmefronten* (Oslo: Dreyers Forlag, 2020), pp. 211–228.

Festersen, J., 'Dänemark und die deutsche Volksgruppe in Nordschleswig 1940–1955', in M. Kittel, H. Möller, J. Pešek and O. Tuma (eds.), *Deutschsprachige Minderheiten 1945: ein europäischer Vergleich* (Oldenbourg: De Gruyter, 2006), pp. 571–582.

Finder, G. N., and Prusin, A. V., *Justice behind the Iron Curtain* (Toronto: University of Toronto Press, 2018).

Flo, I., *Norsk presses historie 1660–2010, Bind IV: Norske aviser fra A til Å* (Oslo: Universitetsforlaget, 2001).

François, D., *Femmes tondues: la diabolisation de la femme en 1944: les bûchers de la Libération* (Coudray-Macouard: Cheminements, 2006).

Frevert, U., *Die Politik der Demütigung: Schauplätze von Macht und Ohnmacht* (Frankfurt am Main: Fischer, 2017).

Frøland, H. O., Hatlehol, G. and Ingulstad, M., 'Regimenting Labour in Norway during Nazi Germany's Occupation', *Unabhängige Historikerkommission zur Geschichte des Reichsarbeitsministeriums, 1933–1945*, Working Paper No. 12, 2017.

Frommer, B., *National Cleansing: Retribution against Nazi Collaborators in Postwar Czechoslovakia* (Cambridge: Cambridge University Press, 2005).

'Denouncers and Fraternizers: Gender, Collaboration, and Retribution in Bohemia and Moravia during World War II and After', in N. M. Wingfield and M. Bucur (eds.), *Gender and War in Twentieth-Century Eastern Europe* (Bloomington: Indiana University Press, 2006), pp. 111–132.

Führer, H., *Nachspiel: die niederländische Politik und die Verfolgung von Kollaborateuren und NS-Verbrechern, 1945–1989* (Münster: Waxmann, 2005).

Funk, M. (ed.), *Hitler, Deutschland und die Mächte: Materialien zur Außenpolitik des Dritten Reiches* (Düsseldorf: Droste, 1976).

Furuseth, A. K., *Norske nazister på flukt: jakten på et nytt hjemland i Argentina* (Oslo: Schibsted, 2013).

Gerhardsen, E., *Fellesskap i krig og fred: erindringer 1940–45* (Oslo: Tiden Norsk Forlag, 1970).

Samarbeid og strid: erindringer 1945–55 (Oslo: Tiden Norsk Forlag, 1971).

Gogstad, A., *'Men seier'n var vår': søkelys på omveltningenes år mellom krig og fred* (Bergen: Universitetet i Bergen, 2003).

Goslan, R. J., 'The Legacy of World War II in France: Mapping Discourses of Memory', in R. N. Lebow, W. Kansteiner and C. Fogu (eds.), *The Politics of Memory in Postwar Europe* (Durham and London: Duke University Press, 2006), pp. 73–101.

Graver, H. P., *Dommernes krig: den tyske okkupasjonen 1940–1945 og den norske rettsstaten* (Oslo: Pax Forlag, 2015).

'Rettsoppgjøret i Norge etter krigen – tid for et nytt juridisk blikk?', *Lov og Rett: Norsk Juridisk Tidsskrift* 54 (2015) 2, pp. 65–86.

Der Krieg der Richter: die deutsche Besatzung 1940–1945 und der norwegische Rechtsstaat (Baden-Baden: Nomos, 2019).

Okkupasjonstidens Høyesterett (Oslo: Pax Forlag, 2019).

Greene, J., and Massignani, A., *Hitler Strikes North: The Nazi Invasion of Norway and Denmark, 9 April 1940* (Barnsley: Frontline Books, 2013).

Greve, T., *Det Norske storting gjennom 150 år*, Vol. 3 (Oslo: I kommisjon hos Gyldendal, 1964).

Grimnes, O. K., *Hjemmefrontens ledelse* (Oslo: Universitetsforlget, 1977).

'Historieskrivingen om okkupasjonen. Det nasjonale konsenssyndromets gjennomslagskraft', *Nytt Norsk Tidsskrift* (1990), pp. 108–121.

'Fra krig til fred', in H. F. Dahl, H. Kirchhoff, J. Lund and L. E. Vaale (eds.), *Danske tilstande – norske tilstande: forskelle og ligheder under tysk besættelse 1940–45* (Copenhagen: Gyldendal, 2010), pp. 259–281.

'Okkupation og politik', in H. F. Dahl, H. Kirchhoff, J. Lund and L. E. Vaale (eds.), *Danske tilstande – norske tilstande: forskelle og ligheder under tysk besættelse 1940–45* (Copenhagen: Gyldendal, 2010), pp. 79–103.

'The Two Norways, 1940–41', in M. H. Clemmesen and M. S. Faulkner (eds.), *Northern European Overture to War, 1939–1941* (Leiden: Brill, 2013), pp. 383–402.

Norge under andre verdenskrig, 1939–1945 (Oslo: Aschehoug, 2018).

Gundersen, O. C., *Noen betraktninger omkring rettsoppgjøret med landssvikerne: foredrag i Oslo krets av den Norske sakførerforening, 18 January 1949* (Oslo: Aschehoug, 1949).

Hagen, I., *Oppgjørets time: om landssvikoppgjørets skyggesider* (Oslo: Spartacus, 2009).

Hambro, C. J., *Dagboksblade og aktstykker til regjeringsdannelsen i 1945* (Oslo: Gyldendal, 1964).

Hamsun, K., *Paa gjengrodde stier* (Oslo: Gyldendal, 1949).

Harper, C. S., 'Rettsoppgjørets behandling av deportasjonen av jødene fra Norge under okkupasjonen 1940–1945' (HL-senterets temahefte nr. 16, 2012).

Harsem, P., *Utrolig men sant!* (Oslo: Private publisher, 1948).

Hassing, A., *Church Resistance to Nazism in Norway, 1940–1945* (Washington: University of Washington Press, 2014).

Hauge, J. C., *Frigjøringen* (Oslo: Gyldendal, 1994).

Heiene, G., *Eivind Berggrav: en biografi* (Oslo: Universitetsforlaget, 1992).

Hem, P., *Megleren Paal Berg 1873–1968* (Oslo: Aschehoug, 2012).

Henke, K.-D., and Woller, H., *Politische Säuberung in Europa: die Abrechnung mit Faschismus und Kollaboration nach dem Zweiten Weltkrieg* (Munich: DTV, 1991).

Hjeltnes, G., *Norge i krig, Bind VI* (Oslo: Aschehoug, 1986).

Avisoppgjøret etter 1945 (Oslo: Aschehoug, 1990).

Holzmann, C. 'Geschlecht vor Gericht. Kollaborationsprozesse und Geschlechterordnung nach dem Zweiten Weltkrieg', *L'HOMME. Europäische Zeitschrift für feministische Geschichtswissenschaft* 35 (2024) 2 (forthcoming).

Huyse, L., 'The Criminal Justice System as a Political Actor in Regime Transitions: The Case of Belgium, 1944–50', in I. Deák, J. T. Gross and T. Judt (eds.), *The Politics of Retribution in Europe: World War II and Its Aftermath* (Princeton: Princeton University Press, 2000), pp. 157–172.

'Belgian and Dutch Purges after World War II Compared', in J. Elster (ed.), *Retribution and Reparation in the Transition to Democracy* (Cambridge: Cambridge University Press, 2006), pp. 164–178.

Jakubec, P., 'Together and Alone in Allied London: Czechoslovak, Norwegian and Polish Governments-in-Exile, 1940–1945', *The International History Review* 42 (2020), pp. 465–484.

Jarausch, K., *Out of Ashes: A New History of Europe in the Twentieth Century* (Princeton: Princeton University Press, 2015).

Johansen, P. O. (ed.), *På siden av rettsoppgjøret* (Oslo: Unipub, 2006).

Judt, T., 'The Past Is Another Country: Myth and Memory in Postwar Europe', in I. Deák, J. T. Gross and T. Judt (eds.), *The Politics of Retribution in Europe: World War II and Its Aftermath* (Princeton: Princeton University Press, 2000), pp. 293–323.

Postwar: A History of Europe since 1945 (London: Penguin, 2010).

Jullum, B., *Det norske arbeiderparti: Landsmøtet, 31. august – 2. september* (Oslo: Arbeidernes Aktietrykkeri, 1947).

Karcher, N., *Kampen om skolen: nazifisering og lærerens motstand i det okkuperte Norge* (Oslo: Dreyers Forlag, 2018).

Karsai, L., 'The People's Courts and Revolutionary Justice in Hungary, 1945–46', in I. Deák, J. T. Gross and T. Judt (eds.), *The Politics of Retribution in Europe: World War II and Its Aftermath* (Princeton: Princeton University Press, 2000), pp. 233–251.

Kellmann, K., *Dimensionen der Mittäterschaft: die europäische Kollaboration mit dem Dritten Reich* (Vienna: Böhlau, 2019).

Koop, V., *'Dem Führer ein Kind schenken': die SS-Organisation Lebensborn e.V.* (Cologne: Böhlau, 2007).

Kornbluth, A., *The August Trials: The Holocaust and Postwar Justice in Poland* (Cambridge, MA: Harvard University Press, 2021).

Koselleck, R., *Sediments of Time: On Possible Histories* (Stanford: Stanford University Press, 2018).

Krog, H., *6te kolonne?: Om den norske storindustriens bidrag til Nazi-Tysklands krigføring* (Oslo: Pax Forlag, 1969).

Kvanmo, H., *Dommen* (Oslo: Gyldendal, 1990).

Lagrou, P., *The Legacy of Nazi Occupation: Patriotic Memory and National Recovery in Western Europe, 1945–1965* (Cambridge: Cambridge University Press, 2004).

Langslet, L. R., *John Lyng: samarbeidets arkitekt* (Oslo: Cappelen, 1989).

Larsen, S. U., 'The Social Foundations of Norwegian Fascism 1933–1945: An Analysis of Membership Data', in S. U. Larsen, B. Hagtvet and J. P. Myklebust (eds.), *Who Were the Fascists? Social Roots of European Fascism* (Bergen/Oslo/Tromsø: Universitetsforlaget, 1980), pp. 595–620.

'Die Ausschaltung der Quislinge in Norwegen', in K.-D. Henke and H. Woller (eds.), *Politische Säuberung in Europa: die Abrechnung mit Faschismus und Kollaboration nach dem Zweiten Weltkrieg* (Munich: DTV, 1991), pp. 241–280.

Lau, C., *Erinnerungsverwaltung, Vergangenheitspolitik und Erinnerungskultur nach 1989: Institute für nationales Gedenken im östlichen Europa im Vergleich* (Göttingen: V & R, 2017).

Lebow, R. N., Kansteiner, W. and Fogu, C. (eds.), *The Politics of Memory in Postwar Europe* (Durham and London: Duke University Press, 2006).

Levin, I., *Vi snakket ikke om Holocaust: mor, jeg og tausheten* (Oslo: Gyldendal, 2020).

Lilienthal, G., *Der 'Lebensborn e.V.': ein Instrument nationalsozialistischer Rassenpolitik* (Stuttgart: Gustav Fischer, 1985).

Loock, H.-D., *Quisling, Rosenberg und Terboven: zur Vorgeschichte und Geschichte der nationalsozialistischen Revolution in Norwegen* (Stuttgart: Deutsche Verlags-Anstalt, 1970).

'Nordeuropa Zwischen Außenpolitik und "großgermanischer" Innenpolitik', in M. Funk (ed.), *Hitler, Deutschland und die Mächte: Materialien zur Außenpolitik des Dritten Reiches* (Düsseldorf: Droste, 1976), pp. 684–706.

Lorek, S., *Rechtsabrechnung-Retsopgør: politische Säuberung nach dem Zweiten Weltkrieg in Nordschleswig* (Neumünster: Wachholtz, 1998).

Lorenz, E., '"Vi har ikke invitert jødene hit til landet" – norske syn på jødene i et langtidsperspektiv', in V. Moe and Ø. Kopperud (eds.), *Forestillinger om jøder: aspekter ved konstruksjonen av en minoritet 1814–1940* (Oslo: Unipub, 2011), pp. 35–52.

Lowe, K., *Savage Continent: Europe in the Aftermath of World War II* (London: Penguin, 2013), pp. 163–178.

Lyng, J., *Forræderiets epoke* (Oslo: Gyldendal Norsk Forlag, 1979).

Mann, C., 'The Norwegian Armed Forces in Britain', in M. Conway and J. Gotovitch (eds.), *Europe in Exile: European Exile Communities in Britain 1940–45* (Oxford: Berghahn, 2001), pp. 153–166.

März, S., *Die langen Schatten der Besatzungszeit: 'Vergangenheitsbewältigung' in Norwegen als Identitätsdiskurs* (Berlin: Berliner Wissenschaftsverlag, 2008).

Mazower, M., *Dark Continent: Europe's Twentieth Century* (New York: Vintage Books, 2000).

Hitler's Empire: Nazi Rule in Occupied Europe (London: Penguin, 2008).

Mendelsohn, O., *Jødene i Norge: historien om en minoritet* (Oslo: Universitetsforlaget, 1992).

Jødenes historie i Norge gjennom 300 år (Oslo: Forlaget Press, 2019).

Michelet, M., *Hva visste hjemmefronten? Holocaust i Norge: varslene, unnvikelsene, hemmeligholdet* (Oslo: Gyldendal, 2018).

Milward, A., *The Fascist Economy in Norway* (Oxford: Clarendon Press, 1972).
Moll, M., 'Kapitulation oder heroischer Endkampf in der "Festung Norwegen"? Die Entscheidung für ein friedliches Ende der deutschen Okkupation Dänemarks und Norwegens im Frühjahr 1945', in R. Bohn and J. Elvert (eds.), *Kriegsende im Norden: vom heißen zum kalten Krieg* (Stuttgart: Steiner, 1995), pp. 43–84.
Morgan, P., *Hitler's Collaborators* (Oxford: Oxford University Press, 2018).
Mykland, K., *Norges historie* (Oslo: Cappelen, 1979).
Naimark, N., *Fires of Hatred: Ethnic Cleansing in Twentieth Century Europe* (Cambridge, MA: Harvard University Press, 2001).
Narud, H. M., Heidar, K. and Grønlie, T. (eds.), *Stortingets historie 1964–2014* (Bergen: Fagbokforlaget, 2014).
Nielsen, A., *Eventyret på Solbris* (Bergen: Martinussen, 1952).
Nietschke, B., *Vertreibung und Aussiedlung der deutschen Bevölkerung aus Polen 1945 bis 1949* (Munich: Oldenbourg, 2003).
Nilssen, T. R. *Da freden brøt løs* (Oslo: Universitetsforlaget, 2015).
Nilssen, T.R., and Reitan, J., *Legacies of the Nazi Camps in Norway: Falstad 1941–49* (Münster: LIT Verlag, 2020).
Noack, J. P., *Det tyske mindretal i Nordslesvig under besættelsen* (Copenhagen: Munksgaard, 1975).
Nøkleby, B., *Josef Terboven: Hitlers mann i Norge* (Oslo: Gyldendal, 1992).
Skutt blir den . . .: tysk bruk av dødsstraff i Norge, 1940–1945 (Oslo: Gyldendal, 1996).
Krigsforbrytelser: brudd på krigens lov i Norge 1940–45 (Oslo: Pax Forlag, 2004).
Norrman, R., *Quislingkyrkan: Nasjonal samlings kyrkopolitik 1940–1945* (Skellefteå: Norma, 1998).
Novick, P., *The Resistance Versus Vichy: The Purge of Collaborators in Liberated France* (London: Chatto & Windus, 1968).
Oosterom, R., *Moffenmeiden: over soldatenliefjes, knippers en omstanders: een geschiedenis in verhalen* (Amsterdam: Meulenhoff, 2019).
Orla-Bukowska, A., 'New Threads on an Old Loom: National Memory and Social Identity in Postwar and Post-Communist Poland', in R. N. Lebow, W. Kansteiner and C. Fogu (eds.), *The Politics of Memory in Postwar Europe* (Durham and London: Duke University Press, 2006), pp. 177–209.
Skodvin, M., 'Elverumsfullmakten', *Store Norske Leksikon* (15 February 2018); https://snl.no/Elverumsfullmakten, last accessed 14 February 2021.
Stenius, H., Österberg, M. and Östling, J. (eds.), *Nordic Narratives of the Second World War: National Historiographies Revisited* (Lund: Nordic Academic Press, 2011).
Papendorf, K., *Siktet som tyskertøs: rettsoppgjøret i videre forstand* (Oslo: Novus Forlag, 2015).
Penter, T., 'Local Collaborators on Trial: Soviet War Crimes Trials under Stalin (1943–1953)', *Cahiers du Monde russe* 49 (2008) 2–3, pp. 341–364.
Prusin, A. V., 'Traitors of War Criminals: Collaboration on Trial in Soviet Courts in the 1940s', in D. M. Crowe (ed.), *Stalin's Soviet Justice* (London: Bloomsbury, 2019), pp. 79–103.

Pryser, T., *Tyske hemmelige tjenester i Norden: spionsaker og aktører 1930–1950* (Oslo: Universitetsforlaget, 2012).

Reisel, B., *'Hvor ble det av alt sammen?': plyndringen av jødene i Norge* (Oslo: Forlaget Press, 2021).

Ringdal, N. J., *Mellom barken og veden: politiet under okkupasjonen* (Oslo: Aschehoug, 1987).

Riste, O., *The Neutral Ally: Norway's Relations with Belligerent Powers in the First World War* (Oslo: Universitetsforlaget, 1965).

London-Regjeringa, Norge i krigsalliansen, Bind I: 1940–1942: Prøvetid (Oslo: Samlaget, 1973).

London-Regjeringa, Norge i krigsalliansen, Bind II: 1942–1945: Vegen heim (Oslo: Det Norske Samlaget, 1979).

Riste, O., and Nökleby, B., *Norway 1940–1945: The Resistance Movement* (Oslo: Tanum, 1970).

Robertson, E., *Bishop of the Resistance: The Life of Eivind Berggrav* (Haddington: Handsel Press, 2001).

Romijn, P., *Snel, streng en rechtvaardig: politiek beleid inzake de bestraffing en reclassering van 'foute' Nederlanders, 1945–1955* (Houten: De Haan, 1989).

'Die Ahndung der Kollaboration in den Niederlanden', in K.-D. Henke and H. Woller, *Politische Säuberung in Europa: die Abrechnung mit Faschismus und Kollaboration nach dem Zweiten Weltkrieg* (Munich: DTV, 1991), pp. 281–310.

Rousso, H., 'L'Épuration: die politische Säuberung in Frankreich', in K.-D. Henke and H. Woller, *Politische Säuberung in Europa: die Abrechnung mit Faschismus und Kollaboration nach dem Zweiten Weltkrieg* (Munich: DTV, 1991), pp. 192–240.

The Vichy Syndrome: History and Memory in France since 1944 (Cambridge, MA: Harvard University Press, 1994).

'The Purge in France', in J. Elster (ed.), *Retribution and Reparation in the Transition to Democracy* (Cambridge: Cambridge University Press, 2006), pp. 89–123.

Sæveraas, T. E., *Wehrmacht i Norge: på vakt i krigens skjebnesone* (Oslo: Pax Forlag, 2022).

Sandmo, E., *Siste ord: Høgsterett i norsk historie 1814–1965, Bind II: 1905–1965* (Oslo: Cappelen, 2005).

Schechtman, J. B., *Postwar Population Transfers in Europe, 1945–1955* (Philadelphia: University of Pennsylvania Press, 1962).

Scherner, J., and White, E. N. (eds.), *Paying for Hitler's War: The Consequences of Nazi Hegemony for Europe* (Cambridge: Cambridge University Press, 2016).

Schrijvers, P., 'The Liberation: A Wild Picture of Emotions', in W. Devos and K. Gony (eds.), *War, Occupation, Liberation: Belgium 1940–1945* (Tielt: Lannoo, 2019), pp. 243–244.

Seemann, A., 'Citizen Outcasts: The Penalty of "Loss of Civil Rights" during the Norwegian Treason Trials, 1945–1953', *Scandinavian Journal of History* 45 (2020) 3, pp. 360–383.

'On War, Loyalty and Reconciliation: The German Minority in North Schleswig during the Second World War and the Post-war Reckoning', in P. Thaler (ed.), *Like Snow in the Sun? The German Minority in Denmark in Historical Perspective* (Berlin: De Gruyter, 2022), pp. 91–114.

Simonin, A., 'L'indignité nationale: un chatiment républicain', in M. O. Baruch (ed.), *Une poignée de misérables l'épuration de la société française après la Seconde Guerre mondiale* (Paris: Fayard, 2003), pp. 37–60.

Simonsen, K. B., 'Antisemittismen i Norge, ca. 1918–1940: former, funksjoner og virkninger', in Ø. Sørensen and K. B. Simonsen (eds.), *Historie og moral: nazismen, jødene og hjemmefronten* (Oslo: Dreyers Forlag, 2020), pp. 21–50.

Sivertsen, A. G., *Rinnan: et nærbilde* (Oslo: Universitetsforlaget, 1995).

Rinnanbanden. Infiltrasjonen. Torturen. Oppgjøret (Oslo: Kagge, 2022).

Skeie, J., *Landssvik* (Oslo: Norli, 1945).

'Trondheimsavtalen 1940', in T. Bergh and H. Ø. Pharo (eds.), *Historiker og veileder: festskrift til Jakob Sverdrup* (Oslo: Tiden Norsk Forlag, 1989), pp. 81–111.

Solbrekken, I., *Landssvikoppgjørets hemmelige historie: brukte norske rettsmyndigheter krigsforbrytere og nazi-metoder ved landssvikoppgjøret?* (Oslo: Tanum, 2015).

Soleim, M. N., *Sovjetiske krigsfanger i Norge, 1941–45: antall, organisering og repatriering* (Oslo: Spartacus, 2018).

Solhjell, D., and Dahl, H. F., *Men viktigst er æren: oppgjøret blant kunstnerne etter 1945* (Oslo: Pax Forlag, 2013).

Solumsmoen, O., and Larsen, O. (eds.), *Med Einar Gerhardsen gjennom 20 år* (Oslo: Tiden Norsk Forlag, 1967).

Sørensen, N. A., 'Narrating the Second World War in Denmark since 1945', *Contemporary European History* 14 (2005) 3, pp. 295–315.

Sørensen, Ø., 'NS-regimet og jødene', in Ø. Sørensen and K. Simonsen (eds.), *Historie og moral: nazismen, jødene og hjemmefronten* (Oslo: Dreyers Forlag, 2020), pp. 51–90.

Sørlie, S., *Solkors eller hakekors: nordmenn i Waffen-SS 1941–1945* (Oslo: Dreyers Forlag, 2015).

Storeide, A., *Norske krigsprofitører: Nazi-Tysklands velvillige medløpere* (Oslo: Gyldendal, 2014).

Stratigakos, D., *Hitler's Northern Utopia: Building the New Order in Occupied Norway* (Princeton: Princeton University Press, 2020).

Sundvall, E. W., *Gerhardsens valg: Arbeiderpartiets tunge avskjed med Sovjetunionen 1917–1949* (Oslo: Gyldendal, 2016).

Szita, S., 'Die Volksgerichtsbarkeit als Teil der politischen Säuberung in Ungarn, 1945–1946', in C. Kuretsidis-Haider and W. R. Garscha (eds.), *Keine „Abrechnung": NS-Verbrechen, Justiz, Gesellschaft in Europa nach 1945* (Leipzig: AVA, 1998), pp. 207–216.

Szöllösi-Janze, M., '"Pfeilkreuzler, Landesverräter und andere Volksfeinde" – Generalabrechnung in Ungarn', in K.-D. Henke and H. Woller (eds.), *Politische Säuberung in Europa: die Abrechnung mit Faschismus und Kollaboration nach dem Zweiten Weltkrieg* (Munich: DTV, 1991), pp. 311–357.

Tamm, D., *Retsopgøret efter besættelsen* (Copenhagen: Jurist- og økonomforbundet, 1984).

Theien, I., 'Det politiske system og den tyske besættelse i året 1940', in H. F. Dahl, H. Kirchhoff, J. Lund and L.-E. Vaale (eds.), *Danske tilstande – norske tilstande: forskelle og ligheder under tysk besættelse 1940–45* (Copenhagen: Gyldendal, 2010), pp. 33–48.

Tiedau, U., 'Die Rechtslage der deutschsprachigen Bevölkerung in Belgien nach dem Zweiten Weltkrieg', in M. Kittel, H. Möller, J. Pešek and O. Tuma (eds.), *Deutschsprachige Minderheiten 1945: ein europäischer Vergleich* (Oldenbourg: De Gruyter, 2006), pp. 435–487.

Ustvedt, Y., *Det skjedde i Norge, 1945–52: den varme freden – den kalde krigen* (Oslo: Gyldendal, 1978).

Vaale, L. E., *Dommen til døden: dødsstraffen i Norge 1945–50* (Oslo: Pax Forlag, 2004).

'Myndighetene og NS-barnene i Norge etter 1945', Report, Ministry of Labour and Social Inclusion, 16 February 2023.

'Høyesterett, Grunnloven og oppgjøret i Norge 1945–1965: rett og politikk i landets øverste domstol under rettsoppgjøret' (unpublished manuscript).

Vaale, L.-E., and Borge, B. H., 'Caught between International Law and National Constitution: The Legal Reckoning with Foreign War Criminals in Norway after 1945', in *Max Planck Institute for Legal History and Legal Theory Research Paper Series*, No. 1, 2022.

Valen, T., *De tjente på krigen: hjemmefronten og kapitalen* (Oslo: Oktober, 1974).

Virgili, F., *La France "virile": des femmes tondues à la libération* (Paris: Payot, 2000).

Voksø, P. (ed.), *Eivind Berggrav: brobygger og kirkeleder, 1884–1984* (Oslo: Gyldendal, 1984).

Warring, A., *Tyskerpiger: under besættelse og retsopgør* (Copenhagen: Gyldendal, 2017).

Welzer, H. (ed.), *Der Krieg der Erinnerung: Holocaust, Kollaboration und Widerstand im europäischen Gedächtnis* (Frankfurt: Fischer, 2007).

Westlie, B., *Fangene som forsvant: NSB og slavearbeiderne på Nordlandsbanen* (Oslo: Spartacus, 2015).

Woller, H., '"Ausgebliebene Säuberung?" Die Abrechnung mit dem Faschismus in Italien', in K.-D. Henke and H. Woller (eds.), *Politische Säuberung in Europa: die Abrechnung mit Faschismus und Kollaboration nach dem Zweiten Weltkrieg* (Munich: DTV, 1991), pp. 148–191.

Zägel, J., *Vergangenheitsdiskurse in der Ostseeregion: Auseinandersetzungen in den nordischen Staaten über Krieg, Völkermord, Diktatur, Besatzung und Vertreibung* (Münster: LIT Verlag, 2007).

Dissertations

Borge, B. H., 'I rettsoppgjørets lange skygger: andre generasjons problemer i lys av moderne transisjonsteori' (PhD Dissertation, University of Bergen, 2012).

Brandal, N., 'Eit politisk strafferettsleg oppgjer: det norske arbeidarpartiet og etterkrigsoppgjeret 1945–50' (Master's Dissertation, University of Oslo, 2002).

Dostál Raska, F., 'The Czechoslovak Exile Government in London and the Sudeten German Issue' (Doctoral Dissertation, Charles University in Prague, 2002).

Hetland, Ø., 'In the Shadow of the SS: Three Norwegian Police Districts, 1940–1945' (PhD Dissertation, University of Oslo, 2021).

Kullerud, M. J., 'Tre kritikere, et rettsoppgjør' (Master's Dissertation, University of Oslo, 2016).

Kvistad, J. M., '"Det unge Norges fylking klar til slag", Nasjonalsosialistisk ungdom i Norge: historien om Nasjonal Samlings Ungdomsfylking, 1933–1945' (PhD Dissertation, University of Oslo, 2011).

Reinaas, T., 'Isfront – Silkefront?: Oslopressen og holdninger til Landssvikoppgjøret 1945–1948' (Master's Dissertation, University of Trondheim, 1980).

Reitan, J., 'Møter med holocaust: Norske perspektiver på tilintetgjørelsens historiekultur' (PhD Dissertation, NTNU, 2015).

Index

Act of State, 36–37
Acting Supreme Court (*Kommissarisk Høyesterett*), 40, 166
Administration Council (*Administrasjonsrådet*), 31–33, 59, 242
Aftenposten, 94–97, 101, 133, 185, 216, 231
Akershus, 35, 228
Alten, Edvin, 120, 122, 124
Andenæs, Johannes, 6, 11–12, 23, 124, 131–132, 139–140, 181, 193, 217, 223, 246, 255–256, 286
antisemitism, 43, 53–55, 212–213, 284
Arbeiderbladet, 95–96, 101–103, 138–139, 163, 185
Arbeiderpartiet, *See* Labour Party (*Arbeiderpartiet*)
Arbeidsdirektoratet, 49
Argentina, 200–203
Arntzen, Sven, 70, 86–87, 100, 114–115, 148, 162, 207, 216, 241
Arrow Cross, 264, 279
Aulie, Andreas, 98, 130, 208–209, 223, 229, 235–241, 244–245, 255
Auschwitz, 57
Austria, 53

Badoglio, Pietro, 265
Belgium, 21, 64, 72, 90, 260, 266, 268–269, 282
Beneš, Edvard, 260, 271
Berg, Kittil, 153
Berg, Paal, 31, 59–60, 62
Bergen, 201
Berggrav, Bishop Eivind, 23, 45, 79–81, 102, 105, 108–109, 129–130, 175–176, 195, 197, 218, 232, 245, 286
Bergh, Henrik, 127
Bergsvik, Arne, 176–177
Berlin, 28–29, 34
bishops, 46, 163, 182
Blücher, 29
Böhme, Franz, 77
Bondepartiet, *See* Centre Party
Bräuer, Curt, 29, 31–32
Brazil, 202–203
Brøgger, Nils Christian, 102–103
Bunkholt, Halvor, 250

Cappelen, Johan, 103, 105–107, 114, 123, 131, 138, 144
censorship, 49–50
Centre Party (*Bondepartiet*), 27, 89, 94, 105, 129, 144–145, 154, 184, 203, 247, 250
Christian Unity Party (*Kristelig Folkeparti*), 144–145
church, 45–47, 94, 105, 108, 195, 218, 232
Circle, the (*Kretsen*), 60–62
civil rights, 5, 64, 67, 71, 116, 120, 132, 165, 176, 220–223, 257, 262, 277, 301
Civilian Criminal Code of 1902, 4, 63–64, 69, 116, 120, 128
Cold War, 2, 8, 199, 205, 211, 214, 227, 239, 244, 255, 281
Communism, 226
Communist Party (*Norges Kommunistiske Parti*), 28, 95
communists, 12, 40, 90, 145, 164, 273, 290
Compensation Directorate (*Erstatningsdirektoratet*), 70–73, 113, 131
Conservative Party (*Høyre*), 88–90, 145, 155, 216
Coordination Committee (*Koordinasjonskomitéen*), 60–62
Czech Lands, *See* Czechoslovakia
Czechoslovakia, 53, 72, 226, 260, 269, 271, 273–274, 276, 279, 282, 284, 290

Dagbladet, 95–96, 101, 133–137
Danish Freedom Council (*Danmarks Frihedsraad*), 264
death penalty, 64–65, 67, 91, 93, 97, 100–108, 114, 116, 118–120, 123, 128–129, 134–135, 181–182, 189, 191, 193, 203–206, 228, 233, 240, 248, 254–255, 262, 274, 277–279

Denmark, 21, 28–29, 77, 87, 263–265, 267–269, 274, 276, 280–282, 284
Didriksen, Bjarne, 140
DNSAP - National Socialist Workers' Party of Denmark (*Danmarks Nationalsocialistiske Arbejderparti*), 279
Donau, 57, 212
Dorenfeldt, Lauritz, 229
Duynstee, Frans, 286

Eastern Front, 26, 41, 169, 191, 212, 214
economic collaboration, 48, 71, 146, 174, 206–210, 262, 283
Egeberg, Hans Birger, 134–136
Einarson, Odd, 159–162, 230
Eitinger, Leo, 127
Elverum, 29–30
Elverum Authorisation (*Elverumsfullmakten*), 30–31, 33, 117–118
Evensmo, Sigurd, 99
executive decrees (*forelegg*), 148–157, 301
exile government, *See* government-in-exile

Falstad, 56
Fanebust, Toralv, 160–162, 164, 230
Feldmann, Jakob, 212
Feldmann, Rakel, 212
Finland, 44, 174
Flensburg, 77
Folkedomstolen, 40, 166
Forbundet for Sosial Oppreisning, 175
forced labourers, 14–15, 41, 48
Førre, Ingvald, 107
France, 9, 21, 33, 48, 72, 75, 87, 127, 259, 266, 268–269, 273, 276, 280, 284–286, 288, 291–293
Friheten, 95–97, 133–137
Fritt Folk, 49, 168
frontfighters, 41, 134–136, 169, 171, 174–175, 192–193
Fuglesang, Rolf Jørgen, 255
fylkesfører, 39, 166

Gamborg-Nilsen, Olaf, 203
Gerhardsen, Einar, 88, 114, 123, 144, 226
Germanske SS Norge, 43
Germany girls (*tyskerjenter*), 97–100, 269
Germany-workers, 49, 170–171
Gestapo, 39–42, 57, 116, 134, 169–170, 227–229, 240–241
Gimle, 78
Gotenland, 57
government-in-exile, 26–31, 58–59, 62–77, 81–89, 116–119, 122, 127, 140, 145, 148–149, 242, 259–263

Granli, Leif, 153
Great Britain, 9, 30, 127
Gundersen, Oscar Christian, 144–146, 152–157, 177–179, 183, 185–186, 191–192, 194–199, 217, 219, 222–224, 236–237, 244, 247, 253

Haakon VII, King of Norway, 30, 33, 81, 86, 259
Haaland, Reidar, 116–124
Hagelin, Albert Viljam, 127, 181–183
Hague Conventions, 31, 173, 206
Haldorsen, Haldor, 203
Halftime Act (*Halvtidsloven*), 197–200, 206, 218–219, 223
Hambro, Carl Joachim, 92–93, 100–101, 145
Hamburg, 241
Hamsun, Knut, 230–231
Hans, Oscar, 184–185
Hanssen, Einar, 124
Hansteen, Viggo, 49, 126, 128
Hauge, Jens Christian, 60, 70
Himmler, Heinrich, 39
Hird (*Hirden*), 43, 56–57, 122, 167–168, 193, 213
Hirsch, Asriel, 127
Hitler, Adolf, 28–38, 56, 77, 230, 264, 282
Holocaust, 14–15, 52–58, 190, 210–215, 269, 284, 292–294
Holtskog, Gard, 228, 240–241, 255
Home Front (*Hjemmefronten*), 61–78, 83–94, 98, 111, 115, 126, 140, 162, 230, 236, 238, 263, 266–268, 270
honour courts, 3
Horthy, Miklós, 264, 280
Høyre, *See* Conservative Party (*Høyre*)
Hungary, 264–267, 269, 273, 279, 282, 289–290, 295

ice front, 96–97, 131, 134–135, 150, 152, 159–164, 178–179, 181, 184, 186, 203
Ilebu, 176
Italy, 265, 268–269, 285–288, 291, 296–297

Jackson, Robert, 9
Jahn, Gunnar, 123
Jews in Norway
  arrests, 56
  before the Second World War, 52–53
  compensation, 293
  deportations, 57–58
  expropriation, 56–57
  punishment of crimes against, 129, 172, 210–213, 215
  registration, 55–56

Johansen, Magnus, 153–154
Joint Party Programme (*Fellesprogrammet*), 90, 143
Juster, Leif, 162

Kaas, Finn Knutinge, 255
Karl Johan Boulevard, 81
Keilhau, Wilhelm, 63
Kingston House, 58
Komorg (Communist resistance), 58
Kråkerøy, 226
Kvinnehirden (Women's Hird), 43

L'Abée-Lund, Lars, 228–229
Labour Party (*Arbeiderpartiet*), 27–28, 89, 144, 153, 226–227, 247
Landssvikarkivet, *See* Treason Archive
Langeland, Oliver, 1–2, 9, 13, 227, 231–246
Langfeldt, Gabriel, 231
Laval, Pierre, 280
Lavik, Nils, 145
Liaison Division (*Sambandsavdelingen*), 84, 228
Liberal Party (*Venstre*), 89, 144, 154, 203
Liberation, 63, 75–78, 81–83, 112, 116, 266–267, 296
Lindberget, Oskar, 249
Lippestad, Johan Andreas, 255
Liquidation Board (*Likvidasjonsstyret*), 56, 213
Løberg, Sverre, 146, 155, 250
London, 4, 26, 30, 58, 62, 67, 78, 118, 144, 234, 259–260, 262
Løvestad, Harald, 212
Lublin Committee, 267, 271
Lyng, John, 145, 153–155, 180, 199, 216, 250–251

Military Criminal Code of 1902, 64, 129
milk strike, 49
Milorg (Military resistance), 60, 70, 83, 231, 246
Morgenbladet, 95, 133, 185
Morgenposten, 94, 229
Moseid, Gabriel, 184, 203
Munich Agreement, 260
Mussert, Anton, 279
Mussolini, Benito, 265

Nasjonal Samling
  and antisemitism, 43–44, 54–55
  criminal status of, 66–68
  foundation of, 42
  ideology, 43–44
  membership numbers, 44
  opposition to, *See* resistance
  passive membership, 67, 79, 142–143, 157, 175–176, 194, 233, 235, 261
  preparations for German invasion, 28
  relationship to Reichskommissariat, 34–35, 37–38
Nationaal Socialistische Beweging, 276, 279
National Police Chief (*Rikspolitisjefen*), 83–84
National Socialism
  Nazification, 36–38
  New Order, 38, 48
Nationalsozialistische Deutsche Arbeiterpartei (NSDAP), 27, 35, 42–44, 50
Nationalsozialistische Deutsche Arbeiterpartei-Nordschleswig (NSDAP-N), 279
Nationen, 96, 133, 247
Netherlands, 21, 72, 87, 267–269, 276, 278, 280, 284–289, 292, 297
Nordic Folk Rising of Norway (*Nordisk Folkereisning i Norge*), 42
Norges Kommunistiske Parti, *See* Communist Party (*Norges Kommunistiske Parti*)
North Schleswig, 281–282
Norwegian merchant fleet, 59
Norwegian Women's Council (*Norske Kvinners Nasjonalråd*), 131
NS, *See Nasjonal Samling*
Nygaardsvold, Johan, 26, 85, 215–216

Operation Weserübung (Weser Exercise), 28
Oppegard, Per, 134–135
Ordnungspolizei, 39
Oslo, 1, 29, 36, 41, 46, 57–58, 77–78, 81, 115, 136–137, 168, 210–211, 228, 230–231
Oslo-Pressen, 85–86

pardons, 191–194, 217–220, 222–223, 251–256
Pardons Committee, 193, 206, 217, 221–224, 230, 251–257
Pedersen, Peder, 212
Pétain, Philippe, 280
Poland, 28, 57, 262
Polish Committee of National Liberation (*Polski Komitet Wyzwolenia Narodowego*, PKWN), 263
Poulsen, Eystein, 159
POWs, *See* prisoners of war
prisoners of war, 7, 14–15, 19, 26, 41, 111, 212–215, 281

Quisling Decree, 66–68, 70–71, 120, 122–123, 142, 179
Quisling, Maria, 129–130

Quisling, Vidkun
  antisemitism, 43–44, 54–55
  arrest, 77
  attempted coup, 29–30
  ideology, 43–44
  Minister President, 35
  pre-war era, 26–31
  trial of, 124–128

Ræstad, Arnold, 63
Ramndal, Lars, 153, 199
Readiness Acts (*Beredskapslovene*), 247–250, 253
Realm Council negotiations (*Riksrådsforhandlingene*), 33, 59
Rediess, Wilhelm, 39
Reichskommissar, *See* Terboven, Josef
Reichskommissariat, 34–39, 42–43, 48, 54–55, 77, 127, 243, 261
resistance, 12–13, 35, 40–42, 45–48, 50, 59–77, 81–84, 88, 96, 112, 125, 134, 145, 159, 162, 165, 171, 200, 211, 246, 263–268, 272–273, 276, 291
retroactivity, 63, 65–66, 69, 72–73, 106–107, 118–119, 129, 264, 275
Riksting, 39
Rinnan group, 134, 181, 281
Rød, Knut, 57, 127, 210–212
Rosenberg, Alfred, 34
Ruge, Otto, 129
rule of law, 4, 81, 95–97, 101–107, 130, 140, 145, 155, 163, 178–179, 193, 239, 250, 255, 258, 261, 274–275, 287, 290, 299–300
Rysstadt, Aani, 153

Saatvedt, Arne Braa, 134–135
Sachsenhausen, 35
Samfundspartiet, *See* Society Party (*Samfundspartiet*)
Scharffenberg, Johan, 101–102, 162, 286
Schjødt, Annæus, 127
Sicherheitsdienst (SD), 40, 134
Sicherheitspolizei (Sipo), 39, 55, 281
silk front (*silkefronten*), 96, 131, 152, 156, 162, 178–179, 182
Skancke, Ragnar, 182–183, 185–187, 205–206
Skeie, Jon, 140, 154
Skogen, Ketil, 153, 199
Society Party (*Samfundspartiet*), 158, 231
Solbris, 200–203
Solem, Erik, 70, 100, 115, 126, 193
Somdalen, Bernt, 228–230, 236–238, 255
Sonderabteilung Lola, *See* Rinnan group
Soviet Union, 174–175, 214, 257–258, 263–265, 273
Spain, 78, 201, 203
Special Courts (*særdomstolene*), 40
Stalinisation, 289–290
Statspolitiet (*Stapo*), 39, 41, 57
Stavang, Einar Magnus, 153
Steinsvik, Marta, 53, 158–162, 230, 239–240
Storting, 30, 33–34, 89, 91–94, 100, 103–108, 135, 143–147, 152–157, 163, 177, 179–181, 183–185, 195, 199, 204, 215–216, 222, 232, 247–251, 293, 298–299
Strand, Knut, 105, 107
Stray, Christian, 106
Supreme Court (*Høyesterett*), 31–33, 37, 40, 59, 86, 113, 115–123, 126, 129, 135, 167–175, 182–186, 209, 211, 213, 247
Sweden, 27, 42, 50, 58, 69, 78, 83, 88, 112, 144–145
Szálasi, Ferenc, 264, 279

Teacher's Front (*Lærersambandet*), 47
teachers' strike, 46–48, 182
Tenerife, 201
Terboven, Josef, 32–36, 47–50, 54, 56, 77–78, 207, 243
The Troll's Mirror (*Trollspeilet*), 160–161
Thommessen, Øystein, 2, 237, 241–244, 246–247
Thune Works (*Thunes Mekaniske Værksted*), 136
Tiso, Jozef, 279
Togliatti, Palmiro, 285, 287
Trædal, Nils, 145
Tranmæl, Martin, 163
transitional justice, 18, 293
transitional politics, 18–19
Treason Act (*Landssvikloven*), 91, 154, 177–181, 194
Treason Archive, 22
Treason Commission (*Landssvikutvalget*), 11, 250–251, 298
Treason Decree (*Landssvikanordningen*), 70–75, 115, 118–120, 123–124, 126, 131–134, 142, 165, 206–208, 234–235, 263
Tromsø, 30
Trøndelag, 56
Trondheim, 52, 56, 134, 145

United Nations War Crimes Commission (UNWCCW), 69

Venstre, *See* Liberal Party
Verdens Gang, 95, 126, 133
Vichy regime, 273, 285, 291

Victoria Terrasse, 41
Vigo, 201

Waffen-SS, 7, 41, 281
Wagner, Wilhelm, 57, 127, 212–213
Wehrmacht, 38, 76–78, 82, 97, 111, 228, 281
Welhaven, Kristian, 245
Weymouth, 201
Wickstrøm, Rolf, 49
Wold, Terje, 68, 86, 103

Youngstorget, 137

www.ingramcontent.com/pod-product-compliance
Lightning Source LLC
LaVergne TN
LVHW011704200926
848484LV00004B/1072